BANKING AND CAPITAL MARKETS

New International Perspectives

BANKING AND CAPITAL MARKETS

New International Perspectives

Lloyd P Blenman

University of North Carolina-Charlotte, USA

Harold A Black

University of Tennessee, USA

Edward J Kane

Boston College, USA

editors

World Scientific

NEW JERSEY • LONDON • SINGAPORE • BEIJING • SHANGHAI • HONG KONG • TAIPEI • CHENNAI

Published by

World Scientific Publishing Co. Pte. Ltd.
5 Toh Tuck Link, Singapore 596224
USA office: 27 Warren Street, Suite 401-402, Hackensack, NJ 07601
UK office: 57 Shelton Street, Covent Garden, London WC2H 9HE

British Library Cataloguing-in-Publication Data
A catalogue record for this book is available from the British Library.

BANKING AND CAPITAL MARKETS
New International Perspectives

ISBN-13 978-981-4273-60-2
ISBN-10 981-4273-60-0

Typeset by Stallion Press
Email: enquiries@stallionpress.com

Printed in Singapore Mainland Press Pte Ltd.

Acknowledgments

Our deepest gratitude for the completion of this volume and to the success of the conference goes to the enthusiastic response of the conference participants and to the authors who contributed and subjected their work to the lengthy screening and selection procedures. Without any doubt, we should also note the persistent and untiring efforts of our editor Shalini Bhupathiraju, who worked with us very cheerfully even when the entire project fell behind schedule. She realized and anticipated many of the complexities that arose during our planning process and invariably came up with the right solutions. Her help was invaluable. We would be amiss if we did not note the support given to us by the Midwest Finance Association in making it possible to bring together scholars, who discussed their research in a friendly and stimulating environment. They gave their support early and the project could not have gone ahead without their support.

Harold A. Black
Lloyd P. Blenman
Edward J. Kane

List of Contributors

Angelo Baglioni
Università Cattolica, Italy
Email: angelo.baglioni@unicatt.it

Jason Ball
Ernst & Young, Australia

Jennifer E. Bethel
Babson College, USA
Email: bethel@babson.edu

Dennis Chung
Simon Fraser University, Canada
dychung@sfu.ca

Diego Cueto
University ESAN, Peru
Email: d_cueto@jmsb.concordia.ca;
diegocueto@esan.org.pe;
d_cueto@jmsb.concordia.ca

Kenneth Daniels
Virgina Commonwealth University, USA
Email: kndaniel@vcu.edu

Arup Daripa
University of London, UK
Email: a.daripa@bbk.ac.uk

Victor Fang
Monash University, Australia
Email: victor.fang@buseco.monash.edu.au

Laurie Krigman
Babson College, USA
Email: lkrigman@babson.edu

Lawrence Kryzanowski
Concordia University, Canada
Email: lkryzan@vax2.concordia.ca

James R. McCown
Toltec Group, USA
Email: jamesmccown@att.net

Lucía Morales
Dublin Institute of Technology, Dublin
Email: lucia.morales@ul.ie; lucia.morales@dit.ie

Irwin Morgan
Bentley College, USA
Email: imorgan@bentley.edu

Jose Moreno
Incarnate University, USA
Email: jfmoreno@utpa.edu

Usha R. Mittoo
University of Manitoba, Canada
Email: umittoo@ms.umanitoba.ca

Arturo Rubalcava
University of Regina, Canada
Email: arturo.rubalcava@uregina.ca

Hendrik Scholz
Catholic University of Eichstätt-Ingolstadt
Email: hendrik.scholz@ku-eichstaett.de

Stephan Simon
University of Erlangen-Nürnberg
Email: stephan_simon@mckinsey.com

Joon-Young Song
University of Findlay, USA
Email: song@findlay.edu

Gökçe Soydemir
University of Texas Pan American, USA
Email: soydemir@utpa.edu

Erhan Uluceviz
Bogozici University, Turkey

Simone Varotto
University of Reading, UK
Email: s.varotto@icmacentre.reading.ac.uk

Rahul Verma
University of Houston, USA
Email: vermar@uhd.edu

Marco Wilkens
Catholic University of Eichstätt-Ingolstadt
Email: marco.wilkens@ku-eichstaett.de

Levent Yildiran
Bogozici University, Turkey
Email: levent.yildiran@boun.edu.tr

John R. Zimmerman
Oklahoma University, USA
Email: jrzimmerman4@yahoo.com

Zhou Zhang
University of Regina, Canada
zhou.zhang@uregina.ca

Introduction and Overview

H.A. Black, L.P. Blenman and E.J. Kane

This book organizes a series of papers that were presented at the Midwest Finance Association meeting in San Antonio, Texas. The collection emphasizes research on international financial markets, but most chapters develop results that are universal in scope and can be applied to national and regional settings as well. A theme that runs through almost all of the chapters is the importance of information asymmetries. Differences in who knows what and when inside information surfaces, constrain the role played by regulators and outside stakeholders in corporations, and the equity share that insiders are willing to retain.

This volume goes to press at a time when several central precepts of asset pricing and finance are under attack. The economic environment is one of the global crisis. Outsized losses have spilled across national boundaries. Most of these losses originated in financial services and real-estate markets, but produced large, but varied cross-sector and cross-country impacts. The difficulty of settling these losses onto particular institutions and taxpayers has spread crisis pressures widely. Each country's crisis traces to a mix of market and regulatory failures, including weaknesses in government supervision, in corporate governance practices, and in how financial risks are assessed and priced. Because this crisis has been both painful and widespread, it has intensified interest in identifying factors that trigger crises and in studying how hedging and risk management might better protect wealth in the future.

The volume covers financial institutions, banking markets, risk management, international investment, corporate governance and their regulation. Much of the volume focuses on banks. Banks play a central role in crisis avoidance and control because they channel liquidity to transactions of all sorts. When banks fail, important payments chains are apt to be disrupted. This is why financial safety nets come into existence. Of course, the modern financial services industry also includes a number of near-banks. These corporations are also apt to be protected by implicit and explicit guarantees and other risk-sharing arrangements. Safety nets span deposit insurance, brokerage account protections and the screening of security issuers, investment banks and insurance companies. The degree of insolvency the world is experiencing underscores a need for safety net and information reform in the financial services industry. The size of bailout expenditures indicates how poorly many risks were accounted for and how pricing and employee compensation structures encouraged inappropriate risk taking.

Even where very flexible exchange rate schemes were in place, volatility spillovers occurred. Few national authorities were able to insulate themselves from harmful effects. In the face of a severe decline in asset prices, interconnection became a disadvantage. The highly touted benefits of globalization evaporated and revealed limitations of national monetary and fiscal policies that few had appreciated during good times.

Some chapters offer policy prescriptions: for averting crises, for upgrading prudential regulation and improving corporate governance. Some chapters develop empirical evidence on these same policy themes. Topics include the role of ownership structures in emerging markets. Other empirical chapters review international evidence on cross-listing, buyout activity and joint ventures.

The volume is divided into two parts. Part I covers Banking and International Finance and Part II covers Corporate Finance and Investments. The order of individual chapters was governed by an effort to establish a logical flow and closeness of fit. Obviously, strong arguments can be made for a different grouping. It should be equally obvious that too many problems beset the world's banking and capital markets to permit us to address them adequately in a single volume. We select writings for their ability to shed light on a subset of the problems that concern us.

The chapters in Part I analyze bank and exchange-rate regulation, paying special attention to the welfare losses that can be created by sub-optimal regulation. When bank supervision is inadequate, eventually safety net protections transfer losses to taxpayers. When supervision is too intrusive, too little lending is apt to occur, so that creditworthy customers find it more costly to carry out their plans. Some chapters in this section investigate the efficacy of value at risk (VaR) as a risk-management tool and whether the risks inherent in bank trading portfolios are properly priced. Maturity transformation strategies and their effectiveness in dealing with interest rate risk are also considered in these chapters. Other chapters deal with narrower topics: coordination failures in international lending, how introducing the euro affected various other asset markets, how variation in the country of origin might influence the success of international joint ventures and the pricing of risk in Latin American markets.

Part II deals with a number of important, but diverse, issues. These include identifying private benefits of control, reviewing corporate governance practices in Latin America and examining the usefulness of precious metals for hedging against inflation and equity risks. Chapter 9 examines whether and how non-standard ways of registering securities can reduce the cost of raising equity capital. Global loan syndication is treated in this part as well, but from a different perspective. Chapter 10 looks at how syndication might reduce underwriting quality because lenders would not coordinate or share adverse information about sovereign borrowers. It also examines how loan syndication affects the costs of borrowing in LBOs. The final two chapters deal with the benefits of cross-listing and the asymmetric impact that good and bad news have on stock return volatility.

Part I: Banking and International Finance

Jason Ball and **Victor Fang** on "Value-at-Risk Disclosures and the Implications on Bank Shareholders" is a study of how VaR disclosures for the trading portfolio impact this class of stakeholder. Even though disclosures are reported with a lag, the authors show that incorporating this information in their analysis improves estimates of betas and forecasts of next period's realized return. The chapter makes the case that even though VaR has been used to report trading risk faced by banks and that risk has to be priced by the market, shareholders are not adequately compensated for that risk. This implies that the risk is either mismeasured or mispriced. Putting aside more technical objections to the use of VaR, this has serious implications for investment banking as previously practiced. The authors suggest that equity investors would be better off holding stakes in banks without large trading portfolios. The finding that bond returns are positively related to VaR positions, is somewhat puzzling, unless size of positions proxies for bank profitability. This is because shareholders face a moral hazard problem and are asymmetrically compensated. They share in few of the benefits from increased profits but are susceptible to bank failures.

Arup Daripa and **Simone Varotto** in "Ex-Ante Versus Ex-Post Regulation of Bank Capital" ask a very important question: What is the optimal form of capital regulation for banks? Information asymmetries ensure that either ex-ante or ex-post regulation is usually dominant in any specific situation, given banks' private information, the reputation and risk aversion profiles of bank managers. However, the authors show that a combination of both regimes is superior to either the ex-ante or the ex-post approach taken in isolation if banks have superior information about the underlying risk of their assets. The authors underline their new approach by modeling a trade-off between "safety loss" and "overprotection loss". In their framework, the bank regulator sets the optimal capital level by minimizing an objective function that is a linear combination of these two elements. The weights set on each element depend on the immediate priority of the regulator, but the authors show that in combination with appropriately regressive penalties, regulators can prescribe for well-capitalized banks, regardless of whether their goal is reducing solvency risk or reducing overprotection losses. Regulatory forbearance and the possibility of banks taking cosmetic measures to reduce perceived risk leave open the question of whether this policy prescription might ultimately be successful.

Erhan Uluceviz and **Levent Yildiran**, in their study "Effects of International Interbank Loans on Twin Crises", address the issue of whether international banks contribute to the development of banking and financial crises by failing to coordinate their lending policies. Evidence presented in the chapter importantly suggests that such coordination failures are more likely to trigger crises in developing countries than in developed countries. Low institutional quality in the former countries establishes preconditions for crisis to the extent that there already exist budgetary deficits, high real rates of interest and low foreign exchange reserves. Relatively more developed economies tend to be less exposed to the advent of crises because they are protected by the quality of the institutional structures in place. The authors make the key point that international flows of funds to some developing countries have had the perverse effect of destabilizing the recipient. Better oversight is needed. In many ways, some of the themes of the previous study resonate here also.

Lucía Morales in her work, "International Transmission Effects of Volatility between Financial Markets in the G-7 since the Introduction of the Euro", looks at the effects on first- and second-order moments of return in asset and exchange markets from introducing the euro. Volatility increased at the announcement, but somewhat-reduced levels of volatility emerged as markets matured. This pattern of response is typical of markets for a new product. The innovation here is that the study is done both within region bilateral rates as well as with the cross rates of the euro currencies with those of prime currencies such as the dollar, pound and yen. Volatility persistence is observed in both currency and stock markets. The evidence seems to show that the effect of volatility in stock returns on the volatility of exchange rates is larger than the influence that runs in the reverse direction. The effects of adopting the euro differ greatly across countries. An unresolved question is why.

Usha R. Mittoo, **Dennis Chung** and **Zhou Zhang**, in "Country-of-Origin Determinants of Value Creation in International Joint Ventures: A Comparison of Hong Kong and U.S. Investments in China", develop a series of insights about what characteristics lead to a successful joint venture. They explore the role of market size, partner size and nationality factors in sourcing foreign direct investment into China from potential Hong Kong and US joint venture partners. "Home country bias" and cultural distance factors would tend to give an advantage to Hong Kong firms, but market size and partner size are countervailing factors. The evidence suggests that for culturally distant firms, there is a learning effect from previous investments in China but no such effect for Hong Kong firms. Several country-of-origin factors prove important in creating wealth in new joint ventures. However, the task of disentangling the precise causative roles of the individual factors is still a work in progress. It turns out that firm size has opposite effects for US and Hong Kong firms in determining a venture's success. Making progress on this problem is rendered especially difficult because of the likelihood that numerous hidden factors are important for investors that wish to engage themselves in this major, but still largely planned economy.

Hendrik Scholz, **Stephan Simon** and **Marco Wilkens**, in their work "Maturity Transformation Strategies and Interest Rate Risk of Financial Institutions: Evidence from the German Market", assess the risk posed to financial institutions by interest rate risk. The risk posed by changes in interest rate is typically assessed by utilizing duration data for both assets and liabilities. In the absence of such data, a two-factor model of a firm's stock returns can be used instead. Regressing firm equity returns on the market portfolio and a bond index over a designated period of investment is another method of assessing the risk. The authors develop what they call maturity transformation factors, derived by orthogonalizing a standard interest rate factor and market rate of return. These factors also enable them to estimate the extent of maturity transformation undertaken by the firms and thereby infer differences in the effective maturities of aggregate assets and liabilities. The new factors are compared with standard interest rate factors in terms of their effectiveness in explaining the exposure of different kinds of financial institutions including banks, life insurance companies and real-estate firms, whose operating results are very interest-rate sensitive. Using industry-level data, the authors present evidence that these two new factors, called "extra-market interest rate sensitivity" and "total interest rate sensitivity", perform better in a two-factor model explaining the sensitivity of returns to interest rate changes, than do other more traditional interest rate factors.

Gökçe Soydemir, **Rahul Verma** and **Jose Moreno**, in "Asymmetries in the Market Price of Risk: Evidence from Latin America", examine how spillovers in risk premiums are transmitted across international markets. In many respects, this chapter explores the same themes as the study by Morales. Whereas Morales examined volatility spillovers across stock and exchange markets, these authors analyze how the Sharpe ratio reacts across markets. They present evidence that the risk-adjusted returns in Latin American markets are higher than those in the U.S. market. In fact, they prove significantly higher than comparable benchmark returns. The evidence also suggests that Latin American markets respond more sharply to negative surprises than to positive surprises. The effects of negative surprises also persist longer. In summary, after showing that Latin American markets move in sympathy with U.S. markets, they paint a picture in which relatively integrated markets each price risk asymmetrically.

Part II: Corporate Finance and Investments

Angelo Baglioni, in "Corporate Governance Institutions as Signaling and Commitment Devices", presents a policy blueprint for dealing with agency costs faced by investors in corporate equities. To the basic problem of moral hazard with managers, entrepreneurs and/or dominant shareholders who have control, he adds a lemon problem. Owing to information asymmetry, investors have no way to distinguish how much scope entrepreneurs in different firms have to extract private benefits. Good managers, shareholders and entrepreneurs do not try to extract private benefits, but so-called bad ones do. When good and bad entrepreneurs sell partial equity stakes in their firms, Baglioni shows that cross-subsidization is implicit in the equilibrium price of sold equity. Good entrepreneurs pay part of the cost extracted by bad entrepreneurs in the form of private benefits, even if third-party governance regulations strive to limit the extraction of such benefits. He shows that self-regulation on the part of all firms raising equity dominates the third-party regulatory strategy. With self-regulation, a separating equilibrium can develop that dictates different strategies for good and bad entrepreneurial types and eliminates the cross-subsidization. The study stresses the advantage of self-regulation.

Jennifer E. Bethel and **Laurie Krigman**, in "Managing the Costs of Issuing Common Equity: The Role of Registration Choice", discuss the costs of raising equity in U.S. capital markets. The choice discussed is that between traditional registrations and shelf registration. Shelf registration unequivocally lowers the costs of raising funds for low-information asymmetry firms, but can substantially raise costs for high-information asymmetry firms that release little information. These opaque firms suffer from costs associated with market overhang. Nevertheless, the authors posit that the main driver behind the use of shelf registrations is *not* cost minimization but risk minimization. Shelf registration offers firms the flexibility to be able to raise funds quickly in the event that their finances warrant it or if fortuitous circumstances arise. However, the authors uncover no evidence that firms have successfully timed the market in raising funds via shelf registrations. Traditional registration generates less ambiguity and information asymmetry than the shelf registration method. Consequently, the costs associated with market overhang are lower for both types of issuers when they use the traditional method.

Kenneth Daniels and **Irwin Morgan**, in "The Impact of Arrangers and Buyout Sponsors on Loan Pricing in LBOs: A Cross Border Study", represent a further exploration of the costs of raising funds in different ways. Here the market is the debt market and the instrument is the syndicated loan. The authors examine in detail the structure of the syndicated loan market and find that arrangers of syndicated loans help to mitigate information asymmetries and help to certify the quality of the debt. In this market, small deal sizes are typically associated with single arrangers. Costs are higher in small deals with single arranger structures because the creditworthiness of small issuers is typically opaque. Sponsored deals also have significantly higher all-in spreads even after controlling for the number of arrangers in the deal. It seems that sponsored deals are highly complex ones that are riskier than the average deal. Hence, the higher yield reflects the additional risks of the deal. The authors also show that all-in spreads on U.S. LBOs are higher than those for comparable European deals. They attribute this cross-country spread to the higher degree of leverage employed in U.S. deals.

Lawrence Kryzanowski and **Arturo Rubalcava**, in their study "Ownership Control and Valuation Changes for Earnings Announcements around U.S. Cross-Listings by Canadian Firms", analyze the factors that drive the benefits of cross-listing on U.S. exchanges. They ask whether the changes that are observed the result of the behavior of non-insiders who hold float shares. They try to disentangle any pure listing effects from effects that are purely earnings-related. The authors find no evidence that when changes in float shares are conditioned on earnings surprises, they play any role in explaining the changes in firm value that occur either in the pre-listing or post-listing periods. However, when they consider the entire listing period (i.e., combining the pre-listing, announcement and post-listing intervals), they find that, conditioned on negative earning surprises, float shares help to explain declines in firm value. They also find evidence of reduced ordering costs in terms of lower bid-asked spreads, but greater risk because price volatility increases. Surprisingly they show that the incidence of insider ownership increases after a U.S. listing. This is contrary to what would be expected *a priori*.

James R. McCown and John R. Zimmerman, in their study, "Analysis of the Investment Potential and Inflation-Hedging Ability of Precious Metals", analyze the long- and short-term hedging abilities of gold and silver. The evidence shows that as an investor's time horizon increases from one month to five years, the correlations between inflation and returns from holding positions in both metals increase and are positive. The increase in the correlations with the length of one's investment horizon is monotonic for gold but not so for silver. For stocks, the evidence shows that the returns on stocks are negatively correlated with returns on positions in both gold and silver. These patterns prove robust to splitting the sample period in two subperiods, in which returns on stocks are strikingly different. Simply taking long positions in either could achieve the goal of hedging, but gold is a demonstrably better hedge against rising inflation. The correlations between the returns on the metals and the stock markets are somewhat weaker. At short time intervals, they are close to zero but becoming increasingly negative over longer horizons. The authors show that the ability of gold and silver to hedge against stock market returns is tied primarily to their ability to hedge against inflation.

Diego Cueto, in his paper "Corporate Governance and Ownership Structure in Emerging Markets: Evidence from Latin America", is also concerned with the problem with the private benefits of control. However, unlike Baglioni's contribution, this is not a policy chapter. It is a cross-country study of the discrepancy between cash-flow rights and voting rights and of the possibility for asset diversion. He provides evidence of a negative effect on firm value when a dominant shareholder exists. Dominant shareholders exert influence within a firm that is disproportionate with their actual voting rights in emerging Latin American markets. In this study, all named shareholders are assigned a unique voting status: either stand alone, member of a business group, member of a blockholder group etc. The panel data analysis shows that investors have negative perceptions about large ownership concentration. Firm value decreases with the percentage of voting rights held by the dominant shareholder, the excess gap between cash-flow rights and voting rights. However, if large ownership concentration is in fact present, investors prefer that the blockholder be a corporation or a family business group.

Joon-Young Song, in "Asymmetric Impact of News on Stock Return Volatility", continues the line of investigation pursued by Morales (Chap. 4) and Gökçe Soydemir, Rahul Verma and Jose Moreno (Chap. 7). Whereas other chapters focused on the asymmetric impact of spillovers across international markets and on the pricing of risk, Song is concerned with whether the volatility spillover is a factor that should formally be captured in an asset-pricing model. He confirms this hypothesis, finding evidence that a stable dynamic relationship exists between movements in the returns of small firms and large firms when a news event occurs. He also finds that small firm stock returns are significantly affected by news about large firms. The returns on large firm stocks are not significantly affected by good news on small firms. Even after sorting portfolios by size, industry affiliation and markets, the asymmetric response persists. The asymmetry in effect is not a factor only of size. However, Song acknowledges that size might be the dominant explanatory factor.

Contents

Part I

Banking and International Finance

1

Value-at-Risk Disclosures and the Implications on Bank Stakeholders

Jason Ball and Victor Fang

1. Introduction

Are bank shareholders compensated for the risk that is contained within the bank's trading portfolio? What are the implications of value-at-risk (VaR) disclosures to the bank debt holders and the level of bank's earnings? To date, there have been no rigorous studies to examine these issues. This is because VaR measures are proprietary information and they are not easily available to the public. Before 1995, very few banks reported VaR numbers voluntarily.

In response to a number of financial disasters involving banks, bank regulators in particular, the Basel Committee on Banking requires banks to disclose their VaR measurements on an annual or quarterly basis in their financial reports. Because of the disclosure requirement of VaR, academic researchers are able to investigate the relationship between the publicly disclosed VaR figures and the bank trading portfolios. But the number of research studies in this area is limited.

For example, Jorion (2002) investigated the relationship between bank VaR measures and the volatility of trading revenues for a group of U.S. banks. In his study, he used eight banks with six years of quarterly and annual VaR figures from December 1994 to 1999. His results suggest that VaR disclosures are informative measures of risks in that they can use to predict the variability of bank's trading revenues. By extending Jorion's finding using a larger sample of 17 banks, Liu *et al.* (2004) show that banks' VaR has predictive power for next period's beta and realized returns.

A recent study by Chipalkatti and Datar (2006) examines the usefulness of VaR disclosures using an event study — the LTCM announcement of the crisis date. Their results show that there is no such association between the trading VaR disclosed by a bank and the magnitude of the abnormal returns and volume reaction around the announcement date. The inconsistent findings on the relationship between VaR disclosures and stock returns also provide a motivation to closely reexamine the VaR disclosures and stock returns.

In this chapter, we attempt to shed light on the above-mentioned issues by investigating (i) the relationship between the VaR figures that banks publicly disclosed in their financial statements and the subsequent beta and returns to shareholders, (ii) the relationship between VaR disclosures and the subsequent returns to bondholders and (iii) the relationship between the VaR disclosures and the changes in the level of earnings.

Using a sample of trading disclosed VaRs that were reported by U.S. banks under FRR No. 48 (1997) from 1997 to 2004, our results show that stock betas and bond returns are sensitive and positively related to reported trading VaR while equity returns are not. Therefore, this suggests that banks with conservative trading operations may represent better investments from a stockholder's perspective because increased trading risk does not influence the stock returns.

In other words, investors find that the VaR disclosures do not provide any incremental useful information to them. In addition, the results also suggest that VaR is inversely related to changes in the level of earnings in previous periods. This finding implies that large trading portfolios may represent a moral hazard to bondholders in particular, because the increase in bank's earnings from taking on more trading risk will not directly benefit them but they may be subject to default risk if banks are faced with large unexpected trading losses.

2. Market Risk and Value-at-Risk Disclosures

VaR summarizes the potential losses a bank could suffer over a given period due to normally observed adverse market movements with a given level of confidence. For example, a one-day 99% VaR of $10 million implies that 99% of the time the trading losses will not exceed $10 million over the next business day. In other words, there is 1% possibility that the trading losses will exceed $10 million over the next business day. In principle, VaR is an effective tool for modeling and disclosing the market risk of any portfolio (including an entire firm), because it incorporates the correlations of the exposures within the portfolio and uses a consistent time interval and confidence level (Liu *et al.*, 2004).

VaR is commonly applied in numerous capacities by practitioners from a wide variety of industries. For example, it can be used to allocate capital, to estimate the impact of price/rate changes on cash flows (known as "Cash Flow at Risk"), to manage credit and operational risks, or to manage trading and non-trading exposures. While VaR provides information about total market risk, investors are primarily more concerned about priced risks such as interest rate risk and exchange rate risk. Although priced risks can be hedged and diversified, we contend that not all banks hedge their trading and non-trading portfolios and not all investors hold diversified portfolios. Hence, it is meaningful to investigate the relationship between trading VaR disclosures[1] and the bank's total market risk.

Under the Basel Accord, banks are required to hold regulatory capital for market risk in proportion to their trading VaR disclosures. In addition, in FRR No. 48 that was introduced in January 1997, the Securities and Exchange Commission (SEC, 1997) requires U.S. publicly traded companies to report quantitative and qualitative information about market risk in their 10-K reports. For quantitative disclosures, the SEC provides three options:

1. Tabular format of fair values and contractual terms sufficient to determine the amount and time of cash flows over each of the next five years;

2. Sensitivity analysis approach which estimates the potential loss of value, and cash flows that result from selected hypothetical changes in market rates or prices; and
3. VaR disclosures approach reports the potential loss in earnings, and cash flows over a selected period with selected likelihood of occurrence.

3. Related Literature and Hypothesis Development

Jorion (2002) demonstrates that the disclosed VaR is positively related to future trading revenues and thus concludes that VaR disclosures can provide a comparison of the relative risk profiles of banks. In addition, Jorion posits that the strength of this relationship should increase over time as firms continue to refine their VaR systems. By extending Jorion (2002) findings, Liu *et al.* (2004) go on to examine the relationship between VaR and banks' total risk (i.e., stock return volatility), priced risk (i.e., beta) and stock returns. Their results indicate that VaR is indeed a good predictor of these factors. Furthermore, they find support for Jorion's conjecture that VaR disclosures should become more informative over time.

Bali and Cakici (2004) examine the relationship between VaR and stock returns from a different perspective. Rather than focus on public VaR disclosures, they estimate the distribution of monthly stock returns for a sample of U.S. companies from 1958 to 2001 and then extract VaR estimates from this distribution by isolating the extreme lower tails. Their results indicate that VaR has explanatory power for cross-sectional stock returns at both the company and portfolio level.

In their study, Chipalkatti and Datar (2006) examine whether investors use the VaR disclosures information to determine the potential loss of banks, directly or indirectly exposed to LTCM, at the time of the crisis announcement. Their results show that there is no such association between the trading VaR disclosed by a bank and the magnitude of the abnormal returns and volume reaction around the announcement date. This finding is inconsistent with previous studies. There are several other important relationships regarding VaR's impact on stakeholders that remain less clear. We classify these other effects into two separate but inter-related categories: (1) the flow-on effects that trading portfolio VaR has on the risk profile of a bank as a whole and (2) firm-specific determinants of VaR.

3.1. *Flow-On Effects of VaR*

Total risk is comprised of systematic and unsystematic risks. Traditional asset-pricing models such as the CAPM rely heavily on estimates of beta to capture the systematic risk inherent in a security. However, we maintain that the question remains as to whether beta accurately reflects the market risk within a bank's trading portfolio. That is, does trading portfolio risk as measured by VaR flow through into the commonly used total risk indicators? We argue that it does, but it does so with a lag.

Beta is a function of the way in which a stock co-varies with the broader market. Hence, it reflects a stock's volatility (or systematic risk) relative to that of the market. Presumably, asset prices react to macroeconomic and firm-specific news announcements both as they occur and based on the market's expectations for the future (Chen *et al.*, 1986). However, VaR figures are not disclosed regularly. As such, the full impact of trading portfolio risk may not be captured by a bank's current beta until the next period. Therefore, investors' perceptions of a bank's true risk profile may be distorted due to the lag with which this information is reflected in market data.

This argument is consistent with the findings of Liu *et al.* (2004) who report that trading portfolio VaR is significantly related to *next* period's beta. Hence, the authors conclude that VaR has predictive power for the following period's beta. We go one step further by suggesting that this lagged relationship is the result of VaR disclosures that are not available on a timely basis. Specifically, since VaR is released in end-of-period disclosures, these data are subsequently impounded into market prices (and thus beta) the next period. This is an intuitive explanation of the lagged relationship that directly corresponds to the construct of beta. Thus, our Hypothesis 1 is:

H1: The market risk of a firm's trading portfolio as captured by VaR is reflected in the following period's beta.

Jorion (2002) examines the relationship between VaR and the variability of trading revenues and finds that disclosed VaR figures provide a good indication of future trading revenue volatility. Liu *et al.* (2004) extend this finding by investigating the link between quarterly VaR disclosures and the following period's stock returns. Their evidence suggests that VaR is indeed a significant factor in determining future stock returns. Following Liu *et al.* (2002), our Hypothesis 2 is:

> *H2: The returns to shareholders in the following period are a positive function of a firm's disclosed trading VaR for the current period.*

It is generally accepted that bondholders of bank debt securities are risk-averse investors and are concerned with bank trading performance. The VaR disclosures made by banks provide useful information to bondholders about the potential trading losses. Previous studies suggest that the higher the trading VaR, the larger will be the unexpected trading losses faced by a bank. Thus, it follows that bondholders will be interested to know the amount of trading portfolio risk that banks assume because it affects their risk level. Thus, our Hypothesis 3 is:

> *H3: The returns to bondholders in the following period are a positive function of a firm's disclosed trading VaR for the current period.*

3.2. *Firm-Specific Determinants of VaR*

A VaR calculation takes as given the assets that a bank holds. However, there may be firm-specific factors that affect VaR by influencing the type of assets banks choose to hold. The most obvious of these factors is earnings because earnings capture the net effects of most material changes in a bank's business operations. For example, do changes in the level of earnings in prior periods influence the level of trading risk banks are willing to bear? This effect could potentially occur when other more traditional product areas such as the lending division are experiencing profit slumps.

The result of this decline in earnings may, in turn, lead management to resort to other avenues, including exposure to increased trading portfolio risk, to restore profits to a more "normal" level. That is, this increased bank trading portfolios may represent increased returns to shareholders but at the expense of the bondholders. If extreme trading losses are incurred due to increased trading risk, it may directly affect the bank's ability to honor its contracts with the bondholders. In this study, we choose the adverse changes in earnings as the firm-specific factor. That is, adverse changes in earnings are likely to lead managers to increase the trading portfolio position, hoping that this increase could restore the previous loss. Thus, our Hypothesis 4 is:

> *H4: Trading VaR is inversely related to bank performance as measured by changes in the level of previous period's earnings.*

4. Data and Methodology

4.1. *Sample*

Publicly disclosed VaR figures are the basis of our analysis. VaR has a relatively short history as a risk management tool, and VaR disclosures, while becoming increasingly more widespread, are still primarily confined to large international institutions. To avoid the serious problem of differences in reporting requirements across countries, our sample consists solely of U.S. banks.

The U.S. market is a suitable choice for this type of research for several reasons. First, SEC rule FRR No. 48, introduced in 1997, requires all publicly listed firms to make some form of market risk disclosure on a quarterly basis. VaR is included as one of three disclosure options which satisfy this requirement. Therefore, a relatively large number of VaR disclosures are expected for U.S. banks. Second, the U.S. banking market is the world's largest, which enables us to study a reasonably large sample.

Due to VaR's complexity and primary function as a trading risk management tool, it was clear that the sample would consist primarily of sophisticated banks with relatively large trading operations. Therefore, we collected VaR data for the top 100 banks in terms of total assets as listed by the Federal Reserve on 31 December 2004 (Federal Reserve Bank of Chicago, 2004).[2] Upon examination of these 100 banks' 10-Q and 10-K reports, only 15 large banks are found to report VaR figures for at least two years from 1997 to the end of 2004. This gives us a total of 322 firm-quarters observations (excluding two banks that report VaR in annual basis).

According to Liu *et al.* (2004), larger banks are likely to have more complex, diverse- and trading-oriented exposures, and thus there is a need to establish VaR-based risk management and disclosure systems.[3] In addition, they are likely to have greater resources and technical sophistications to develop those systems. The other banks that we assess disclose their market risk under FRR No. 48 using some combination of the tabular format and sensitivity approaches. Table 1 reports the sample banks and a brief description of their respective VaR models as described in their company reports.

A decision rule was needed to determine how VaR data would be selected for inclusion in the sample. This issue arises because of the difference in timing between institutions as to when VaR disclosures began and the format of their respective disclosures (e.g., high/low, average, end-of-period etc.). As Jorion (2002) notes, it is not possible to standardize such a collection of VaR figures. Therefore, we employed his criteria for gathering VaR data as follows:

1. End-of-quarter VaR,
2. Average quarterly VaR,
3. End-of-year VaR, and
4. Average annual VaR.

Quarterly data are preferred over annual data because the higher frequency leads to a larger sample. Quarterly data were collected for the period 1997(1) to 2004(4) from 10-Q and 10-K reports filed with the SEC. In the event that a bank did not begin disclosing VaR until after 1997, the sample period for that bank begins at the time the first disclosure was made.[4]

Because VaR models and parameters differ across banks, reported VaR figures were standardized to produce a comparable data set. In particular, it was necessary to control for the different intervals and confidence levels at which VaRs were calculated. This process, as

Table 1. Sample details.

Bank	Ranking	VaR methodology	Confidence level (%)	First observation	No. of observation	Frequency
Bank of America	3	Proprietary model	99	4Q:1999	21	Quarterly
Bank of New York	15	Monte Carlo simulation	99	4Q:1999	29	Quarterly
JP Morgan Chase	2	Historical simulation	99	1Q:1998	28	Quarterly
Citigroup	1	NA	99	4Q:1997	29	Quarterly
Wachovia	4	Variance/co-variance & Historical simulation	97.5	4Q:1997	29	Quarterly
U.S. Bancorp	8	Volatility-based measures	99	44Q:1999	21	Quarterly
Mellon	34	Historical simulation	95	1Q:1997	32	Quarterly
PNC	20	NA	99	4Q:1997	29	Quarterly
National City	10	Historical simulation	97.5	4Q:1998	7	Annually
Suntrust	9	Bloomberg analytics, risk metrics	99	1Q:2003	8	Quarterly
Key	18	Historical simulation	95	4Q:1997	29	Quarterly
Wells Fargo	5	NA	99	4Q:2001	4	Annually
State Street	17	Historical simulation	99	4Q:1997	28	Quarterly
Bank One*	NA	Various	99	4Q:1998	22	Quarterly
Fleet Boston†	NA	Industry standard techniques	99	4Q:1999	17	Quarterly

Note: Table 1 lists the sample banks and a brief description of their VaR model as reported in company disclosures. The "Ranking" column shows each bank's respective rank in terms of total assets as reported by the Federal Reserve on 31 December 2004. The "First observation" column denotes the starting point for VaR data collection for each bank in the study. The differences between banks as to the first observation reflect the fact that some banks began disclosing VaR before others. The "Frequency" column illustrates the regularity with which VaR disclosures are made by each bank.

*Bank One merged with JP Morgan Chase as of July 2004.

†Fleet Boston merged with Bank of America as of June 2004. Therefore, the observations for these firms are limited to the periods in which they operated as independent entities.

outlined below, is consistent with both Jorion (2002) and Liu *et al.* (2004).

Periodic trading VaR disclosures, which represent a one-day risk estimate unless otherwise noted, are transformed using the square root of time rule to achieve quarterly measure as shown below:

$$\text{VaR}_t(\text{quarter}) = \text{VaR}_t(\text{day})\sqrt{63}.$$

Differences in confidence levels across banks are accounted for by scaling reported VaR figures by the respective standard normal variable α that corresponds to the reported confidence level as described below (e.g., $\alpha = 2.33$ for a confidence level of 99%):

$$\text{Standardized VaR} = \text{VaR}_t/\alpha.$$

These standardized VaR figures represent VaR_t, which is then used in the regression analysis for each hypothesis.

4.2. *Additional Variables*

The following additional data are collected from quarterly Y9-C reports[5] filed with the Federal Reserve: notional amounts of derivatives, 0–1 year repricing gap, total trading assets, total risk-based capital and after-tax income.[6] These variables serve as controls for the regression models. Quarterly betas were estimated by regressing the daily returns of each stock on the daily S&P 500 return for each quarter in the form:

$$R_{i,t} = \alpha + \beta R_{m,t} + \varepsilon_t. \tag{1}$$

In addition, daily bond price data were collected from Datastream to examine VaR's implications for debtholders.[7]

Descriptive statistics for each data series are provided in Table 2. As shown in Panel A, all of the balance sheet data distributions exhibit positive skewness and leptokurtosis. In particular, the VaR figures varied widely across the sample banks ranging between 300 and 123,000. This dramatic variation in risk levels across banks is not surprising considering the size of the banks' trading operations also

Table 2. Descriptive statistics.

	Mean	Median	Max.	Min.	Std. dev.	Skewness	Kurtosis
Panel A (in thousands)							
VaR	19,651	8,000	123,000	300	25,349	1.7465	5.5571
GAP	67,276	34,896	329,000	−8,543	68,290	1.4750	4.3839
NOT	3,880,000	118,000	43,800,000	1,601	7,740,000	2.8159	11.6279
TTA	31,873	3,759	289,000	1,200	61,308	2.4565	8.3292
Total RBC	23,960	13,440	101,000	2,117	22,585	1.4193	4.2750
ATE	2,010	1,011	17,853	−1,359	2,705	2.9234	13.0524
Panel B							
Stock returns	0.0270	0.0269	0.7426	−0.4604	0.1526	0.2294	4.5889
S&P 500 returns	0.0165	0.0255	0.2462	−0.1602	0.0976	−0.0451	2.6933
Bond returns	0.0053	0.0001	0.1035	−0.0615	0.0274	0.5379	3.5320
10YT-bond yield	0.0501	0.0507	0.0690	0.0356	0.0092	0.1406	1.8998
1YT-bond yield	0.0381	0.0428	0.0623	0.0107	0.0187	−0.2159	1.4299

Note: This table illustrates the nature of the distribution for each of the variables in the sample. VaR is the raw VaR figure reported by each bank in 10-Q and 10-K filings with the SEC. GAP reflects the difference between assets and liabilities that will be repriced within the next year (i.e., 0–1 repricing gap), excluding those items with indefinite terms (e.g., demand deposits). NOT is the total amount of outstanding derivatives held by each bank. TTA is the total amount of trading assets. Total RBC is the total amount of risk-based capital and ATE is the reported after-tax earnings. All financial asset yields and returns are reported on a quarterly basis.

varied widely as shown by the statistics for the total amount of trading assets (TTA).

Panel B displays statistics for the asset return and yield distributions. They are closer to normal than the balance sheet data distributions, but they too exhibit some significant departures from normality. Specifically, stock returns varied quite dramatically over the sample period as reflected by the standard deviation of 0.1526 while the treasury yield series are characterized by flat distributions.

We build our analysis around the models employed by Liu *et al.* (2004) but make some changes to the way in which the models are implemented. Liu *et al.* scale the variables VaR_t, NOT_t and GAP_t by firm size measures. They use the book value of equity as a measure for firm size. They rationalize this scaling procedure by citing Ahmed *et al.* (1999) who analyze the impact of interest rate changes on stock price *sensitivity*. As beta is also a measure of stock sensitivity, this seems to be a plausible method for scaling the variables.

Instead of scaling the variables by firm size, we take their natural log. This is because it isolates the effect of each independent variable on the dependent variable without introducing a bias of any type into the model. As Liu *et al.* note, there are no structural models of the relationship between trading VaR and priced risk measures such as beta. Hence, they estimate variations of the commonly used market model in an effort to explain this relationship. This model is outlined below[10]:

$$\beta_{t+1} = \alpha + \gamma_1 \mathrm{VaR}_t + \gamma_2 \mathrm{NOT}_t + \gamma_3 \mathrm{GAP}_t + \gamma_4 \beta_t + \varepsilon_{t+1}, \qquad (2)$$

where

$\mathrm{VaR}_t =$ the natural log of the standardized trading VaR in period t,
$\mathrm{NOT}_t =$ the natural log of the outstanding notional derivatives for period t,
$\mathrm{GAP}_t =$ the natural log of the 0–1 year repricing gap for period t and
$\beta_t =$ the respective firm beta for period t.

The total notional amount of outstanding derivatives is commonly used as a gauge of risk exposure (see Liu *et al.*, 2004). Hence, it has been included here to control for the impact that this risk exposure would be expected to have on beta. However, this variable provides no indication of the magnitude of risk because it does not reflect the extent to which offsetting instruments hedge each other. VaR_t is expected to have an incremental effect on beta in addition to NOT_t because it is indicative of the magnitude of risk.

Similarly, the one-year repricing gap controls for the effect of short-term interest rate risk and its effect on beta. Again, VaR_t is expected to contribute additional explanatory power for beta because it is a more comprehensive risk metric.

4.3. *Hypothesis 2*

Equation (2) suggests that next period's beta is influenced by trading VaR, the amount of notional derivatives and the one-year repricing gap. Therefore, we use Eq. (2) as a basis for examining share returns by substituting it into the commonly used market model as follows[11]:

$$R_{t+1} = \alpha + R_{m,t+1}(\gamma_1 \mathrm{VaR}_t + \gamma_2 \mathrm{NOT}_t + \gamma_3 \beta_t) + \varepsilon_{t+1}, \quad (3)$$

where

VaR_t = the natural log of the standardized trading VaR in period t,
NOT_t = the natural log of outstanding notional derivatives for period t,
β_t = the respective firm beta for period t and
$R_{m,t+1}$ = the return on the S&P 500 Index for the following period.

Equation 3 differs from that of Liu *et al.* insofar as they do not include VaR_t and NOT_t as part of the interaction term. However, Ke (2004) argues that since VaR_t, NOT_t, and beta are alternative systematic risk proxies, they should be treated alike. That is, if beta is a function of these other variables, then these other variables should be treated in the same manner as beta for the purposes of examining share returns. Therefore, we contend that Eq. (3) is more suitable for our purposes than the model proposed by Liu *et al.* (2004). Following the theory of risk and return, we anticipate a positive relationship between trading VaR and shareholder returns. A significant coefficient for VaR_t would confirm that VaR has a priced component and imply that shareholders are in fact compensated for the risk contained in bank trading portfolios.

4.4. *Hypothesis 3*

Much work has been done regarding the determinants of bond returns and it is commonly accepted that they are primarily determined by changes in the level, slope and curvature of the interest rate term structure (e.g., Driessen *et al.*, 2003; Knez *et al.*, 1994; Litterman and Scheinkman, 1991). Therefore, we do not intend to completely reexamine this issue here but rather conduct a test of VaR's role in debt markets by examining the relationship between VaR disclosures and bond returns.

We aim to examine whether bondholders are compensated for the trading risk assumed by banks. Specifically, we estimate the following model:

$$\mathrm{BR}_{t+1} = \alpha + \gamma_1 \mathrm{VaR}_t + \gamma_2 \Delta\mathrm{SP}_{t+1} + \gamma_3 \Delta\mathrm{IR}_{t+1} + \gamma_4 \Delta\mathrm{YC}_{t+1} + \varepsilon_{t+1}, \quad (4)$$

where

BR_{t+1} = the return on the corresponding bond in period $t+1$,
VaR_t = the natural log of the standardized trading VaR in period t,
$\Delta\mathrm{SP}_{t+1}$ = the change in the firm's stock price in period $t+1$,
$\Delta\mathrm{IR}_{t+1}$ = the change in the 10-year U.S. treasury bond yield in period $t+1$ and
$\Delta\mathrm{YC}_{t+1}$ = the change in the slope of the U.S. treasury yield curve in period $t+1$.

Our hypothesis states that trading VaR and bond returns should exhibit a positive relationship. The change in stock price within the period serves as a proxy for idiosyncratic risk. We include it on the assumption that stock prices reflect the firms' business prospects as investors' beliefs are continually impounded to stock prices. Hence, stock price change in this case essentially represents an indirect control for credit risk.

The term structure of interest rates has been shown to be a major determinant of bond returns. Thus, we control for this effect by including the change in treasury rates and slope of the yield curve to determine if VaR has incremental explanatory power for bond returns beyond these traditional variables. Consistent with the prior models, the natural log of VaR_t was taken to better approximate the scale of the dependent variable. The remaining independent variables are already consistent with the scale of the dependent variable.

This model is subject to several limitations. First, it is widely known that bonds with differing maturities and coupons also have differing levels of price sensitivity and therefore differing expected returns.

However, due to our small sample it is not possible to collate a sufficiently large sub-sample of bonds with similar characteristics. In fact, some of the smaller institutions had only one outstanding bond series on issue during the sample period. Second, we do not have a direct control for credit quality differences between bonds. Stock return volatility is included to provide an indirect control for this factor, but credit ratings would provide a more direct control for this effect.

4.5. *Hypothesis 4*

The objective here is to examine whether high-trading VaR is motivated by successive losses in earnings. Thus, we use the following model:

$$\begin{aligned}\mathrm{VaR}_t = \alpha + \gamma_1 \Delta\mathrm{ATE}_t + \gamma_2 \Delta\mathrm{ATE}_{t-1} + \gamma_3 \mathrm{RBC}_t + \gamma_4 \mathrm{TTA}_t \\ + \gamma_5 \mathrm{MI}_{t-1} + \gamma_6 \Delta\mathrm{IR}_{t-1} + \varepsilon_t, \qquad (5)\end{aligned}$$

where

$\Delta\mathrm{ATE}_t =$ the change in after-tax earnings for periods t and $t-1$ respectively,
$\mathrm{RBC}_t =$ the natural log of the total amount of risk-based capital for period t,
$\mathrm{TTA}_t =$ the natural log of total trading assets for period t,
$\Delta\mathrm{MI}_{t-1} =$ the change in the S&P 500 market index during period $t-1$,
$\Delta\mathrm{IR}_{t-1} =$ the change in the 10-year U.S. treasury rate for period $t-1$.

We conjecture that changes in the level of earnings for the two previous periods may affect the level of trading risk that firms choose to bear. The choice of these two periods is arbitrary but it seems logical that if there is a relationship between earnings and VaR, it should be strongest for the most recent periods. The coefficients of concern for this model are γ_1 and γ_2. The model controls for the level of risk capital, total trading assets and both equity market and interest rate volatility as, intuitively, these factors will affect the risk of the trading portfolio. For example, VaR is constrained by the level of capital held and the value of assets in the portfolio. Similarly, VaR is, by definition, a function of market volatility.

Ideally, tier 3 capital (market risk capital) is preferable relative to total risk-based capital because it directly corresponds to trading risk. However, because the market risk capital charge was not binding for some firms within the sample, tier 3 capital could not be used.

5. Empirical Results

5.1. *Hypothesis 1*

Table 3 reports the pooled OLS estimation[10] of Eq. (2). This model regresses beta in period $t+1$ on VaR_t, NOT_t, GAP_t and the lagged dependent variable. The results based on the full sample are shown

Table 3. Pooled OLS estimation of Eq. (2).

$$\beta_{t+1} = \alpha + \gamma_1 \text{VaR}_t + \gamma_2 \text{NOT}_t + \gamma_3 \text{GAP}_t + \gamma_4 \beta_t + \varepsilon_{t+1}$$

	Coefficient	Std. error	*t*-statistic	*p*-value
Panel A				
Full sample				
α	0.5981	0.1849	3.24	0.0007
VaR_t	0.0214	0.0104	2.06	0.0200
NOT_t	0.0095	0.0052	1.81	0.0356
GAP_t	−0.0430	0.0143	−3.00	0.0015
β_t	0.7680	0.0468	16.40	0.0000
Adj. R^2	0.27			
N	322			
Panel B				
Ex. 3Q–4Q 1998				
α	0.5790	0.2141	2.71	0.0037
VaR_t	0.0301	0.0133	2.27	0.0121
NOT_t	0.0082	0.0058	1.43	0.0776
GAP_t	−0.0429	0.0167	−2.57	0.0055
β_t	0.7142	0.0667	10.7	0.0000
Adj. R^2	0.27			
N	305			

Note: The dependent variable is the beta estimate for period $t+1$ obtained from Eq. (1). VaR_t is the natural log of the standardized trading VaR. NOT_t is the natural log of total notional amount of outstanding derivatives. GAP_t refers to the natural log of the 0–1 year repricing gap excluding those items with indefinite repricing such as demand deposits and β_t is the lagged dependent variable.

in Table 3 Panel A. The coefficient on VaR_t is significant at the 5% level. The results support Hypothesis 1 and thus it can be inferred that disclosed VaR figures are indeed significantly related to next period's beta.

Due to the extreme volatility of financial markets in the last half of 1998, we also run the pooled OLS regression excluding the third and fourth quarters of that year to determine whether that volatility had any material impact on the initial results. The results are reported in Panel B. These results are consistent with those reported in Panel A. Our results are consistent with the findings of Liu *et al.* (2004) despite the difference in the way in which the independent variables are transformed. In addition, the adjusted R-squared of 27% suggests that our transformation may in fact be more suitable than that used by Liu *et al.* (adjusted R-squared is 6%).

Based on these results, we draw two conclusions. First, as Liu *et al.* (2004) argue, VaR appears to capture a priced component of risk. Second, consistent with Hypothesis 1, disclosed trading VaR is reflected in the following period's beta. We contend that this lagged relationship reflects the fact that VaR disclosures are impounded in stock prices during the following period once these data are made public in end-of-period disclosures. This explanation seems more plausible because it more closely corresponds to the construct of beta.

5.2. *Hypothesis 2*

We test Hypothesis 2 by incorporating an interaction term with respect to VaR_t and NOT_t such that these variables are treated in the same manner as beta. The aim of this model is to determine whether shareholders are compensated for the market risk borne by banks in their trading portfolios as measured by VaR. We estimate this relationship by regressing stock returns for period $t + 1$ on the market return for period $t + 1$ and an interaction term including VaR_t, NOT_t, and beta. The results of this regression are shown in Table 4. Panel A reports the results of the model based on the full sample while Panel B shows the results excluding the latter half of 1998.

Table 4. Pooled OLS estimation of Eq. (3).

$$R_{t+1} = \alpha + R_{m,t+1}(\gamma_1 \text{VaR}_t + \gamma_2 \text{NOT}_t + \gamma_3 \beta_t) + \varepsilon_{t+1}$$

	Coefficient	Std. error	t-statistic	p-value
Panel A				
Full sample				
α	0.0098	0.0064	1.53	0.0552
VaR_t	−0.0432	0.0761	−0.56	0.2703
NOT_t	0.0373	0.0411	0.91	0.1489
β	0.5750	0.2100	2.74	0.0141
Adj. R^2	0.40			
N	322			
Panel B				
Ex. 3Q–4Q 1998				
α	0.0151	0.0066	2.28	0.0094
VaR_t	0.0493	0.0855	0.58	0.2682
NOT_t	0.0071	0.0471	0.15	0.4377
β	0.157	0.2737	0.57	0.3124
Adj. R^2	0.29			
N	305			

Note: The dependent variable is realized holding period returns for period $t + 1$. All independent variables are as described in Table 3. However, in this model, they have each been interacted with the market return as discussed earlier. The results of the model in each panel have been adjusted for autocorrelation with one lag. The reported t-statistics have been adjusted to account for heteroskedasticity using White's process.

The results in Table 4 do not support the hypothesis that disclosed VaR is significantly related to the following period's stock return. This finding contradicts that of Liu *et al.* (2004) who show VaR_t to be significantly related to the following period's realized returns. Moreover, the result is perplexing in that if VaR_t and NOT_t are significantly related to beta, then the CAPM would suggest a significant relationship between these variables and realized returns as well. An additional confounding result is that the coefficient of β_t is insignificant in Panel B. We suspect that the insignificance of VaR_t and NOT_t may be due to multicollinearity considering their relatively high correlation of 79.45%. Therefore, we reestimate the model excluding NOT_t. The results of this estimation are shown in Table 5.

Excluding NOT_t from the model has no significant impact on the coefficient for VaR_t. It remains insignificant as noted by the p-value

Table 5. Pooled OLS estimation of Eq. (3) excluding NOT_t.

$$R_{t+1} = \alpha + R_{m,t+1}(\gamma_1 \text{VaR}_t + \gamma_2 \beta_t) + \varepsilon_{t+1}$$

	Coefficient	Std. error	t-statistic	p-value
Full sample				
α	0.01	0.0062	1.62	0.0527
VaR_t	0.0221	0.0284	0.78	0.2184
β	0.6286	0.2618	2.40	0.0085
Adj. R^2	0.40			
N	322			

Note: All variables are as described in Table 4. However, NOT_t has been dropped from the model to determine whether multicollinearity affected the results of the original regression. VaR_t was again interacted with the market return as described earlier. This model has been adjusted with one lag to eliminate autocorrelation in the residuals. The reported t-statistics have been adjusted to account for heteroskedasticity using White's process.

of 0.2184. Hence, there is still no statistical evidence of a significant relationship between disclosed VaR and the following period's stock returns and thus we are forced to reject Hypothesis 2.

The lack of VaR_t's significance in both of these models brings into question the conclusion drawn from Eq. (2), which suggested that VaR has a priced component. If in fact VaR contains a priced component, the CAPM would suggest that the coefficient on VaR_t should be statistically significant when examining stock returns as well. This lack of significance suggests that shareholders are not compensated for the risk contained in bank trading portfolios. Hence, from a shareholder's perspective, banks with a conservative approach to trading may represent better investments relative to banks that trade aggressively.

5.3. *Hypothesis 3*

To examine the relationship between disclosed VaR and returns to bondholders, we run a pooled OLS regression by including changes in treasury yields and the slope of the yield curve as control variables. The results are displayed in Panels A and B (excluding VaR_t in order to ascertain its impact on the results) of Table 6.[11]

Table 6. Pooled OLS estimation of Eq. (4).

$$\mathrm{BR}_{t+1} = \alpha + \gamma_1 \mathrm{VaR}_t + \gamma_2 \Delta\mathrm{SP}_{t+1} + \gamma_3 \Delta\mathrm{IR}_{t+1} + \gamma_4 \Delta\mathrm{YC}_{t+1} + \varepsilon_{t+1}$$

	Coefficient	Std. error	*t*-statistic	*p*-value
Panel A				
Full sample				
α	−0.0182	0.0072	−2.55	0.0061
VaR_t	0.0018	0.0007	2.64	0.0005
$\Delta\mathrm{SP}_{t+1}$	0.0018	0.0007	2.64	0.0005
$\Delta\mathrm{IR}_{t+1}$	−5.4557	0.3187	−17.12	0.0000
$\Delta\mathrm{YC}_{t+1}$	1.6657	0.2548	6.54	0.0000
Adj. R^2	0.75			
N	322			
Panel B				
Full Sample Ex. VaR				
α	0.0012	0.0009	1.28	0.1013
$\Delta\mathrm{SP}_{t+1}$	0.0213	0.0058	3.67	0.0000
$\Delta\mathrm{IR}_{t+1}$	−5.1735	0.2652	−19.5	0.0000
$\Delta\mathrm{YC}_{t+1}$	1.7463	0.3338	5.23	0.0000
Adj. R^2	0.72			
N	322			

Note: The dependent variable is the bond-holding period return for period $t+1$. VaR_t is as described earlier. $\Delta\mathrm{SP}_{t+1}$ is the change in stock price. $\Delta\mathrm{IR}_{t+1}$ refers to the change in the level of interest rates as measured by the yield on 10-year U.S. treasury bonds and $\Delta\mathrm{YC}_{t+1}$ is the change in the slope of the yield curve equal to the difference between 2- and 10-year treasury bond yields. The model has been adjusted for autocorrelation with two lags. The reported *t*-statistics have been adjusted for heteroskedasticity using White's process.

All variables are highly significant for each version of the model as indicated by the extremely low *p*-values. Thus, despite VaR's insignificance with respect to equity returns, the results indicate that there is a highly significant relationship with the following period's bond returns. In addition, the adjusted *R*-squared of 75% indicates that this regression model explains much of the variation in bond returns. Furthermore, as shown in Panel B, excluding VaR_t from the model reduces the adjusted *R*-squared by 3%. This is an encouraging result which suggests that VaR_t does indeed have explanatory power for bond returns above and beyond the traditional variables.

In order to check the robustness of the relationship between VaR_t and the dependent variable, the model is respecified in various ways.[12]

VaR's robustness to these changes in specification is indicative of a strong relationship with bond returns. Overall, the results suggest that bond returns are indeed sensitive to the level of trading risk within bank trading portfolios.

5.4. *Hypothesis 4*

Hypothesis 4 states that changes in earnings in previous periods affect the level of trading risk that banks choose to assume. We estimate this relationship by regressing VaR_t on the changes in after-tax earnings in periods $[t - (t - 1)]$ and $[t - 1 - (t - 2)]$ while controlling for the level of trading assets, total risk-based capital and equity market and interest rate volatility during the previous period. The results are displayed in Panels A and B of Table 7.

The results indicate that there is a statistically significant relationship between changes in earnings and trading VaR levels in both the full sample and sub-sample. More importantly, the coefficients for ΔATE_t and ΔATE_{t-1} are both negative, indicating that decreases in earnings may lead to increased trading risk as proposed by Hypothesis 4. Furthermore, the adjusted R-squared of 58% indicates that this model does a good job of explaining the variation in VaR_t. Moreover, the results are not materially changed in Panel B when the last two quarters of 1998 are excluded. In addition, the result is unaffected by the changes in model specification[13]:

Collectively, the results show that there is a strong statistical relationship between VaR and adverse changes in earnings. Therefore, we contend that the trading portfolio may indeed represent a moral hazard to bondholders and depositors insofar as the level of risk within it seems to be, at least in part, determined by adverse changes in earnings. The existence of deposit insurance obviously diminishes this effect for depositors because in the event that trading losses cause a bank to become insolvent, they would be reimbursed. However, this insurance generally only applies up to a certain amount. Depositors would lose amounts in excess of the insurance limit. Furthermore, the existence of deposit insurance essentially transfers the moral hazard effect from depositors to the insurer.

Table 7. Pooled OLS estimation of Eq. (5).

$$\text{VaR}_t = \alpha + \gamma_1 \Delta\text{ATE}_t + \gamma_2 \Delta\text{ATE}_{t-1} + \gamma_3 \text{RBC}_t + \gamma_4 \text{TTA}_t + \gamma_5 \Delta\text{MI}_{t-1} + \gamma_6 \Delta\text{IR}_{t-1} + \varepsilon_t$$

	Coefficient	Std. error	t-statistic	p-value
Panel A				
Full sample				
α	0.6882	3.2806	0.21	0.4170
ΔATE_t	−0.0460	0.0200	−2.29	0.0115
ΔATE_{t-1}	−0.0602	0.0197	−3.05	0.0013
RBC_t	0.3327	0.2117	1.57	0.0687
ITA_t	0.2666	0.0706	3.77	0.0001
ΔMI_{t-1}	−0.1579	0.1125	−1.40	0.1118
ΔIR_{t-1}	7.2684	3.5171	2.07	0.0199
Adj. R^2	0.58			
N	322			
Panel B				
EX. 3Q–4Q 1998				
α	1.1648	3.6700	0.32	0.3757
ΔATE_t	−0.0467	0.0194	−2.40	0.0086
ΔATE_{t-1}	−0.0566	0.0200	−2.83	0.0026
RBC_t	0.2646	0.2303	1.15	0.1259
ITA_t	0.3085	0.0754	4.09	0.0001
ΔMI_{t-1}	−0.1006	0.1252	−0.80	0.2112
ΔIR_{t-1}	6.7737	3.6294	1.87	0.0317
Adj. R^2	0.54			
N	305			

Note: The dependent variable is the standardized VaR figure for period t. ΔATE_t is after-tax earnings for the designated period. RBC_t is the total amount of risk-based capital. TTA_1 refers to the amount to trading assets held by each firm. ΔMI_{t-1} and ΔIR_{t-1} reflect the change in the S&P 500 Index and 10-year treasury bond yields respectively. Each version of the model has been adjusted for autocorrelation with two lags.

6. Conclusion

As the use of VaR has become increasingly more widespread in the recent past, the underlying theory on which it is based, its various models and regulatory uses have been tested and examined by researchers. However, one gap within the literature relates to VaR's implications for the various groups of bank stakeholders. This gap is a paradox of sorts since the risk/return trade-off is a fundamental concept within the finance discipline. This chapter has attempted to address that gap by reexamining two previously proposed hypotheses as well as introducing two new conjectures to the literature.

Based on Hypotheses 1 and 3, VaR appears to have a priced component because it is significantly related to beta and bond returns. However, this result does not carry over to stock returns in Hypothesis 2. This inconsistency is quite perplexing. The different relationship between VaR and stock and bond returns may potentially be due to the relatively large amount of interest sensitive assets in bank trading portfolios. However, this reason cannot explain the diverging results of Eqs. (2) and (3) with respect to beta and stock returns. Based on the underlying theory of the CAPM, it seems that VaR should be significantly related to stock returns because it appears to be significantly related to beta which implies that VaR contains a priced component of risk. Yet, the data do not support this.

Overall, the results presented herein suggest that beta and bond returns are sensitive to the level of trading risk a bank assumes while equity returns are not. Thus, it would seem that, based on this finding, conservative banks may represent better investments from a stockholder's perspective. In addition, the results for Hypothesis 4 suggest that VaR has implications beyond the trading portfolio because it appears to be affected by changes in the level of earnings in previous periods. This could imply that the trading portfolio may represent a moral hazard to some groups of stakeholders, bondholders in particular, because the increase in expected returns from taking on more trading risk does not directly accrue to them but indeed they can be affected by the increase in risk.

VaR certainly seems to be a useful measure of risk despite many arguments to the contrary. Therefore, it seems prudent for regulators to continue to integrate VaR and its disclosure into the regulatory framework. As the VaR modeling process and the aforementioned empirical testing models become more refined, VaR's importance for the various stakeholder groups will become increasingly more apparent.

Endnotes

1. In the context of this chapter, VaR or trading VaR refers to the market risk within bank trading portfolio.

2. VaR disclosures data was sourced from the Federal Reserve Bank of Chicago website (http://www.chicagofed.org).
3. Due to data limitation, only large banks reported VaR figures during the sample period, hence, selection bias is inevitable.
4. In some cases, data had to be excluded from the sample because disclosure policies were not consistent for the duration of the sample period. For example, Bank of America initially made two sets of VaR disclosures; one based on the assumption of perfect positive correlation between trading assets and another based on the assumption of zero correlation. The company then changed its disclosure format in 1999 to include a single figure which accounted for diversification effects across assets. Therefore, these later disclosures are not comparable to prior periods due to the change in the manner in which VaR was disclosed. Hence, the earlier data were excluded from the study to create a comparable data set. In the event that a firm subsequently adjusted data from prior years to facilitate comparison with later data, the amended figures were included in the sample so as to increase the number of observations. This decision is based on the assumption that the restated figures still accurately reflect actual risk levels.
5. Y-9C reports consist of a balance sheet, an income statement and detailed supporting schedules, including a schedule of off-balance sheet items.
6. These data are sourced from the Federal Reserve Bank of Chicago's website (http//www.chicagofed.org).
7. Clean prices were used as the basis for bond returns to standardize the data across different bond series. All bond price returns reflect quarterly holding period returns that correspond to VaR data.
8. We did not include leverage as part of interest rate risk measure because banks debt equity ratios are substantially higher (due to the nature of their business — that is borrowing funds to lend them; hence, inevitably they will have a great dependence on liabilities as sources of funds) than those of non-financial institutions; hence, it may not provide meaningful information of risk measure. In addition, this model is consistent with Liu *et al.* (2004).
9. GAP has been dropped from this model due to its directional indication of risk.
10. In the analysis, we assume the correlations of error terms across banks are zero.
11. The results for this model could not be broken down into a sub-sample excluding the last half of 1998 as was done for other models because the bond return sample begins after this period.
12. Specifically, VaR_t's significance is unaffected by the following changes in model specification: (i) exclusion of the yield curve slope, 10-year treasury yield, and stock return volatility, (ii) inclusion of the level of interest rates measured as the yield on 10-year treasury bonds (as opposed to the change in that yield) and (iii) inclusion of the lagged dependent variable.
13. We exclude ΔMI_{t-1} and ΔIR_{t-1} and substitute the slope of the treasury yield curve for ΔIR_{t-1}.These results have not been reported due to space constraints. However, interested readers may obtain a copy from the author upon request.

Acknowledgment

We would like to thank Rob Brown and Robert Faff for their helpful comments.

References

Ahmed, A, A Beatty and B Bettinghaus (1999). Evidence on the efficacy of market risk disclosures by commerial banks. Working paper, Pennsylvania State University.

Bali, T and N Cakici (2004). Value at risk and expected stock returns. *Financial Analysts Journal*, 60, March/April, 57–73.

Chen, NF, R Roll and SA Ross (1986). Economic forces and the stock market. *Journal of Business*, 59, 383–403.

Chipalkatti, N and V Datar (2006). The relevance of VaR disclosures: Evidence from the LCTM crisis. *Journal of Financial Regulation and Compliance*, 14(2), 174–184.

Driessen, J, B Melenberg and T Nijman (2003). Common factors in international bond returns. *Journal of International Money and Finance*, 22(5), 629–656.

Federal Reserve Bank of Chicago (2004). http://www.chicagofed.org.

Jorion, P (2002). How informative are value-at-risk disclosures? *Accounting Review*, 77(4), 911–931.

Ke, B (2004). Discussion of "How banks value-at-risk disclosures predict their total and priced risk: Effects of bank technical sophistication and learning over time". *Review of Accounting Studies*, 9(2–3), 295–299.

Knez, P, R Litterman and J Scheinkman (1994). Explorations into factors explaining money market returns. *Journal of Finance*, 49(5), 1861–1882.

Litterman, R and J Scheinkman (1991). Common factors affecting bond returns. *Journal of Fixed Income*, 1, 54–61.

Liu, C, S Ryan and H Tan (2004). How banks' value-at-risk disclosures predict their total and priced risk: Effects of bank technical sophistication and learning over time. *Review of Accounting Studies*, 9(2–3), 265–294.

Securities and Exchange Commission (SEC) (1997). Disclosure of accounting policies for derivative financial instruments and derivative commodity instruments and disclosure of quantitative and qualitative information about market risk inherent in derivative financial instruments. Release No. 33-7386, FRR No. 48, Washington, D.C.

2

Ex-Ante Versus Ex-Post Regulation of Bank Capital

Arup Daripa and Simone Varotto

1. Introduction

The principal justification for capital regulation of banks rests on two factors. First, it has a role in ameliorating moral hazard induced by deposit insurance.[1] The problem would not arise if deposit insurance premiums reflect true portfolio risk. However, typically, the regulator does not have full information on the portfolio risk of a particular bank, which makes setting actuarially fair risk-based premiums difficult (see Chan *et al.*, 1992).[2] This implies a scope for additional solvency regulation. Indeed, as several authors have shown, risk-based capital regulation plays a role in designing incentive-compatible risk-sensitive deposit insurance under asymmetric information.[3]

Second, capital regulation also serves to mitigate negative externalities arising from the failure of a bank. The importance of this "systemic risk" problem[4] has been underlined by the recent financial turmoil in the credit markets that has led to massive central bank and government interventions in many countries around the world. While the above discusses reasons behind capital regulation,[5] this chapter focuses on a related but different question. Given that capital regulation is an integral part of bank regulation, what form should it take?

In this chapter, we construct a simple framework to analyze this issue. In our model, the risk carried by a bank as well as managerial risk preference are a bank's private information. Our contribution can be summarized as follows. We show that ex-ante regulation wastes the private risk information of a bank, while ex-post regulation makes full use of it. However, we show that the latter is more vulnerable to the problem of unknown managerial risk aversion. The results imply that the two forms of regulation are complements, rather than substitutes. We characterize the optimal mix, and describe the scenario in which ex-post regulation emerges as the dominant element in the optimal combination, and that in which ex-ante regulation dominates. Finally, we use the results to shed light on current concerns arising from Basel II and the credit crunch.

Broadly speaking, there are two distinct forms of capital regulation: ex-ante and ex-post. One approach is to specify minimum capital requirements as a proportion of a bank's risk-weighted assets. This imposes an ex-ante constraint on risk taking by a bank, and forces an exogenous link between risk and capital. An alternative design gives a bank freedom to choose capital and portfolio risk. Regulatory intervention is triggered if losses exceed a certain threshold. The threat of intervention endogenously induces a link between risk and capital. Since such a scheme conditions on the outcome of bank actions, this is referred to as ex-post regulation.

Basel I, introduced in 1988, imposed pure ex-ante constraints. This regime is gradually being replaced by Basel II, the new capital adequacy framework which combines ex-post features with ex-ante constraints. Pillar 1 of Basel II is dominated by ex-ante rules, while Pillar 2 introduces explicit ex-post elements. Therefore, natural questions arise about the efficiency of different forms of capital regulation, and how they fit together. In spite of the considerable practical importance of this issue, the theoretical literature offers little consensus or clarity on the comparison of different forms of capital regulation. This chapter is an attempt to fill this gap. In doing so, we clarify the theoretical reasons for inclusion of Pillar 2 alongside Pillar 1. To the best of our knowledge, this is the first paper to address this issue.

Under the condition of full information, all regimes are equally efficient. However, as Fama (1985) and others have noted, information asymmetries are endemic to the problem of regulating banks. Once this is taken into account, we show that ex-ante and ex-post regimes have very different properties. Therefore, questions about when a particular form should be used, and how different forms fit together are not only theoretically interesting but also of immediate practical relevance. As Fama (1985) points out, banks typically have private information on their clients, and this is fundamental to explaining the special nature of banks.[6] Therefore, a bank can usually make a more precise estimate of its own portfolio risk compared to the regulator.

A further source of information asymmetry is the risk preference of a bank, which is typically the bank's private information. In the event of bankruptcy, shareholders usually lose only the capital they contribute. Such limited liability increases their appetite for risk. On the other hand, the risk preference of bank managers ultimately depends on the firm-specific human capital of the manager, reputational concerns, as well as the form of management compensation.

The level of bank capital can also influence the manager's degree of risk aversion. An additional factor is the extent to which the bank is controlled by the management. Management-controlled institutions tend to be more conservative than stockholder-controlled organizations. For example, Saunders and colleagues (1990) study the relationship between bank ownership structure and risk taking. They find support for the hypotheses that stockholder-controlled banks take more risk compared to manager-controlled banks, and that deregulation makes this difference more pronounced.

The above-mentioned discussion motivates our modeling of informational structure. True portfolio risk and the degree of managerial risk aversion are private information of a bank. We judge the success of any regulatory regime against this backdrop of multidimensional information asymmetries. Our main results are as follows. We show that an ex-ante regime makes poor use of the expertise of a bank in measuring risk. An ex-post regime, on the other hand, fully incorporates the superior private information of a bank about underlying risk; but in doing so, becomes more sensitive to the problem of unknown managerial risk aversion compared to an ex-ante regime.

This implies that the two regimes are vulnerable to different dimensions of information asymmetry, and their comparison depends on the relative importance of the sources of informational asymmetries. This also suggests that a combination of the two regimes is potentially welfare improving. Even though Basel II combines the two forms of regulation, the theoretical literature largely treats them as substitutes and advocates one or the other.

In contrast, we show that a combined regime outperforms either regime. Moreover, if ex-post penalties are sufficiently regressive,[7] (we show that a linear penalty function can satisfy this), we get a striking characterization: when solvency is the main regulatory concern, and the bank is well capitalized, the optimal mixture involves a strong form of ex-post regulation, combined with a much weaker version of ex-ante regulation. For banks with low capital (a situation faced by several institutions following recent subprime-related losses), even early intervention penalties might be problematic. In such cases, ex-ante regulation plays a more dominant role.

The results above are derived assuming that a bank has superior information on underlying risk. If, however, the bank's ability to assess risk is poor, we show that it is optimal to use only ex-ante regulation. The result underlines the importance of tailoring regulation according to the regulator's assessment of the risk-management ability of a bank through, for example, backtesting or stress testing of a bank's internal risk-measurement models.[8]

Such customization is indeed a feature of Basel II. We relate our results to current trends in regulation and draw policy conclusions. The rest of the chapter is organized as follows. Sections 2 and 3 introduce the model and specify the regulatory benchmark. Sections 4 and 5 analyze ex-ante and ex-post regulations. Section 6 characterizes the optimal combination. Section 7 deals with some special cases on information provision. Section 8 considers extensions of the model. Section 9 relates our results to Basel II, offers policy suggestions, and discusses extensions. Finally, Sec. 10 concludes.

2. The Model

The model is adapted for the case of bank regulation from our work on safety provision Daripa and Varotto (2008). Let us briefly summarize the model at the outset. There are two players: a bank manager and a regulator. The manager can invest in a riskless asset and a risky asset, and chooses a portfolio to maximize expected utility. The regulator does not know either the exact risk of the risky asset, or the degree of risk aversion of the manager. The regulator can observe the fraction invested in the risky asset as well as the bank's capital, and wants to limit the probability of bankruptcy. However, given the information asymmetries, the regulator cannot ensure first best. The actual probability of bank default might deviate from the optimal probability.

A safety loss occurs if the probability of default is too high, and overprotection loss occurs if it is too low. The regulator's objective is to minimize a weighted average of the two kinds of losses. We start describing the model by specifying the investment opportunities facing the bank and its objective function. The bank's total investment is normalized to 1. The bank chooses efficient portfolios of assets. Portfolios are constructed by investing a fraction $(1-\alpha)$ on a riskless asset, and a fraction $\alpha \in \Re$ on a risky asset.[10]

The log return[11] from the risky asset is normally distributed with mean m and standard deviation s. The return from the riskless asset is normalized to 0 and the efficient frontier is a ray from the origin given by $m = \beta s$. Let $\tilde{V}$ denote the log return from the bank's portfolio, where $\tilde{V} \sim N(\alpha m, \alpha s)$. Let σ denote the portfolio risk. Then $\sigma = \alpha s$ and $\tilde{V} \sim N(\beta\sigma, \sigma)$.

2.1. *The Bank's Objective Function*

The objective is to specify the choice of α (the fraction of the portfolio invested in the risky asset) for any given capital level. This is the relevant relation because the regulator can observe both capital and α, and therefore specifies regulation to affect precisely this relationship. For any given level of bank capital, the manager chooses α as follows. A more risky portfolio not only earns a higher expected return but also generates a higher probability of bankruptcy.

As noted in the introduction, default is costly for the manager for several reasons including loss of firm-specific human capital investment, erosion of reputation and loss of future income in the wake of bankruptcy, as well as personal liability issues. Taking into account the level of capital (which affects the probability of bankruptcy for any risk level), personal bankruptcy costs, own risk preferences, as well as the benefit from higher risk, the manager decides on a portfolio risk σ. The benefit of higher risk is parameterized by β. For any given β, the manager's choice of risk depends on his/her sensitivity to the other factors affecting risk preference. The optimal choice of risk therefore varies over some positive interval $[\sigma_L, \sigma_H] \subseteq (0, \infty)$. For any given β, we can express the optimally chosen $\sigma \in [\sigma_L, \sigma_H]$ as

$$\sigma^* = \frac{\beta}{\rho}, \tag{1}$$

where $\rho \in [\rho_L, \rho_H]$ and $\beta/\rho_H = \sigma_L$ and $\beta/\rho_L = \sigma_H$.

This formulation captures the complex factors affecting the manager's decision problem through a managerial "type" ρ. This can be interpreted as the manager's risk aversion factor.[11] This factor increases in bankruptcy costs and private risk aversion. While observing capital conveys information on the managerial type ρ,[12] our analysis rests on the fact that it is not a deterministic function of the level of capital, so that for any given capital level, the regulator faces uncertainty about managerial risk aversion. The informational structure is specified after we set up the regulator's objective function.

2.2. *The Regulator's Objective Function*

As noted by Kim and Santomero (1988), Dimson and Marsh (1995), and Hellmann *et al.* (2000) and other authors, regulators face a trade-off when determining the amount of regulatory capital to be set. Very high capital requirements impose inefficiently high costs on banks.[13] Such a requirement might also inhibit competition by acting as an entry barrier (Dimson and Marsh, 1995). On the other hand, low capital impairs solvency. Therefore, a regulator faces a trade-off between safety and efficiency, which determines a socially optimal probability of default. The regulator attempts to ensure that portfolio risk and capital in a bank are consistent with this probability.

Therefore, in the social optimum, capital and portfolio risk ($\sigma = \alpha s$) should be such that portfolio losses exceed the capital with a specified probability p (e.g., 0.05% when using annual returns). The recent crisis has led to calls for more systemic banks to face tighter regulation. Note that our analysis can accommodate such concerns — the specified p can be bank specific, and can vary across a parameter capturing the degree of systemic importance of a bank. Our conclusions about optimal capital regulation would then also vary across this parameter.

Let $\hat{K}$ denote the capital level. Given that the initial value of the bank's assets is normalized to 1, the bank is in default when $\exp(\tilde{V}) < 1 - \hat{K}$ or, equivalently, when $\tilde{V} < \ln(1 - \hat{K}) \equiv -K$. In what follows we refer to this K as capital.[14] This harmless abuse of terminology allows for a clearer presentation.

Given capital K, portfolio choice should ideally be such that $\Pr(\tilde{V} < -K) = p$. This can be written as $\Phi(-K/\sigma - \beta) = p$, where Φ denotes the standard normal cumulative distribution function. It follows that for any given capital level K, and any σ, the socially optimal portfolio risk is given implicitly by

$$\frac{K}{\sigma} = \Phi^{-1}(1 - p) - \beta \equiv C.$$

Therefore, the socially optimal risk (denoted by σ_0) is

$$\sigma_0 = \frac{K}{C}. \tag{2}$$

We assume that $C > 0$.[15]

Note that the socially optimal risk is different for banks with different levels of capital. Indeed, regulatory regimes would be different for different levels of capital. For any given K, whenever actual risk is different from the socially optimal risk, there is an efficiency loss. If the actual risk ratio exceeds the optimal risk, we say there is a "loss of safety" because the probability that the bank defaults is higher than the regulatory optimum. On the other hand, when the actual risk falls below the optimal risk, we say that there is an "overprotection loss".

Given the capital K held by the bank, the regulator attempts to implement the socially optimal portfolio risk σ_0. This is a non-trivial problem under asymmetric information. The usual optimization problem is simply to minimize the deviation of the actual portfolio risk from the optimal risk. However, this is not necessarily appropriate for bank regulation. Given a level of capital, if the actual portfolio risk is lower than the optimal risk (i.e., overprotection loss occurs), it principally penalizes the shareholders of the bank.

The reason is that under limited liability the payoff of shareholders is a convex function of the return from investment, implying that they prefer higher risk. If, on the other hand, actual risk is higher than the optimal level (i.e., safety loss occurs), it is primarily a problem for depositors, whose payoff is a concave function of the return from investment, implying a preference for lower risk. In general, the regulator might attach different weights to the interests of shareholders and depositors, i.e., different weights to overprotection and safety loss. Dewatripont and Tirole (1994) argue that solvency (i.e., protection against safety loss) is the main goal of bank regulation because banks are not like other financial institutions. The important difference is that banks have a large number of small depositors who face a free-riding problem resulting in poor provision of monitoring of the bank. Therefore, the regulator, who represents the interests of the depositors, has a monitoring role.

A further argument in favor of relatively greater regulatory concern about solvency is the presence of externalities from bank failure. Given significant systemic risk, the regulator needs to ensure that banks internalize the externality. In such cases, the regulator would attach a greater weight to safety loss. On the other hand, overprotection loss might be of importance when it is important to encourage banks to expand lending.[16]

We propose a formulation that encompasses such concerns through a regulatory objective function that allows for safety loss and overprotection loss to be weighted differently. The loss is given by:

$$L = w \max\left(1 - \frac{\sigma_0}{\sigma}, 0\right) + (1 - w) \max\left(\frac{\sigma_0}{\sigma} - 1, 0\right), \qquad (3)$$

where $w \in [0, 1]$. The loss function is the weighted sum of the two types of losses described above. The first element of the sum is the weighted safety loss and the second element is the weighted overprotection loss. We should emphasize that allowing w to take any value in the unit interval makes this a more general regulatory objective function compared to simple loss minimization. The weight w can be thought of as the regulator's "*safety bias*". $w > 0.5$ represents a positive safety bias. Clearly, if $w = 0$, no regulation is trivially the best solution. We ignore this trivial case and assume $w > 0$.

2.3. *Information*

Finally, we specify the informational structure. The regulator faces two dimensions of asymmetric information. First, the standard deviation s of the risky asset is a random variable uniformly distributed on the interval $[s_L, s_H]$. The realization of s is the private information of the bank manager. The regulator knows only the distribution of s.

Second, the type ρ is the bank manager's private information. From the perspective of the regulator, ρ is a random variable which is uniformly distributed on the interval $[\rho_L, \rho_H]$. To ensure that regulation is non-trivial, we need to make a further assumption about the distribution of ρ. This is clarified below.

From Eq. (2), the socially optimal portfolio risk is given by K/C. From Eq. (1), the optimal portfolio risk of a bank with risk aversion ρ is β/ρ. If $K/C < \beta/\rho$, there is a safety loss. Of course, for regulation to have any bite at all, there must be some types of bank managers such that $K/C < \beta/\rho$. Let ρ_0 be the type whose optimal portfolio coincides with the socially optimal portfolio. Thus,

$$K/C < \beta/\rho_0. \tag{4}$$

We proceed with the following general specification. We assume that the managerial risk aversion is not a deterministic function of bank capital. Specifically, we assume that for any finite K chosen by the manager, the support of the distribution of ρ is such that

$$\rho_H \geq \rho_0 > \rho_L. \tag{5}$$

If K is infinite, the regulatory problem is obviously trivial, as the risk chosen by the manager is never greater than the socially optimal risk, which itself is infinite. However, for any K that is not unboundedly large, so long as the above inequality holds,[17] there are types $\rho < \rho_0$ whose optimal risk is higher than the socially optimal risk in the absence of regulation. It follows that, if the regulator observes a finite K in a bank, he/she faces non-trivial uncertainty about the bank manager's type,[18] and the regulatory problem is non-trivial.

2.4. *A Picture of the Model*

Figure 1 summarizes the model. For any given type ρ, the portfolio risk $\sigma = \alpha s$ is a constant given by β/ρ. Thus, in (α, s) space, the optimal choice of ρ is a rectangular hyperbola. The socially optimal portfolio risk is K/C, another constant. Thus, this is also a rectangular hyperbola — it coincides with the optimal choice of type ρ_0.

The figure shows the hyperbolas associated with types ρ_H, ρ_L and ρ_0. The positions of the three hyperbolas reflect assumption (5). For

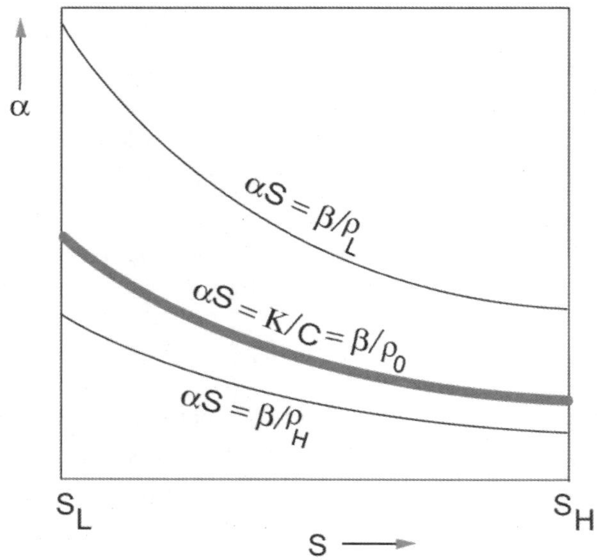

Figure 1. The unregulated optimum. For any type ρ, the optimal portfolio function is the rectangular hyperbola $\alpha s = \beta/\rho$. The thicker hyperbola is the socially optimum portfolio risk function $\alpha s = K/C$. This is also, by definition, the optimal hyperbola of type ρ_0. Types $\rho < \rho_0$ take more than socially optimal risk (optimal hyperbolas above the thicker hyperbola), generating safety loss, and types $\rho > \rho_0$ take less than socially optimal risk (optimal hyperbolas below the thicker hyperbola), generating overprotection loss.

each type $\rho < \rho_0$, the optimal choice hyperbola is entirely above the hyperbola of type ρ_0. Each such type ρ generates a safety loss (but no overprotection loss). For example, the area between the topmost and the middle hyperbolas is the safety loss generated by type ρ_L. Similarly, each type $\rho > \rho_0$ generates an overprotection loss (but no safety loss). For example, the area between the middle and lowest hyperbolas is the overprotection loss generated by type ρ_H. The regulator's objective is to minimize a weighted average of these losses, where w denotes the weight attached to safety loss. We show next how ex-ante and ex-post regimes attempt to achieve this objective. However, we need to specify the regulatory benchmark first.

3. The Regulatory Benchmark

Our aim is to model well-known regulatory regimes and study their properties. Regulators typically only restrain risk taking. They do not set out to encourage conservative banks to take on further risk. Accordingly, we impose the restriction that under full information, for any $\rho > \rho_0$, no regulation is imposed. We should emphasize that realism is the main reason for this modeling choice. Removing the restriction would complicate the algebra considerably, but leave our policy relevant results qualitatively unchanged.[19] Imposing the restriction also makes it clear that the results comparing the two regimes are not influenced by any relative advantage/disadvantage of any regime in encouraging risk taking.

For any $\rho < \rho_0$, and for any s, the optimal regulation forces a choice of α (either through an ex-ante constraint or through ex-post penalties) such that $\alpha s = \beta/\rho_0$. The only loss then is the overprotection loss arising from types $\rho > \rho_0$. Therefore, the *regulatory benchmark loss* (denoted by EL_0) is strictly positive and given by $(1-w)\int_{\rho_0}^{\rho_H}(\sigma_0/\sigma-1)(d\rho/(\rho_H-\rho_L))$. Using $\sigma = \alpha^* s$ and Eqs. (1), (2) and (4), $\sigma_0/\sigma < \rho/\rho_0$. Therefore,

$$EL_0 = (1-w)\int_{\rho_0}^{\rho_H}\left(\frac{\rho}{\rho_0}-1\right)\frac{d\rho}{(\rho_H-\rho_L)}. \tag{6}$$

The fact that under full information, regulation cannot attain zero loss is of course due to our assumption that regulation does not encourage risk taking, and therefore cannot eliminate the overprotection loss arising from types that adopt lower risk than is socially optimal.

For any regulation, $(EL - EL_0)$ is the *distortion* caused by the presence of asymmetric information. It is useful to note that the *unregulated distortion* provides an upper bound to regulatory distortion. If the distortion under any regulation exceeds this level, that regulation is clearly useless and should not be applied. The unregulated distortion is given by $(EL_U - EL_0) = w \int_{\rho_L}^{\rho_0} \int_{s_L}^{s_H} (1 - \sigma_0/\sigma)((ds/s_H - s_L)(d\rho/\rho_H - \rho_L))$, which can be rewritten as:

$$EL_U - EL_0 = w \int_{\rho_L}^{\rho_0} \left(1 - \frac{\rho}{\rho_0}\right) \frac{d\rho}{(\rho_H - \rho_L)}. \tag{7}$$

4. Ex-Ante Regulation

Ex-ante regulation in Basel II (Pillar 1) is characterized by a rule that establishes a direct link between capital and portfolio risk. The regulator can observe capital and α. If the underlying risk s were also observable, the regulator would simply set a capital requirement $K = C\alpha s$. The portfolio risk would then coincide with the socially optimal risk (given by Eq. (2)), achieving a zero loss.

However, the realization of s is the bank's private information, and regulation is based on the risk as measured by the regulator. For any given level of K, the regulator, by minimizing regulatory loss, specifies a "*regulatory risk estimate*" $\hat{s} \in [s_L, s_H]$.[20] This implies an estimated portfolio risk $\alpha\hat{s}$. Given this estimate, the regulator asks the bank to adopt portfolios such that estimated portfolio risk does not exceed the optimal risk K/C.

For any given capital level K, and for any choice of regulatory estimate $\hat{s} \in [s_L, s_H]$, such regulation leads to a maximum permissible α, denoted by $\bar{\alpha}$, and given by $\bar{\alpha}\hat{s} = K/C$, i.e.,

$$\bar{\alpha} = \frac{K}{C\hat{s}}. \tag{8}$$

This implies that choosing an $\hat{s}$ is equivalent to choosing a portfolio constraint $\bar{\alpha}$, shown by the horizontal line in Fig. 2. A higher

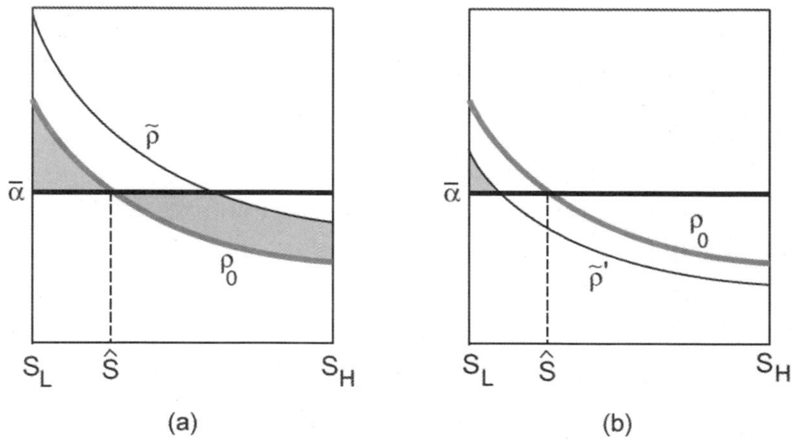

Figure 2. The thick hyperbola is the regulatory optimum (i.e., the optimal hyperbola of type ρ_0), while the horizontal line is the portfolio constraint. Figure 2(a) shows the safety loss and overprotection loss from an ex-ante constraint for any type $\tilde{\rho} < \rho_0$. In Fig. 2(b), the area between the two curves plus the shaded area is the overprotection loss from any type $\tilde{\rho}' < \rho_0$.

regulatory risk estimate leads to a lower $\bar{\alpha}$, that is, a more stringent portfolio constraint. In what follows, we use $\bar{\alpha}$ and $\hat{s}$ interchangeably.

Next, we need to characterize the optimal choice of $\hat{s}$, obtained by minimizing the expected loss. The next section shows that in minimizing expected loss, the regulator faces a trade-off.

For types $\rho < \rho_0$, both safety loss and overprotection loss occur. Figure 2(a) shows that for a type $\tilde{\rho} < \rho_0$, an overprotection loss occurs for $s < \hat{s}$ (the constrained portfolio is below the socially optimum portfolio). This is shown as the shaded area to the left of $\hat{s}$. Further, a safety loss occurs for $s > \hat{s}$ (the shaded area to the right of $\hat{s}$). For types $\rho > \rho_0$, only an overprotection loss occurs. Figure 2(b) shows the overprotection loss for a type $\tilde{\rho}' > \rho_0$ for which the constraint binds for some values of s. The overprotection loss is given by the area between the two hyperbolas and the shaded area. The area between the hyperbolas is part of benchmark loss. The shaded area is the extra overprotection loss over and above benchmark loss.

Finally, if the choice of $\hat{s}$ is moved to the left, this reduces overprotection loss from any type constrained by regulation, but increases safety loss. The opposite happens if $\hat{s}$ is moved to the right. Thus, a trade-off arises between safety and overprotection. The optimal regulatory estimate $\hat{s}^*$ optimally balances the twin losses, minimizing expected regulatory loss. As the safety bias w increases (i.e., the regulator becomes more conservative), the regulatory risk estimate becomes upwardly biased. An ex-ante regime makes poor use of the expertise of a bank in measuring its risk exposure. The regulator imposes a portfolio upper bound, and for all values of s at which this binds, the bank is forced to adopt the same portfolio.

Therefore, the information of the bank on those values of s is lost, creating a distortion. Further, the distortion (given by $(EL^* - EL_0)$, where EL^* denotes minimized loss) rises as the uncertainty about s increases. It follows that the extent of uncertainty about s is crucial. The following result states this. As noted above, the results are adapted for the case of bank regulation from Daripa and Varotto (2008), which contains the detailed proofs.

4.1. *Result 1 (Importance of Information on Underlying Risk)*

As the uncertainty about s *increases, the distortion under an ex-ante regime increases so that beyond a certain level of uncertainty, no regulation is optimal. Next, as the uncertainty about* s *vanishes, an ex-ante regime attains the regulatory benchmark.*

The next result shows that the precision of information about ρ is not as important. It is the uncertainty about s that is crucial in evaluating the performance of an ex-ante regime.

4.2. *Result 2 (Relative Unimportance of Information on Managerial Risk Aversion)*

As the uncertainty on managerial risk aversion parameter ρ increases, the expected loss is bounded above. Next, as the uncertainty about ρ vanishes, the expected loss goes to a strictly positive lower bound for any type on which regulation binds.

The intuition for part (a) is that all types for which the constraint binds are pooled at the portfolio upper bound. Thus, managers are not free to choose high-risk portfolios. This reduces the sensitivity of ex-ante regulation to the uncertainty about risk preference of the bank manager. The intuition for part (b) is that whenever the regulatory upper bound binds, no use is made of the bank's private information about s, which generates a distortion.

5. Ex-Post Regulation

Under ex-post regulation, the bank is allowed to choose portfolio risk without any ex-ante constraint. If the losses exceed a specified tripwire, corrective action is imposed. This induces a link between capital and portfolio risk. Such a regime can be thought of as generating an endogenous "soft-link" between capital and portfolio risk that contrasts with the exogenous "hard-link" under ex-ante regulation.

Kupiec and O'Brien (1997) proposed an ex-post scheme for capital regulation of market risk. Market risk refers to risk in the trading book of the bank, which is a fraction of the total investment by a bank. Under this proposal, known as the "pre-commitment" approach, a bank announces a certain level of capital for market risk, and chooses portfolio risk without any ex-ante constraint. However, if the bank suffers losses that exceed the pre-announced level of capital, it is fined. A large fine in the event of a loss might be credible if the trading book capital is a small part of total capital.

Here, we investigate ex-post regulation for the whole bank. The above approach may not work as fines are difficult to enforce when losses are large relative to the total capital of the bank. Therefore, we should note at the outset that our aim is not to prescribe pure ex-post regulation for all banks. Indeed, as the next section shows, the optimal regime combines the two forms of regulation.[21] But as a first step in our analysis, we need to study a pure ex-post approach to understand its properties.

Let us now discuss our approach to ex-post incentives. To obviate the problem of fines that may be difficult or even undesirable to impose on a bank that has already suffered losses, one can resort to more general penalties available in the form of gradual interventions by the regulator. For instance, imposing stricter constraints on future portfolio choice could reduce the market value of bank capital. A well-known example is the structured early intervention and resolution proposed originally by Benston and Kaufman (1988), clarified further by the Shadow Financial Regulatory Committee (SFRC (1989)), and subsequently revised and incorporated as "prompt corrective actions" in the Federal Deposit Insurance Corporation Improvement Act (FDICIA) of 1991.[22] As SFRC (2000) notes, "it is conceivable that the gradual penalties embodied in the structured early intervention and resolution system ... could help to make the pre-commitment approach, as applied to the entire bank, credible."[23] So long as capital is not too low, this approach is feasible.

We model regulatory intervention following this idea. We assume that corrective actions impose a cost on the shareholders as well as the manager of the bank, and the gradual nature of intervention implies that this cost is an increasing function of the extent of loss. While the cost on the shareholders is limited by the level of capital, the regulator might be able to impose additional private costs on the manager. For example, the regulator might initiate action to prevent a manager of a failed bank from being appointed to a similar job for a few years.[24] Disqualification following regulatory action could be detrimental to the manager's (and the bank's) reputation. In what follows, the word "penalty" refers to such regulation-imposed costs. We assume that the expected managerial cost through penalties increases in the total losses of the bank.

We assume that a penalty applies when $\tilde{V} < -\theta K$, $0 \leq \theta < 1$. In general, the penalty function is an increasing function of the extent of portfolio losses in excess of θK (given by $|\tilde{V}| - \theta K = -\tilde{V} - \theta K$). Here, θK is the regulatory tripwire. A general form of the penalty function is given by $f(-\tilde{V} - \theta K)$, where $f' > 0$. In general, θ can vary across different banks. For example, in the FDICIA approach, penalties are applied when capital falls below some specified percentage of asset value. Then θ depends on a bank's initial capital to asset ratio. For example, if the initial capital of bank A is 20% of total assets and that of bank B is 10% of total assets, and the tripwire is set at a capital to asset ratio of 5%, θ equals 0.25 and 0.5 for banks A and B, respectively.

For banks with very low capital, there might be limited scope for early intervention by the regulator. In such cases, feasible penalties may provide weak incentives, and not able to control all types of managers. Since we simply want to study the properties of ex-post regulation here, we assume throughout this section that ex-post control is possible (implicitly assuming well-capitalized banks). Section 8.2 characterizes the solution when this is relaxed.

Under an ex-post regime, two different types cannot be induced to choose the same portfolio.[25] If some type adopts the socially optimal portfolio risk, more risk averse types adopt portfolios with lower risk, causing an overprotection loss to arise, while less risk averse types adopt higher-risk portfolios, and generate a safety loss. A greater penalty leads to lower risk taking by all types. This reduces safety loss (i.e., reduces the proportion of types adopting greater than socially optimal risk) — but at the same time increases overprotection loss. Thus, a trade-off arises between safety and overprotection.

Clearly, the reason behind the trade-off here is fundamentally different from that under ex-ante regulation. The latter regime faces a trade-off because it makes poor use of the bank's private information about risk. Here, on the other hand, the trade-off is purely due to the uncertainty about the bank manager's type.

5.1. *Result 3 (Use of Bank's Expertise)*

Under ex-post regulation, all information on s *is used so that the expected regulatory loss is independent of the distribution of the underlying risk.*

The result implies that even if the regulator's information on s is very poor, this is not a matter for concern, since ex-post regulation makes full use of the information of the bank. Ex-ante regulation imposes a cap on the share of the risky component in the bank's portfolio, preventing full use of the bank's superior information on risk. Under an ex-post regime, the prospect of punishment makes a bank choose a lower portfolio risk for each level of s compared to the unrestricted optimum. However, a bank can still choose different portfolios for different realizations of s, making full use of their superior information on risk.

Result 3 notes that in sharp contrast with ex-ante regulation, under an ex-post regime the uncertainty about s is irrelevant, as such a regime makes full use of the bank's private information on s. However, the opposite is true of the regulator's information on the degree of risk aversion of the bank manager. The following result shows that unlike in an ex-ante regime, uncertainty about ρ is very important under ex-post regulation.

5.2. *Result 4 (Importance of Information on the Manager's Type)*

The expected loss is increasing in the uncertainty about ρ. Next, as uncertainty about ρ vanishes, an ex-post regime attains the regulatory benchmark.

6. Combining Ex-Ante and Ex-Post Regulation

From Propositions 1 and 2 the extent of information on s — rather than that on ρ — is the critical factor in evaluating the performance of an ex-ante regime. As the uncertainty about s increases starting from zero, the distortion goes from zero to the maximum (the unregulated level). Further, Result 3 shows that information on s is irrelevant for the performance of ex-post regulation, and Result 4 shows that the extent of information on ρ is critical for evaluating the performance of an ex-post regime. Therefore, the comparison of the two regimes depends on the relative spreads of the distributions of ρ and s. If the spread of the distribution of s is high relative to that of ρ, ex-post regulation produces a lower regulatory loss, and vice versa. The complementary nature of the two regimes implies that a combination might be useful. The following result characterizes the optimal combination.

6.1. *Result 5*

The optimal combination always includes a non-trivial version of ex-ante constraints.

Finally, if the regulator is mostly concerned about depositor protection and/or faces significant systemic risk, so that w is close to 1, we get a striking characterization. In this case, the optimal mixture is asymmetric. One regime is applied in a strong form, and the other in a weak form. The following result shows the exact nature of the asymmetry.

6.2. *Result 6 (Asymmetry Under High Safety Bias)*

For w *close to 1, the optimal combination is asymmetric and involves either (a) strong ex-post penalties and weak ex-ante constraints, or (b) strong ex-ante constraints and weak ex-post penalties. Further, if the strongest possible* *ex-post regime generates a lower (greater) overprotection loss compared to the strongest possible ex-ante regime, case (a) $(case$ $(b))$ obtains.*

The intuition is as follows. Given strong ex-post penalties (say), safety loss is very low. At this point, a marginal increase in ex-ante constraints does not reduce safety loss very much further, but it does increase overprotection loss. Therefore, if strong ex-post penalties are already in place, ex-ante constraints should be weakened, and vice versa. In addition, either regime, applied in a strong enough form, is capable of eliminating safety loss. It follows that the regime chosen to be applied in a strong form is the one that generates a lower overprotection loss when applied in a strong form.

Which regime is likely to have a lower overprotection loss when applied in a strong form? Clearly, the answer is ex-post regulation if the uncertainty about the manager's type ρ is low relative to that about the underlying risk s. However, the same answer might apply even if the latter condition is not satisfied. A desirable property of penalties is that the penalty is "*regressive*" in the sense that the marginal impact of a rise in penalties is higher on less risk averse types. Since the marginal reduction in risk is lower for more risk averse types, the optimal risks adopted by the different types get "bunched" together as the penalty level rises.

This *bunching effect* reduces the effective spread of the distribution of ρ. Thus, if a penalty structure is sufficiently regressive, the overprotection loss generated by a strong form of ex-post regulation is lower than that under a strong form of ex-ante regulation. Therefore, an ex-post regime is the dominant element of the optimal combination (case (a) in the result above). The following example shows that linear penalties satisfy this property.

7. Regressive Property and Bunching Effect: An Example with Linear Penalties

As an example of ex-post penalty functions, we look at the case of linear penalties. A linear penalty function is given by $f(-\tilde{V} - \theta K) = \delta(-\tilde{V} - \theta K)$, where δ is a positive constant.[26] For general penalties, we used $\hat{\rho}$ as the index of the level of penalties. We can do the same here, but now δ is an equivalent but more natural index of penalties.

In what follows, we will use δ to index penalties for ease of calculation. Since $\hat{\rho}$ maps one-for-one into δ, this is without loss of generality.

To calculate the effect of the penalty explicitly, we need to specify a managerial utility function. As noted in Endnote 12, the manager's preferences can be represented by a vN-M utility function $-\exp(-\rho\tilde{V})$. With this specification, expected utility under linear penalty is given by:

$$EU = -\exp\left(-\rho\left[\beta\sigma + Z\delta\sigma - \frac{\rho}{2}\sigma^2(1+\delta)^2\right]\right)\Phi(-Z+\sigma\rho(1+\delta))$$
$$-\exp\left(-\rho\left[\beta\sigma - \frac{\rho}{2}\sigma^2\right]\right)\Phi(Z-\sigma\rho),$$

where $Z = \theta K/\sigma + \beta$ and $\sigma = \alpha s$. Let σ^* denote the optimal risk. The marginal impact of penalties on risk is given by $\partial\sigma^*/\partial\delta$, which is negative. As described before, a penalty structure is regressive if the absolute value of this derivative is decreasing in ρ at each δ. Formally, a penalty is regressive if

$$\frac{\partial}{\partial\rho}\left|\frac{\partial\sigma^*}{\partial\delta}\right| < 0 \quad \forall\delta > 0. \text{ (Regressive Penalties)}$$

As mentioned above, if this is the case, as δ increases, the optimal risk of lower types fall faster and thus the optimal risks across types get "bunched". We show the behavior through simulations. Figure 3 plots

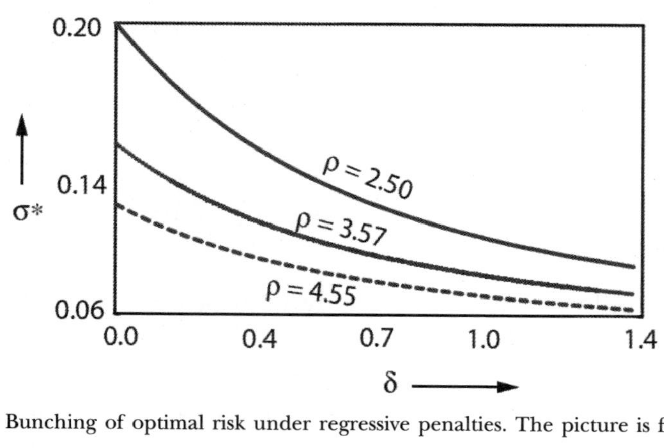

Figure 3. Bunching of optimal risk under regressive penalties. The picture is for the case $\theta = 0.5$.

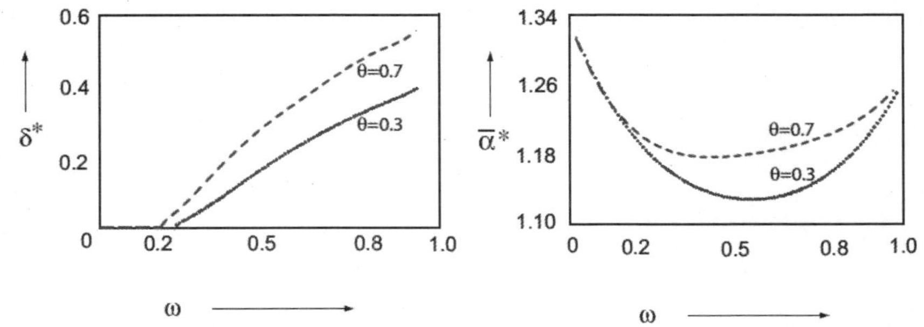

Figure 4. The ex-post penalty level (δ^*) and the ex-ante constraint ($\bar{\alpha}^*$) in the optimal combination for different values of the safety bias w. Lower θ implies that the penalties kick in at lower levels of loss. In this case, penalties are lower and the ex-ante constraint is stricter for most values of w.

the optimal choice of σ for different types ρ as the penalty rises. This shows that linear penalties are regressive and give rise to a bunching effect. Next, Fig. 4 shows the optimal combination of the two regimes for different values of safety bias. Ex-post penalties kick in once w exceeds a critical level, and then steadily get stronger. The ex-ante constraint $\bar{\alpha}$ displays a "U" shape as a function of w. Initially, the constraint gets stronger ($\bar{\alpha}^*$ falls). As w rises, the optimal regulation relaxes ex-ante constraints and employs more stringent ex-post measures. Accordingly, for high safety bias, ex-post regime is dominant. Note that the spread of s is relatively small, yet a strong bunching effect makes ex-post the dominant regime for high safety bias.

Interestingly, different combinations emerge under high and low values of θ. Lower θ implies that the penalties kick in at lower levels of loss. In this case, penalties are lower and the ex-ante constraint is stricter for most values of w. A high value of θ implies that penalties apply only after large losses, but in such cases penalties are severe. If penalties with large losses are credible, they generate strong incentives allowing weaker ex-ante constraints.

To obtain the results reported in Figs. 3 and 4, we use the following parameter values: $\rho_L = 2.5$, $\rho_H = 4.6$, $s_L = 0.1$, $s_H = 0.2$, $\beta = 0.5$, $K = 0.15$ and $p = 0.05$. $C \equiv \Phi^{-1}(1-p) - \beta = 1.644 - 0.5 = 1.144$. The socially optimal risk is $K/C = 0.13$. Further, the type for which the optimal risk coincides with the socially optimal risk is given by $\rho_0 = \beta C/K = 3.8$. Therefore, types $\rho \in (3.8, 4.6)$ initially adopt risk below the socially optimal risk and types below 3.8 initially adopt risk exceeding the socially optimal risk. We have carried out simulations for a wide range of parameter values, and obtained similar results in all cases.

8. Two Special Cases

8.1. *Poor Bank Information on Risk*

We have assumed so far that the bank knows the true portfolio risk. However, as the current crisis clearly suggests, this may not always be the case.

What if we relax this assumption? Recall that the principal virtue of ex-post regulation is that it makes full use of the bank's specialized information on underlying risk. If the bank has no such specialized information, the advantage vanishes. On the other hand, the relative advantage of ex-ante regulation, arising from the fact that it is less sensitive to regulatory uncertainty about the risk preference of the bank, still holds. Therefore, for a bank with poor risk management, pure ex-ante regulation is optimal. Only when regulators are satisfied that a bank has developed sufficient expertise in measuring risk should they move towards including ex-post incentives. This is the intuition behind the following result.

8.2. *Result 7*

If the bank has no private information on s, *regulating through only ex-ante constraints is optimal.*

8.3. *Absence of Full Control Through Penalties*

In Sec. 5, we assumed that the regulator can control all types with penalties. However, for banks with very low capital, there might be limited scope for early intervention. In such cases, feasible penalties may generate weak incentives, and not able to control all types of managers. To extend our analysis to such cases, suppose there is a critical type $\rho_0 < \rho_C < \rho_L$ such that the optimal risk of types $\rho \in [\rho_L, \rho_C]$ is very high even under penalties. Given any ex-ante constraint $\bar{\alpha}$, these types adopt $\bar{\alpha}$ for all s. The analysis of a combined regime does not change qualitatively. However, for high values of w, ex-post penalties cannot reduce the regulatory loss below a certain level since types below ρ_C do not reduce risk taking under feasible penalties. Ex-ante regulation, on the other hand, remains as effective as before. This gives us the following result, which follows immediately from Result 6.

8.4. *Result 8*

Suppose a bank is undercapitalized, so that feasible penalties are unable to prevent some types of managers taking very high risk. In this case, for w *close to* 1, *the optimal combination is asymmetric and involves strong ex-ante constraints and weak ex-post penalties.*

9. Ex-Ante and Ex-Post Regulation in Basel II

The first international standard for risk-based bank capital requirements was proposed in 1988 by the Basel Committee on Banking Supervision. A new capital adequacy framework (Basel II) has now replaced the old agreement in most developed economies. While the 1988 Accord imposes a fairly rigid ex-ante regime, the three pillars that constitute Basel II include both ex-ante and ex-post forms of regulation.[27] The pillars are: (1) minimum capital requirements, (2) supervisory review of capital adequacy and (3) market discipline.

Our results provide a theoretical explanation for the approach taken in Pillar 1 and the inclusion of Pillar 2. First, let us consider how our results relate to Pillar 1. For banks with poor expertise in risk measurement, we show that only ex-ante regulation should be used. On the other hand, banks that can prove their ability to measure risks accurately should be regulated through a mixture of ex-ante and ex-post regulations. This is consistent with Pillar 1, in which banks are subject to different regimes according to the quality of their risk management practices. For example, as stated in Pillar 1, banks can opt for a pure ex-ante credit risk regime known as the Standardized Approach, which is very similar to the 1988 Basel Accord.[28] More sophisticated banks are given the option of choosing an internal rating-based (IRB) approach,[29] in which some risk factors are specified by banks themselves, thus combining ex-ante and ex-post features.

The fact that some aspects of risk are specified by the banks introduces an element of ex-post regulation in an otherwise ex-ante environment. As Rochet (1999) points out, there is little theoretical difference between a system in which banks decide their own capital and risk and are penalized ex-post (our model), and a system in which banks use their internal models to measure and report risk, and the regulator checks whether the model is accurate through backtesting or stress testing.

Even though Pillar 1 makes some room for ex-post measures, it is still dominated by ex-ante requirements. The hybrid nature of Basel II is more importantly highlighted by Pillar 2, which introduces explicit ex-post features. Pillar 2 requires banks to hold additional capital for the risk not taken into account in Pillar 1.[30] The banks are directly responsible for measuring these additional risks and hold capital against them. If additional risks are deemed not to be assessed properly, the regulator intervenes with measures that appear to be similar to the corrective actions in the FDICIA (1991).[31] Here losses could well be an indicator for poor risk management, which would make our modeling of ex-post regulation fit well with actual Pillar 2 interventions.[32] Finally, Pillar 3 requires greater disclosure from banks, and can potentially introduce ex-post penalties in the form of an adverse market reaction to bad news (e.g., when banks disclose higher risk exposure). However, market discipline is outside the scope of this chapter.

10. Conclusion

The 1988 Basel Accord imposed ex-ante capital regulation. In contrast, Basel II has moved toward more hybrid regimes. This motivates our question about the role of different approaches to capital regulation. Despite its practical importance, the theoretical literature offers little clarity on this issue. Our contribution is to specify a simple framework adapted from Daripa and Varotto (2008) to analyze the properties of different forms of capital regulation, helping to determine the optimal regime under a variety of circumstances.

We show that in both ex-ante and ex-post regimes, the regulator must resolve a trade-off between safety loss and overprotection. Interestingly, the nature of the trade-off is very different under the two regimes. Ex-ante regulation is not very sensitive to the information asymmetry about managerial risk aversion, but makes poor use of the private information of the bank on underlying risk. Ex-post regulation, on the other hand, makes full use of the bank's private information on risk, but is more vulnerable to the problem of unknown managerial risk preference.

It follows that the relative importance of the two sources of regulatory uncertainty determines which regime is preferable. Further, the fact that the two regimes are sensitive to different dimensions of information asymmetry suggests that a combination is useful. Indeed, we show that a combined regime outperforms either regime. Moreover, under penalties with a plausible regressive property, we get a striking characterization for well-capitalized banks: if the regulator is mostly interested in protecting depositors and/or faces significant systemic risk (so that safety is the overwhelming concern), the optimal regime combines a strong version of ex-post regulation with a weak version of ex-ante regulation.

On the other hand, in banks with low capital, ex-post penalties may not be very effective. If ex-post penalties cannot prevent some types of managers from adopting high risk, ex-ante regulation becomes the dominant element in safety-first regulation. The discussion above assumes that the bank has superior information on underlying risk. If, however, the bank's information on risk is poor, it is optimal to use only ex-ante regulation. This explains why it is important for the regulator to assess the risk-management abilities of a bank before choosing the appropriate form of regulation.

While our analysis generates robust insights, there are certain practical problems with ex-ante and ex-post regulations that are beyond the scope of our simple model. As Jones (2000) points out, banks might make cosmetic adjustments that reduce the regulatory measure of risk, and therefore capital requirement, even though actual risk is unchanged. Such "regulatory capital arbitrage" reduces the effectiveness of ex-ante regulation. The regulatory arbitrage engaged by banks prior to the current crisis whereby CDOs of mortgage backed securities were treated under market risk capital regulation, instead of the more stringent credit risk capital rules, may well be one of the main factors behind the widespread underestimation of risk and inadequate capital levels that became apparent as the crisis unfolded.

A second practical problem faced by both regimes is regulatory forbearance, which undermines enforcement. As Calomiris (1999) as well as SFRC (2000) discuss, a potential solution is to make use of market discipline induced by market price signals of mandatory subordinated debt. However, the efficacy of such a solution is questionable in times of crisis, since asset prices become unreliable signals of underlying value. A formal analysis of these problems is a matter for future research.

Endnotes

1. Kahane (1977), Koehn and Santomero (1980), Kim and Santomero (1988) and Rochet (1992) show that a flat-rate capital requirement might increase risk in bank portfolio. Relaxing the assumption of zero net present value assets, Gennotte and Pyle (1991) show that capital standards based on accounting value could lead to an increase in risk taking. Kim and Santomero (1988) and Rochet (1992) show how a move to risk-adjusted capital requirements might solve the problem and calculate optimal risk weights in a setting with no asymmetric information. Besanko and Kanatas (1996) consider a model with moral hazard, and show that capital regulation can cause risk of bank assets to increase because regulation leads to effort aversion by bank management. See Calomiris (1999) for a succinct overview of the reasons behind and the problems arising from deposit insurance.
2. For example, papers by Bond and Crocker (1993), Giammarino and colleagues (1993) and Freixas and Gabillon (1998) adopt a mechanism-design approach to derive risk-based deposit insurance. Further, Flannery (1991) shows that if the regulator observes bank risk with an error, the negative impact of the error can be minimized by combining capital requirements with risk-based deposit insurance premiums.
3. Since the mid-90s there has been a growing literature on systemic risk. See de Bandt and Hartmann (2000) for a detailed survey.
4. The systematic nature of the bank failure is the principal motivation behind the current spate of bailouts, government-induced sales of banks and significant capital injections in both the U.S. and U.K. examples include the Northern Rock bail out and the partial nationalization of Royal Bank and Scotland and Lloyds Bank in the U.K., and the Fed-engineered sale of Bear Sterns and Merrill

Lynch, as well as large capital injections into AIG, Fannie Mae, Freddie Mac and a growing list of banks including Wells Fargo, JP Morgan Chase, Bank of America, Morgan Stanley and Goldman Sachs in the U.S.

5. See Santos (2000) for an extensive survey of the literature on capital regulation.
6. See James (1987) for empirical evidence of this. See also Freixas and Rochet (1997) (Chap. 2) for a discussion on the role of asymmetric information in justifying the existence of banks.
7. A penalty structure is regressive if a higher penalty has a greater marginal impact on the optimal choice of types with lower risk aversion.
8. The Federal Reserve has recently required major U.S. banks to undertake a comprehensive stress-testing exercise under the "Supervisory Capital Assessment Program", to be completed by April 2009, to ascertain their ability to withstand a protracted scenario of economic recession. In January 2009, the Basel Committee also proposed to require banks to calculate a stressed VaR for their market risk positions.
9. This can also be thought of as the tangency portfolio between the efficient frontier with all assets and that with only risky assets.
10. Using log return is the standard practice. Log return has the entire real line as range, and therefore allows the use of a normal distribution.
11. Indeed, the managerial preference ordering as described can be represented by the following vN-M utility function: $u(\tilde{V}) = -\exp(-\rho\tilde{V})$, where $\tilde{V}$ is the log final value of the bank's assets (since the initial asset value is 1, the final asset value is given by $\exp(\tilde{V})$, implying that its log is simply $\tilde{V}$). Expected utility is then given by $-\exp(-\rho(s\alpha\beta - s^2\alpha^2\rho/2))$. It follows that the manager can simply maximize $s\alpha\beta - s^2\alpha^2\rho/2$ with respect to α. The optimal choice is $\alpha^* = \beta/(s\rho)$. Therefore, the optimal risk of type ρ is $\sigma^* = \alpha^* s = \beta/\rho$.
12. Our analysis does not require any specific relation between K and ρ. In general, it is likely that ρ decreases in K. However, for very low capital, some types might take high risk. See also Endnote 18.
13. Seminal work by Leland and Pyle (1977) shows how a cost of capital can arise due to information asymmetry, which distorts investment decisions when the bank must raise funds from uninformed outsiders. Besanko and Kanatas (1996) show that recapitalization might dilute managerial effort-provision incentives and lower share price. Indeed, as Hellmann *et al.* (2000) note, if capital were not costly, the problem of excessive risk taking (in the pursuit of private gains) by the bank ownership would hardly be as severe as empirical evidence suggests, as regulators would simply set high capital requirements and banks would comply willingly.
14. Given that initial asset value is 1, it follows that $0 < 1-\hat{K} < 1$ implying $\ln(-\hat{K}+1)$ is well defined (and negative), and that $K > 0$.
15. This is not unreasonable, since for p not too high (which should be the case), $\Phi^{-1}(1-p)$ is large, and the slope of the efficient frontier β is typically less than 1.
16. Clearly, in a situation such as the current crisis, which is characterized by both widespread bank fragility and a credit crunch, the choice of how to weight overprotection loss and safety loss is particularly difficult. On the one hand, banks need to be encouraged to lend. On the other hand, it is important to lower

leverage to restore confidence in banks. So far, regulators and governments in the U.S. and U.K. have attempted to address the problem through tighter bank capital regulation (high weight on safety loss), and complemented with unprecedented levels of central bank interventions to restore lending and alleviate the credit crunch.

17. For example, a sufficient condition for this is that the distribution of ρ shifts down (in the sense of being first order stochastically dominated) at a high enough rate as K increases, so that at any level of K there are types who want to take more risk than the socially optimal risk.
18. If $\rho_0 \leq \rho_L$, regulation is unnecessary. On the other hand, if we make the stronger assumption that $\rho_0 > \rho_H$, our results remain qualitatively unaffected.
19. Removing the restriction would imply that for low values of w, optimal regulation involves a lower limit on risk (ex-ante) and a reward for higher risk (ex-post). This would make the algebra much more complicated, but not gain in terms of policy relevant results since standard regulatory regimes studied here have no lower limit provisions.
20. Risk can also be measured by banks under restrictive guidelines set by the regulator. In this case, we can think of the regulator forcing a particular estimate of s through the restrictions.
21. Imposing some ex-ante limit puts an upper bound on risk taking, which substantially increases the usability of ex-post incentives.
22. These include compulsory capital restoration plans, asset growth limits, restriction on transactions with affiliates, restrictions on deposit interest rates and liquidation. See Benston and Kaufman (1997) for a review of the effectiveness of the act.
23. Taylor (2002) discusses a similar idea.
24. Such measures are not uncommon. For example, in the U.K., a director of an insolvent company can be legally disqualified even in the absence of any dishonest behavior, if the director was negligent or incompetent. Under the 1986 Company Directors Disqualification Act, individuals can be forbidden from acting as a director for up to 15 years.
25. To see this, suppose two different types adopt the same portfolio for some value of s. Given that they face the same penalty function, they must face the same distribution of outcomes. But if two different types face exactly the same distribution of returns, their optimal choice of portfolio cannot be the same, which contradicts the original statement.
26. Note that when log return equals minus infinity the actual loss is finite and equal to the initial value of the bank's assets. Since penalties are also therefore defined in the log return domain, they are finite.
27. The same is true for the 1996 Amendment that is concerned with capital requirements for the bank's trading book.
28. However, unlike Basel 1988 where each debt attracts a capital charge that only depends on the type of debtor (sovereign, bank, corporate and householder), the Standardized Approach is also based on "external" credit ratings.
29. The IRB approach itself includes two variants: a "foundation" version which is close to the standardized approach, and an "advanced" version, which allows

greater flexibility. Similarly, for operational risk an ex-ante regime called the Basic Indicator Approach is offered as an alternative to a hybrid regime, the Advanced Measurement Approach.

30. These are (i) risks considered under Pillar 1 that are not fully captured by the Pillar 1 process (e.g., credit concentration risk), (ii) factors not taken into account by the Pillar 1 process (e.g., interest rate risk in the banking book, business and strategic risk) and (iii) factors external to the bank (e.g., business cycle effects).
31. Principle 4 of Pillar 2 explicitly incorporates early intervention "to prevent capital from falling below the minimum levels required to support the risk characteristics of a particular bank and should require rapid remedial action if capital is not maintained or restored".
32. The Accord has not clearly specified what triggers intervention. The Basel Committee on Banking Supervision (2004) states "Supervisors are expected to evaluate how well banks are assessing their capital needs relative to their risks and to intervene, when appropriate ... when deficiencies are identified, prompt and decisive action can be taken to reduce risk or restore capital".

References

Basel Committee on Banking Supervision (2004). *Basel II: International Convergence of Capital Measurement and Capital Standards: A Revised Framework.* Bank for International Settlements.

Benston, GJ and GG Kaufman (1988). Risk and solvency regulation of depository institutions: Past policies and current options. Monograph Series in *Finance and Economics*, Salomon Center, Stern School of Business, New York University, Monograph 1988–1.

Benston, GJ and GG Kaufman (1997). FDICIA after 5 years. *Journal of Economic Perspectives*, 11(3), 139–158.

Besanko, D and G Kanatas (1996). The regulation of bank capital: Do capital standards promote bank safety? *Journal of Financial Intermediation*, 5, 160–183.

Bond, EW and KJ Crocker (1993). Bank capitalisation, deposit insurance, and risk categorisation. *Journal of Risk and Insurance*, 60(3), 547–569.

Calomiris, CW (1999). Building an incentive-compatible safety net. *Journal of Banking and Finance*, 23(10), 1499–1519.

Chan, Y-S, S Greenbaum and A Thakor (1992). Is fairly-priced deposit insurance possible? *Journal of Finance*, 47, 227–245.

Daripa, A and S Varotto (2008). *Standards Versus Liability: A Theory of Safety Provision.* Working Paper, Birkbeck College.

de Bandt, O and P Hartmann (2000). *Systemic Risk: A Survey.* Working Paper No. 35, European Central Bank.

Dewatripont, M and J Tirole (1994). *The Prudential Regulation of Banks.* Cambridge, Massachusetts: MIT Press.

Dimson, E and P Marsh (1995). Capital requirements for securities firms. *Journal of Finance*, 50(3), 821–851.

Fama, EF (1985). What's different about banks? *Journal of Monetary Economics*, 15, 29–39.

Flannery, MJ (1991). Pricing deposit insurance when the insurer measures bank risk with an error. *Journal of Banking and Finance*, 15(4–5), 975–998.

Freixas, X and E Gabillon (1998). *Optimal Regulation of a Fully Insured Deposit Banking System.* Mimeo, University Pompeu Fabra, Barcelona.

Freixas, X and J-C Rochet (1997). *Microeconomics of Banking.* Cambridge, Massachusetts: MIT Press.

Gennotte, G and D Pyle (1991). Capital controls and bank risk. *Journal of Banking and Finance*, 15(4–5), 805–824.

Giammarino, RM, TR Lewis and DEM Sappington (1993). An incentive approach to banking regulation. *Journal of Finance*, 48, 1523–1542.

Hellmann, TF, KC Murdock and JE Stiglitz (2000). Liberalization, moral hazard in banking, and prudential regulation: Are capital requirements enough? *American Economic Review*, 90(1), 147–165.

James, C (1987). Some evidence on the uniqueness of bank loans. *Journal of Financial Economics*, 19, 217–235.

Jones, D (2000). Emerging problems with the basel capital accord: Regulatory capital arbitrage and related issues. *Journal of Banking and Finance*, 24(1–2), 35–58.

Kahane, Y (1977). Capital adequacy and the regulation of financial intermediates. *Journal of Banking and Finance*, 1, 207–218.

Kim, D and AM Santomero (1988). Risk in banking and capital regulation. *Journal of Finance*, 43(5), 1219–1233.

Koehn, M and AM Santomero (1980). Regulation of bank capital and portfolio risk. *Journal of Finance*, 35, 1235–1244.

Kupiec, PH and JM O'Brien (1997). *The Pre-Commitment Approach: Using Incentives to Set Market Risk Capital Requirements.* Federal Reserve Board, Finance and Economics Discussion Series No. 97–14, March.

Leland, HE and DH Pyle (1977). Informational asymmetries, financial structure and financial intermediation. *Journal of Finance*, 32(2), 371–387.

Rochet, J-C (1992). Capital requirements and the behaviour of commercial banks. *European Economic Review*, 36, 1137–1178.

Rochet, J-C (1999). Solvency regulations and the management of banking risks. *European Economic Review*, 43, 981–990.

Santos, M (2000). *Bank Capital Regulation in Contemporary Banking Theory: A Review of the Literature.* BIS Working Paper No. 90.

Saunders, A, E Strock and NG Travlos (1990). Ownership structure, deregulation, and bank risk taking. *Journal of Finance*, 45(2), 643–654.

Shadow Financial Regulatory Committee (1989). Statement No. 41: An outline of a program for deposit insurance and regulatory reform. Published in the *Journal of Financial Services Research*, 1992, Supplement: 78–82.

Shadow Financial Regulatory Committee (2000). Reforming Bank Capital Regulation. *AEI Publication.*

Taylor, C (2002). *A New General Approach to Capital Adequacy: A Simple and Comprehensive Alternative to Basel 2.* Paper No. 59, Centre for the Study of Financial Innovation, London and New York.

3

Effects of International Interbank Loans on Twin Crises

Erhan Uluceviz and Levent Yildiran

1. Introduction

The 1980s were characterized by capital account liberalizations and banking deregulations. It has been argued that, with capital account liberalizations, savings would flow from low- to high-return countries, thus fostering the world-wide growth and enrichment of low-income countries. Banking deregulations, on the other hand, aimed at allowing the market forces to shape the evolution of financial system. Thus, with the Basel Capital Accord in 1988 (Basel I) classical banking regulations that restricted activities, assets, deposit rates, capital flows etc. were replaced by capital regulations that obliged banks to hold equity at least 8% of their risk-weighted assets.[1]

However, since then, banking and financial crises have become more frequent and widespread. The large amount of short-term capital inflows, mostly in the form of international interbank loans (IIBL),[2] to developing countries was pointed out as the major reason of the recent crises (e.g., Greenspan, 1998; Bernard and Bisignano, 2000; Tirole, 2002; Lindgren *et al.*, 1996; Miskhin, 1996). It has been argued that, after Basel I, in order not to reduce their asset portfolios or increase their equities, banks had switched their asset portfolio allocations from consumer and corporate loans to government securities and interbank loans (esp. to OECD countries), as the latter required less bank equity, 0% and 1.6%(= 20%*8%), respectively.[3]

Figure 1 shows that in some of the recent episodes IIBL indeed rose considerably prior to the outset of the crises, reaching 59% of GDP in Jordan (1989), 51% in Thailand (1997), 42% in Argentina (1989), 35% in Malaysia (1985), 28% in Venezuela (1993) and 25% in Turkey (2000).[4] If the amount of short-term capital inflows (hot money) is indeed an important factor that increases the likelihood of crisis in a developing country (which, in turn, decreases the likelihood that international investors will recoup their investments), then the following question is a relevant one: why do not international investors limit their loans to developing countries? In both theoretical and empirical corporate finance literature, it is well documented that credit-rationing exists, i.e., although borrowers are ready to pay high interest rates, lenders do not satisfy all credit demands of borrowers due to adverse selection or moral hazard concerns. Lenders would think that high interest rates would drive good borrowers out or reduce borrowers' incentives to behave in a way that lenders would prefer.

However, when there are multiple lenders things are more complicated, borrowers may not be credit rationed due to the externalities or asymmetric information among lenders. In the context of IIBL, for example, the return of an individual international bank depends on the total indebtness of the developing country. Although the international bank can contract with the local bank that it lends, it may have no means/incentives to control the indebtness of the other local banks. The negative externalities or asymmetric information among international investors, thus, may well lead to over lending to developing countries. Another important argument for the absence of credit rationing in the international interbank market (IIBM) is that international banks expect that IMF will not leave the ailing countries alone and will in fact bail them out in case of a severe crisis.

The main objective of this work is to empirically investigate the IIBL to developing countries and to determine whether and how these loans affect the likelihood of crises, an issue which has

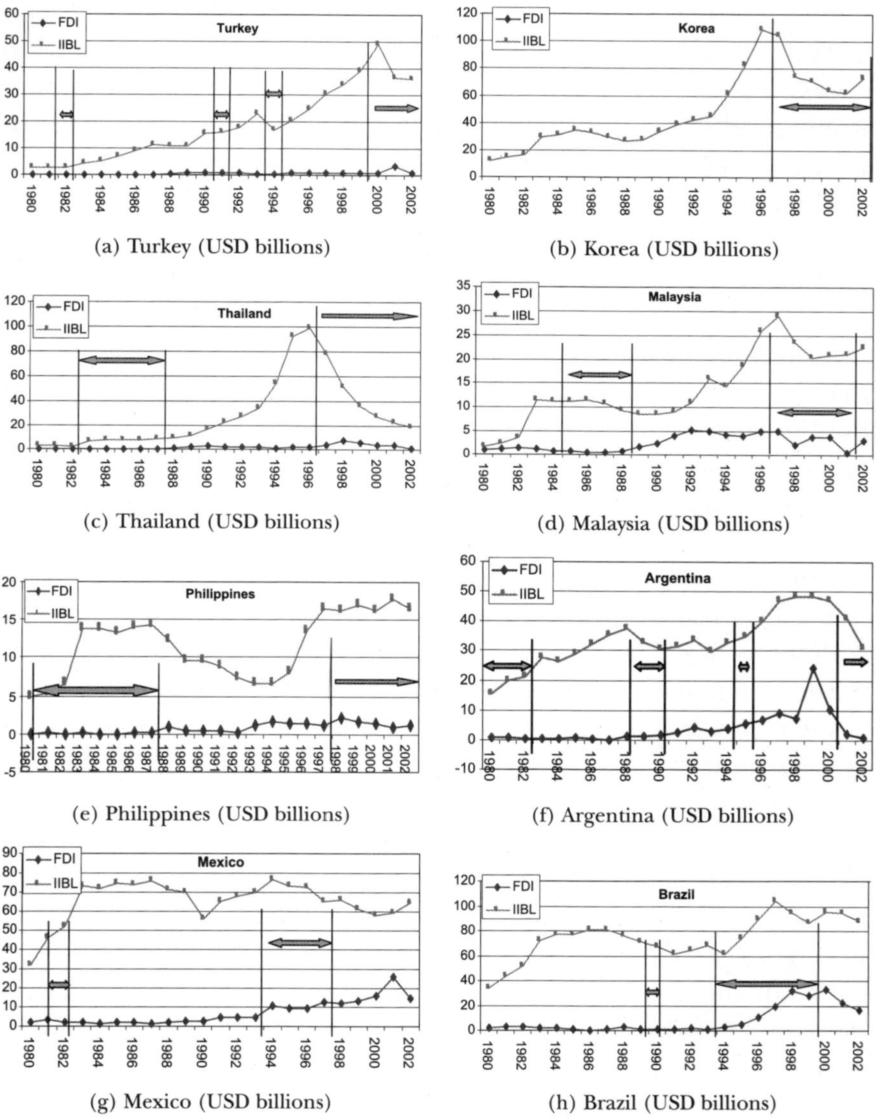

(a) Turkey (USD billions)

(b) Korea (USD billions)

(c) Thailand (USD billions)

(d) Malaysia (USD billions)

(e) Philippines (USD billions)

(f) Argentina (USD billions)

(g) Mexico (USD billions)

(h) Brazil (USD billions)

Figure 1. Crises years, IIBL and FDI levels for the selected countries.

not yet been addressed to the best of our knowledge. Finding that IIBL is a significant factor that increases the likelihood of crises has some important implications. In that case, although some important amendments have already been proposed to refine sovereign and corporate risks in Basel II attention still must be paid to the coordination failures among international banks that would lead to excessive loans to developing countries. In addition, regulations that would limit these loans should possibly be incorporated in Basel II, which is expected to replace Basel I in the near future.

The empirical literature that tries to identify the factors associated with crises follows two main approaches: signaling and qualitative response modeling. The ultimate aim of this literature is to explain crises by determining the significant factors, and to use those factors as tools for forecasting and taking precautionary actions that may prevent a forthcoming banking crisis. Signaling approach is developed for predicting the turning points of business cycles. Its application as early warning indicators for banking crises is due to Kaminsky and Reinhart (1996), which is later refined by Kaminsky (1998).

In this methodology, monthly data are used and the behavior of selected indicators in the 24 months prior to the crisis is compared with the behavior during tranquil times. Under this set-up, a variable is said to signal a crisis if at any time it crosses a particular threshold. If the signal is followed by a crisis within the next 24 months, it is considered correct; otherwise, it is considered as noise. The threshold for each variable is chosen by performing a grid search over a range of critical regions to minimize the in-sample noise to signal ratio. The best early warning signals were found to be the loss of foreign exchange reserves, high real interest rates, low output growth and decline in stock prices.

In qualitative response modeling, it is assumed that the dependent variable is drawn from a continuous probability distribution, usually the logistic (logit) or normal (probit) distribution. Regression analysis is done to capture the effect of movements in the indicator variables on the probability of the crisis occurring. The dependent variable is coded by discrete values according to the realization of some predefined event (episodes of banking crises in this case).

The study by Demirgüç-Kunt and Detragiache (1998) is the first systematic study employing qualitative response modeling in the banking crises literature to consider the effects of macroeconomic, financial and institutional variables. In their multivariate logit analysis, Demirgüç-Kunt and Detragiache used the annual data of 65 countries for the time period 1980–1994 and obtained the following results. The likelihood of a banking crisis increases in the presence of macroeconomic imbalances, i.e., slow growth, high inflation. Higher real interest rates that may emanate from financial liberalization is an effective factor paving the road to crisis. In addition, the institutional environment is a significant determinant in the likelihood of the occurrence of crises. For countries with low institutional quality, the existence of explicit deposit insurance leads to moral hazard and poor portfolio diversification problems, which in turn increase the likelihood of a crisis. A detailed survey on related studies can be found in Eichengreen and Arteta (2000).

As methodology we follow Demirgüç-Kunt and Detragiache (1998). Along with some other factors suggested by the theory and case studies, we study the effect of IIBL on the likelihood of crises in a multivariate logit specification with annual data. Our panel includes 64 market economies whose data were available over the period 1980–2002. The results are in line with the previous work and have some policy implications. We find that IIBL significantly increase the probability of crises in developing countries. The very high levels of IIBL/GDP ratios in the recent crisis episodes suggest the existence of coordination failures among international banks and the need for regulations to control such loans. Moreover, confirming the previous work, we find that low GDP growth, high real interest rates, budget deficits and low GDP per capita, which is a reflection of low-institutional quality, significantly increase the likelihood of crises.

2. Econometric Model and Data Sources

2.1. *Sample*

Our dataset covers 1980–2002 period. We chose countries from the IMF's International Financial Statistics (IFS) Database. We excluded the centrally planned economies and economies in transition since these countries were of a distinctive nature. We also excluded the countries whose main macroeconomic and financial data series were missing or incomplete. Finally, Bahrain and Singapore were also eliminated because they were outliers with respect to our main regressor, IIBL/GDP. Thus, we ended up with 64 countries. The list of these countries is in Appendix 1. Our major data sources for the independent variables, besides the IFS Database, were the World Bank's World Development Indicators (WDI) Database and the Quarterly Review of the Bank for International Settlements (BIS).

2.2. *Econometric Model*

For a given country i and a given year t, we estimate the probability of a banking crisis using multivariate logit econometric model. Under this set-up, dependent variable, y_{it}, a 0/1 crisis dummy, is assumed to be drawn from a logistic distribution where cumulative distribution function is denoted by

$$\text{Prob}(y_{it} = 1|x_{it}, \beta) = (\exp(x'_{it}\beta))/(1 + \exp(x'_{it}\beta)) = F(x'_{it}\beta).$$

Crisis dummy, y_{it}, equals one if the country i is in crisis in year t. It equals zero otherwise. To estimate the unknown coefficients, we solve to maximize the log-likelihood of the model.

$$l = \sum_{t=1}^{n}\sum_{t=1}^{T}\{y_{it}\ln[F(x'_{it}\beta)] + (1 - y_{it})\ln[1 - F(x'_{it}\beta)]\},$$

where

x_{it}: the vector of explanatory variables for country i in year t
β: the vector of unknown coefficients.

In logit, it is assumed that the log of odds ratio is a linear function of independent variables; $\ln(p_{it})/(1 - p_{it}) = x'_{it}\beta$, where p_{it} is the probability that the country i experiences a crisis in year t. Therefore, the coefficients do not reflect the effect of a unit change in the explanatory variables on the probability of crisis. Rather, they reflect the changes in $\ln(p_{it})/(1 - p_{it})$. The total change in probability depends on the initial probability and the pdf of the logistic distribution evaluated at $x'_{it}\beta$. Since the cdf of the logistic distribution is rather flat at both tails, if the initial crisis probability is low or high, the effect of corresponding change in the explanatory variable will be low; whereas change will be high if the initial probability is in the intermediate range. But the signs of coefficients indeed reflect the direction of change in the probability.

With our model, we estimate a reduced form relationship without deriving it from a structural model of the economy. Thus, the associations among some variables should be interpreted cautiously, as they may not always reflect direct causality. If the effects of a crisis propagate promptly to the rest of the economy, contemporaneous regressors may not be exogenous. Low GDP growth, high real interest rates, high inflation may be the manifestations of the economic downturn caused by the crisis itself. However, this criticism is not applicable to our main regressor IIBL, as it is not reasonable to claim that IIBL increase due to a (possible) crisis.

Through some feedback effects, the crisis may affect the future regressors as well. For example, IIBL and credits that are likely to fall after a crisis will naturally reduce the future GDP growth. Real interest rate is another variable that is likely to be affected by the crisis, as the monetary authority, by applying loose monetary and banking policy, may distort it. To reduce such endogeneity problems with future regressors, one way is to eliminate from the panel all the observations after the crisis, which will result in the loss of all multiple crises episodes. A less costly alternative is to eliminate only the observations while the crisis is going on. The drawback of this method is, however, that determining when the effects of a crisis disappear is quite difficult and the decision is rather judgmental. Of these methods, we pick the latter, as Demirgüç-Kunt and Detragiache (1998) also did.[5]

2.3. *Dependent Variable*

Dependent variable, a 0/1 dummy, takes the value of value 1 if the country is in crisis, and 0 otherwise. Our source for dependent variable is Demirgüç-Kunt and Detragiache (2005). As all other authors who empirically study banking crises do, Demirgüç-Kunt and Detragiache distinguish borderline and systemic banking crises somewhat arbitrarily. They construct banking crisis dummy by finding a consensus in dating schemes of various studies on banking crises. If in doubt, they rely on self judgment. An incidence is defined as a full-fledged banking crisis if one or more of the below criteria are met. If none holds, then it is identified as "localized and/or relatively minor".

1. The ratio of non-performing assets to total assets in the banking system exceeded 10 percent.
2. The cost of rescue operation was at least two percent of GDP.
3. Banking sector problems resulted in a large scale nationalization of banks.
4. Extensive bank runs took place or emergency measures such as deposit freezes, prolonged bank holidays or generalized deposit guarantees were enacted by the government in response to the crisis.

Table 1 shows the banking crises by country. Caprio and Klingebiel (2003) provide another list of banking crises dates used in several empirical studies. Caprio and Klingebiel identify a banking crisis by relying on two pieces of information on the incidence:

1. Exhaustion of much or all of banking system capital.
2. Judgment of business professionals in that country.

We also replicated our study based on the dependent variable dataset in Caprio and Klingebiel (2003). We do not report these results as the conclusions essentially do not change. This validates our findings' robustness to slight changes in the dependent variable. In our sample, we have 44 countries which experienced 58 banking crises in total. For some incidences, data availability problems emerge in the year the crisis erupts. Depending on the specification and the availability of the data, number of crises observations is between 45 and 56 in the first part of our analysis.

2.4. *Independent Variables*

Our choice of independent variables is based on the theory, case studies and data availability. The summary of the sources and

Table 1. Banking crises by country.

Country	Crises date(C)
Argentina	1980–1982, 1989–1990, 1995, 2001–2002*
Brazil	1990, 1994–1999
Burundi	1994–1997
Chile	1981–1997
Colombia	1982–1985, 1999–2000
Congo. Dem. Rep.	1994–2002*
Congo. Rep.	1992–2002*
Ecuador	1995–2002*
El Salvador	1989
Finland	1991–1994
Guyana	1993–1995
India	1991–1994
Indonesia	1992–1995, 1997–2002*
Israel	1983–1984
Italy	1990–1995
Jamaica	1996–2000
Japan	1992–2002*
Jordan	1989–1990
Kenya	1993–1995
Korea	1997–2002
Malaysia	1985–1988, 1997–2001
Mali	1987–1989
Mexico	1982, 1994–1997
Nepal	1988–1991
Niger	1983–1986
Nigeria	1991–1995
Norway	1987–1993
Papua N. Guinea	1989–1992
Paraguay	1995–1999
Peru	1983–1990
Philippines	1981–1987, 1998–2002*
Portugal	1986–1989
Senegal	1983–1988
South Africa	1985
Sri Lanka	1989–1993
Swaziland	1995
Sweden	1990–1993
Tanzania	1988–1991
Thailand	1983–1987, 1997–2002*
Turkey	1982, 1991, 1994, 2000–2002*
Uganda	1994–1997
United States	1980–1992
Uruguay	1981–1985, 2002*
Venezuela	1993–1997

*in crises as of 2005.

definitions of the variables used in this study is in Appendix 2. Some macroeconomic and financial variables are employed as independent variables to account for the performance of the economy and to consider the risks that banks face during their operations. Banks, as financial intermediaries, collect the small and liquid deposits of lenders (households) and finance the big, illiquid projects of borrowers (firms), whose types and behaviors are unobservable by lenders. These vital functions of banks expose them to some risks. Credit risk is a major risk that banks face. Though there are several ways that banks use to reduce this risk, such as screening, setting up long-term customer relationships, requiring collateral, diversifying etc., it is not possible to completely eliminate this risk without severely curtailing the role of banks as financial intermediaries.

Appropriate screening can ensure that projects that are unprofitable ex-ante are not financed; but risky projects that are profitable in an ex-ante sense may still fail ex-post. This failure can be due to either idiosyncratic risk or an adverse shock that affects the whole economy. Thus, we hypothesize that when economy is going down (low GDP growth), credit risk is higher and banking sector problems are more likely.

Interest rate risk is another risk that banks face. As banks borrow short and lend long, in case there is a rise in short-term real interest rates, banks' cost of funds may exceed their income from the long-term loans. This would deteriorate the banking sector's profitability. Thus, we hypothesize that when short-term real interest rates are high, banking sector problems are more likely. It is found that liberalization results in higher real interest rates. Therefore, real interest rates can also proxy financial liberalization. Liberalization may increase the likelihood of banking crises through microeconomic channels.

High inflows of money are likely to lead to excessive risk taking and looting[6] on the side of bank management, if governing institutions are not well established. In the empirical literature that investigates the effects of the quality of institutions, several indexes (corruption, enforcement of law, bureaucracy etc.) are used to measure this quality, and GDP per capita is found to capture all the information summarized by these indexes. That is, countries with high GDP per capita are also the countries with high-quality institutions. Thus, we hypothesize that higher the GDP per capita is, the higher the quality of the institutions and the less likely the existence of banking sector problems.

Foreign exchange rate risk is another important risk that banks have to deal with. Banks might have borrowed funds denominated in foreign currency and given credits denominated in local currency. In this case, the depreciation of the local currency makes it difficult for banks to repay their foreign currency debt. To reduce their foreign exchange rate risk, banks may choose to give their credits also denominated in foreign currency; but in this case, depreciation will increase the credit risk. Thus, our hypothesis is that, if banks have liabilities in foreign currency, then the depreciation of the local currency increases the likelihood of banking sector problems.

Inflation is another frequently cited factor associated with banking sector problems. It implies persistent macroeconomic mismanagement and high nominal interest rates. However, it is difficult to disentangle its independent effect from that of real interest rate and depreciation. Budget deficit was identified as an important factor in the early crisis models, as it reduced the governments' willingness and capacity of applying the correct macroeconomic and regulatory policies against crises. Thus, we hypothesize that Surplus/GDP reduces the likelihood of crises.

Although they are somewhat correlated, we include (several lags of) both IIBL and credit growth to our independent variable set, based on the following stylized story reported by many of the recent case studies: ... upon some information signaling the political and economic stability in a developing country, international investors, in a herd-like behavior, race among themselves to give foreign currency denominated short-term credit to that country, mostly through IIBM. In response, the developing country enters into a prosperous period: imports explode, consumer credits expand, stock and real estate prices inflate etc.

The substantial amount of short-term foreign loans borrowed by the local banks are directed as credit in large part to the government, non-tradable sector (i.e., real estates, stocks and the sector that creates consumption goods for local use) and individuals, rather than to the foreign currency generating tradable sector (i.e., export or tourism). Although the government of a developing country can affect the level and use (consumption vs. investment) of the foreign borrowing, it often either fails, or is reluctant to do so.

A few years later, some observable information, such as the increasing short-term foreign debt to foreign exchange reserves ratio and/or the decreasing current account to outstanding foreign debt ratio, signals to international investors that the developing country's potential to repay its debt is diminishing. Upon these observable signals, international investors, again in a herd-like behavior, refuse to roll over their loans. Capital outflow breaks out, devaluation follows, some of the local banks fall insolvent, credit crunch arises and the real economy collapses.

So we hypothesize that the (lags of) IIBL and credit growth[7] increase the likelihood of crises. Finally, some authors (e.g., Baghwati, 1998), claim that only long-term foreign direct investment is beneficial for financial integration and all short-term capital flows should be banned, as they create significant financial instability. Thus, to contrast with the short-term capital flows, we also include the foreign direct investments as an independent variable. Table 2 summarizes the dependent and independent variables.

Our research problem, identifying the relevant factors affecting the likelihood of crises, warrants employing several variables that

Table 2. Data summary.

Variables	Mean	Median	Max.	Min.	Std. dev.	Observations
Crises	0.05	0	1	0	0.21	1275
Growth	3.0	3.1	83.4	−16.8	4.7	1501
Depreciation	37.0	5.6	13296	−37.1	439.4	1482
Real interest	3.12	2.65	449	−99	22.64	1477
Inflation	57.8	7.1	26762	−29.2	741.6	1505
Surplus/GDP	−3.76	−0.03	0.18	−282	25.44	1240
$\text{Credgrow}_{\tau-2}$	7.03	5.26	821	−63	29.13	1431
GDP/CAP	9116	5356	32554	447	8253	1506
FDI/GDP	0.02	0.01	0.40	−0.03	0.03	1443
IIBL/GDP	0.23	0.17	2.07	0	0.23	1464

Table 3. Results with rich effect for sample [1990–2002].

Variables	Model 1	Model 2	Model 3	Model 4	Model 5
Growth	−0.224***	−0.131***	−0.116**	−0.131**	−0.142***
	[0.001]	[0.007]	[0.022]	[0.013]	[0.001]
Real interest	0.016**	0.013*	0.016*	0.014	0.009
	[0.023]	[0.062]	[0.081]	[0.155]	[0.438]
Surplus/GDP		−0.022**	−0.023**	−0.023**	−0.023**
		[0.014]	[0.012]	[0.012]	[0.013]
Inflation			0.0005	0.0006	0.002
			[0.407]	[0.406]	[0.298]
Credgrow_{t-2}				0.009	0.008
				[0.245]	[0.392]
Depreciation					−0.001
					[0.524]
IIBL/GDP	1.933*	2.294*	2.415*	2.512**	2.570**
	[0.086]	[0.065]	[0.057]	[0.046]	[0.040]
$R_{90} \times \left(\frac{IIBL}{GDP} - \frac{FDI}{GDP}\right)$	−4.799***	−6.824***	−6.526***	−6.607***	−6.724***
	[0.007]	[0.008]	[0.009]	[0.008]	[0.008]
FDI/GDP	−2.338	1.208	2.737	2.696	2.598
	[0.783]	[0.869]	[0.677]	[0.699]	[0.713]
Number of crises	32	29	29	27	26
Number of obs.	668	531	531	504	502
% Correct	68	68	72	71	69
% Crises correct	59	59	59	67	65
% No-crises correct	67	67	71	71	69
Model χ^2	31***	29.9***	36.9***	33.3***	28.2***
Pseudo R^2	0.12	0.12	0.16	0.15	0.14
AIC	0.36	0.39	0.38	0.38	0.39

Note: Terms in square brackets are the *p*-values. ***, **, * indicate significance at 1%, 5% and 10% levels, respectively.

are normalized by GDP. In this literature, other researchers such as Demirgüç-Kunt and Detragiache (1998) and Kaminsky (1998) also had to use multiple such variables in their analyses. But, our results are robust to this potential multicollinearity problem. Correlations among these variables are not significant, and hence estimations for our main regressor IIBL/GDP given in Table 3 are insensitive to the inclusion/exclusion of the other variables that are normalized by GDP. Also, GDP/CAP variable is not used in obtaining our main results in Table 3, where it is replaced by a rich country dummy Rt that separates rich and poor countries.

3. Analysis and Results

After making numerous trials with different specifications, we present our primary results in five specifications in Table 4. The overall quality of model specification is assessed based on three criteria: Model χ^2, Akaike information criterion (AIC) and in-sample classification accuracy. Model χ^2 tests the joint significance of the independent variables by comparing the log-likelihood of the model with that of a model with only the intercept.

As Table 4 shows, the null hypothesis that coefficients of the explanatory variables jointly equal to zero is rejected at 1% significance level in all specifications. In terms of AIC, which is smaller for better models, the most parsimonious specification, Model 1, seems to outperform the others. To assess the prediction accuracy of the

Table 4. Results for benchmark models.

Variables	Model 1	Model 2	Model 3	Model 4	Model 5
Growth	−0.125***	−0.109***	−0.101***	−0.106***	−0.107***
	[0.0001]	[0.001]	[0.003]	[0.003]	[0.003]
Real interest	0.013***	0.012***	0.012**	0.025***	0.025***
	[0.0011]	[0.003]	[0.040]	[0.001]	[0.005]
Surplus/GDP		−0.004	−0.004	−0.004	[−0.005]
		[0.407]	[0.397]	[0.352]	[0.353]
Inflation			0.0004	0.0003	0.0003
			[0.504]	[0.388]	[0.836]
Credgrow_{t-2}				0.007	0.007
				[0.233]	[0.242]
Depreciation					0.0005
					[0.970]
GDP/CAP	−0.00005**	−0.00006**	−0.00006**	−0.00005**	−0.00006**
	[0.045]	[0.022]	[0.028]	[0.038]	[0.038]
IIBL/GDP	−0.1125	0.156	0.206	0.019	0.010
	[0.897]	[0.871]	[0.831]	[0.984]	[0.992]
Number of crises	56	50	50	46	45
Number of obs.	1233	1026	1026	979	977
% correct	68	66	68	70	69
% crises correct	59	66	64	63	69
% no-crises correct	68	66	67	70	69
Model χ^2	40.7***	31.23***	38.4***	38.6***	32.4***
Pseudo R^2	0.09	0.07	0.09	0.10	0.09
A1C	0.34	0.37	0.37	0.36	0.36

Note: Terms in square brackets are the *p*-values. ***, **, *indicate significance at 1%, 5% and 10% levels, respectively.

specifications, we report the total percentage of observations that are correctly classified, according to which models seem to predict fairly well.[8]

The independent variables, GDP growth, real interest rate and GDP per capita are found to have the expected signs with high significance and be robust to specification changes. Thus, low GDP growth and high real interest rates are significantly associated with high probability of crisis. As mentioned earlier, our estimation is subject to endogeneity criticisms, and thus it is possible to interpret the low growth and high interest rates as a manifestation of the economic downturn caused by the crisis itself. We do not use instrumental variables to deal with such possible endogeneity problems for two reasons.

Firstly, our major concern, IIBLs are free from endogeneity problems, as they are not likely to increase due to a (possible) crisis. Secondly, as indicated by the previous literature, some factors suggest that the cyclical downturn accompanying the crises is exogenous. For example, Kaminsky and Reinhart (1996), by examining the monthly data for 23 crises, find that output is likely to peak almost eight months before the outset of a crisis, that is, downturn precedes the crisis. Moreover, anecdotal evidence in several episodes shows that the economic downturn was triggered by a specific exogenous event.[9]

The other significant variable GDP per capita, as explained earlier, should be interpreted as a proxy for the quality of institutions. Thus, lower GDP per-capita ratios, which indicate more opportunities to loot and lower ability to carry out effective prudential supervision, are associated with higher likelihood of crisis.

The other independent variables are not found to be significant in any of the specifications we tried. We present our results in five specifications to show that the inclusion or exclusion of the insignificant variables do not change the results for the other variables. All these insignificant variables, except IIBL/GDP, actually had the expected signs. That is, we find that surplus/GDP tends to decrease the likelihood of crises, inflation increases, credit growth (lag 2 of which is found to be more meaningful) increases and finally depreciation of local currency increases the likelihood of crises, but their p-values are not significant. However, IIBL/GDP,[10] which is our main concern, does not seem to be relevant in these specifications.

In the next stage, considering that low levels of IIBL/GDP may be beneficial, we hypothesize that IIBL/GDP increases the likelihood of crises if it is above a certain threshold. Thus, we define the variable ThresJ as ThresJ = {1 if IIBL/GDP $\geq$ J% and 0 otherwise} and instead of regressing on IIBL/GDP level, we regress on ThresJ. To test whether there is a certain threshold above which IIBL/GDP is significantly associated with the likelihood of crises, we inspect all the thresholds from 2 to 51, the range for which we can solve the log-likelihood functions uniquely. Since all other variables are robust to ThresJ for all specifications, we focus only on ThresJ. Figure 2 summarizes the results. In this figure, the x-axis runs from Thres2 to Thres51. The bars on the graphs, scaled by the y-axis on the left, are

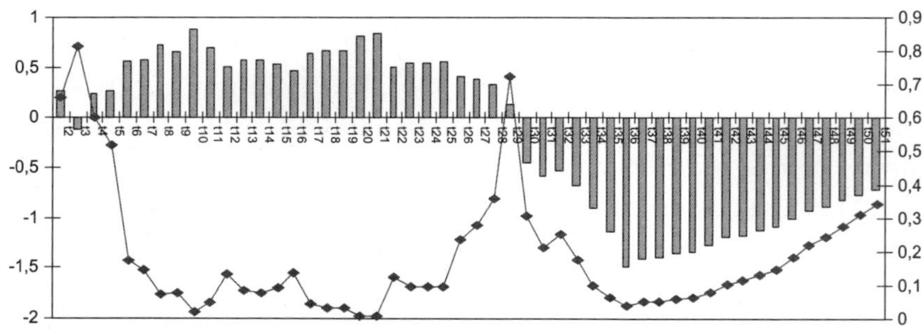

(a) Model 1

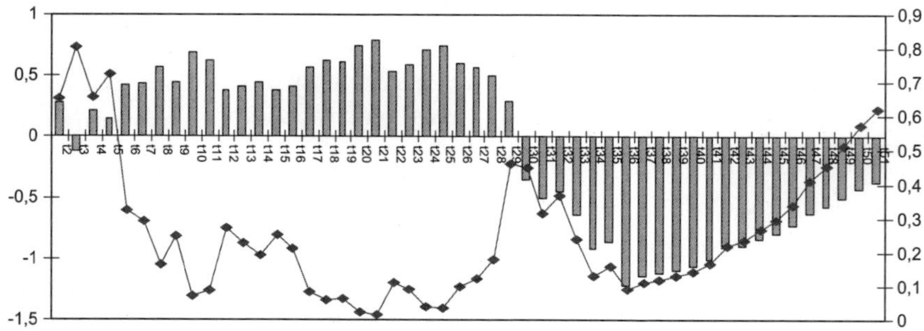

(b) Model 2

Figure 2. ThresJ, coefficients and p-values.

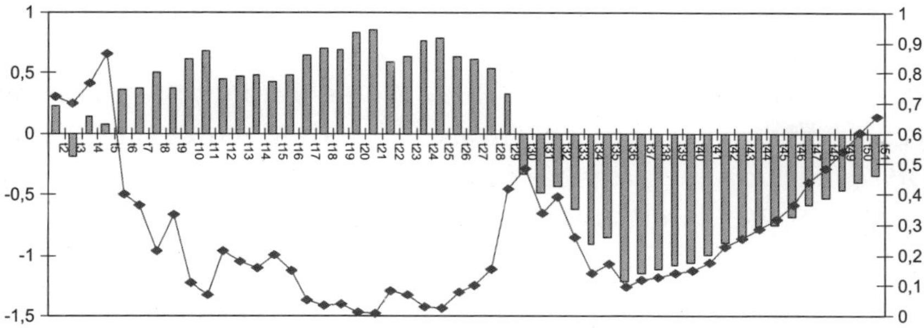

(c) Model 3

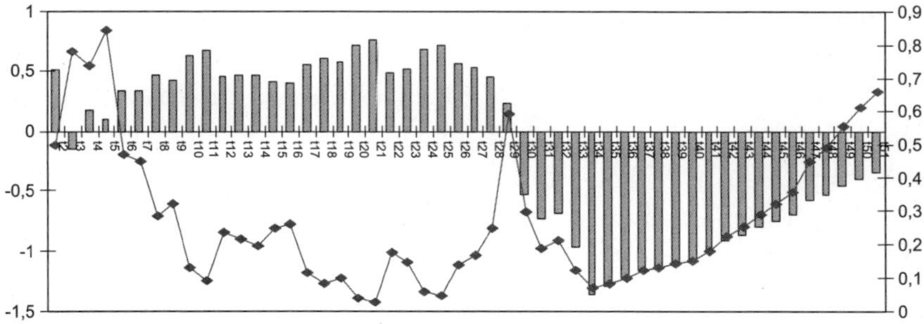

(d) Model 4

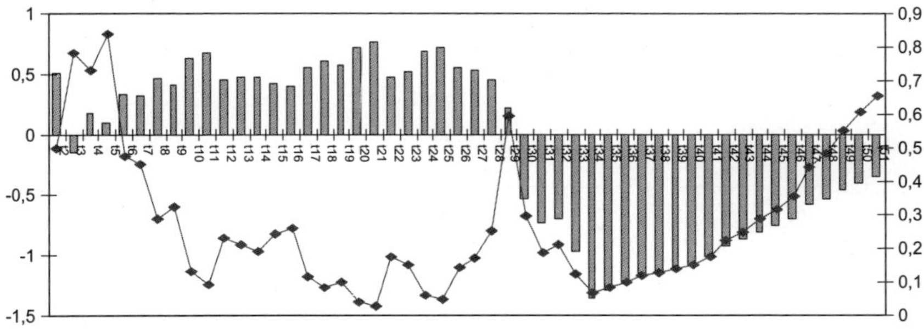

(e) Model 5

Figure 2. (*Continued*)

the estimated coefficients of ThresJ. The lines, scaled by *y*-axis on the right, on the other hand, represent the *p*-values of these estimations. Figure 2(a) at Thres21 is read as follows; if specification 1 is run on Thres21, we estimate Thres21's coefficient to be 0.89 with *p*-value 0.005. Other figures are read similarly.

Examining Fig. 2 carefully, we observe that all thresholds (except 3) up to 30 have positive coefficient estimates. Significances vary slightly but thresholds 20 and 21 are significant at 1–3% in all specifications, implying that borrowing from IIBM more than 20% of GDP significantly increases the country's probability of experiencing a crisis. Another interesting result from this analysis is that for all thresholds after 30, the coefficient estimates turn to negative in all specifications. The significances vary in this range as well, but threshold 36 is significant at less than 10% in all specifications, implying that for the countries that borrow more than 36% of their GDP, crises are significantly less likely. To get a better grasp of these seemingly confusing results, we plot, in Fig. 3, the average IIBL/GDP levels from 1977 Q4 to 2002 Q4 of all countries in three groups: Rich, the countries listed as industrialized in the IFS Database, except Turkey and South Africa; Poor without crises, the poor countries which did not experience any banking crisis during the study period; Poor with crises after 1990, the poor countries which experienced at least one crisis after 1990. The list of the countries in each group is in Appendix 1.

In Fig. 3, we observe that there is a jump in IIBL/GDP ratios in 1984, then they become more stable after 1990s and reside in a band of 15–20% for poor countries with crises and 10–15% for

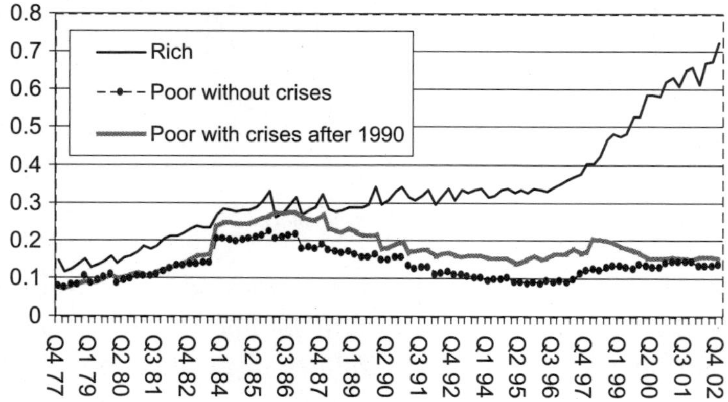

Figure 3. Average IIBL/GDP levels for sample countries.

poor countries without crises. For rich countries, on the other hand, these ratios increase steadily over time and are almost always above 30% after 1984. These observations help clarify the conclusions in the previous paragraph. Thus, the conclusion which states that borrowing more than 36% of GDP from IIBM decreases the likelihood of crises is true because such countries are mostly rich countries and in such countries crises are much less likely. The conclusion which states that borrowing more than 20% of GDP from that market increases the likelihood of crises is also true because crises in rich countries are much fewer and thus do not heavily affect the estimated coefficient for threshold 20.

The above conclusions hint that there is a fixed effect for rich countries, where institutions are of high quality. To introduce this effect, we define a rich country dummy, Rt, as Rt = {1 if rich (for year starting with t) and 0 otherwise} and interact it with IIBL/GDP. We include IIBL/GDP and Rt * IIBL/GDP as regressors and exclude GDP per capita, since Rt * IIBL/GDP captures the institutional characteristics of rich countries. The effect of IIBL on the crisis probability for the poor countries is measured by the coefficient estimate of IIBL/GDP, whereas it is the sum of those of IIBL/GDP and Rt * IIBL/GDP for rich countries.

The time dimension that runs from 1980 to 1999, abbreviated as y80 to y99, is our sample selection tool and used to test whether conclusions depend on the sample period. In this notation, y80 denotes the sample period 1980–2002 and y99 denotes 1999–2002. Ignoring the robust results for other variables, we summarize the results for IIBL/GDP and Rt * IIBL/GDP in Fig. 4. Figure 4(a–e) traces the results for IIBL/GDP. In the figure, the horizontal axis runs from y80 to y99. Bars on the graph, scaled by the vertical axis on the left, are the estimates for the coefficients of IIBL/GDP. The vertical axis on the right represents the *p*-values, traced by the line. We read the graphs as follows: Take for example Fig. 4(a) with y90. Figure 4(a), corresponding to Specification 1, reveals to us that when we run the regression using the sample [1990–2002] the estimate for IIBL/GDP is 2.011 with *p*-value 0.076. Figure 4(f–j) is read similarly to infer about Rt * IIBL/GDP.

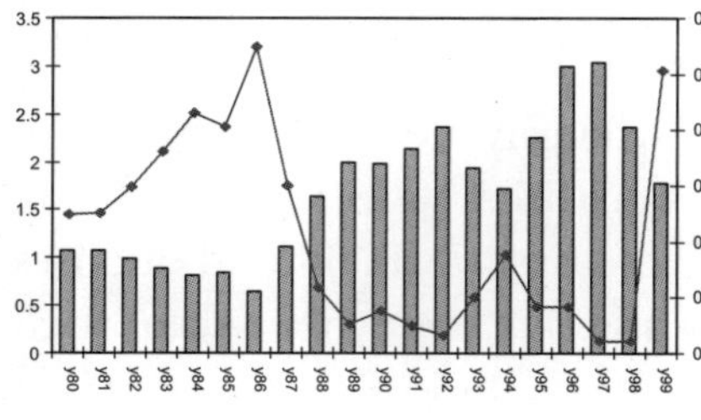

(a) IIBL/GDP Model 1

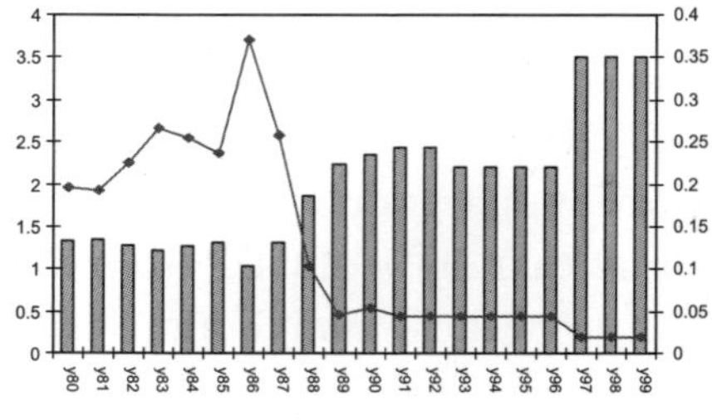

(b) IIBL/GDP Model 2

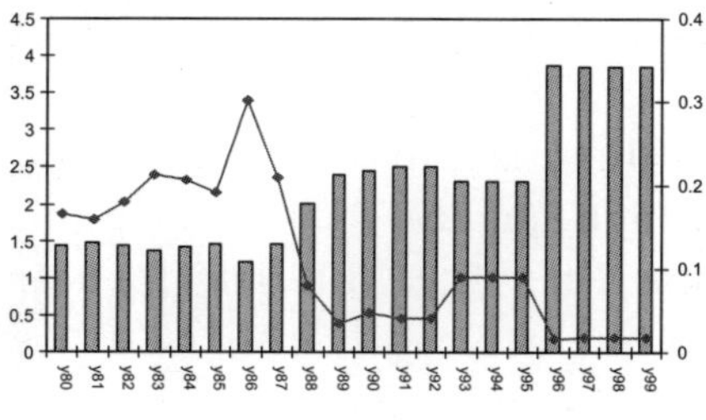

(c) IIBL/GDP Model 3

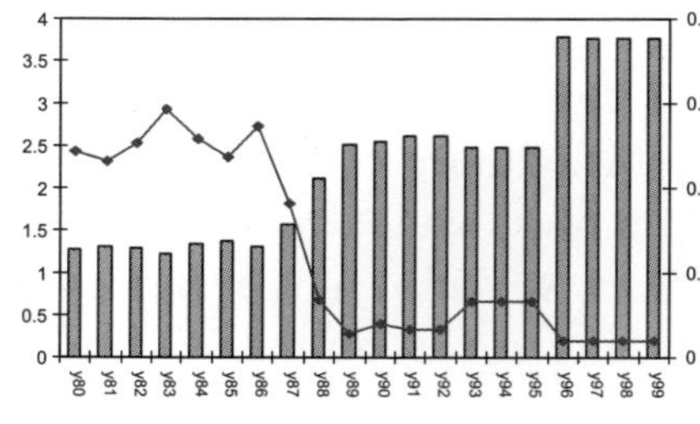

(d) IIBL/GDP Model 4

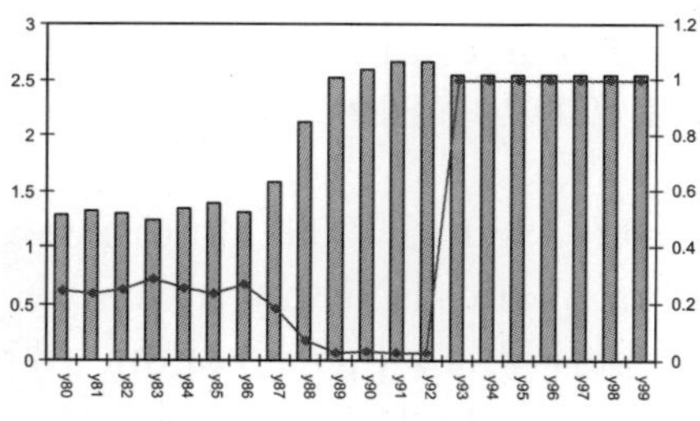

(e) IIBL/GDP Model 5

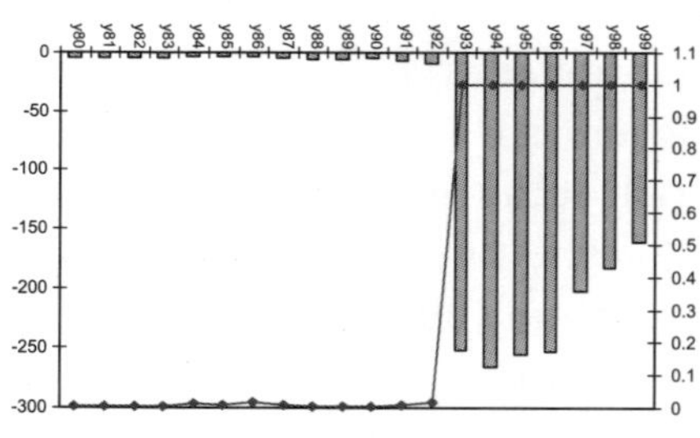

(f) R_t * (IIBL/GDP) Model 1

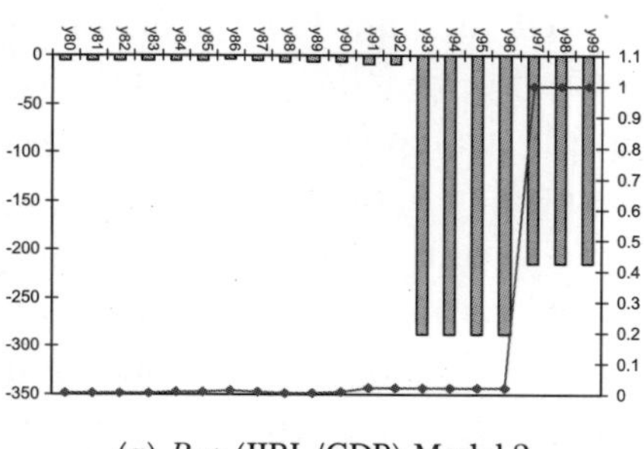

(g) R_t * (IIBL/GDP) Model 2

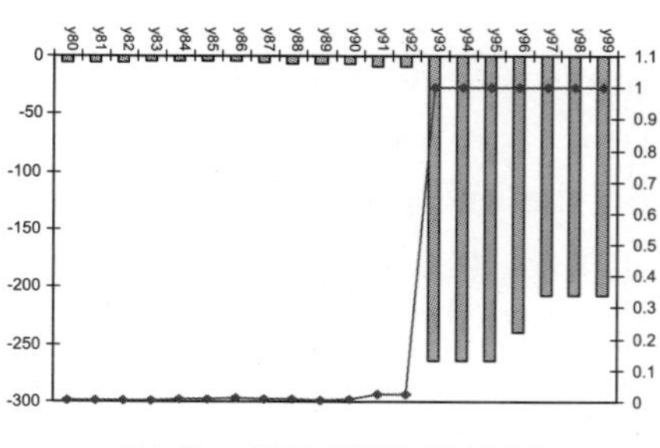

(h) R_t * (IIBL/GDP) Model 3

Figure 4. IIBL/GDP and R_1 * (IIBL/GDP), coefficient estimates and p-values.

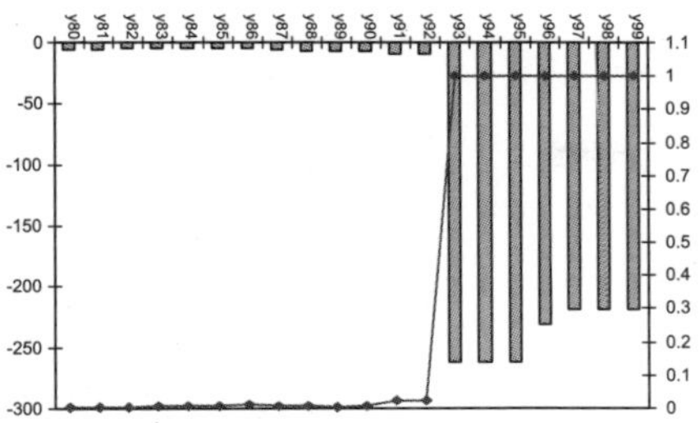

(i) $R_t *$ (IIBL/GDP) Model 4

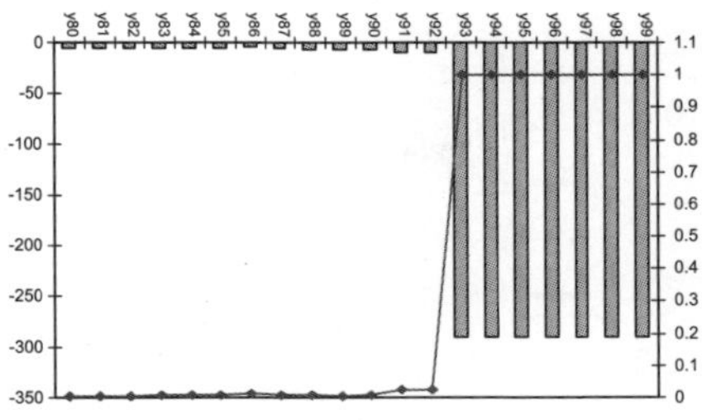

(j) $R_t *$ (IIBL/GDP) Model 5

Figure 4. (*Continued*)

We have significant (all at 1% level) and negative estimates for Rt* IIBL/GDP in all specifications for all sample periods up to and including 1992. That is, for all samples from 1980–2002 to 1992–2002, a rich country has a lower probability of experiencing a crisis than a poor one, given that they have the same values for all explanatory variables. For the sample periods above 1992, computational difficulties arise, making estimation results unreliable.

IIBL/GDP has positive estimates in all specifications for all sample periods. Although they do not seem to be significant till 1989, significances improve in and around the 1990s, implying that IIBL started to significantly affect the likelihood of crises after the 1990s. Accordingly, our best sample period, employing several criteria such as pseudo R^2, AIC and prediction successes, turns out to be 1990–2002. This conclusion seems to be in line with the literature because it is frequently cited that crises in the 1990s are of a different nature, and hence named as twin crises. Figure 3 can shed a light on this conclusion. Although IIBL/GDP ratios are higher on average for developing countries in the 1980s (specially in the second half), of 58 crises in our sample 25 occurred in the 1980s and 33 occurred in the 1990s. That is, IIBL were not as influential in the 1980s as they were in the 1990s. For example, the high IIBL/GDP ratios did not result in a crisis in the following countries (Fig. 5) in the 1980s, but they did in the 1990s.

For the sample period 1990–2002, we proceed to investigate the effects of another source of capital inflow, foreign direct investments

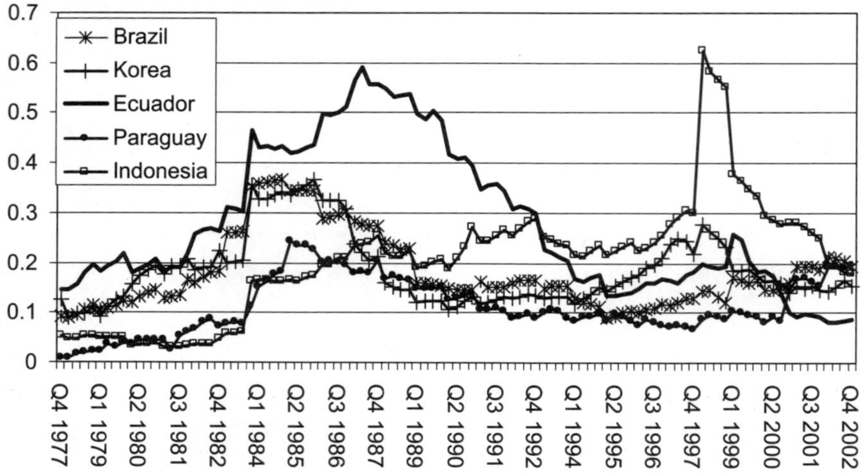

Figure 5. IIBL/GDP levels for selected countries.

(FDI), on the likelihood of crises. So, to our analysis we incorporate FDI/GDP and its interaction with Rich Dummy, Rt. The results are summarized in Table 3.

We observe that IIBL/GDP has positive and significant (at 5% to 10% levels) coefficients, implying that interbank borrowings significantly increase the likelihood of crises in poor countries after the 1990s. R_{90} * (IIBL/GDP + FDI/GDP), total amount of capital inflows to rich countries, has negative and significant (at 1%) coefficients in all specifications, thus concluding that crises are much less likely in rich countries. Coefficient estimates for FDI/GDP have positive and negative signs depending on the specification, and they are highly insignificant in all specifications.

Thus, we conclude that FDI/GDP has no significant effect on the probability of crises and thus is irrelevant. A careful examination of Fig. 1 actually confirms this result. There we observe that, although FDI generally move together with IIBL, that is, rise before crises and fall after crises, in terms of magnitude and volatility they are much less significant. Moreover, we observe that although the significance of real interest rate has fallen slightly, the coefficients of Surplus/GDP have become negative and significant in a robust way. Thus, we conclude that governments with budget deficits, as they benefit from capital flows, do not have the willingness and capacity to apply the correct regulatory and macroeconomic policies against excessive capital flows.

As a result of the nonlinearity of the logit model, coefficients do not reflect the effect of a unit change in the explanatory variables on the dependent variable as coefficients in linear models do. Total change in probability depends on the coefficients and the initial values of the explanatory variables. To get a better insight on the relative impact of independent variables, we compute the elasticities for three recent episodes of banking crises, Turkey (2000), Argentina (2001) and Indonesia (1997). In computing the elasticities, we select Model 3 in Table 4 as our benchmark model by relying on several model selection criteria such as Model χ^2, pseudo R^2, AIC and prediction successes.

We employed a 10% increase to the initial values in the significant explanatory variables. Table 5 summarizes the results. For Turkey and Indonesia, real GDP growth rate and IIBL/GDP have the largest elasticities. If growth rate for Turkey in 2000 were 10% higher, the estimated crisis probability would be 7.9% lower than the initial crisis probability. It would be 5.9% higher if initial IIBL/GDP were 10% higher. For Argentina, IIBL/GDP has the largest effect on the estimated probability with a corresponding 3.3% increase. In Indonesia (1997) crisis, IIBL/GDP has the largest marginal effect, a 6.9% increase, on the probability of crisis. Real interest rate has also positive effects. In all episodes, Surplus/GDP has a minor marginal effect on the crisis probability.

Table 5. Percent change in estimated probabilities after a 10% increase in initial values of significant variables for various crises.

Variables	Turkey (2000)	Argentina (2001)	Indonesia (1997)
Growth	−7.9	−0.8	−4.9
Real interest	1.7	2.5	0.9
Surplus/GDP	0.0	0.0	0.0
IIBL/GDP	5.9	3.3	6.9

4. Conclusions

We analyzed whether and how IIBL affected the probability of crises in the period 1980–2002. We find that although IIBL peaked in the second half of the 1980s, they were not a significant determinant of the probability of crises in that period. However, after the 1990s, we find that IIBL significantly increased the likelihood of crises in developing countries, while the same is not true for developed countries. Well-established institutions in developed countries seem to prevent the possible adverse effects of short-term capital flows. The excessive amounts of IIBL/GDP ratios, reaching 40–50% in some episodes, suggest the existence of coordination failures among international banks. Thus, regulations that would coordinate and limit short-term capital flows from this market to developing countries seem to be justified. We analyzed also some other factors suggested by the theory and case studies, and find that, in accordance with the previous literature, the low output growth, high short-term real interest rates and budget deficits tend to increase the likelihood of crises.

Appendix

A.1. *List of Countries*

Countries used in this study and their classification as rich and poor are given below. Classification is due to IFS Database. We classified Turkey and South Africa as developing countries, even though they are in the industrialized (rich) countries list in the IFS Database.

Rich (20): Australia, Austria, Belgium, Canada, Denmark, Finland, France, Germany, Greece, Ireland, Italy, Japan, Netherlands, New Zealand, Norway, Portugal, Sweden, Switzerland, United Kingdom and United States.

Poor (44): Chile, Colombia, Ecuador, El Salvador, Guatemala, Guyana, Honduras, Jamaica, Mexico, Paraguay, Peru, Uruguay, Venezuela, Cyprus, Egypt Arab Rep., Israel, Jordan, Syrian Arab Rep., India, Indonesia, Korea, Malaysia, Nepal, Philippines, Sri Lanka, Thailand, Burundi, Congo Dem. Rep., Congo Rep., Kenya, Mali, Niger, Nigeria, Senegal, Swaziland, Tanzania, Togo, Uganda, Zambia, Papua New Guinea, Argentina, Brazil, South Africa and Turkey.

Countries in Figure 1

Rich (20): Australia, Austria, Belgium, Canada, Denmark, Finland, France, Germany, Greece, Ireland, Italy, Japan, Netherlands, New Zealand, Norway, Portugal, Sweden, Switzerland, United Kingdom and United States.

Poor with crises after 1990 (24): Argentina, Brazil, Burundi, Colombia, Congo Dem. Rep., Congo Rep., Ecuador, Guyana, India, Indonesia, Jamaica, Kenya, Korea, Malaysia, Mexico, Nigeria, Paraguay, Philippines, Swaziland, Thailand, Turkey, Uganda, Uruguay and Venezuela.

Poor without crises (20): Chile, Cyprus, Egypt Arab Rep., El Salvador, Honduras, Guatemala, Israel, Jordan, Mali, Nepal, Niger, Papua New Guinea, Peru, Senegal, South Africa, Sri Lanka, Syrian Arab Rep., Tanzania, Togo and Zambia.

A.2. *Data Sources and Definitions*

Table A.2. Description of the explanatory variables and sources.

Variable	Definition	Source
Crisis	Dummy variable that equals one if country is in crisis, zero otherwise.	Demirgüç-Kunt and Detragiache (2005)
Growth	Rate of growth of real GDP	WDI: GDP, PPP (constant 1995 international $)
Inflation	Rate of change of GDP deflator	WDI
Depreciation	Rate of change of US$ exchange rate. For U.S., rate of change of the nominal effective exchange rate	IFS: line ae, for U.S., line neu.
Real interest	$\left\{\left[\frac{1+\frac{\text{nominal rate}}{100}}{1+\frac{\textit{inflation}}{100}}\right]-1\right\}*100$	IFS: Nominal interest rate is the treasury bill rate (line 60c). or if not available is the discount bank rate (line 60), or if not available is the deposit rate (line 601).
Surplus/GDP	Ratio of central government budget surplus to GDP	IFS: Surplus, Line 80.
CredGrow	Rate of growth of real domestic credit	IFS line 32d divided by the WDI GDP deflator.

(*Continued*)

Table A.2. (*Continued*)

Variable	Definition	Source
$\frac{GDP}{CAP}$	Real GDP per capita.	WDI: GDP/capita, PPP (cons. 1995 int.l $)
$\frac{FDI}{GDP}$	Ratio of foreign direct investment net inflows to GDP	WDI: EDI net inflows (BoP current US$).
$\frac{IIBL}{GDP}$	Ratio of International Interbank Lending to GDP	BIS quarterly review: IIBL. Table 6A (assets)

A.3. *IIBL/GDP Ratios in Crises*

Table A.3. IIBL/GDP ratios in crises.

Year	Country	IIBL/GDP	Year	Country	IIBL/GDP
1980	Argentina	0.20	1982	Mexico	0.30
1989	Argentina	0.43	1994	Mexico	0.18
1995	Argentina	0.13	1988	Nepal	0.02
2001	Argentina	0.15	1983	Niger	0.22
1990	Brazil	0.15	1991	Nigeria	0.21
1994	Brazil	0.11	1987	Norway	0.25
1994	Burundi	0.02	1989	Papua New Guinea	0.22
1981	Chile	0.23	1995	Paraguay	0.08
1982	Colombia	0.12	1983	Peru	0.34
1999	Colombia	0.15	1981	Philippines	0.15
1994	Congo, Dem. Rep.	0.10	1998	Philippines	0.25
1992	Congo, Rep.	0.33	1986	Portugal	0.29
1995	Ecuador	0.14	1983	Senegal	0.15
1989	El Salvador	0.08	1985	South Africa	0.30
1991	Finland	0.27	1989	Sri Lanka	0.12
1993	Guyana	0.11	1995	Swaziland	0.02
1991	India	0.05	1990	Sweden	0.33
1992	Indonesia	0.29	1988	Tanzania	0.04
1997	Indonesia	0.30	1983	Thailand	0.17
1983	Israel	0.26	1997	Thailand	0.52
1990	Italy	0.21	1982	Turkey	0.04
1996	Jamaica	0.10	1991	Turkey	0.11
1992	Japan	0.23	1994	Turkey	0.13
1989	Jordan	0.59	2000	Turkey	0.25
1993	Kenya	0.20	1994	Uganda	0.02
1997	Korea	0.22	1980	United States	0.03
1985	Malaysia	0.35	1981	Uruguay	0.07
1997	Malaysia	0.29	2002	Uruguay	0.26
1987	Mali	0.02	1993	Venezuela	0.29

Endnotes

1. Banks' assets were categorized into four groups according to their risk weights: Loans to OECD countries' governments (0%), loans to banks in OECD countries (20%), real-estate loans (50%), loans to consumers and corporations (100%).
2. The implicit/explicit guarantees given by governments to protect the international payment system and the lower capital requirements in the 1988 Basel Capital Accord for the interbank loans are generally considered as the reasons why short-term capital flowed mostly through interbank loans.
3. Another important criticism raised against Basel-I was that risk groups were too broad and imprecise. Thus, banks can easily switch to the higher risk, higher return alternatives within the same risk weighing group of assets so that they can both meet the capital standards and take on more risk. Jackson *et al.* (1999) and Jones (2000) provide examples of such techniques.
4. The whole list is in the Appendix.
5. They try both alternatives and conclude that the latter performs better.
6. Looting is rather a concern for small banks. The managers of the small banks, who are also the biggest shareholders, extract the value of the bank by insider lending, when they discover that the prospects of their banks are deteriorating. Akerlof and Romer (1994) argue that looting accounts almost 30% ($50 billion) of the losses incurred during the savings and loans (S&L) crisis in the U.S.
7. Two period lags seem to be the most relevant ones.
8. The critical issue in computing the prediction successes is the choice of the cut-off probability, P* (i.e., if $F(x'_{it}\beta) > P^*$, a crisis is predicted in that year). As Greene (2003) states "... there is no correct answer as to the best value to choose for P*. Therefore, as Demirgüç-Kunt and Detragiache (1998) also did, we choose the in-sample frequency for the particular model.
9. For example, the external debt crisis in Mexico 1982, the end of Argentina Tablita in Uruguay in 1981, the collapse of trade with Soviet Union in Finland 1990, the sharp decline in oil prices in Norway 1986, and the shift in the monetary policy in the U.S. 1980.
10. No lag is found to be more meaningful than the variable itself.

References

Akerlof, G and P Romer (1994). Looting: The economic underworld of bankruptcy for profit. *Brooking Papers on Economic Activity*, September, 1–60.

Bernard, H and J Bisignano (2000). Information, liquidity and risk in the international interbank market: Implicit guarantees and private credit market failure. *BIS Working Papers*, No. 86.

Bhagwati, J (1998). The capital myth: The difference between trade in widges and trade in dollars. *Foreign Affairs*, 77, 7–12.

Caprio, G and D Klingebiel (2003). *Episodes of Systemic and Borderline Financial Crises.* Working Paper, World Bank.

Demirgüç-Kunt, A and E Detragiache (2005). Cross-country empirical studies of systemic bank distress: A survey. *National Institute Economic Review*, 192(1), 68–83.

Demirgüç-Kunt, A and E Detragiache (1998). The determinants of banking crises in developing and developed countries. *IMF Staff Papers*, 45, March, 81–109.

Eichengreen, B and C. Arteta (2000). *Banking Crises in Emerging Markets: Presumptions and Evidence.* Centre for International Development Economics Research Working Paper, No. 115. Haas School of Business. University of California Berkeley.

Greene, W (2003). *Econometric Analysis*, 5th edition, pp. 685. Prentice-Hall.

Greenspan, A (1998). Remarks at the 34th Annual Conference on Bank Structure and Competition, Federal Reserve Bank of Chicago.

Jackson, P, C Furfine, H Groeneveld, D Hancock, D Jones, W Perraudin, L Redecki and N Yoneyama (1999). Capital requirements and bank behaviour: The impact of the Basel Accord. Basel Committee on Bank Supervision, Working Paper 1.

Jones, D (2000). Emerging problems with the Basel Capital Accord: Regulatory capital arbitrage and related issues. *Journal of Banking and Finance*, 24, 35–56.

Kaminsky, G and C Reinhart (1996). *The Twin Crises: The Causes of Banking and Balance of Payments Problems.* International Finance Discussion Paper, No. 544. Federal Reserve Board. Washington DC.

Kaminsky, G (1998). *Currency and Banking Crises: The Early Warnings of Distress.* Board of Governors of the Federal Reserve System. International Finance Discussion Paper, No. 629.

Lindgren, C, G Garcia and M Saal (1996). *Bank Soundness and Macroeconomic Policy.* Washington DC: International Monetary Fund.

Miskhin, F (1996). Understanding financial crises: A developing country perspective. *Annual World Bank Conference on Development Economics*, Michael Bruno and Boris Pleskovic (eds.). Washington DC: World Bank, 29–62.

Tirole, J (2002). *Financial Crises. Liquidity and International Monetary Systems.* Princeton University Press.

4

International Transmission Effects of Volatility Between Financial Markets in the G-7 Since the Introduction of the Euro

Lucía Morales

1. Introduction

The aim of this chapter is to investigate the interdependence of stock returns and exchange rates changes for the G-7 financial markets and the main exchange rates, with the objective of identifying which currencies will generate a stronger impact in the financial markets in the G-7 before and after the introduction of the Euro. Several theoretical models have found empirical evidence that the exchange rate between two currencies is affected by stock price changes in the respective countries; for example, Zapatero (1995) shows that in fully integrated financial markets, there is an explicit linkage between the volatility of stock prices and the volatility of the exchange rate.

More recently, Yang and Doong (2002) note that given the rapid integration and deregulation of international financial markets in recent years, exchange rates have become more sensitive to stock market innovations. A number of studies have investigated the extent of volatility spillovers between stock markets and exchange rates in the G-7 countries (e.g., Yang and Doong, 2004; Kanas, 2000,

2002). However no study to date has specifically investigated volatility spillovers between stock markets and exchange rates in the G-7 since the introduction of the Euro.

In addition to this, there is a lack of evidence of studies studying this issue taking into account the effect of exchange rates other than for the domestic currency on the stock returns of these countries. Therefore, we attempt to address the gap in the literature in this area by conducting an in-depth analysis of the relationship between these two variables. Our objective is to add to the general literature in this area by investigating spillovers between stock markets and exchange rates for a number of exchange rates. Current evidence for the G-7 has focused exclusively on spillovers between the domestic currency and the stock market; for this reason, we analyze the relationship between these two variables in a wider way. Section 2 sets out the theoretical and empirical evidence on the nature of linkages between stock markets and exchange rates. Section 3 describes the methodology we use to assess the nature of volatility spillovers between the stock and foreign exchange markets, and we discuss our data. Section 4 presents empirical results and Sec. 5 concludes the chapter.

2. Literature Review

Several theoretical models have analyzed the link between stock markets and currency markets. The asset market approach to exchange rate determination (Branson, 1983; Frankel, 1983) posits that causality will run from stock prices to exchange rate changes as expectations of financial asset price movements affect the dynamics of exchange rates. Smith (1992) derives an estimable equation for the exchange rate where the stock price is included as an explanatory variable. The goods market approach suggests causality runs in the opposite direction, from exchange rates to stock prices (Mundell, 1963, 1964; Dornbusch and Fisher, 1980). In these models, movements in exchange rates affect the international competitiveness of firms which affects real income and output and eventually stock prices.

Much of the available empirical evidence on the linkages between stock markets and exchange rates has concentrated on the first moments.[1] Yang and Doong (2004) note that there is a dearth of empirical evidence that concentrates on the linkages between the second moments of the distribution of the variables. A number of studies however have examined the extent to which volatility from one stock market spills over into other stock markets or between different assets[2] (e.g., Nelson, 1991; Koutmos and Booth, 1995; Laopodis, 1998). Kanas (2000) was one of the first studies which analyzed volatility spillovers from stock returns to exchange rate changes in the U.S.A., the U.K., Japan, Germany, France and Canada.

Kanas found evidence of spillovers from stock returns to exchange rate changes for all countries except Germany, suggesting that the asset approach to exchange rate determination is valid when formulated in terms of the second moments of the exchange rate distribution for the countries included in his analysis. Volatility spillovers from exchange rate changes to stock returns were insignificant for all countries. Assoé (2001) investigates the dynamic interrelationship between exchange rate changes and stock market performance in 11 emerging markets and five developed markets, using a trivariate Exponential-GARCH model. His results indicate that shocks in foreign exchange markets significantly increase volatility in emerging stock markets. He also found evidence of asymmetric volatility spillover from FX markets to stock markets for some of the countries that were included in his analysis.

The asymmetric nature of volatility transmission suggest that investors in these markets react more to adverse innovations in foreign exchange markets than to positive shocks. Yang and Doong (2004) explored the nature of the mean and volatility transmission mechanism between stock and foreign exchange markets for the G-7 countries. The results point to significant volatility spillovers and an asymmetric effect from the stock market to the foreign exchange market for France, Italy, Japan and the U.S., suggesting integration between stock and foreign exchange markets in these countries. Kanas (2000) and Yang and Doong (2004) concentrate exclusively on the domestic currency and do not investigate the extent of spillovers from other currencies to the domestic stock market.

Wu (2005) examines volatility spillovers between stock prices and exchange rates for Japan, South Korea, Indonesia, the Philippines, Singapore, Thailand and Taiwan for the period 1997–2000, splitting the sample into crises and recovery periods. He found a bi-directional relationship between the volatility of stock returns and exchange rate changes during the recovery period in all countries except South Korea, as well as significant contemporaneous relationships between the two markets for most of the countries. Furthermore, he found volatility spillovers increased in the recovery period. Qayyum and Kemal (2006) examine volatility spillover between the stock market and the foreign exchange market in Pakistan, through a bivariate EGARCH model.

Their results show that the behavior of both the stock exchange and the foreign exchange markets are interlinked. The returns of one market are affected by the volatility of the other market. In particular, the returns of the stock market are sensitive to the returns as well as the volatility of foreign exchange markets. They found evidence of strong relationship between the volatility of foreign exchange market and the volatility of returns in stock market. Leeves (2007) analyzes the conditional volatility in stock returns in Indonesia over the period covered by the Asian crisis. He used three asymmetric models of conditional volatility (GJR, NGARCH and AGARCH), he found evidences of significant asymmetric impacts from conditional volatility shocks, with negative shocks causing greater volatility than positive shocks, during the Asian crisis. We add to the existing literature in this area by providing up-to-date evidence on this issue for the G-7 and provide new evidence on the extent to which volatility spillovers vary between different currencies and the domestic stock market in each country.

3. Data and Methodology

The analysis will be conducted with the purpose of investigating volatility spillovers between stock returns and exchange rate changes for the G-7 (Canada, France, Germany, Italy, Japan, the U.K. and the U.S.A.) for the period 1 January 1996 to 31 December 2006. In order to analyze the relationship between these two variables, we split our sample into three sub-samples, which provide more detail and a better understanding of volatility spillovers between stock returns and exchange rates. Therefore, we initially analyze the relationship between these two variables before the introduction of the Euro. So our first sub-sample will analyze the period 1996–1998.

Then we analyze the period after the introduction of the Euro from 1999 to 2006. We are interested in examining whether the first years of the single currency in the European financial markets affected the relationship between our variables, so we split our sample into two subperiods; 1999–2001 covers the period that markets were working with the single currency but without it being physically introduced. Finally, we analyze the period from 2002 to 2006 where the Euro was physically introduced in the financial markets, allowing us to observe the behavior of our variables when the Euro settled in European Monetary Union. The data set consists of daily closing values for the stock market indices in each country, as well as daily closing values for the exchange rates of each country against the Euro, Deutsche mark, British pound, Swiss franc, Japanese yen and the US dollar.

We include these exchange rates to examine whether volatility spillovers are stronger from certain currencies during the sample period. The original data set was subject to some modifications, all holidays and other closing days were removed from the sample to avoid inconsistencies with the data set and also to avoid problems in the modeling estimation. Data were taken from DataStream and the Federal Reserve Statistic Release, giving a total of 2766 observations for each series. Following Kanas (2000), we use continuously compounded stock returns and exchange rate changes calculated as the first differences of the natural log. That is, S = stock prices; $S_t = \ln(P_t^s) - \ln(P_{t-1}^s)$ and E = exchange rates; $E_t = \ln(P_t^e) - \ln(P_{t-1}^e)$.

As an initial step, we provide descriptive statistics for stock returns and exchange rates to summarize the statistical characteristics of our sample. We then proceed to perform a stationarity test on each of the relevant variables that are included in our analysis to ensure that the results from the analysis are not spurious. We apply the Dickey-Fuller (DF) test or Augmented Dickey-Fuller test (ADF) procedure if serial correlation is present. We also apply the Lagrange Multiplier (LMF) test, to ensure that a sufficient number of lags have been added in the ADF test to ensure that there is no serial correlation present and the results of the ADF test are valid. The LMF test is applied given that it is valid in the presence of lagged dependent variables as well as having the advantage of testing for first and higher orders of serial correlation.

We then proceed with our volatility analysis and apply a bivariate extension of the EGARCH (p,q) model to examine whether the volatility of stock returns affects and is affected by the volatility of exchange rate changes within each economy. The EGARCH specification (Nelson, 1991) is used to test whether the volatility spillover effects are asymmetric. For example, an asymmetric spillover from stock returns to exchange rate changes would suggest that the effect of "bad" stock market news on the exchange rate change is greater than the effect of "good" news. The model is specified as follows:

$$S_t = a_{s,0} + \sum_{i=1}^{r} a_{s,i} S_{t-i} + \sum_{i=1}^{r} a_{e,i} E_{t-i} + e_{S,t} \tag{1}$$

$$E_t = a_{E,0} + \sum_{i=1}^{r} a_{E,i} E_{t-i} + \sum_{i=1}^{r} a_{S,i} S_{t-i} + e_{E,t} \tag{2}$$

$$\frac{e_{S,t}}{\Omega_{t-1}} \approx N(0, \sigma^2_{S,t})$$

$$\frac{e_{E,t}}{\Omega_{t-1}} \approx N(0, \sigma^2_{E,t}).$$

The conditional variances of stock returns and exchange rates changes are specified as follows:

$$\log \sigma^2_{S,t} = \exp\left\{ c_{S,0} + \sum_{j=1}^{ps} b_{S,j} \log(\sigma^2_{S,t-j}) + \delta_{S,S}[(|z_{S,t-1}| - E|z_{S,t-1}| \right.$$
$$+ \theta_{S,Sz_{s,T-1}}) + \delta_{S,E}[(|z_{E,t-1}| - E|z_{E,t-1}| + \theta_{S,EzE,t-1})]] \tag{3}$$

$$\log \sigma^2_{E,t} = \exp\left\{ c_{E,0} + \sum_{j=1}^{ps} b_{E,j} \log(\sigma^2_{E,t-j}) + \delta_{E,E}[(|z_{E,t-1}| - E|z_{E,t-1}| \right.$$
$$\left. + \theta_{E,Ez_{s,T-1}}) + \delta_{E,S}[(|z_{S,t-1}| - E|z_{S,t-1}| + \theta_{E,SzE,t-1})]] \right. \quad (4)$$
$$\sigma_{S,E,T} = \rho_{S,E}\sigma_{S,t}\sigma_{E,t}.$$

We summarize each of the relevant terms in Eqs. (1)–(4) in Table 1.

Asymmetry of spillovers is such that $\theta_{S,E} < 0$, $\theta_{E,S} < 0$, implies that negative exchange rate shocks increase the volatility of stock returns more than positive shocks. The number of lags for the conditional mean Eqs. (1) and (2) are specified using the HQ criterion; Griffin *et al.* (2007), Andersen and Bollerslev (1998) all note that the Hannan-Quinn selection criterion is preferable to the more commonly used Akaike's Information Criteria (AIC), as the latter tends to overparameterize the models.[3] Next the likelihood ratio (LR) test is applied to determine the lag truncation length, p.

Table 1. Description of parameters Eqs. (1)–(4).

	Stock returns	Exchange rate returns
Stochastic error terms	$e_{S,t}$	$e_{E,t}$
Information set at time $t-1$	Ω_{t-1}	Ω_{t-1}
Conditional (time varying) variances	$\sigma^2_{S,t}$	$\sigma^2_{E,t}$
Standardized residuals assumed to be normally distributed with 0 mean and variances of $\sigma^2_{S,t}$, $\sigma^2_{E,t}$	$z_{S,t} = e_{S,t}/\sigma_{S,t}$ $e_{S,t}/\Omega_{t-1} \sim \text{N}(0, \sigma^2_{S,t})$	$z_{E,t} = e_{E,t}/\sigma_{E,t}$ $e_{E,t}/\Omega_{t-1} \sim \text{N}(0, \sigma^2_{E,t})$
Persistence of volatility	$\sum_{j=1}^{ps} b_{S,j}$	$\sum_{j=1}^{pE} b_{E,j}$
ARCH effect where the parameters $\theta_{S,S}$, $\theta_{E,E}$ allow this effect to be asymmetric	$[\lvert z_{S,t}\rvert - E\lvert z_{S,t}\rvert + \theta_{S,Sz_{S,t}}]$	$[\lvert z_{E,t}\rvert - E\lvert z_{E,t}\rvert + \theta_{E,Ez_{E,t}}]$
Volatility spillover	$\delta_{S,E}[\lvert z_{E,t-1}\rvert - E\lvert z_{E,t-1}\rvert + \theta_{S,Ez_{E,t-1}}]$	$\delta_{E,S}[\lvert z_{S,t-1}\rvert - E\lvert z_{S,t-1}\rvert + \theta_{E,Sz_{SSt-1}}]$
Measures of spillovers	$\delta_{S,E}$	$\delta_{E,S}$
Asymmetry of spillovers	$\theta_{S,E}$	$\theta_{E,S}$
Correlation coefficient for standardized residuals	$\rho_{S,E}$	$\rho_{E,S}$

This technique is implemented separately, so an LR test on the stock returns and exchange rate conditional variance Eqs. (3) and (4) is run to determine the optimal lag length for the EGARCH specification of each equation. Hamilton (1994) defines the LR test as follows: $2\lfloor L(\hat{\theta}) - L(\tilde{\theta})\rfloor \approx \chi^2(m)$, where $L(\hat{\theta})$ denotes the value of the log likelihood function at the unrestricted estimate and $L(\tilde{\theta})$ denotes the value of the log likelihood function of the restricted estimate. Bollerslev-Woolridge robust *t*-statistics are derived to take into account possible nonnormality of the residuals.

4. Empirical Results

4.1. *Descriptive Statistics*

This section begins by providing descriptive statistics for stock returns and exchange rates, in order to summarize the statistical characteristics of the sample.[4] For the stock returns of each country for 1996–1998 the means are positive in all the cases, with the exception of the NIKKEI 225. During 1999–2001, the sample means of stock returns are positive in the case of Canada, France and the U.S., while for Germany, Italy, Japan and the U.K. stock returns means are negative. During 2002–2006, the means of all the indices are positive. The standard deviations (SD) of the stock returns provide information about the volatility of the markets during the three periods. In general, all the markets show higher volatility during the initial years of the introduction of the Euro on financial markets that is during 1999–2001. The SD ranges from 1.23% (Dow Jones) to 1.58% (DAX 30). The SD for 2002–2006 range from 0.81% (S&P/TSX composite) to 1.61% (DAX 30). The skewness and kurtosis coefficients indicate that stock returns are leptokurtic relative to the normal distribution, which Caporale *et al.* (2002) note is a common finding for stock returns. The Jarque-Bera test also rejects the hypothesis that stock returns are normally distributed in all the cases.

The descriptive statistics for the exchange rate returns are presented for each country, to capture the behavior of the exchange rates on an individual basis. Overall, there is a wide variation in the sign and magnitude of the means and SD both over time, across countries and across the various bilateral exchange rates included in the analysis. For Canada, during 1996–1998, the means of the exchange rates are positive in the case of C$/$, C$/£ and C$/¥, while C$/CHF and C$/DM means are negative. During 1999–2001, the means for the C$/€, C$/$ are positive while C$/£, C$/¥ and C$/CHF are negative, and during 2002–2006, the mean for all the exchange rates are negative. The SD shown that as with the stock returns, the exchange rates are more volatile during the first years of the introduction of the Euro on financial markets, the SD range from 0.36% (C$/$) to 0.79% (C$/¥).

For the period prior to the introduction of the Euro for France, the means are positive in the case of Franc/$, Franc/£ and Franc/¥, while the means are negative for Franc/CHF and Franc/DM. For Germany, the means for D/$, DM/£, DM/¥ are positive, while DM/CHF mean is negative. For Italy, for this period the means are positive for Lira/$, Lira/£, while Lira/¥, Lira/CHF and Lira/DM are negative. During 1999–2001, the €/$ and €/£ means are negative while the €/¥ and €/CHF are positive. This situation reverses during 2002–2006, where the €/$ and €/£ means are positive and the €/¥ and €/CHF means are negative. As with Canada, it is also found that in this case the volatility in the exchange rates is higher during the 1999–2001 than in the other periods, ranging from 0.24% (€/CHF) and 0.90% (€/¥).

For Japan, during 1996–1998, the means for the ¥/$ and ¥/£ are positive while ¥/CHF and ¥/DM are negative, during 1999–2001, the ¥/€ and ¥/CHF the means are negative while ¥/$ and ¥/£ are positive, and finally during 2002–2006, the means are positive in all the cases with the exception of ¥/$ which is negative. The volatility of these markets was higher during 1999–2001 period, as in the previous cases, with the SD range from 0.71% (¥/$) to 1% (¥/CHF). For the U.K. for 1996–1998 the means for all the exchange rates are negative. During 1999–2001, the means are positive in all the cases with the exception of £/CHF, and during 2002–2006, the means are negative in all cases. The SD coefficients indicates that the exchange markets were more volatile during 1999–2001 than in the other periods, where volatility range from 0.51% (£/€ and £/$) to 1% (£/¥).

For the U.S., the mean coefficients are positive during 1996–1998 in all the cases, with the exception of \$/£. During 1999–2001, the means are negative in all the cases with the exception of €/£ were the means are positive, and finally during 2002–2006, the means are positive with the exception of \$/€ that is negative. The SD coefficients show that again the exchange rates were more volatile during 1999–2001 than in the rest of the period, ranging from 0.49% (\$/£) to 0.7% (\$/¥). The skewness and kurtosis statistics for all countries and bilateral exchange rates in all periods indicate that the distribution of exchange rate returns in all the cases for all the countries are nonnormal and the Jarque-Bera test also rejects the hypothesis of normally distributed returns for all periods for all exchange rates.

4.2. *Unit Root Tests*

The results[5] from the ADF test statistics indicate the null hypothesis of the existence of unit root in levels can be rejected for all variables in all periods indicating that all series are $I(0)$.[6] Given that all variables are integrated of the same order, and also given that they are $I(0)$ processes it is possible to proceed directly to perform the volatility analysis using EGARCH (p,q) modeling.

4.3. *Likelihood Ratio Test*

In order to establish the correct lag length for the EGARCH model, the likelihood ratio test is applied, as it was mentioned previously in the methodology. Dealing firstly with the stock return equations, for the 1996–1998 period, the EGARCH (1,1) model is chosen for the DM/\$ for Germany and for the \$£, \$/¥ and \$DM for the U.S. For the 1999–2001 period, the EGARCH (1,1) is selected for Canada for the C\$/\$, C\$/¥ and C\$/CHF. For Germany and Japan, for this period, this model was also chosen for all bilateral exchanges rates. For the 2002–2006 period, for France for the €/\$ and €/¥, as well as for Germany for the €/¥ and for Japan for all bilateral exchange rates the (1,1) model was selected on the basis of the LR results. For all countries for all other exchange rates for the EGARCH (2,1) model was selected for the stock return equation.

For the exchange rate equation, for the 1996–1998 period, the EGARCH (1,1) model is chosen for Canada for C$/$, for France for FR/DM, for Germany for DM/$ and for Japan for Y/CHF. For the 2002–2006 period, again for Canada the (1,1) model is selected for C$/$ and C$/£, for France and Italy for €/$, for the U.K. for £/€, $/CHF and finally for the U.S. for the $/€ and $/£. Again for all countries for all other exchange rates in each period, the EGARCH (2,1) model was chosen for the exchange rate equation. The estimated parameters from the EGARCH estimation are set out in Tables 2 to 10, for the three periods of analysis (1996–1998, 1999–2001 and 2002–2006).

4.4. *Volatility Persistence*

The coefficients on the volatility persistence term are presented through Tables 2 to 4. The results vary depending on the country, or on the equation under consideration, but the majority of terms are significant for both the stock returns and exchange rate changes. This is not surprising given that persistence is a feature of many financial markets data. Regarding the significance of volatility persistence in stock returns, Italy was the only country for which the volatility persistence term was significant in all periods across all bilateral exchange rates; France also showed consistency across all time periods for all exchange rates with only the €/CHF not significant in 2002–2006.

There appears to be more consistency between the pre-Euro period and the 2002–2006 period for certain countries; for example, for Canada and the U.K., all bilateral exchange rates are significant for the stock return equation in both periods but insignificant for the 1998–2001 period. While all coefficients were significant across all exchange rates for Japan in the pre-Euro period, there was no significant persistence evident in after the introduction of the Euro. In contrast, there was no significant volatility persistence in the U.S. apart from the $/CHF prior to the Euro and for the 1999–2001 period, but for 2002 all bilateral exchange rates in the stock return.

Table 2. EGARCH results volatility persistence 1996–1998.

Canada	**C$/$**	**C$/¥**	**C$/DM**	**C$/CHF**	**C$/£**
Stock returns	0.2749	0.2083	0.2766	0.2706	0.2828
	(0.000)*	(0.000)*	(0.000)*	(0.000)*	(0.000)*
Exchange rates	0.1335	0.2671	0.2173	0.1132	0.0866
	(0.004)*	(0.002)*	(0.004)*	(0.038)**	(0.005)*
France	**FR/$**	**FR/£**	**FR/¥**	**FR/CHF**	**FR/DM**
Stock returns	0.1279	0.1314	0.1270	0.1278	0.1322
	(0.000)*	(0.000)*	(0.000)*	(0.000)*	(0.000)*
Exchange rates	0.0171	0.0569	0.1826	0.0436	0.6480
	(0.837)	(0.0386)**	(0.000)*	(0.088)***	(0.000)*
Germany	**DM/$**	**DM/£**	**DM/¥**	**DM/CHF**	
Stock returns	0.1345	−0.0596	0.1538	−0.0314	
	(0.000)*	(0.4952)	(0.000)*	(0.7285)	
Exchange rates	−0.1973	−0.1532	−0.1936	−0.1417	
	(0.652)	(0.026)**	(0.000)*	(0.0311)**	
Italy	**Lira/CHF**	**Lira/¥**	**Lira/DM**	**Lira/£**	**Lira/$**
Stock returns	0.2081	0.2652	0.1914	0.2522	0.2534
	(0.000)*	(0.000)*	(0.000)*	(0.000)*	(0.000)*
Exchange rates	0.0303	0.2463	0.1422	0.1098	0.1059
	(0.207)	(0.006)*	(0.000)*	(0.002)*	(0.003)*
Japan	**¥/$**	**¥/£**	**¥/CHF**	**¥/DM**	
Stock returns	0.0450	0.0607	0.0528	0.0483	
	(0.033)**	(0.008)*	(0.0130)**	(0.0215)**	
Exchange rates	0.2261	0.2589	0.1903	0.1523	
	(0.0235)**	(0.004)*	(0.093)***	(0.000)*	
U.K.	**£/$**	**£/¥**	**£/CHF**	**£/DM**	
Stock returns	0.0741	0.0851	0.0873	0.0862	
	(0.002)*	(0.001)*	(0.001)*	(0.001)*	
Exchange rates	−0.0017	0.2637	0.0549	0.0638	
	(0.891)	(0.002)*	(0.107)	(0.017)**	
U.S.	**$/£**	**$/¥**	**$/CHF**	**$/DM**	
Stock returns	−0.0332	−0.0306	0.1396	−0.0381	
	(0.741)	(0.760)	(0.005)*	(0.723)	
Exchange rates	0.0063	0.2147	0.0425	−0.0863	
	(0.647)	(0.017)**	(0.570)	(0.287)	

Note: *1% significance level, **5% significance level and ***10% significance level.

For the persistence of volatility of exchange rates, an interesting feature to highlight is that the analysis of more than one exchange rate the coefficient for persistence of volatility of exchange rates varies depending on which bilateral exchange rate is included in

Table 3. EGARCH results volatility persistence 1999–2001.

Canada	**C$/$**	**C$/¥**	**C$/CHF**	**C$/£**	**C$/€**
Stock returns	−0.11603	−0.1227	−0.1101	−0.1016	−0.1172
	(0.286)	(0.237)	(0.279)	(0.327)	(0.304)
Exchange rates	−0.1667	0.0292	−0.0409	0.0959	−0.0225
	(0.159)	(0.189)	(0.274)	(0.220)	(0.746)
France	**€/$**	**€/£**	**€/¥**	**€/CHF**	
Stock returns	0.1021	0.0966	0.0978	0.0939	
	(0.028)**	(0.042)**	(0.027)**	(0.041)**	
Exchange rates	−0.1106	0.2804	0.1108	0.1558	
	(0.072)***	(0.001)*	(0.068)***	(0.002)*	
Germany	**€/$**	**€/£**	**€/¥**	**€/CHF**	
Stock returns	−0.1973	−0.1532	−0.1936	−0.1417	
	(0.013)**	(0.080)***	(0.021)**	(0.109)	
Exchange rates	−0.1122	0.2794	0.0965	0.1614	
	(0.103)	(0.001)*	(0.092)***	(0.001)*	
Italy	**€/CHF**	**€/¥**	**€/£**	**€/$**	
Stock returns	0.2301	0.2535	0.2627	0.2671	
	(0.001)*	(0.000)*	(0.000)*	(0.000)*	
Exchange rates	0.1536	0.1058	0.2543	−0.1050	
	(0.003)*	(0.079)***	(0.003)*	(0.124)	
Japan	**¥/€**	**¥/$**	**¥/£**	**¥/CHF**	
Stock returns	−0.1268	−0.1209	−0.1261	−0.1059	
	(0.2795)	(0.272)	(0.251)	(0.085)	
Exchange rates	0.0929	0.0430	0.0171	−0.1059	
	(0.097)***	(0.066)***	(0.503)	(0.334)	
U.K.	**£/€**	**£/$**	**£/¥**	**£/CHF**	
Stock returns	0.0691	0.0689	0.0599	0.0660	
	(0.059)***	(0.106)	(0.106)	(0.073)***	
Exchange rates	0.0858	0.1377	0.1879	0.0728	
	(0.211)	(0.115)	(0.000)*	(0.130)	
U.S.	**$/€**	**$/£**	**$/¥**	**$/CHF**	
Stock returns	0.0550	0.0860	0.0388	0.0540	
	(0.147)	(0.238)	(0.292)	(0.124)	
Exchange rates	−0.0537	0.0860	0.0516	−0.0557	
	(0.272)	(0.238)	(0.028)**	(0.458)	

Note: *1% significance level, **5% significance level and ***10% significance level.

the EGARCH model. Overall, there appears to be more widespread persistence in the 1996–1998 period and the 2002–2006 period than the 1999–2001 period for Canada, Japan, Germany and Italy. Only for the U.S. and France was there more significant volatility persistence

Table 4. EGARCH results volatility persistence 2002–2006.

Canada	C$/$	C$/¥	C$/CHF	C$/£	C$/€
Stock returns	0.0886	0.0794	0.0821	0.0871	0.0981
	(0.001)*	(0.004)*	(0.002)*	(0.002)*	(0.001)*
Exchange rates	0.1044	0.0548	0.1240	0.0371	0.0455
	(0.014)**	(0.044)**	(0.000)*	(0.597)	(0.386)
France	**€/$**	**€/£**	**€/¥**	**€/CHF**	
Stock returns	−0.0568	−0.0618	−0.0672	0.0947	
	(0.492)	(0.417)	(0.406)	(0.000)*	
Exchange rates	−0.1165	0.0402	0.0466	0.0957	
	(0.115)	(0.005)*	(0.029)**	(0.001)*	
Germany	**€/$**	**€/£**	**€/¥**	**€/CHF**	
Stock returns	0.1116	0.1063	−0.0230	0.1035	
	(0.000)*	(0.000)*	(0.781)	(0.000)*	
Exchange rates	0.0596	0.0377	0.0459	0.0914	
	(0.005)*	(0.008)*	(0.036)**	(0.002)*	
Italy	**€/CHF**	**€/¥**	**€/£**	**€/$**	
Stock returns	0.0660	0.0774	0.0741	0.0832	
	(0.000)*	(0.000)*	(0.000)*	(0.000)*	
Exchange rates	0.0919	0.0488	0.0447	−0.0934	
	(0.001)*	(0.029)**	(0.002)*	(0.209)	
Japan	**¥/€**	**¥/$**	**¥/£**	**¥/CHF**	
Stock returns	−0.0693	−0.0437	−0.0461	−0.0606	
	(0.359)	(0.581)	(0.555)	(0.442)	
Exchange rates	0.0491	−0.0040	0.0942	0.1363	
	(0.019)**	(0.962)	(0.259)	(0.007)*	
U.K.	**£/€**	**£/$**	**£/¥**	**£/CHF**	
Stock returns	0.0814	0.0883	0.0741	0.0720	
	(0.000)*	(0.000)*	(0.000)*	(0.000)*	
Exchange rates	0.1052	−0.0158	0.0226	−0.0887	
	(0.070)***	(0.131)	(0.431)	(0.233)	
U.S.	**$/€**	**$/£**	**$/¥**	**$/CHF**	
Stock returns	0.0663	0.0654	0.0585	0.0664	
	(0.000)*	(0.000)*	(0.001)*	(0.000)*	
Exchange rates	−0.0843	0.1561	0.0136	0.0544	
	(0.254)	(0.007)*	(0.873)	(0.007)*	

Note: *1% significance level, **5% significance level and ***10% significance level.

across exchange rates in the 2002–2006 period than in the periods prior to this, while for the U.K. the 2002–2006 period showed a decline in the significance of volatility persistence across exchange rates compared to the earlier periods.

Table 5. EGARCH results volatility spillovers 1996–1998.

Canada	**C$/$**	**C$/¥**	**C$/DM**	**C$/CHF**	**C$/£**
Stock returns	−0.1079	−0.0585	−0.0998	−0.0987	−0.0954
	(0.005)*	(0.023)**	(0.010)*	(0.010)*	(0.008)*
Exchange rates	0.0147	0.0834	0.0744	0.0458	0.0583
	(0.577)	(0.067)***	(0.145)	(0.356)	(0.121)
France	**FR/$**	**FR/£**	**FR/¥**	**FR/CHF**	**FR/DM**
Stock returns	−0.0531	−0.0655	−0.0599	−0.0635	−0.0688
	(0.017)**	(0.003)*	(0.010)*	(0.003)*	(0.002)*
Exchange rates	−0.0309	0.0270	0.0208	0.0265	0.1147
	(0.537)	(0.117)	(0.558)	(0.229)	(0.018)**
Germany	**DM/$**	**DM/£**	**DM/¥**	**DM/CHF**	
Stock returns	−0.0339	−0.0750	−0.0494	−0.0603	
	(0.170)	(0.005)*	(0.040)**	(0.018)*	
Exchange rates	−0.0367	0.0176	0.0128	0.0362	
	(0.441)	(0.247)	(0.716)	(0.255)	
Italy	**Lira/$**	**Lira/£**	**Lira/¥**	**Lira/CHF**	**Lira/DM**
Stock returns	0.0204	−0.0376	−0.0141	−0.0341	−0.0376
	(0.495)	(0.303)	(0.627)	(0.327)	(0.290)
Exchange rates	0.0195	0.0601	0.0162	0.0174	0.0121
	(0.074)	(0.157)	(0.577)	(0.419)	(0.692)
Japan	**¥/$**	**¥/£**	**¥/CHF**	**¥/DM**	
Stock returns	0.1320	−0.1324	−0.1364	−0.1416	
	(0.000)*	(0.000)*	(0.000)*	(0.000)*	
Exchange rates	0.0586	−0.0587	−0.1899	−0.0116	
	(0.1997)	(0.307)	(0.005)*	(0.736)	
U.K.	**£/$**	**£/¥**	**£/CHF**	**£/DM**	
Stock returns	0.16	−0.0653	−0.0596	−0.0629	
	(0.000)*	(0.000)*	(0.000)*	(0.000)*	
Exchange rates	0.0402	0.0580	−0.0063	−0.0136	
	(0.035)**	(0.304)	(0.686)	(0.352)	
U.S.	**$/£**	**$/¥**	**$/CHF**	**$/DM**	
Stock returns	0.1577	−0.1601	−0.1363	−0.1583	
	(0.000)*	(0.000)*	(0.000)*	(0.000)*	
Exchange rates	0.0493	0.0392	0.0904	−0.0332	
	(0.019)**	(0.384)	(0.072)***	(0.506)	

Note: *1% significance level, **5% significance level and ***10% significance level.

Thus, the impact of the introduction of the Euro on the persistence of the volatility of stock returns and exchange rates has not had a uniform impact across the financial markets in the G-7. Wu (2005) notes that a necessary condition for the volatility persistence terms to be stable is that the value of the estimated coefficients should be less

Table 6. EGARCH results volatility spillovers 1999–2001.

Canada	**C$/$**	**C$/¥**	**C$/CHF**	**C$/£**	**C$/€**
Stock returns	−0.1014	−0.1031	−0.1078	−0.1093	−0.0619
	(0.000)*	(0.000)*	(0.000)*	(0.000)*	(0.029)**
Exchange rates	−0.0693	0.0252	−0.0054	0.0244	0.0180
	(0.259)	(0.117)	(0.794)	(0.556)	(0.743)
France	**€/$**	**€/£**	**€/¥**	**€/CHF**	
Stock returns	−0.0954	−0.0805	−0.0806	−0.0671	
	(0.002)*	(0.009)*	(0.011)**	(0.024)**	
Exchange rates	−0.0210	−0.0753	0.0824	0.1331	
	(0.639)	(0.255)	(0.008)*	(0.008)*	
Germany	**€/$**	**€/£**	**€/¥**	**€/CHF**	
Stock returns	−0.1217	−0.1131	−0.1106	−0.1075	
	(0.001)*	(0.002)*	(0.002)*	(0.002)*	
Exchange rates	−0.0158	−0.0800	0.0665	0.1333	
	(0.723)	(0.232)	(0.023)**	(0.008)*	
Italy	**€/CHF**	**€/¥**	**€/£**	**€/$**	
Stock returns	−0.0815	−0.0928	−0.0961	−0.1009	
	(0.002)*	(0.018)**	(0.011)**	(0.008)*	
Exchange rates	−0.1292	−0.0770	−0.0793	−0.0143	
	(0.011)**	(0.013)**	(0.229)	(0.745)	
Japan	**¥/€**	**¥/$**	**¥/£**	**¥/CHF**	
Stock returns	−0.0939	−0.0896	−0.0894	−0.0840	
	(0.0505)***	(0.004)*	(0.004)*	(0.001)*	
Exchange rates	−0.0617	−0.0349	−0.0242	−0.0840	
	(0.031)**	(0.094)***	(0.3777)	(0.006)*	
U.K.	**£/€**	**£/$**	**£/¥**	**£/CHF**	
Stock returns	−0.1015	−0.1166	−0.1117	−0.1101	
	(0.052)***	(0.035)**	(0.041)**	(0.039)**	
Exchange rates	−0.1385	−0.0556	−0.0024	0.0515	
	(0.002)*	(0.227)	(0.956)	(0.073)***	
U.S.	**$/€**	**$/£**	**$/¥**	**$/CHF**	
Stock returns	−0.1372	0.0740	−0.1324	−0.1306	
	(0.000)*	(0.0831)***	(0.000)*	(0.000)*	
Exchange rates	0.0270	0.0740	0.0323	−0.0004	
	(0.560)	(0.083)***	(0.136)	(0.989)	

Note: *1% significance level, **5% significance level and ***10% significance level.

than one; this condition applies in all cases for the three periods for the persistence terms for both stock returns and exchange rates where it is possible to appreciate that the magnitude of the coefficients are all less than one.

Table 7. EGARCH results volatility spillovers 2002–2006.

Canada	**C$/$**	**C$/¥**	**C$/CHF**	**C$/£**	**C$/€**
Stock returns	−0.0803	−0.0850	−0.0836	−0.0833	−0.0939
	(0.000)*	(0.000)*	(0.000)*	(0.000)*	(0.000)*
Exchange rates	−0.0081	−0.0104	0.0073	0.0145	0.0977
	(0.656)	(0.657)	(0.751)	(0.012)**	(0.097)***
France	**€/$**	**€/£**	**€/¥**	**€/CHF**	
Stock returns	−0.1149	−0.1304	−0.1156	−0.1297	
	(0.000)*	(0.000)*	(0.000)*	(0.000)*	
Exchange rates	0.0032	0.0043	0.0032	−0.0023	
	(0.814)	(0.727)	(0.863)	(0.925)	
Germany	**€/$**	**€/£**	**€/¥**	**€/CHF**	
Stock returns	−0.0949	−0.1109	−0.1083	−0.0991	
	(0.000)*	(0.000)*	(0.000)*	(0.000)*	
Exchange rates	0.0069	0.0053	0.0004	−0.0041	
	(0.571)	(0.664)	(0.982)	(0.866)	
Italy	**€/CHF**	**€/¥**	**€/£**	**€/$**	
Stock returns	−0.0983	−0.0923	−0.0996	−0.0868	
	(0.000)*	(0.000)*	(0.000)*	(0.000)*	
Exchange rates	0.0022	−0.0031	0.0035	0.0032	
	(0.925)	(0.867)	(0.775)	(0.799)	
Japan	**¥/€**	**¥/$**	**¥/£**	**¥/CHF**	
Stock returns	−0.0506	−0.0598	−0.0595	−0.0583	
	(0.0477)**	(0.025)**	(0.026)**	(0.029)**	
Exchange rates	0.0007	0.0241	−0.1276	−0.0055	
	(0.971)	(0.682)	(0.033)**	(0.892)	
U.K.	**£/€**	**£/$**	**£/¥**	**£/CHF**	
Stock returns	−0.1205	−0.1189	−0.1244	−0.1278	
	(0.000)*	(0.000)*	(0.000)*	(0.000)*	
Exchange rates	0.0958	−0.0340	0.0218	−0.0024	
	(0.041)**	(0.000)*	(0.2887)	(0.757)	
U.S.	**$/€**	**$/£**	**$/¥**	**$/CHF**	
Stock returns	−0.0802	−0.0810	−0.0852	−0.0777	
	(0.000)*	(0.000)*	(0.000)*	(0.000)*	
Exchange rates	−0.0080	−0.1030	−0.0662	−0.0035	
	(0.494)	(0.020)**	(0.272)	(0.801)	

Note: *1% significance level, **5% significance level and ***10% significance level.

4.5. *Volatility Spillovers*

In terms of the coefficients for the volatility spillover effects, the results are presented in Tables 5 through 7. Firstly, there is a large degree of consistency across countries and periods for spillovers

Table 8. EGARCH results asymmetric spillovers 1996–1998.

Canada	**C$/$**	**C$/¥**	**C$/DM**	**C$/CHF**	**C$/£**
Stock returns	0.9642	0.9742	0.9665	0.9674	0.9660
	(0.000)*	(0.000)*	(0.000)*	(0.000)*	(0.000)*
Exchange rates	0.9874	0.9027	−0.1972	0.8954	0.9896
	(0.000)*	(0.000)*	(0.598)	(0.000)*	(0.000)*
France	**FR/$**	**FR/£**	**FR/¥**	**FR/CHF**	**FR/DM**
Stock returns	0.9899	0.9907	0.9893	0.9902	0.9876
	(0.000)*	(0.000)*	(0.000)*	(0.000)*	(0.000)*
Exchange rates	−0.3573	0.9926	0.9804	0.9811	0.9507
	(0.104)	(0.000)*	(0.000)*	(0.000)*	(0.000)*
Germany	**DM/$**	**DM/£**	**DM/¥**	**DM/CHF**	
Stock returns	0.9931	0.9843	0.9895	0.9859	
	(0.000)*	(0.000)*	(0.000)*	(0.000)*	
Exchange rates	0.4816	0.9930	0.9846	0.9767	
	(0.289)	(0.000)*	(0.000)*	(0.000)*	
Italy	**Lira/$**	**Lira/£**	**Lira/¥**	**Lira/CHF**	**Lira/DM**
Stock returns	0.9613	0.9355	0.9634	0.9406	0.9351
	(0.000)*	(0.000)*	(0.000)*	(0.000)*	(0.000)*
Exchange rates	0.9945	0.9390	0.9983	0.9829	0.9749
	(0.000)*	(0.000)*	(0.000)*	(0.000)*	(0.000)*
Japan	**¥/$**	**¥/£**	**¥/CHF**	**¥/DM**	
Stock returns	0.9874	0.9856	0.9870	0.9861	
	(0.000)*	(0.000)*	(0.000)*	(0.000)*	
Exchange rates	0.9405	0.9097	0.5479	0.9867	
	(0.000)*	(0.000)*	(0.000)*	(0.000)*	
U.K.	**£/$**	**£/¥**	**£/CHF**	**£/DM**	
Stock returns	0.9947	0.9937	0.9948	0.9943	
	(0.000)*	(0.000)*	(0.000)*	(0.000)*	
Exchange rates	0.994	0.9102	0.9871	0.9924	
	(0.000)*	(0.000)*	(0.000)*	(0.000)*	
U.S.	**$/£**	**$/¥**	**$/CHF**	**$/DM**	
Stock returns	0.9372	0.9399	0.9615	0.9475	
	(0.000)*	(0.000)*	(0.000)*	(0.000)*	
Exchange rates	0.9964	0.9554	0.7299	−0.4999	
	(0.000)*	(0.000)*	(0.000)*	(0.472)	

Note: *1% significance level, **5% significance level and ***10% significance level.

from stock returns to exchange rate changes. Significant spillover effects are found at 5% level for Canada, France, Japan and the U.K. for all periods for all bilateral exchange rates. For Germany, in the period prior to the introduction of the Euro, the DM/$ was the only exchange rate for which there was no significant volatility spillovers

Table 9. EGARCH results asymmetric spillovers 1999–2001.

Canada	**C$/$**	**C$/¥**	**C$/CHF**	**C$/£**	**C$/€**
Stock returns	0.9385	0.9398	0.9413	0.9365	0.9682
	(0.000)*	(0.000)*	(0.000)*	(0.000)*	(0.000)*
Exchange rates	0.3974	0.9778	0.9169	−0.6604	−0.7229
	(0.285)	(0.000)*	(0.000)*	(0.047)**	(0.329)
France	**€/$**	**€/£**	**€/¥**	**€/CHF**	
Stock returns	0.9415	0.9437	0.9484	0.9483	
	(0.000)*	(0.000)*	(0.000)*	(0.000)*	
Exchange rates	−0.8955	−0.0025	0.9047	0.9597	
	(0.000)*	(0.994)	(0.000)*	(0.000)*	
Germany	**€/$**	**€/£**	**€/¥**	**€/CHF**	
Stock returns	0.9181	0.9084	0.9152	0.9118	
	(0.000)*	(0.000)*	(0.000)*	(0.000)*	
Exchange rates	−0.8885	−0.0042	0.9204	0.9614	
	(0.000)*	(0.990)	(0.000)*	(0.000)*	
Italy	**€/CHF**	**€/¥**	**€/£**	**€/$**	
Stock returns	0.9426	0.9385	0.9375	0.9371	
	(0.000)*	(0.000)*	(0.000)*	(0.000)*	
Exchange rates	0.9608	0.9054	0.0176	−0.8917	
	(0.000)*	(0.000)*	(0.963)	(0.000)*	
Japan	**¥/€**	**¥/$**	**¥/£**	**¥/CHF**	
Stock returns	0.9325	0.9337	0.9325	0.9391	
	(0.000)*	(0.000)*	(0.000)*	(0.000)*	
Exchange rates	0.9236	0.9795	0.9611	0.9391	
	(0.000)*	(0.000)*	(0.000)*	(0.000)*	
U.K.	**£/€**	**£/$**	**£/¥**	**£/CHF**	
Stock returns	0.9306	0.9173	0.9214	0.9183	
	(0.000)*	(0.000)*	(0.000)*	(0.000)*	
Exchange rates	−0.7294	−0.7077	0.9824	0.9439	
	(0.000)*	(0.000)*	(0.000)*	(0.000)*	
U.S.	**$/€**	**$/£**	**$/¥**	**$/CHF**	
Stock returns	0.9662	−0.7464	0.9643	0.9698	
	(0.000)*	(0.000)*	(0.000)*	(0.000)*	
Exchange rates	−0.9072	−0.7464	0.9831	0.7417	
	(0.000)*	(0.000)*	(0.000)*	(0.102)	

Note: *1% significance level, **5% significance level and ***10% significance level.

from the stock market with significant spillovers evident from the stock market to all exchange rates post-1999.

Thus, the volatility of stock returns has been an important influence and determinant of volatility of all bilateral exchange rates in the analysis in these countries. Furthermore, the impact of stock market

Table 10. EGARCH results asymmetric spillovers 2002–2006.

Canada	**C$/$**	**C$/¥**	**C$/CHF**	**C$/£**	**C$/€**
Stock returns	0.9658	0.9649	0.9658	0.9651	0.9562
	(0.000)*	(0.000)*	(0.000)*	(0.000)*	(0.000)*
Exchange rates	0.9763	0.9703	0.9570	0.9923	−0.6080
	(0.000)*	(0.000)*	(0.000)*	(0.000)*	(0.002)*
France	**€/$**	**€/£**	**€/¥**	**€/CHF**	
Stock returns	0.9858	0.9844	0.9864	0.9858	
	(0.000)*	(0.000)*	(0.000)*	(0.000)*	
Exchange rates	0.9824	0.9983	0.9946	0.9669	
	(0.000)*	(0.000)*	(0.000)*	(0.000)*	
Germany	**€/$**	**€/£**	**€/¥**	**€/CHF**	
Stock returns	0.9878	0.9871	0.9857	0.9874	
	(0.000)*	(0.000)*	(0.000)*	(0.000)*	
Exchange rates	0.9868	0.9986	0.9947	0.9662	
	(0.000)*	(0.000)*	(0.000)*	(0.000)*	
Italy	**€/CHF**	**€/¥**	**€/£**	**€/$**	
Stock returns	0.9880	0.9878	0.9869	0.9877	
	(0.000)*	(0.000)*	(0.000)*	(0.000)*	
Exchange rates	0.9670	0.9944	0.9975	0.9842	
	(0.000)*	(0.000)*	(0.000)*	(0.000)*	
Japan	**¥/€**	**¥/$**	**¥/£**	**¥/CHF**	
Stock returns	0.9750	0.9698	0.9695	0.9699	
	(0.000)*	(0.000)*	(0.000)*	(0.000)*	
Exchange rates	0.9943	−0.2654	0.0039	0.8993	
	(0.000)*	(0.894)	(0.991)	(0.000)*	
U.K.	**£/€**	**£/$**	**£/¥**	**£/CHF**	
Stock returns	0.9872	0.9877	0.9876	0.9876	
	(0.000)*	(0.000)*	(0.000)*	(0.000)*	
Exchange rates	−0.2906	0.9963	0.9589	0.9936	
	(0.368)	(0.000)*	(0.000)*	(0.000)*	
U.S.	**$/€**	**$/£**	**$/¥**	**$/CHF**	
Stock returns	0.9925	0.9924	0.9930	0.9925	
	(0.000)*	(0.000)*	(0.000)*	(0.000)*	
Exchange rates	0.9889	−0.0108	−0.3173	0.9810	
	(0.000)*	(0.970)	(0.687)	(0.000)*	

Note: *1% significance level, **5% significance level and ***10% significance level.

volatility on exchange rates has not been altered significantly by the introduction of the Euro in the sense that the cross exchange rates against the $, ¥, £ and CHF existed prior to the introduction of the Euro as well as after it across nearly all G-7 markets. In addition to this, it was found that for the pre-Euro period, Italy was the only country in the G-7 for which there was no volatility spillover effects from the stock market to any of the bilateral exchange rates included in this analysis. After the Euro was introduced, the \$/£ exchange rate was the only exchange rate where no volatility spillovers were evident from the U.S. stock market at 5% level, although this was significant at 10% level.

The significant coefficients indicate that the volatility of stock returns was a determinant of the volatility of the exchange rate and that information contained in stock prices impacted on the behavior of exchange rates in these markets. Significant coefficients are also indicative of integration between stock markets and exchange rate markets; given that the G-7 markets are the most developed financial markets globally, the existence of integration is not surprising. In addition, the lack of these spillovers in Italy in the pre-Euro period can be taken as evidence that the stock and money markets in Italy were not as integrated as in other more developed G-7 countries. Furthermore, where the coefficients are insignificant indicates that prior to the introduction of the Euro there was some potential for diversification between stock markets and currency markets in these countries.

In terms of volatility spillovers from exchange rates to stock markets, the results are less significant across countries and over time. For the 1996–1998 period, Canada, Germany and Italy had no significant spillovers. For the other countries included in the analysis, there were a number of bilateral exchange rates where significant spillovers were evident from exchange rates to stock returns at 5% level; for the period prior to the introduction of the Euro, they were for France for the FR/DM, for Japan for the ¥/CHF, for the U.K. for the £/\$ and for the U.S. for the \$/£ exchange rates. After the Euro there is some commonality regarding which exchange rates are found significant volatility spillover effects for stock markets. That is, for the €/¥ and ¥/CHF the volatility spillovers were significant for the stock markets in France, Germany and Italy, the ¥/€ and ¥/CHF for the Japanese stock market, the £/€ and £/CHF for the U.K. and the \$/\$ for the U.S. For the 2002–2006 period, again there was only a small number of all exchange rates included for which it was an observed significant volatility spillovers into stock markets; for Canada for the C$/£, for Japan for ¥/£, for the U.K. for the £/€ and £/$. No significant spillovers were evident in France, Germany or Italy.

The lack of significant spillovers from exchange rate changes to stock returns found here for some countries across a number of exchange rates are consistent with results from Jorion (1990) as well as with Yang and Doong (2004). Jorion (1990) explained the lack of spillovers as possibly due to positive exchange rate volatility on stock returns for some firms offsetting negative exchange rate volatility on stock returns for other firms to give an insignificant or weak effect overall. In addition to this, the use of instruments to hedge exchange rate risk, may reduce the impact of exchange rate volatility on stock markets. Grant and Marshall (1997), and Bodnar *et al.* (1995) both note that the use of hedging instruments to ameliorate exchange rate risk is pervasive among larger companies which are the main components of national stock market indices. The lack of significant spillovers from exchange rates to stock markets in the pre-Euro period could be indicative of wider use of hedging by firms listed on the stock markets in these countries than after the introduction of the Euro. It may also be the case that the adoption of the Euro brought greater volatility to certain stock markets given the global nature of the currency which they would not have been exposed to prior to the Euro's introduction.

A positive sign on the spillover coefficient indicates that an increase in volatility in one market is associated with increased volatility in the other market while a negative coefficient indicates that increased volatility in one market is associated with decreased volatility in the other market. The results presented show a mixture of positive and negative significant coefficients for the two spillover terms in all periods; this indicates that the impact of volatility from exchange rate markets to stock markets or vice versa is not constant either over time for the same country, or across countries for the same period.

4.6. *Asymmetric Spillovers*

For the asymmetric spillover effects from stock returns to exchange rates the results are presented through Tables 8 to 10. The major findings show that the coefficients are significant in all the cases for all the periods. However, when analyzing asymmetric spillover effects from exchange rates to stock returns some differences are found, during 1996–1998 the coefficients are significant in almost all the cases, with the exception of Canada where the C$/DM is insignificant. France shows an insignificant coefficient in the case of FR/$; for Germany, DM/$ is insignificant and finally, the $/DM for U.S. is insignificant as well. During 1999–2001, in general terms the coefficients are significant but there are few exceptions in relation to the following countries where the coefficients are insignificant: in the case of Canada, we found that the coefficients are insignificant for C$/$, C$/£ and C$/€, for France, Germany and Italy the €/£ and finally for the U.S., the $/CHF.

Analyzing the last period 2002–2006, the results show that again the coefficients are significant in almost all the cases. Just a few exceptions were found where the coefficients are insignificant, namely for Japan the ¥/$ and the ¥/£, for the U.K. the £/€ and for the U.S. the $/£ and the $/¥. Thus, the general significance of most of the asymmetry coefficients justifies the use of the EGARCH model to capture this asymmetry in the impact of good and bad news. The existence of insignificant coefficients indicates that the spillover effects in these instances are symmetric, that is, that positive and negative shocks have the same impact on volatility.

4.7. *Diagnostic Tests*

The Jarque-Bera test indicates that the hypothesis that the residuals are normally distributed is rejected. Hence, this justifies the use of the Bollerslev-Woolridge robust *t*-statistics. The Ljung-Box statistics for all three periods for all countries indicate that there are no residual linear or nonlinear dependencies. There are some exceptions where the coefficient was not significant but the problem was corrected after introducing more lags into the test. Finally, to check the validity of the assumption of constant correlation adopted in the estimation of the bivariate models (Kanas, 2000), the LB statistics for the cross products

Table 11. EGARCH results volatility persistence 2002–2006.

Canada	**C$/$**	**C$/¥**	**C$/CHF**	**C$/£**	**C$/€**
Stock returns	0.0886	0.0794	0.0821	0.0871	0.0981
	(0.001)	(0.004)	(0.002)	(0.002)	(0.001)
Exchange rates	0.1044	0.0548	0.1240	0.0371	0.0455
	(0.014)	(0.044)	(0.000)	(0.597)	(0.386)
France	**€/$**	**€/£**	**€/¥**	**€/CHF**	
Stock returns	−0.0568	−0.0618	−0.0672	0.0947	
	(0.492)	(0.417)	(0.406)	(0.000)	
Exchange rates	−0.1165	0.0402	0.0466	0.0957	
	(0.115)	(0.005)	(0.029)	(0.001)	
Germany	**€/$**	**€/£**	**€/¥**	**€/CHF**	
Stock returns	0.1116	0.1063	−0.0230	0.1035	
	(0.000)	(0.000)	(0.781)	(0.000)	
Exchange rates	0.0596	0.0377	0.0459	0.0914	
	(0.005)	(0.008)	(0.036)	(0.002)	
Italy	**€/CHF**	**€/¥**	**€/£**	**€/$**	
Stock returns	0.0660	0.0774	0.0741	0.0832	
	(0.000)	(0.000)	(0.000)	(0.000)	
Exchange rates	0.0919	0.0488	0.0447	−0.0934	
	(0.001)	(0.029)	(0.002)	(0.209)	
Japan	**¥/€**	**¥/$**	**¥/£**	**¥/CHF**	
Stock returns	−0.0693	−0.0437	−0.0461	−0.0606	
	(0.359)	(0.581)	(0.555)	(0.442)	
Exchange rates	0.0491	−0.0040	0.0942	0.1363	
	(0.019)	(0.962)	(0.259)	(0.007)	
U.K.	**£/€**	**£/$**	**£/¥**	**£/CHF**	
Stock returns	0.0814	0.0883	0.0741	0.0720	
	(0.000)	(0.000)	(0.000)	(0.000)	
Exchange rates	0.1052	−0.0158	0.0226	−0.0887	
	(0.070)	(0.131)	(0.431)	(0.233)	
U.S.	**$/€**	**$/£**	**$/¥**	**$/CHF**	
Stock returns	0.0663	0.0654	0.0585	0.0664	
	(0.000)	(0.000)	(0.001)	(0.000)	
Exchange rates	−0.0843	0.1561	0.0136	0.0544	
	(0.254)	(0.007)	(0.873)	(0.007)	

of the standardized residuals from the stock returns equation and from the exchange rate equation are calculated and these statistics indicated that the assumption of constant correlation over time can be accepted (Tables 11–24).

Table 12. EGARCH results volatility spillovers 1996–1998.

Canada	**C$/$**	**C$/¥**	**C$/DM**	**C$/CHF**	**C$/£**
Stock returns	−0.1079	−0.0585	−0.0998	−0.0987	−0.0954
	(0.005)	(0.023)	(0.010)	(0.010)	(0.008)
Exchange rates	0.0147	0.0834	0.0744	0.0458	0.0583
	(0.577)	(0.067)	(0.145)	(0.356)	(0.121)
France	**FR/$**	**FR/£**	**FR/¥**	**FR/CHF**	**FR/DM**
Stock returns	−0.0531	−0.0655	−0.0599	−0.0635	−0.0688
	(0.017)	(0.003)	(0.010)	(0.003)	(0.002)
Exchange rates	−0.0309	0.0270	0.0208	0.0265	0.1147
	(0.537)	(0.117)	(0.558)	(0.229)	(0.018)
Germany	**DM/$**	**DM/£**	**DM/¥**	**DM/CHF**	
Stock returns	−0.0339	−0.0750	−0.0494	−0.0603	
	(0.170)	(0.005)	(0.040)	(0.018)	
Exchange rates	−0.0367	0.0176	0.0128	0.0362	
	(0.441)	(0.247)	(0.716)	(0.255)	
Italy	**Lira/$**	**Lira/£**	**Lira/¥**	**Lira/CHF**	**Lira/DM**
Stock returns	−0.0204	−0.0376	−0.0141	−0.0341	−0.0376
	(0.495)	(0.303)	(0.627)	(0.327)	(0.290)
Exchange rates	−0.0195	0.0601	0.0162	0.0174	0.0121
	(0.074)	(0.157)	(0.577)	(0.419)	(0.692)
Japan	**¥/$**	**¥/£**	**¥/CHF**	**¥/DM**	
Stock returns	−0.1320	−0.1324	−0.1364	−0.1416	
	(0.000)	(0.000)	(0.000)	(0.000)	
Exchange rates	−0.0586	−0.0587	−0.1899	−0.0116	
	(0.1997)	(0.307)	(0.005)	(0.736)	
U.K.	**£/$**	**£/¥**	**£/CHF**	**£/DM**	
Stock returns	−0.0516	−0.0653	−0.0596	−0.0629	
	(0.000)	(0.000)	(0.000)	(0.000)	
Exchange rates	−0.0402	0.0580	−0.0063	−0.0136	
	(0.035)	(0.304)	(0.686)	(0.352)	
U.S.	**$/£**	**$/¥**	**$/CHF**	**$/DM**	
Stock returns	−0.1577	−0.1601	−0.1363	−0.1583	
	(0.000)	(0.000)	(0.000)	(0.000)	
Exchange rates	0.0493	0.0392	0.0904	−0.0332	
	(0.019)	(0.384)	(0.072)	(0.506)	

5. Conclusions

Relationships between equity returns and exchange rates are of particular interest to academics and practitioners due to the fact that these two variables play a crucial role in portfolio and risk

Table 13. EGARCH results volatility spillovers 1999–2001.

Canada	**C$/$**	**C$/¥**	**C$/CHF**	**C$/£**	**C$/€**
Stock returns	−0.1014	−0.1031	−0.1078	−0.1093	−0.0619
	(0.000)	(0.000)	(0.000)	(0.000)	(0.029)
Exchange rates	−0.0693	0.0252	−0.0054	0.0244	0.0180
	(0.259)	(0.117)	(0.794)	(0.556)	(0.743)
France	**€/$**	**€/£**	**€/¥**	**€/CHF**	
Stock returns	−0.0954	−0.0805	−0.0806	−0.0671	
	(0.002)	(0.009)	(0.011)	(0.024)	
Exchange rates	−0.0210	−0.0753	0.0824	0.1331	
	(0.639)	(0.255)	(0.008)	(0.008)	
Germany	**€/$**	**€/£**	**€/¥**	**€/CHF**	
Stock returns	−0.1217	−0.1131	−0.1106	−0.1075	
	(0.001)	(0.002)	(0.002)	(0.002)	
Exchange rates	−0.0158	−0.0800	0.0665	0.1333	
	(0.723)	(0.232)	(0.023)	(0.008)	
Italy	**€/CHF**	**€/¥**	**€/£**	**€/$**	
Stock returns	−0.0815	−0.0928	−0.0961	−0.1009	
	(0.002)	(0.018)	(0.011)	(0.008)	
Exchange rates	−0.1292	−0.0770	−0.0793	−0.0143	
	(0.011)	(0.013)	(0.229)	(0.745)	
Japan	**¥/€**	**¥/$**	**¥/£**	**¥/CHF**	
Stock returns	−0.0939	−0.0896	−0.0894	−0.0840	
	(0.0505)	(0.004)	(0.004)	(0.001)	
Exchange rates	−0.0617	−0.0349	−0.0242	−0.0840	
	(0.031)	(0.094)	(0.3777)	(0.006)	
U.K.	**£/€**	**£/$**	**£/¥**	**£/CHF**	
Stock returns	−0.1015	−0.1166	−0.1117	−0.1101	
	(0.052)	(0.035)	(0.041)	(0.039)	
Exchange rates	−0.1385	−0.0556	−0.0024	0.0515	
	(0.002)	(0.227)	(0.956)	(0.073)	
U.S.	**$/€**	**$/£**	**$/¥**	**$/CHF**	
Stock returns	−0.1372	0.0740	−0.1324	−0.1306	
	(0.000)	(0.0831)	(0.000)	(0.000)	
Exchange rates	0.0270	0.0740	0.0323	−0.0004	
	(0.560)	(0.083)	(0.136)	(0.989)	

management. Equity returns and exchange rate movements may be used to hedge portfolios against currency movements, where risk management has to take into consideration the linkages between these two markets to design appropriate strategies.

This chapter set out to examine the volatility linkages between stock returns and exchange rates in the G-7 markets. While there

Table 14. EGARCH results volatility spillovers 2002–2006.

Canada	**C$/$**	**C$/¥**	**C$/CHF**	**C$/£**	**C$/€**
Stock returns	−0.0803	−0.0850	−0.0836	−0.0833	−0.0939
	(0.000)	(0.000)	(0.000)	(0.000)	(0.000)
Exchange rates	−0.0081	−0.0104	0.0073	0.0145	0.0977
	(0.656)	(0.657)	(0.751)	(0.012)	(0.097)
France	**€/$**	**€/£**	**€/¥**	**€/CHF**	
Stock returns	−0.1149	−0.1304	−0.1156	−0.1297	
	(0.000)	(0.000)	(0.000)	(0.000)	
Exchange rates	0.0032	0.0043	0.0032	−0.0023	
	(0.814)	(0.727)	(0.863)	(0.925)	
Germany	**€/$**	**€/£**	**€/¥**	**€/CHF**	
Stock returns	−0.0949	−0.1109	−0.1083	−0.0991	
	(0.000)	(0.000)	(0.000)	(0.000)	
Exchange rates	0.0069	0.0053	0.0004	−0.0041	
	(0.571)	(0.664)	(0.982)	(0.866)	
Italy	**€/CHF**	**€/¥**	**€/£**	**€/$**	
Stock returns	−0.0983	−0.0923	−0.0996	−0.0868	
	(0.000)	(0.000)	(0.000)	(0.000)	
Exchange rates	0.0022	−0.0031	0.0035	0.0032	
	(0.925)	(0.867)	(0.775)	(0.799)	
Japan	**¥/€**	**¥/$**	**¥/£**	**¥/CHF**	
Stock returns	−0.0506	−0.0598	−0.0595	−0.0583	
	(0.0477)	(0.025)	(0.026)	(0.029)	
Exchange rates	0.0007	0.0241	−0.1276	−0.0055	
	(0.971)	(0.682)	(0.033)	(0.892)	
U.K.	**£/€**	**£/$**	**£/¥**	**£/CHF**	
Stock returns	−0.1205	−0.1189	−0.1244	−0.1278	
	(0.000)	(0.000)	(0.000)	(0.000)	
Exchange rates	0.0958	−0.0340	0.0218	−0.0024	
	(0.041)	(0.000)	(0.2887)	(0.757)	
U.S.	**$/€**	**$/£**	**$/¥**	**$/CHF**	
Stock returns	−0.0802	−0.0810	−0.0852	−0.0777	
	(0.000)	(0.000)	(0.000)	(0.000)	
Exchange rates	−0.0080	−0.1030	−0.0662	−0.0035	
	(0.494)	(0.020)	(0.272)	(0.801)	

is a significant body of evidence which investigates the relationship between the first moments of exchange rates and stock returns, the evidence on volatility linkages between the two markets is scarce and has generally been confined to investigation of the relationship for stock returns and a single exchange rate. This analysis was thus broader in scope than existing research in that a number of

Table 15. EGARCH results asymmetric spillovers 1996–1998.

Canada	**C$/$**	**C$/¥**	**C$/DM**	**C$/CHF**	**C$/£**
Stock returns	0.9642	0.9742	0.9665	0.9674	0.9660
	(0.000)	(0.000)	(0.000)	(0.000)	(0.000)
Exchange rates	0.9874	0.9027	−0.1972	0.8954	0.9896
	(0.000)	(0.000)	(0.598)	(0.000)	(0.000)
France	**FR/$**	**FR/£**	**FR/¥**	**FR/CHF**	**FR/DM**
Stock returns	0.9899	0.9907	0.9893	0.9902	0.9876
	(0.000)	(0.000)	(0.000)	(0.000)	(0.000)
Exchange rates	−0.3573	0.9926	0.9804	0.9811	0.9507
	(0.104)	(0.000)	(0.000)	(0.000)	(0.000)
Germany	**DM/$**	**DM/£**	**DM/¥**	**DM/CHF**	
Stock returns	0.9931	0.9843	0.9895	0.9859	
	(0.000)	(0.000)	(0.000)	(0.000)	
Exchange rates	−0.4816	0.9930	0.9846	0.9767	
	(0.289)	(0.000)	(0.000)	(0.000)	
Italy	**Lira/$**	**Lira/£**	**Lira/¥**	**Lira/CHF**	**Lira/DM**
Stock returns	0.9613	0.9355	0.9634	0.9406	0.9351
	(0.000)	(0.000)	(0.000)	(0.000)	(0.000)
Exchange rates	0.9945	0.9390	0.9983	0.9829	0.9749
	(0.000)	(0.000)	(0.000)	(0.000)	(0.000)
Japan	**¥/$**	**¥/£**	**¥/CHF**	**¥/DM**	
Stock returns	0.9874	0.9856	0.9870	0.9861	
	(0.000)	(0.000)	(0.000)	(0.000)	
Exchange rates	0.9405	0.9097	0.5479	0.9867	
	(0.000)	(0.000)	(0.000)	(0.000)	
U.K.	**£/$**	**£/¥**	**£/CHF**	**£/DM**	
Stock returns	0.9947	0.9937	0.9948	0.9943	
	(0.000)	(0.000)	(0.000)	(0.000)	
Exchange rates	0.9934	0.9102	0.9871	0.9924	
	(0.000)	(0.000)	(0.000)	(0.000)	
U.S.	**$/£**	**$/¥**	**$/CHF**	**$/DM**	
Stock returns	0.9372	0.9399	0.9615	0.9475	
	(0.000)	(0.000)	(0.000)	(0.000)	
Exchange rates	0.9964	0.9554	0.7299	−0.4999	
	(0.000)	(0.000)	(0.000)	(0.472)	

bilateral exchange rates were included in the study, which permitted to examine whether volatility spillovers exist to the same extent across exchange rates, so increasing the general understanding of the nature of integration between stock and exchange rate markets in the G-7 countries.

Table 16. EGARCH results asymmetric spillovers 1999–2001.

Canada	**C$/$**	**C$/¥**	**C$/CHF**	**C$/£**	**C$/€**
Stock returns	0.9385	0.9398	0.9413	0.9365	0.9682
	(0.000)	(0.000)	(0.000)	(0.000)	(0.000)
Exchange rates	0.3974	0.9778	0.9169	−0.6604	−0.7229
	(0.285)	(0.000)	(0.000)	(0.047)	(0.329)
France	**€/$**	**€/£**	**€/¥**	**€/CHF**	
Stock returns	0.9415	0.9437	0.9484	0.9483	
	(0.000)	(0.000)	(0.000)	(0.000)	
Exchange rates	−0.8955	−0.0025	0.9047	0.9597	
	(0.000)	(0.994)	(0.000)	(0.000)	
Germany	**€/$**	**€/£**	**€/¥**	**€/CHF**	
Stock returns	0.9181	0.9084	0.9152	0.9118	
	(0.000)	(0.000)	(0.000)	(0.000)	
Exchange rates	−0.8885	−0.0042	0.9204	0.9614	
	(0.000)	(0.990)	(0.000)	(0.000)	
Italy	**€/CHF**	**€/¥**	**€/£**	**€/$**	
Stock returns	0.9426	0.9385	0.9375	0.9371	
	(0.000)	(0.000)	(0.000)	(0.000)	
Exchange rates	0.9608	0.9054	0.0176	−0.8917	
	(0.000)	(0.000)	(0.963)	(0.000)	
Japan	**¥/€**	**¥/$**	**¥/£**	**¥/CHF**	
Stock returns	0.9325	0.9337	0.9325	0.9391	
	(0.000)	(0.000)	(0.000)	(0.000)	
Exchange rates	0.9236	0.9795	0.9611	0.9391	
	(0.000)	(0.000)	(0.000)	(0.000)	
U.K.	**£/€**	**£/$**	**£/¥**	**£/CHF**	
Stock returns	0.9306	0.9173	0.9214	0.9183	
	(0.000)	(0.000)	(0.000)	(0.000)	
Exchange rates	−0.7294)	−0.7077	0.9824	0.9439	
	(0.000)	(0.000)	(0.000)	(0.000)	
U.S.	**$/€**	**$/£**	**$/¥**	**$/CHF**	
Stock returns	0.9662	−0.7464	0.9643	0.9698	
	(0.000)	(0.000)	(0.000)	(0.000)	
Exchange rates	−0.9072	−0.7464	0.9831	0.7417	
	(0.000)	(0.000)	(0.000)	(0.102)	

In addition to this, no research to date has explicitly focused on the impact of the introduction of the Euro on volatility spillovers between these financial markets. In order to address this gap in the literature, three main periods were examined, covering the period before the introduction of the Euro, immediately after the

Table 17. EGARCH results asymmetric spillovers 2002–2006.

Canada	**C$/$**	**C$/¥**	**C$/CHF**	**C$/£**	**C$/€**
Stock returns	0.9658	0.9649	0.9658	0.9651	0.9562
	(0.000)	(0.000)	(0.000)	(0.000)	(0.000)
Exchange rates	0.9763	0.9703	0.9570	0.9923	−0.6080
	(0.000)	(0.000)	(0.000)	(0.000)	(0.002)
France	**€/$**	**€/£**	**€/¥**	**€/CHF**	
Stock returns	0.9858	0.9844	0.9864	0.9858	
	(0.000)	(0.000)	(0.000)	(0.000)	
Exchange rates	0.9824	0.9983	0.9946	0.9669	
	(0.000)	(0.000)	(0.000)	(0.000)	
Germany	**€/$**	**€/£**	**€/¥**	**€/CHF**	
Stock returns	0.9878	0.9871	0.9857	0.9874	
	(0.000)	(0.000)	(0.000)	(0.000)	
Exchange rates	0.9868	0.9986	0.9947	0.9662	
	(0.000)	(0.000)	(0.000)	(0.000)	
Italy	**€/CHF**	**€/¥**	**€/£**	**€/$**	
Stock returns	0.9880	0.9878	0.9869	0.9877	
	(0.000)	(0.000)	(0.000)	(0.000)	
Exchange rates	0.9670	0.9944	0.9975	0.9842	
	(0.000)	(0.000)	(0.000)	(0.000)	
Japan	**¥/€**	**¥/$**	**¥/£**	**¥/CHF**	
Stock returns	0.9750	0.9698	0.9695	0.9699	
	(0.000)	(0.000)	(0.000)	(0.000)	
Exchange rates	0.9943	−0.2654	0.0039	0.8993	
	(0.000)	(0.894)	(0.991)	(0.000)	
U.K.	**£/€**	**£/$**	**£/¥**	**£/CHF**	
Stock returns	0.9872	0.9877	0.9876	0.9876	
	(0.000)	(0.000)	(0.000)	(0.000)	
Exchange rates	−0.2906	0.9963	0.9589	0.9936	
	(0.368)	(0.000)	(0.000)	(0.000)	
U.S.	**$/€**	**$/£**	**$/¥**	**$/CHF**	
Stock returns	0.9925	0.9924	0.9930	0.9925	
	(0.000)	(0.000)	(0.000)	(0.000)	
Exchange rates	0.9889	−0.0108	−0.3173	0.9810	
	(0.000)	(0.970)	(0.687)	(0.000)	

introduction of the Euro but when the currency was still not in circulation, and finally the period covering when the currency was physically introduced.

The results overall show that the volatility of stock prices affects the volatility of exchange rates in a much more widespread way than

Table 18. Diagnostic test on EGARCH models — Canada.

1996–1998	**C$/$**	**C$/¥**	**C$/DM**	**C$/CHF**	**C$/£**
Stock returns					
JB	389	757	395	429	324
LB(20)	50.584	53.727	54.751	53.283	53.897
	(0.000)	(0.000)	(0.000)	(0.000)	(0.000)
$LB^2(20)$	12.507	10.434	11.927	12.919	12.595
	(0.898)	(0.960)	(0.919)	(0.881)	(0.894)
Exchange rates					
JB	46	187	74	245	67
LB(20)	19.539	24.336	18.246	12.319	28.708
	(0.487)	(0.228)	(0.571)	(0.905)	(0.094)
$LB^2(20)$	15.77	8.0373	36.107	12.992	13.47
	(0.731)	(0.992)	(0.015)	(0.878)	(0.856)
Cross products					
LB(20)	17.635	29.27	18.606	14.511	16.194
	(0.611)	(0.083)	(0.548)	(0.804)	(0.705)
$LB^2(20)$	14.614	49.117	20.332	11.218	2.9102
	(0.798)	(0.000)*	(0.437)	(0.940)	(1.000)
1999–2001	**C$/$**	**C$/¥**	**C$/CHF**	**C$/£**	**C$/€**
Stock returns					
JB	83	86	73	82	56
LB(20)	18.661	18.547	17.752	18.386	25.749
	(0.544)	(0.551)	(0.604)	(0.562)	(0.174)
$LB^2(20)$	6.9292	7.6807	7.5534	7.2135	7.6796
	(0.997)	(0.994)	(0.991)	(0.996)	(0.994)
Exchange rates					
JB	18	18	21	16	17
LB(20)	22.9	14.777	31.638	26.505	32.342
	(0.304)	(0.789)	(0.047)	(0.150)	(0.040)
$LB^2(20)$	44.719	12.831	15.091	17.999	25.543
	(0.001)*	(0.885)	(0.771)	(0.587)	(0.181)
Cross products					
LB(20)	15.066	15.896	14.089	18.742	17.966
	(0.773)	(0.723)	(0.826)	(0.539)	(0.590)
$LB^2(20)$	4.1503	11.937	4.692	9.877	12.113
	(1.000)	(0.918)	(1.000)	(0.970)	(0.912)
2002–2006	**C$/$**	**C$/¥**	**C$/CHF**	**C$/£**	**C$/€**
Stock returns					
JB	22	25	28	23	28
LB(20)	15.884	14.465	13.859	14.316	12.92
	(0.724)	(0.806)	(0.838)	(0.814)	(0.881)
$LB^2(20)$	18.499	18.248	19.627	19.883	13.238
	(0.555)	(0.571)	(0.481)	(0.465)	(0.867)

(*Continued*)

Table 18. (*Continued*)

Exchange rates					
JB	9	20	7	7	3
LB(20)	16.257	49.509	77.078	20.578	14.005
	(0.701)	(0.000)*	(0.000)*	(0.422)	(0.830)
$LB^2(20)$	28.365	16.122	18.381	27.212	59.112
	(0.101)	(0.709)	(0.562)	(0.129)	(0.000)*
Cross products					
LB(20)	21.31	16.748	23.474	20.657	32.503
	(0.372)	(0.669)	(0.266)	(0.418)	(0.038)
$LB^2(20)$	12.337	11.382	6.741	15.677	28.945
	(0.904)	(0.936)	(0.997)	(0.736)	(0.089)

*$LB^2(32)$:53.005(0.011); $LB^2(9)$:18.074(0.034); LB(41):64.861(0.010); $LB^2(9)$: 16.766(0.053).

Table 19. Diagnostic test on EGARCH models — France.

1996–1998	**FR/$**	**FR/£**	**FR/¥**	**FR/CHF**	**FR/DM**
Stock returns					
JB	11	4	7	10	7
LB(20)	23.11	23.531	19.37	21.582	22.482
	(0.283)	(0.263)	(0.498)	(0.364)	(0.315)
$LB^2(20)$	7.9367	7.8246	6.7154	7.6451	7.8243
	(0.992)	(0.993)	(0.998)	(0.994)	(0.993)
Exchange rates					
JB	19	39	114	44	66
LB(20)	12.61	14.973	15.39	12.926	76.764
	(0.903)	(0.778)	(0.754)	(0.881)	(0.000)*
$LB^2(20)$	36.008	20.254	12.692	17.608	13.205
	(0.015)	(0.442)	(0.890)	(0.613)	(0.868)
Cross products					
LB(20)	17.791	21.004	20.382	28.745	14.915
	(0.601)	(0.397)	(0.434)	(0.093)	(0.781)
$LB^2(20)$	23.717	30.86	10.219	22.426	46.381
	(0.255)	(0.057)	(0.964)	(0.18)	(0.000)*
1999–2001	**€/$**	**€/£**	**€/¥**	**€/CHF**	
Stock returns					
JB	4	7	5	7	
LB(20)	24.666	21.273	20.502	21.265	
	(0.215)	(0.381)	(0.427)	(0.382)	
$LB^2(20)$	29.966	30.199	28.182	25.834	
	(0.070)	(0.067)	(0.105)	(0.171)	

(*Continued*)

Table 19. (*Continued*)

Exchange rates				
JB	44	28	26	392
LB(20)	37.236	30.548	21.012	21.817
	(0.011)	(0.061)	(0.396)	(0.351)
$LB^2(20)$	39.916	39.213	16.808	14.392
	(0.005)*	(0.006)*	(0.665)	(0.810)
Cross products				
LB(20)	32.65	28.389	16.104	19.462
	(0.043)	(0.101)	(0.710)	(0.492)
$LB^2(20)$	18.399	19.35	8.3721	4.3363
	(0.561)	(0.499)	(0.989)	(1.000)
2002–2006	**€/$**	**€/£**	**€/¥**	**€/CHF**
Stock returns				
JB	13	17	13	6
LB(20)	25.928	22.238	24.27	22.211
	(0.168)	(0.328)	(0.231)	(0.329)
$LB^2(20)$	22.69	20.096	17.824	18
	(0.304)	(0.452)	(0.599)	(0.616)
Exchange rates				
JB	15	52	133	95
LB(20)	31.227	22.607	31.314	15.604
	(0.052)	(0.308)	(0.051)	(0.741)
$LB^2(20)$	20.226	23.067	13.627	12.875
	(0.444)	(0.286)	(0.849)	(0.883)
Cross products				
LB(20)	56.758	33.204	35.872	26.591
	(0.000)*	(0.032)	(0.016)	(0.147)
$LB^2(20)$	36.13	56.568	18.915	10.732
	(0.015)	(0.000)*	(0.527)	(0.953)

*$LB^2(29)$:48.588(0.013); $LB^2(24)$:42.949(0.010); $LB^2(22)$:39.664(0.012); LB(13):27.359 (0.011); $LB^2(20)$:20.027(0.067).

the volatility of exchange rates are affecting the volatility of stock prices. These results are thus consistent with those of Kanas (2000) and Yang and Doong (2004) who both found evidence of volatility spillovers from stock returns to exchange rates but no evidence of spillovers in the opposite direction. The lack of significant spillovers in these markets indicates that there is potential for diversification between stock markets and currency markets in certain instances. The difference between this chapter's results and existing studies on

Table 20. Diagnostic test on EGARCH models — Germany.

1996–1998	**DM/$**	**DM/£**	**DM/¥**	**DM/CHF**
Stock returns				
JB	14	10	16	15
LB(20)	20.324	18.855	19.441	17.805
	(0.438)	(0.531)	(0.493)	(0.600)
$LB^2(20)$	17.356	14.312	14.403	10.094
	(0.630)	(0.814)	(0.809)	(0.966)
Exchange rates				
JB	45	32	122	78
LB(20)	15.335	15.316	18.458	9.9396
	(0.757)	(0.758)	(0.557)	(0.969)
$LB^2(20)$	15.131	16.535	10.94	7.8623
	(0.769)	(0.683)	(0.948)	(0.993)
Cross products				
LB(20)	17.878	16.525	18.333	24.856
	(0.595)	(0.684)	(0.565)	(0.207)
$LB^2(20)$	8.362	42.49	4.6912	32.65
	(0.989)	(0.000)*	(1.000)	(0.037)
1999–2001	**€/$**	**€/£**	**€/¥**	**€/CHF**
Stock returns				
JB	25	7	9	4
LB(20)	26.326	24.048	23.657	23.181
	(0.155)	(0.240)	(0.258)	(0.280)
$LB^2(20)$	14.727	22.581	21.721	24.475
	(0.792)	(0.310)	(0.356)	(0.222)
Exchange rates				
JB	43	28	30	386
LB(20)	36.744	30.946	21.015	22.57
	(0.013)	(0.056)	(0.936)	(0.310)
$LB^2(20)$	35.205	35.908	16.443	16.11
	(0.019)	(0.016)	(0.689)	(0.710)
Cross products				
LB(20)	29.798	28.851	7.9922	12.198
	(0.073)	(0.091)	(0.967)	(0.909)
$LB^2(20)$	46.009	44.686	59.215	4.1369
	(0.001)*	(0.000)*	(0.000)	(1.000)
2002–2006	**€/$**	**€/£**	**€/¥**	**€/CHF**
Stock returns				
JB	13	19	13	9
LB(20)	21.871	18.607	21.222	18.232
	(0.348)	(0.547)	(0.384)	(0.572)
$LB^2(20)$	14.605	10.43	10.754	13.172
	(0.799)	(0.960)	(0.952)	(0.870)

(*Continued*)

Table 20. (*Continued*)

Exchange rates				
JB	11	48	143	104
LB(20)	27.739	22.121	32.216	16.027
	(0.116)	(0.334)	(0.041)	(0.715)
$LB^2(20)$	24.533	22.368	11.979	13.763
	(0.220)	(0.321)	(0.917)	(0.842)
Cross products				
LB(20)	50.826	35.423	28.179	29.039
	(0.000)*	(0.018)	(0.105)	(0.087)
$LB^2(20)$	42.541	19.792	25.965	13.963
	(0.002)*	(0.471)	(0.167)	(0.832)

*LB^2(29)49.719(0.01); LB^2(12)8.884(0.712); LB(29):48.757(0.012); LB^2(2.112(0.953)); LB(14):19.432(0.149); LB(14):6.907(0.938).

Table 21. Diagnostic test on EGARCH models — Italy.

1996–1998	**Lira/CHF**	**Lira/¥**	**Lira/DM**	**Lira/£**	**Lira/$**
Stock returns					
JB	15	31	20	26	43
LB(20)	23.848	23.466	29.863	23.745	22.535
	(0.249)	(0.266)	(0.0072)	(0.254)	(0.312)
$LB^2(20)$	19.997	16.592	17.702	17.048	14.667
	(0.458)	(0.679)	(0.607)	(0.650)	(0.795)
Exchange rates					
JB	46	137	106	21	38
LB(20)	11.204	15.531	31.792	19.333	13.682
	(0.941)	(0.745)	(0.046)	(0.500)	(0.846)
$LB^2(20)$	19.695	6.613	18.171	19.550	37.219
	(0.477)	(0.989)	(0.576)	(0.486)	(0.011)
Cross products					
LB(20)	24.965	10.677	29.421	29.74	12.336
	(0.203)	(0.954)	(0.080)	(0.074)	(0.904)
$LB^2(20)$	8.8149	0.5807	8.7528	4.9999	0.6451
	(0.985)	(1.000)	(0.986)	(1.000)	(1.000)
1999–2001	**€/CHF**	**€/¥**	**€/£**	**€/$**	
Stock returns					
JB	6	9	6	5	
LB(20)	27	23.386	23.145	23.009	
	(0.142)	(0.270)	(0.282)	(0.288)	
$LB^2(20)$	16.578	18.114	16.437	19.109	
	(0.680)	(0.580)	(0.689)	(0.515)	

(*Continued*)

Table 21. (*Continued*)

Exchange rates				
JB	411	31	28	48
LB(20)	22.291	20.469	28.594	30.995
	(0.325)	(0.429)	(0.096)	(0.055)
$LB^2(20)$	15.365	16.068	40.263	41.967
	(0.755)	(0.712)	(0.005)*	(0.003)*
Cross products				
LB(20)	23.862	13.011	20.214	29.864
	(0.248)	(0.877)	(0.445)	(0.072)
$LB^2(20)$	10.566	23.052	42.596	23.923
	(0.957)	(0.286)	(0.000)*	(0.246)
2002–2006	**€/CHF**	**€/¥**	**€/£**	**€/$**
Stock returns				
JB	43	86	85	58
LB(20)	16.12	18.992	17.646	16.745
	(0.709)	(0.522)	(0.611)	(0.669)
$LB^2(20)$	10.368	7.4098	9.1597	8.4719
	(0.961)	(0.995)	(0.981)	(0.988)
Exchange rates				
JB	93	136	51	11
LB(20)	17.629	31.613	21.434	28.688
	(0.612)	(0.048)	(0.372)	(0.094)
$LB^2(20)$	12.27	13.515	20.009	20.979
	(0.906)	(0.854)	(0.457)	(0.398)
Cross products				
LB(20)	21.918	34.941	19.785	48.811
	(0.345)	(0.020)	(0.471)	(0.000)*
$LB^2(20)$	16.934	15.265	11.048	40.239
	(0.657)	(0.761)	(0.945)	(0.000)*

volatility spillovers between exchange rates and stock markets could reflect the larger number of bilateral exchange rates included in this analysis. Thus, further research along these lines is required to establish more comprehensively the true nature of spillovers from exchange rates to equity markets, which should provide valuable information on the real possibilities for diversifying holdings of stocks and currencies in investment portfolios, as well as the potential for hedging among these assets.

Table 22. Diagnostic test on EGARCH models — Japan.

1996–1998	**¥/$**	**¥/£**	**¥/CHF**	**¥/DM**
Stock returns				
JB	19	19	20	18
LB(20)	22.284	21.886	22.615	21.775
	(0.325)	(0.347)	(0.308)	(0.353)
$LB^2(20)$	21.559	21.049	19.74	20.219
	(0.365)	(0.394)	(0.474)	(0.444)
Exchange rates				
JB	326	90	62	123
LB(20)	19.902	16.514	24.144	16.816
	(0.464)	(0.684)	(0.236)	(0.665)
$LB^2(20)$	7.9373	16.626	33.145	15.829
	(0.992)	(0.677)	(0.033)	(0.727)
Cross products				
LB(20)	33.631	26.711	25.479	31.28
	(0.029)	(0.144)	(0.184)	(0.052)
$LB^2(20)$	21.444	36.965	56.363	60.027
	(0.371)	(0.012)	(0.000)*	(0.000)*
1999–2001	**¥/€**	**¥/$**	**¥/£**	**¥/CHF**
Stock returns				
JB	53	47	49	47
LB(20)	26.779	19.037	18.436	18.984
	(0.142)	(0.519)	(0.559)	(0.523)
$LB^2(20)$	16.558	16.617	16.666	16.984
	(0.681)	(0.678)	(0.675)	(0.654)
Exchange rates				
JB	27	38	39	24
LB(20)	19.029	23.154	13.439	18.985
	(0.520)	(0.281)	(0.858)	(0.523)
$LB^2(20)$	15.846	15.85	10.015	16.984
	(0.726)	(0.726)	(0.968)	(0.654)
Cross products				
LB(20)	29.685	15.131	25.552	27.177
	(0.075)	(0.769)	(0.181)	(0.130)
$LB^2(20)$	8.7263	8.3058	13.934	25.255
	(0.986)	(0.990)	(0.834)	(0.192)
2002–2006	**¥/€**	**¥/$**	**¥/£**	**¥/CHF**
Stock returns				
JB	49	56	58	59
LB(20)	18.17	9.7344	10.083	9.7879
	(0.576)	(0.973)	(0.967)	(0.972)
$LB^2(20)$	11.799	9.5823	8.9081	9.1307
	(0.923)	(0.975)	(0.984)	(0.981)

(*Continued*)

Table 22. (*Continued*)

Exchange rates				
JB	133	138	210	14
LB(20)	33.128	14.661	38.73	108.15
	(0.033)	(0.0795)	(0.007)*	(0.081)
$LB^2(20)$	14.095	15.632	19.803	21.138
	(0.826)	(0.739)	(0.470)	(0.389)
Cross products				
LB(20)	22.665	11.788	26.826	23.449
	(0.306)	(0.923)	(0.140)	(0.267)
$LB^2(20)$	6.4011	4.5495	7.5342	8.6938
	(0.998)	(1.000)	(0.995)	(0.986)

*$LB^2(17)$:21.662(0.198); $LB^2(47)$:71.638(0.012); LB(19):35.643(0.012).

Table 23. Diagnostic Test on EGARCH models — U.K.

1996–1998	**£/$**	**£/¥**	**£/CHF**	**£/DM**
Stock returns				
JB	10	8	6	7
LB(20)	47.888	47.738	44.158	45.919
	(0.000)*	(0.000)*	(0.001)*	(0.000)*
$LB^2(20)$	58.783	11.777	12.154	11.437
	(0.01)	(0.924)	(0.911)	(0.934)
Exchange rates				
JB	76	86	95	29
LB(20)	24.07	18.808	13.424	14.581
	(0.239)	(0.534)	(0.858)	(0.800)
$LB^2(20)$	17.066	17.252	23.698	18.187
	(0.649)	(0.637)	(0.256)	(0.575)
Cross products				
LB(20)	26.58	26.051	25.491	34.752
	(0.148)	(0.164)	(0.183)	(0.021)
$LB^2(20)$	10.934	15.851	16.253	8.8589
	(0.948)	(0.726)	(0.701)	(0.984)
1999–2001	**£/€**	**£/$**	**£/¥**	**£/CHF**
Stock returns				
JB	234	202	207	206
LB(20)	26.745	30.979	25.967	29.358
	(0.143)	(0.055)	(0.167)	(0.081)
$LB^2(20)$	5.7629	6.2182	5.4999	6.4189
	(0.999)	(0.999)	(0.999)	(0.998)

(*Continued*)

Table 23. (*Continued*)

Exchange rates				
JB	8	24	3223	22
LB(20)	24.57	23.766	29.275	16.863
	(0.218)	(0.253)	(0.082)	(0.662)
$LB^2(20)$	36.393	32.442	30.984	9.0466
	(0.014)	(0.039)	(0.055)	(0.982)
Cross products				
LB(20)	26.884	31.666	21.115	18.832
	(0.139)	(0.047)	(0.390)	(0.533)
$LB^2(20)$	7.9564	15.329	4.0625	5.4335
	(0.992)	(0.757)	(1.000)	(0.999)
2002–2006	**£/€**	**£/$**	**£/¥**	**£/CHF**
Stock returns				
JB	23	15	18	18
LB(20)	26.756	24.823	28.599	25.534
	(0.142)	(0.208)	(0.096)	(0.182)
$LB^2(20)$	21.107	25.827	20.965	20.784
	(0.391)	(0.172)	(0.399)	(0.410)
Exchange rates				
JB	67	41	40	10
LB(20)	24.17	23.881	14.056	24.817
	(0.235)	(0.248)	(0.826)	(0.209)
$LB^2(20)$	37.431	8.4694	8.8236	11.119
	(0.010)	(0.988)	(0.985)	(0.943)
Cross products				
LB(20)	15.163	21.101	26.346	17.58657
	(0.767)	(0.391)	(0.155)	(0.619)
$LB^2(20)$	14.253	21.698	36.9	9.869
	(0.817)	(0.357)	(0.012)	(0.994)

*LB(36):58.783(0.01); LB(35):54.471(0.01); LB(26):44.940(0.012); LB(33):54.145(0.012).

Table 24. Diagnostic test on EGARCH models — U.S.

1996–1998	**\$/£**	**\$/¥**	**\$/CHF**	**\$/DM**
Stock returns				
JB	65	68	83	59
LB(20)	21.725	23.438	19.656	19.921
	(0.356)	(0.268)	(0.480)	(0.463)
$LB^2(20)$	11.428	13.012	11.334	14.469
	(0.934)	(0.877)	(0.937)	(0.806)
Exchange rates				
JB	107	343	170	62
LB(20)	21.159	19.364	12.969	14.482
	(0.388)	(0.498)	(0.879)	(0.805)

(*Continued*)

Table 24. (*Continued*)

$LB^2(20)$	21.159	8.499	12.15	40.929
	(0.780)	(0.988)	(0.911)	(0.004)*
Cross products				
LB(20)	21.05	20.279	12.649	24.885
	(0.394)	(0.441)	(0.892)	(0.206)
$LB^2(20)$	4.575	2.4032	9.0539	13.222
	(1.000)	(1.000)	(0.982)	(0.868)
1999–2001	**\$/€**	**\$/£**	**\$/¥**	**\$/CHF**
Stock returns				
JB	76	81	96	71
LB(20)	19.532	19.67	20.675	21.004
	(0.488)	(0.479)	(0.416)	(0.397)
$LB^2(20)$	11.639	14.04	15.032	12.9
	(0.928)	(0.828)	(0.775)	(0.882)
Exchange rates				
JB	33	8	53	30
LB(20)	31.226	20.37	21.298	26.351
	(0.052)	(0.435)	(0.380)	(0.155)
$LB^2(20)$	30.887	40.126	17.674	17.541
	(0.057)	(0.005)*	(0.609)	(0.618)
Cross products				
LB(20)	31.403	35.834	31.644	51.048
	(0.050)	(0.016)	(0.047)	(0.123)
$LB^2(20)$	21.925	17.642	70.464	27.469
	(0.345)	(0.611)	(0.000)*	(0.123)
2002–2006	**\$/€**	**\$/£**	**\$/¥**	**\$/CHF**
Stock returns				
JB	2	2	2	2
LB(20)	30.322	30.579	31.15	30.37
	(0.065)	(0.061)	(0.053)	(0.064)
$LB^2(20)$	37.394	36.853	33.944	37.26
	(0.01)	(0.012)	(0.027)	(0.011)
Exchange rates				
JB	7	24	165	9
LB(20)	27.634	18.196	16.158	27.059
	(0.118)	(0.578)	(0.707)	(0.134)
$LB^2(20)$	26.3	79.138	15.104	22.776
	(0.156)	(0.000)*	(0.770)	(0.300)

(*Continued*)

Table 24. (*Continued*)

Cross products				
LB(20)	13.342	27.081	28.998	9.7734
	(0.862)	(0.133)	(0.088)	(0.972)
$LB^2(20)$	21.508	43.29	27.996	22.778
	(0.368)	(0.000)*	(0.110)	(0.300)

*$LB^2(6)$5.044; LB(9):18.533(0.029); LB(4):7.545(0.01); $LB^2(16)$:7.66(0.958); LB(5): 6.097(0.297); LB(5):1.5454(0.9).

Endnotes

1. See Nieh and Lee (2001) and Yau and Nieh (2006) for recent evidence on this topic.
2. For brevity, here the number of lags selected for the conditional mean equations for stock prices and exchange rates for each period are not reported.
3. For brevity, these results are not presented in the text, but they are available from the author upon request.
4. Results are available from the author upon request.
5. The LMF test results indicated that the ADF tests were free from serial correlation; for brevity, the test results are not shown here.
6. For brevity, the results have not been displayed in this document, but they are available upon request.

References

Andersen, TG and T Bollerslev (1998). Answering the skeptics: Yes, standard volatility models do provide accurate forecasts. *International Economic Review*, 39, 885–905.

Assoé, K (2001). Volatility spillovers between foreign exchange and emerging stock markets. *CETAI* (Centre d'études en administration internationale). Cahier de recherché, 2001–04.

Bodnar, G, S Hayt, R Marston and C Smithson (1995). Wharton survey of derivatives usage by US non-financial firms, *Financial Management*, 24, 104–114.

Branson, W (1983). Macroeconomic determinants of real exchange rate risk. In *Managing Foreign Exchange Risk*, R Herring (ed.), Cambridge University Press.

Caporale, M, N Pittis and N Spagnolo (2002). Testing for causality-in-variance: An application to the East Asian markets. *International Journal of Finance and Economics*, 7, 235–245.

Dornbusch, R and S Fischer (1980). Exchange rates and the current account. *American Economic Review*, 12, 7–12.

Frankel, J (1983). Monetary and portfolio-balance models of exchange rate determination. In *Economic Interdependence and Flexible Exchange Rates*, J. Bhandari and B. Putman (eds.). Cambridge, MA: MIT Press.

Grant, K and A Marshall (1997). Large UK companies and derivatives. *European Financial Management*, 3, 191–208.

Griffin, JM, F Nardari and RM Stulz (2007). Do investors trade more when stocks have performed well? Evidence from 46 Countries. *Review of Financial Studies*, 20, 905–951.

Hamilton, J (1994). *Time Series Analysis*. Princeton: Princeton University Press.

Jorion, P (1990). The exchange rate exposure of US multinationals. *Journal of Business*, 63, 331–345.

Kanas, A (2000). Volatility spillovers between stock returns and exchange rate changes: International evidence. *Journal of Business Finance and Accounting*, 27, 447–467.

Kanas, A (2002). Is exchange rate volatility influenced by stock return volatility? Evidence from the US, the UK and Japan. *Applied Economics Letters*, 9, 501–503.

Koutmos, G and G Booth (1995). Asymmetric volatility transmission in international stock markets. *Journal of International Money and Finance*, 14, 747–762.

Laopodis, N (1998). Asymmetric volatility spillovers in Deutsche mark exchange rates. *Journal of Multinational Financial Management*, 8, 413–430.

Leeves, G (2007). Asymmetric volatility of stock returns during the Asian crisis: Evidence from Indonesia. *International Review of Economics and Finance*, 16, 272–286.

Mundell, R (1963). Capital mobility and stabilization policy under fixed and flexible exchange rate. *Canadian Journal of Economics and Political Science*, 29, 475–467.

Mundell, R (1964). A reply: Capital mobility and size. *Canadian Journal of Economics and Political Science*, 30, 421–431.

Nelson, D (1991). Conditional heteroscedasticity in asset returns: A new approach. *Econometrica*, 59, 347–370.

Nieh, CC and CF Lee (2001). Dynamic relationship between stock prices and exchange rates for G-7 countries. *The Quarterly Review and Finance*, 41, 477–490.

Qayyum, A and AR Kemal (2006). Volatility spillover between the stock market and the foreign exchange market in Pakistan. Munich Personal RePEc Archive. Paper No. 1715.

Smith, C (1992). Stock markets and the exchange rate: A multi-country approach. *Journal of Macroeconomics*, 14, 607–629.

Wu, R (2005). International transmission effect of volatility between the financial markets during the Asian financial crises. *Transition Studies Review*, 15, 19–35.

Yang, S and S Doong (2004). Price and volatility spillovers between stock prices and exchange rates: Empirical evidence from the G-7 countries. *International Journal of Business and Economics*, 3, 139–153.

Yau, H and CC Nieh (2006). Interrelations among stock prices of Taiwan and Japan and NTD/Yen exchange rate. *Journal of Asian Economics*, 17, 535–552.

Zapatero, F (1995). Equilibrium asset prices and exchange rates. *Journal of Economic Dynamics and Control*, 19, 787–811.

5

Country-of-Origin Determinants of Value Creation in International Joint Ventures: A Comparison of Hong Kong and U.S. Investments in China

Usha R. Mittoo, Dennis Chung and Zhou Zhang

1. Introduction

Whether the nationality of a firm affects its foreign direct investment strategy has attracted the attention of many researchers in recent years. A large number of international business studies have documented that country-of-origin factors influence many aspects of a firm's business strategy including its competitiveness, entry mode, ownership preference and industrial characteristics of foreign investments (see e.g., Kogut and Singh, 1988; Schroath *et al.*, 1993; Erramilli, 1996; Pan, 1997; Hennart and Larimo, 1998; Makino and Beamish, 1998). Relatively few studies have, however, explored whether the nationality of a firm also plays a role in the success of foreign ventures, an issue that is of particular interest to corporate managers and shareholders. If the firm's nationality is indeed an important determinant of its international expansion strategy, then it would also influence the performance and success of the foreign ventures. This chapter attempts to fill this void in the literature by analyzing the determinants of the wealth effect of joint venture investments into China for firms from two different markets, Hong Kong and the U.S.

We focus on two country-of-origin factors that have been hypothesized to have strong impact on the foreign investments: the cultural distance between the home and host country and the size of the home markets. These factors have opposite predictions for our sample countries. The cultural proximity of Hong Kong to China provides its firms an information advantage over their U.S. counterparts in negotiating, establishing and operating Chinese ventures. The existence of the world's largest capital and product markets in the U.S., on the other hand, provides its firms an edge over their Hong Kong counterparts in undertaking Chinese ventures, especially in the high technology and capital intensive areas. To what extent these home country advantages influence the value creation in Chinese ventures is the focus of our study. Specifically, we ask three questions related to the country-of-origin factors: (1) Are the Chinese joint ventures value enhancing for both Hong Kong and U.S. firms? (2) Are the cultural distance and the size of the home markets important determinants of wealth gains in these ventures? and (3) Do firms from either home market have a comparative advantage in undertaking these ventures?

Our main contribution to the literature is that we use a multidisciplinary approach in this study by integrating perspectives from international business and finance disciplines. The theoretical literature in international business links a firm's nationality to the performance and success of the international joint ventures but these theoretical models have not been rigorously tested (e.g., Hofstede, 1980; Dunning, 1988; Porter, 1990). An abundance of finance studies, on the other hand, have examined the wealth effects of international joint ventures but few have explored the role of a firm's nationality in value creation (e.g., Finnerty *et al.*, 1986; Lee and Wyatt, 1990; Lummer and McConnell, 1990; Crutchley *et al.*, 1991; Chen *et al.*, 1991; Hu *et al.*, 1992; Chung *et al.*, 1993; Borde *et al.*, 1998).

While these studies use stock market data and powerful statistical methods, the linkages of their empirical analysis with the theoretical literature are generally not strong. In this chapter, we draw upon the international business literature to develop hypotheses pertaining to the national origin factors, and employ the event study methodology, commonly used in finance literature, to test these hypotheses. The event study methodology is based on the notion that in efficient markets, the stock price reaction to the announcement of the joint ventures will reflect investors' marginal valuation of the probability of success or failure of the joint ventures. This allows us to infer the significance of country-of-origin factors from the valuation effect incorporated in market prices data.

Our study also provides insights into the determinants of value creation in international joint ventures. Despite the abundance of previous research in this area, there is no consensus on which factors drive the cross-sectional variation in wealth effects. Our research design facilitates a comparison of the previous evidence which is based on the experience of the U.S. firms with that of firms based in a different market, Hong Kong. Our results suggest that the national origin factors, ignored in previous finance literature, play an important role in wealth gains in international joint ventures. The rest of the chapter is organized as follows. Section 2 reviews previous literature and develops testable hypotheses. Section 3 outlines the data sources, sample description and event study methodology. We present empirical results in Sec. 4 and the conclusions in Sec. 5.

2. Literature Review and Testable Hypotheses

In this section, we review the literature on the country-of-origin effects and develop testable hypotheses. We focus on two national origin factors — cultural distance between home and host country and the size of the home market, which are likely to have a strong impact on the success of the international joint ventures. We also discuss the reasons for selecting the host and home countries.

2.1. *Cultural Distance Between Home and Host Country*

A rich theoretical literature on international business suggests that a company's culture is strongly influenced by the culture of its home country (see e.g., Hofstede, 1980; Norburn *et al.*, 1990). Firms expanding beyond national borders have to adjust to the foreign national culture and this adjustment process is likely to be more demanding when the foreign culture is substantially different from the home country culture. The success of the foreign ventures, therefore, is likely to depend partly on the cultural distance, that is, difference between the home and host country cultures.

The existing empirical evidence suggests a strong link between the cultural barriers and the foreign expansion strategies of firms, especially in the entry mode and the ownership preference in foreign markets. For example, Kogut and Singh (1988) find that cultural barriers influence the entry mode of foreign firms in the U.S. market. They report that firms domiciled in countries with large cultural distance from the U.S. have a higher probability of choosing a joint or wholly owned green-field investment over a majority or full acquisition. Hennart and Larimo (1998) find that the cultural distance between the home base of the investing firm and the target country exerts a powerful influence on the ownership of the foreign subsidiaries. Pan (1996) also documents significant differences in the ownership strategies of equity joint ventures in China among the U.S., European and Japanese firms and reports that as the cultural distance increases, the foreigner partners are more likely to acquire an equal or a majority ownership stake instead of a wholly owned venture.

The literature also suggests that the adjustment to foreign culture is likely to be more demanding when firms engage in international joint ventures because in such cases firms have to contend with two foreign cultures: a national culture and a corporate culture. Barkema and colleagues (1996) find support for this hypothesis in their study of the longevity of foreign entries using data on 225 entries by 13 Dutch firms. They document that cultural distance is a major factor in foreign entry whenever this involves another firm. They report that the termination of joint ventures and acquisitions was more susceptible to cultural distance than wholly owned subsidiaries and startups.

Makino and Beamish (1998) examine the performance and survival of Japanese joint ventures in Asia with different modes of ownership and show that the inter-partner cultural distance has a significant impact on the performance and survival of the joint venture. Barkema *et al.* (1996) also examine whether firms can reduce the negative impact of cultural barriers on foreign investment by learning over time. They find that the longevity of foreign entries with a majority stake improved whenever the expanding firm engaged in prior entries in the same country and in other countries within the same cultural block. This evidence supports that learning helps to offset the negative impact of cultural barriers on the performance of foreign ventures. Meschi (2004) analyzes 67 Sino-French joint ventures during the period of 1994–2002 and shows that French companies create more value when they accumulate more alliance experience in China.

In summary, the prior literature suggests that cultural distance is an important determinant in the success of foreign ventures, and its effect is likely to be negatively correlated with joint ventures that are located in culturally distant countries. The negative impact of the cultural barriers would decrease as firms expand operations in the host country because of enhanced learning and adaptation to local culture. Thus, we hypothesize:

H1: The greater the cultural distance between the investing firm's home and host country, the smaller the investing firm's wealth gains in international joint ventures, all else being equal.

H2: The greater the cultural distance between the investing firm's home and host country, the larger would be the positive impact of the investing firm's previous expansion in that country on wealth gains in international joint ventures, all else being equal.

2.2. *Home Market Size*

The competitive advantage of home market size in foreign investments is emphasized in two strands of international business literature: the national comparative advantage theory and the internalization theory. Porter (1990) extends the notion of comparative advantage in international trade to international investments and argues that the national competitive advantage in foreign investments is created by the interaction of both economic and strategic factors of the home country. In particular, Porter underscores the importance of the size and characteristics of the domestic market as sources of competitive advantage. He suggests that competing in large and sophisticated markets gives companies opportunities to exploit economies of scale, ability to satisfy the most demanding buyers, and acquire a great deal of self-confidence. Consequently, firms based in countries with large markets tend to be more innovative and competitive which provides them an edge in foreign expansion.

Dunning (1979, 1980, 1988) links the unique firms-specific endowments to the national endowments by extending the theoretical framework of the internalization theory. This theory posits that a firm's foreign investment strategy is driven mainly by its need to internalize the market for its unique firm-specific intangible assets such as patents, superior production or marketing skills. Dunning emphasizes that the existence of large domestic product and capital markets is a potential source of firm-specific endowments along with other factors such as government support of technological innovation, availability of highly trained managerial talent and local availability of natural resources. He argues that large and standardized markets with little restriction on firm size lead to larger firm size, and hence provide the advantages of the economy of scale. Similarly, the existence of sophisticated and reliable capital markets, and high-quality professional advice leads to advantages in the form of capital availability and financial expertise.

The literature suggests that competitive advantages of the home markets are more likely to be reflected in large firms. Porter (1987) and Dunning (1992) suggest that the size of a firm is positively correlated with the ability to raise the needed resources for large-scale projects, the flexibility to leverage across country markets, and to plan and act on a long-term basis. Several studies provide support for the hypothesis that the size of the firm's home markets influences the firm's international investment strategy. Erramilli (1996) examines the influence of national cultural characteristics and the home market size on the ownership preferences of American and European multinationals. He reports that the home market size has a positive influence on the firm's propensity for a majority ownership, although the effect weakens as the size becomes larger.

Osland and Cavusgil (1996) find that the U.S. partners had higher satisfaction with performance of their joint ventures in China when their local partners were relatively small. Pan and Li (2000) also document significant differences in the advantages of doing business in China between large and small multinationals. They document that large foreign firms have higher equity shares, are in a better position to maintain a network of cooperative partners and foreign alliances, and are less sensitive to short-term changes in Chinese business environment.

The empirical evidence on the relation between firm size and wealth gains is, however, not clear. For example, Ueng *et al.* (2000) find no significant relation between wealth gains and firm size for a sample of U.S. firms that engaged in international joint ventures during the 1990–1995 period. Crutchley *et al.* (1991) find that in the U.S. and Japanese joint ventures, the U.S. partner's gain is inversely related to the partner's size but the opposite is true for the Japanese partners, suggesting that the relation may be sensitive to different host and home countries. In summary, the international business literature suggests that firms domiciled in countries with relatively large product and capital markets have a competitive advantage over firms located in small markets, and that large firms would be better able to exploit these competitive advantages. Therefore, we hypothesize:

> *H3: The larger the size of the investing firm's home markets, the higher the investing firm's wealth gains in international joint ventures, all else being equal.*

> *H4: The larger the size of the investing firm, the higher the investing firm's wealth gains in international joint ventures, all else being equal.*

2.3. *Selection of Host and Home Countries*

When data from multiple host countries are used, the determinants of wealth gains may be seriously confounded by other factors such as the host country's institutional structure, political risk and economic conditions. By limiting to one host country, and explicitly comparing the experience of firms from two different markets, we minimize these confounding effects in our study. The choice of China as a host country offers some advantages. First, China has attracted foreign direct investment on an unprecedented scale ever since it opened its door to foreigners in 1979. The annual foreign investment in China grew from less than $4 billion in the 1980s to over $25 billion in the early 1990s. More importantly, a large number of firms from all parts of the world have set up joint ventures in China, mostly with state-owned enterprises, providing a very fertile ground for testing theories on national origin factors. A large number of studies have analyzed the influence of country-of-origin factors on foreign investments in China.

Empirical evidence strongly suggests that national origin factors are important determinants of the entry mode, competitiveness, joint venture characteristics and performance in China (e.g., Schroath *et al.*, 1993; Osland and Cavusgil, 1996; Pan, 1996; Tse *et al.*, 1997). Thus, on an ex-ante basis, if national origin factors are indeed major determinants of the value creation in international joint ventures, we would expect to find some corroborating evidence in the analysis of the international joint ventures in China.

Both Hong Kong and the U.S. have unique home country advantages of doing business in China. Table 1 compares the differences on the cultural and economic dimensions. Panel A shows Hofstede's scores on four dimensions of national culture for Hong Kong, China and the U.S. and the cultural distance indices using Kogut and Singh (1988)'s constructs. These indices confirm that compared to Hong Kong, the U.S. is culturally more distant from China; the cultural distance of the U.S. from China is almost 22 times that of Hong Kong.

Panel B of Table 1 shows the comparative advantage of the U.S. over Hong Kong in terms of the size of the economy and capital markets. Although Hong Kong is ranked very close to the U.S. on

Table 1. Comparison of the U.S. and Hong Kong based on the cultural and economic dimensions.

	U.S.	Hong Kong	China
Panel A:			
Power distance index (PDI)	40	68	80
Uncertainty avoidance index (UAI)	46	29	30
Individualism index	91	25	20
Masculinity index	62	57	66
Cultural distance to China (based on the measure in Kogut and Singh, 1988)	3.12	0.14	
Panel B:			
Size of economy			
Gross national product ($B)	$7,434	$153	$906
(Rank in world)	(1)	(27)	(7)
Industrial output ($B, 1995)	$1,808	$24	$335
(Rank in world)	(1)	(37)	(7)
Exports (% of world exports)	14.22%	0.37%	2.41%
(Rank in world)	(1)	(39)	(10)
Size of capital markets			
Stock market capitalization ($M, 1996)	$8,484,433	$449,381	$113,755
(Rank in world)	(1)	(7)	(22)
Size of firms			
Number of firms among world's 40 largest businesses	11	0	0
Number of banks among world's 40 largest banks	8	0	0
Global competitiveness	1	3	24

Note: Panel A shows Hofstede's scores on four dimensions of national culture (see http://www.geert-hofstede.com/hofstede_dimensions.php) and Kogut and Singh (1988)'s cultural distance indices for the U.S., Hong Kong and China. Panel B compares the size of the economy and capital markets among the U.S., Hong Kong, and People's Republic of China. The figures in panel B are based on *The Economist, World in Figures*, 1999 edition.

global competitiveness, the U.S. has a clear advantage in possessing the world's largest capital markets, and in its status as the world's largest producer and exporter of industrial goods. The U.S. economy is about 48 times larger than that of Hong Kong while its stock market capitalization is nearly 18 times larger than that of Hong Kong's. These differences in the size of the home markets are also reflected in the relative size of the firms. For example, among the 40 largest firms in the world, 11 are domiciled in the U.S. while none belongs to Hong Kong. Similar is the case for banks; eight U.S. banks are included among the 40 largest banks in the world whereas none of the Hong Kong banks is included.

In summary, both Hong Kong and U.S. possess distinct advantages and the two theories of national origin have the opposite implications for both countries. The gains in joint ventures would be expected to be much higher for Hong Kong firms under the cultural distance theory while the opposite would hold under the home market size theory. The net effect for firms in the two countries would depend on the trade-off between the two factors in the context of China.

3. Data and Methodology

3.1. *Data and Sample Description*

Our sample consists of Hong Kong and U.S. joint ventures in China from 1989 to 1995. This sample period is useful to test the impact of cultural distance on joint ventures for several reasons. First, our sample begins with the early period of joint venture expansion in China when the cultural barriers are likely to be important in foreign firms' investment decisions in China. Second, our sample begins in 1989 when Hong Kong was a dependent territory of the U.K. (since 1842) and ends in 1995, two years prior to 1997, when U.K. transferred Hong Kong's sovereignty to the People's Republic of China and it became the Hong Kong Special Administrative Region (SAR) of China. Finally, our measures of cultural distance, market size and firm size are based on the studies in late 1980s, which are more appropriate for our study as these measures are also likely to change significantly over time with the globalization of product and capital markets. Thus, our sample period is less likely to include major confounding effects for Hong Kong, such as close political connection between Hong Kong and China.

The initial sample of Hong Kong and U.S. joint ventures in China was identified from the news announcements related to joint venture activities of all Hong Kong and U.S. firms in the *Financial Times EXTEL Company Research Database*, *PR Newswire* and the *Dow Jones News Retrieval Services.* The text of each announcement was carefully reviewed to identify the initial first time announcement of each joint venture, the announcement date, the identities of the parties involved, and the nature of the intended operations of the joint venture. To be included in the final sample, the data for Hong Kong firms must be available in the Pacific Basin Capital Markets (PACAP) database, and for U.S. firms in the Center for Research in Securities Prices (CRSP) database.

The final sample consists of 138 joint venture announcements by the U.S. firms and 99 announcements by the Hong Kong firms. These deals were undertaken by 107 U.S. firms and 78 Hong Kong firms, respectively. Panel A of Table 2 presents the year-wise frequency distribution of the joint ventures. About 85% of our sample is concentrated in the 1993–1995 period, which is consistent with the general pattern of foreign direct investment in China which experienced a rapid growth in the early 1990s. Panel B shows that the percentage of firms with at least two deals (about 20%) is also similar in both samples.

Table 2. Sample distribution of Hong Kong and U.S. joint ventures in China 1989–1995.

Panel A: Distribution of number of firms and joint venture deals over the years

Year	U.S.	Hong Kong
1989	0	4
1991	6	6
1992	11	2
1993	29	14
1994	45	53
1995	47	20
Total	138	99

Panel B: Distribution of number of firms with multiple joint venture deals

Number of companies	U.S.	Hong Kong
One JV deal	87	62
Two JV deals	13	12
Three JV deals	3	3
Four JV deals	4	1
Total firms	107	78

3.2. *Comparison of the Firm and Industry Characteristics*

The firm and industry characteristics, presented in Table 3, reveal significant differences between the two samples on several dimensions. First, as expected, the U.S. firms are significantly larger than the Hong Kong firms. The average book value of assets of a U.S. firm is US$22.9 billion compared to US$1.8 billion for its Hong Kong counterpart, and the difference is statistically significant at the 1% level ($t = 4.78$). The U.S. sample is dominated by very large firms; 63% of the U.S. firms have book value of assets over one billion dollars whereas only 27% of the Hong Kong firms fall in this category. Second, the international focus of firms also differs substantially in the two samples. The Hong Kong firms are primarily focused in China while the U.S. firms are concentrated in non-Chinese and non-Asian regions. About 50% of the Hong Kong firms have subsidiaries in China compared to only 17% of the U.S. firms. Moreover, a typical Hong Kong firm has an average of 2.6 subsidiaries in China compared to only 0.4 subsidiaries per U.S. firm, and the difference is significant at less than the 1% level ($t = 3.94$). By contrast, the majority of the U.S. firms (about 60%) are focused in non-Asian regions; only about 25% of the Hong Kong firms have subsidiaries in these regions. The average number of foreign subsidiaries in the non-Asian regions for U.S. firms is also significantly higher compared to those for the Hong Kong firms ($p < 0.05$), although the degree of involvement in the Southeast Asia is similar in both samples.

Finally, the industrial characteristics of joint ventures also differ in the two samples (Table 3, Panel B). The majority of the U.S. joint ventures (about 80%) are in the manufacturing sector while the Hong Kong ventures are evenly spread between the manufacturing and non-manufacturing sectors. The U.S. joint ventures are also concentrated in the high technology industries (62%), especially in the capital intensive sectors, such as automotive, pharmaceutical, electrical power plants, oil and gas. In contrast, only 35% of the Hong Kong joint ventures are in high technology industries, mostly in the labor intensive industries, such as air conditioners, cellular phones, toys and food products.

Table 3. Firm and industry characteristics: Hong Kong and U.S. joint ventures in China.

Panel A: Firm characteristics

	U.S.		Hong Kong		
	N	Average	N	Average	*t*-test
Firm size (million U.S. dollars)					
Book value of total assets	125	22,864.90	97	1,757.12	4.78***
(median)		(2,897.00)		(197.47)	
Market capitalization	126	11,689.69	99	1,448.83	5.97***
(median)		(2,149.69)		(198.59)	
International focus					
Number of firms with foreign subsidiaries	129	14.64	90	11.72	1.18
Number of subsidiaries in China	24	0.37	45	2.59	3.94***
Number of subsidiaries in Southeast Asia	55	1.5	36	2.05	0.97
Number of subsidiaries in the world (except in China and Southeast Asia)	84	12.58	24	7.05	2.67**

Panel B: Industry characteristics

	U.S.		Hong Kong		
	N	% of Total	N	% of Total	Z-stat
Number of joint ventures for which data are available	136		96		
Manufacturing	105	78.20	48	50	−4.31***
High Tech Capital	41	30.10	11	11.50	−1.96*
High Tech Labor	42	31.90	23	24	0.92
Low Tech Capital	1	0.70	3	3.10	1.91
Low Tech Labor	21	15.40	11	11.50	0.41
Non-Manufacturing	31	21.80	48	50	4.31***
Financial Services	0	0	13	13.50	3.17***
Non-Financial Services	15	11	14	14.60	−1.73*
Real Estate	0	0	21	21.90	4.30***
Utilities	16	11.80	0	0	−5.59***

N = number of observations for which data are available. Test-statistic is *t*-test for difference in means and *Z*-test is the Fisher test for the difference in proportions between the two samples. *Significant at the 0.10 level, **significant at the 0.05 level and ***significant at the 0.01 level. *Note*: Table 3 reports the firm characteristics (firm size and the degree of internationalization) and industry characteristics (manufacturing vs. non-manufacturing, high-tech vs. low-tech and capital intensive vs. labor intensive) of Hong Kong and U.S. joint ventures in China during 1989–1995.

The differences between the two samples are even more striking in the non-manufacturing sector. About 22% of the Hong Kong joint ventures are in the real estate sector whereas none of the U.S. ventures are in this sector. A majority of the U.S. joint ventures in the non-manufacturing sector are concentrated in the utility and non-financial service sectors; none of the Hong Kong ventures is in the utility sector. The chi-square (χ^2) test supports that the proportions of firms in different industrial categories is different between the two samples ($\chi^2 = 72.7$).

Overall, these differences support the theory that firm-specific endowments are partly driven by the country-of-origin factors. The larger size of the U.S. firms relative to their Hong Kong peers can be attributed partly to the larger size of the U.S. economy while the differences in the international focus between the Hong Kong and U.S. firms are consistent with the geo-cultural distance of their respective home markets from the target country. The differences in industry characteristics of the joint ventures between the Hong Kong and U.S. samples are consistent with the findings of Schroath *et al.* (1993) and support Dunning's theory that foreign investment patterns are influenced by the country-of-origin endowments.

3.3. *Event Study Methodology*

To assess the announcement effect of joint ventures, we use the standard event study methodology with a market model. The market model is estimated as:

$$R_{jt} = \alpha_j + \beta_j R_{Mt} + \varepsilon_{jt}, \tag{1}$$

where R_{jt} is the rate of return on security j on day t, R_{Mt} is the rate of return on the market index on day t, α_j is the intercept for firm j, β_j is the beta relative to the market, and ε_{jt} is the residual error term. The market index is proxied by the CRSP value-weighted returns for the U.S. firms and by the PACAP value-weighted index for the Hong Kong firms. The daily stock and market returns for the U.S. firms are obtained from the CRSP database and those for the Hong Kong firms and the Hong Kong market index are obtained from the PACAP database.

The daily abnormal returns (ARs) are computed by estimating the market model parameter over the estimation period from $t = -200$ to $t = -51$, relative to the announcement day $t = 0$. The joint venture events are reported by the newswire as they occur, and are normally published in the newspapers the next day. The average abnormal return (AARs) for any day t is calculated by summing the ARs for the N firms in the sample and dividing by N. Cumulative abnormal returns (CARs) are calculated by summing the ARs over the T days window.

4. Empirical Evidence

4.1. *Average Wealth Effects of Joint Venture Announcements*

Table 4 compares the daily average abnormal returns for the U.S. and Hong Kong firms around the announcement date ($t = 0$) of the joint ventures for the 11-day period ($t = -5, +5$). The evidence shows that the announcements of the Chinese joint ventures are, on average, associated with positive abnormal returns for both Hong Kong and U.S. firms. The Hong Kong firms have an abnormal return of 0.85% on day +1 and 59% of them experienced positive ARs on that day. It is also the largest one-day return in the entire event period and is statistically significant at the 1% level. The U.S. firms also experience positive average abnormal gains of 0.65% and 0.42% on days 0 and +1, respectively, although the *Z*-statistics is significant only at the 10% level on day +1. The U.S. results are consistent with the previous evidence by Chen *et al.* (1991) who document significant positive excess returns on the announcement date of the U.S.–China joint ventures in the 1979–1990 period.

We also report the CARs in different event period windows around the joint venture announcements to account for the possible leakage of information or a delayed effect of the announcements. The CARs are reported in Panel B for two intervals: a three-day interval $(-1, +1)$ and a five-day interval $(-2, +2)$. As Panel B shows, the CARs for the Hong Kong firms are positive and significant at the

Table 4. Abnormal returns around the announcements of the joint ventures in China: U.S. versus Hong Kong sample.

Panel A: Average abnormal returns around the announcement date

Day	Average abnormal return (%)	Positive:Negative	Patell Z
U.S.–China Joint Ventures			
−5	−0.05	62:76	0.107
−4	0.02	65:73	−0.165
−3	0.24	68:70	0.463
−2	0.31	68:70	0.933
−1	−0.07	65:73	0.065
0	0.65	65:73	1.044
1	0.42	70:68	1.657*
2	−0.03	69:69	0.187
3	0.03	60:78	0.265
4	−0.15	69:69	1.233
5	0.37	66:72	1.297
Hong Kong–China Joint Ventures			
−5	0.58	43:38	2.253**
−4	−0.06	39:55	−0.492
−3	0.24	43:52	1.257
−2	−0.06	38:60	−0.282
−1	0.20	46:50	1.287
0	−0.20	44:49	−0.567
1	0.85	56:39	3.449***
2	0.25	42:56	1.057
3	0.27	46:50	0.662
4	−0.19	43:53	−0.508
5	0.21	47:48	0.336

Panel B: Cumulative abnormal returns (CARs)

	U.S. JVs		Hong Kong JVs		Difference in the U.S. and Hong Kong CARs	
Event windows	CARs	Patell Z	CARs	Patell Z	CARs	*t*-test
[−1,1]	1.00%	1.60	0.83%	2.43**	0.17%	0.23
[−2,2]	1.27%	1.74*	1.01%	2.21**	0.26%	0.24

Note: *Significant at the 0.10 level, **significant at the 0.05 level and ***significant at the 0.01 level. Table 4 reports the abnormal returns around announcement day for the Hong Kong and U.S. joint ventures in China during 1989–1995. The ARs are computed by estimating the market model parameter over the estimation period from $t = -200$ to $t = -51$, relative to the announcement day $t = 0$. The AARs for any day t is calculated by summing the ARs for the N firms in the sample and dividing by N. CARs is calculated by summing the ARs over the T days window.

5% level under both event windows. The CARs are also positive for the U.S. sample, but are significant only for the five-day interval. In summary, the Chinese joint ventures are, on average, value-enhancing for both Hong Kong and U.S. firms but there is a cross-sectional variation in both samples. The difference in CARs between the two country samples is not significant in either event window at any conventional level.

4.2. *Cross-Sectional Regressions*

The cross-sectional determinants of the wealth gains are examined by running the following regression in each country sample:

$$\text{CARs}_j(-2, +2) = \alpha_0 + \beta_1\text{LRNDEAL} + \beta_2\text{FIRMSIZE} + \beta_3\text{MULTN} + \beta_4\text{SEASIA} + \beta_5\text{HITECH}, \quad (2)$$

where CARs_j is the five-day (−2, +2) CAR for each firm. Our explanatory variables include two main variables (LRNDEAL and FIRMSIZE) that test the country-of-origin hypothesis and three control variables (MULTN, SEASIA and HITECH). LRNDEAL is the number of JV announcements by each firm in our sample. Both international business and finance literature suggest that previous expansion in the host country provides valuable learning experience since knowledge accumulated through this experience helps a firm in avoiding costly mistakes and reduces the risk of failure of the venture.

LRNDEAL proxies for learning about the Chinese culture and is predicted to be positively related with wealth gains for both the U.S. and Hong Kong firms. However, the magnitude of the impact is expected to be much larger for the U.S. firms since the marginal value of learning about foreign culture is expected to be higher for firms in culturally distant countries. FIRMSIZE is the log of the book value of the total assets for each firm in the year ending prior to undertaking the joint venture. The home market size hypothesis predicts that the relation between FIRMSIZE and wealth gains would be positive for both U.S. and Hong Kong firms, but the impact is likely to be much larger for the U.S. firms.[1]

MULTN is the number of foreign subsidiaries of a firm in all countries except in Southeast Asia and China. The international business theories suggest that the value creation in international-stems largely from a firm's ability to arbitrage the distortions in the capital or product markets and its ability to internalize the market for its intangible assets such as superior managerial or production skills. Thus, MULTN is expected to be positively related to the wealth effects of JV announcements. However, the prior literature does not support this prediction. For instance, Chen *et al.* (1991) find no relation between the degree of international involvement and gains in Chinese ventures for the U.S. firms. Hu *et al.* (1992) find that gains are much higher for firms with smaller degree of international involvement, opposite to that predicted by the multinational network theory.[2]

SEASIA is the number of subsidiaries of a firm in Southeast Asia. The gains in JVs are expected to be higher for firms that move to distant countries after having established a presence in the similar cultural block countries, although the impact is expected to be weaker compared to that of earlier expansions in the same country. Chen *et al.* (1991), however, find no significant relation between the previous presence in Southeast Asia and wealth gains in the U.S. joint ventures in China. HITECH is a dummy variable that is equal to one for the high technology joint ventures and zero otherwise. Schroath *et al.* (1993) report that the U.S. and European firms had a much higher percentage of Chinese joint ventures in high technology and capital intensive industries compared to Hong Kong firms.

The literature also suggests that whether the joint venture is with a foreign government or a foreign firm is an important determinant of the value creation in joint ventures (see e.g., Lummer and McConnell, 1990). However, since most joint ventures in China are formed with the state-owned enterprises, we do not control for this variable in our study. Several prior studies report that the strength of home currency could also impact the wealth gains in international joint ventures (see Crutchley *et al.*, 1991; Harris and Ravenscraft, 1991). We do not include foreign exchange rate in the regression because Hong Kong's currency is pegged to the U.S. dollar, and the Chinese currency is convertible to the U.S. dollar on the trade account.

4.3. *Regression Results: The Determinants of Wealth Gains*

The cross-sectional regression result, reported in Table 5, show significant differences in the two-country samples. In the U.S. sample, two main variables LRNDEAL and FIRMSIZE are significant whereas none of the explanatory variables in the Hong Kong sample is significant at any level. The coefficient on LRNDEAL is positive and significant at the 10% level in the U.S. sample, supporting the

Table 5. Cross-sectional regressions.

	U.S. JVs			Hong Kong JVs		
	All (1)	Large firms (2)	Small firms (3)	All (4)	Large firms (5)	Small firms (6)
Intercept	17.93	11.26	34.51	−0.15	−6.90	−25.66
	(3.39**)	(0.92)	(2.33**)	(−0.02)	(−0.64)	(−0.89)
LRNDEAL	1.20	0.80	−0.65	−0.92	−0.73	−1.89
	(1.77*)	(1.55)	(−0.24)	(−1.09)	(−0.98)	(−1.01)
FIRMSIZE	−0.80	−0.49	−1.60	0.09	0.37	1.68
	(2.97**)	(−0.90)	(2.16**)	(0.21)	(0.70)	(1.02)
MULTN	0.01	0.01	0.06	0.11	0.19	−0.33
	(0.33)	(0.58)	(0.39)	(1.52)	(3.40**)	(−1.37)
SEASIA	−0.31	−0.46	0.08	−0.06	0.02	−0.45
	(−1.02)	(−2.21**)	(0.11)	(−0.35)	(0.15)	(−0.92)
HITECH	−2.09	−1.05	−2.15	−0.07	−2.80	2.14
	(−1.64)	(−0.96)	(−0.93)	(−0.05)	(−1.72*)	(0.91)
R^2	0.13	0.17	0.13	0.04	0.33	0.11

Note: *Significant at the 0.10 level, **significant at the 0.05 level and ***significant at the 0.01 level. Estimated coefficients and *t*-statistics (in parentheses) from regressing the five-day ($t = -2$ to $t = +2$) CARs (−2, 2) at the announcements of Chinese joint ventures by Hong Kong and U.S. firms on hypothesized variables:

$$\text{CARs}_{j(-2,+2)} = \alpha_0 + \beta_1\text{LRNDEAL} + \beta_2\text{FIRMSIZE} + \beta_3\text{MULTN} + \beta_4\text{SEASIA} + \beta_5\text{HITECH}$$

LRNDEAL is the number of joint venture deals by investing firms during 1989–1995 period. FIRMSIZE is the log of book value of total assets measured in U.S. dollars for investing firm. MULTN is the number of foreign subsidiaries of investing firm except in Southeast Asia and China. SEASIA is the number of subsidiaries in Southeast Asia for investing firms. HITECH is a dummy variable with 1 for high technology joint ventures and 0 otherwise. Firms with book value of assets less than the median book value in their country sample are defined as small firms in that country sample, the rest as the large firms.

hypothesis that the larger the cultural distance, the higher is the impact of prior business experience on shareholder value for foreign partners.

The coefficient on FIRMSIZE, on the other hand, has a negative sign for the U.S. firms, implying that the larger firm size is a competitive disadvantage rather than an advantage for the U.S. firms in Chinese ventures, contrary to the home market size hypothesis. For Hong Kong firms, firm size has the predicted positive sign but is not significant at any reasonable level. The prior experience in Southeast Asia (SEASIA) and the high technology ventures (HITECH), on the other hand, have negative impact on value creation for the U.S. firms. For the Hong Kong firms, gains are positively related to the degree of the multinational network (MULTN), consistent with the prediction of the multinational network hypothesis. We also examine whether our results are sensitive to the inclusion of year dummies and industry dummies. We find the results remain the same (results not reported here).

Furthermore, we perform a robustness check for the non-size firm characteristics by splitting the sample into large and small firms based on the median size of firms in each sample. The differences in the results for the two countries are even more pronounced in these size-based sub-samples. Two important conclusions can be drawn from this analysis. First, the U.S. sample analysis shows that learning experience (LRNDEAL) is important for large firm (as the *t*-statistics change from 1.77 in column (1) to 1.55 in column (2)) whereas the negative impact of firm size on wealth effect is more pronounced for small firms (as the coefficient on FIRMSIZE increases from −0.80 in column (1) to −1.60 in column (3)).

This implies that the smaller is a U.S. firm, the larger is the abnormal gain associated with the announcement of the joint ventures. We also observe that the coefficient on SEASIA for the U.S. large firms is negative and significant at the 5% level, implying that having a large number of subsidiaries in Southeast Asia does not lead to higher abnormal returns. Second, the comparison between the large and small Hong Kong firms shows that the main significance of the regression comes from the large firms. The coefficient of

MULTN for large Hong Kong firms is positive and significant at the 1% level, suggesting that experience in non-Asian countries also increases shareholder values. The coefficient on HITECH is negative and marginally significant at the 10% level.

In summary, the differences in the regression results in the two country samples support the notion that country-of-origin factors play an important role in value creation in international joint ventures in China. These results are generally consistent with the cultural distance theory but do not support that home market size is an advantage for the U.S. firms.

5. Summary and Conclusions

A rich theoretical and empirical literature on international business supports that a firm's nationality has a strong influence on its foreign investment strategy, yet few studies have explored whether it also plays a role in the success of the foreign ventures. In this study, we examine this issue by comparing the determinants of wealth effects in joint ventures in China for firms based in Hong Kong and U.S.

Our analysis shows three major findings. First, previous business experience in China is positively related to the wealth gains for the U.S. firms but it has no effect for the Hong Kong firms. This evidence is consistent with the prediction of the cultural distance theory that learning about the host country culture is important for the success of these ventures, especially for firms domiciled in culturally distant countries. Second, the evidence on the home market size theory is mixed and unclear. Firm size is negatively related to the wealth gains in the U.S. sample, contrary to that predicted by the home market size theory.

This variable has a positive sign in the Hong Kong sample but its coefficient is not significant at any reasonable level. Furthermore, the influence of firm size is driven largely by the smaller firms. The smaller Hong Kong firms, on average, earn large abnormal returns while their smaller U.S. counterparts experience losses around the announcements of the Chinese joint ventures, holding other factors constant. Finally, our results support the notion that the influence of the hypothesized determinants of the wealth effects in joint ventures is also different in the two country samples.

Our results should be interpreted with caution because of several limitations of our study. First, although we have controlled for several firm- and industry-specific factors suggested in the literature, such controls are imperfect. This limitation arises partly because our knowledge of the determinants of gains in international joint ventures is limited, and more importantly, because it is difficult to obtain comparable firm-level data for the non-U.S. firms. Second, several measures used in our study need further refinement. In particular, the number of deals in China is likely to be an inadequate measure of the learning of Chinese culture because such learning is a complex process and difficult to measure. Similarly, firm size may not be a good proxy for reflecting the advantages of the larger home markets.

In our sample, firm size is also highly positively correlated with the number of deals in China accentuating the problem of testing hypotheses. Moreover, many small- and medium-size investors from the Western countries form alliances with the Hong Kong firms to bridge the cultural gap for investing in China (Beamish and Wang, 1989; Plummer and Montes, 1995). Because of data limitations, we are unable to explicitly control for this effect in our study. These limitations weaken the power of our tests and provide some puzzling results. For example, it is difficult to understand why firm size would have the opposite sign for the U.S. and Hong Kong firms. Furthermore, why would this effect be dominant only in the smaller sub-samples.

One possibility is that firm size is also a proxy for the increased uncertainty associated with the Chinese institutional and political environment which has been evolving over the last two decades. Since larger firms generally undertake larger ventures compared to their smaller counterparts, the negative size effect in the U.S. sample may reflect the higher risk for these larger projects. Smaller projects for the U.S. firms also provide the firms valuable options to expand in future and thus may be perceived to be more valuable and less risky in the option valuation framework.

This interpretation is consistent with the findings by Chen *et al.* (1991) who find that the size of the foreign investment is the only determinant of the wealth gains in the Chinese joint ventures and is negatively related with the announcements effects for the U.S. firms in China. Alternatively, as argued by some researchers, it is plausible that larger U.S. firms may be motivated primarily by the desire to obtain prestige, and to engage in empire building rather than to maximize shareholder wealth (see e.g., Jensen, 1986; Rugman, 1980). These explanations need to be explored in future studies.

Despite these limitations, the striking differences in the cross-sectional regression results between our two-country samples suggest that the country-of-origin factors, ignored in previous studies, may play an important role in the wealth effects of the international joint ventures. Although, we have been unable to pinpoint the source of these differences in our study, our empirical findings suggest that predictions of the theories of foreign direct investment may be sensitive to different home and host country settings. More research is needed to fully identify and understand the sources of these differential effects. This is left for future research.

Endnotes

1. The book value of total assets for the U.S. and Hong Kong firms are denominated as the U.S. dollar and are reported as of the year ending immediately prior to the announcement of the joint venture. We collect the data for U.S. firms from the Compustat database and for Hong Kong firms from their annual reports.
2. Hu *et al.* (1992) suggest that China may be a special case because the Chinese way of conducting business is quite different from that in the developed countries. Since firms, with or without an established network, will experience similar problems in China, they may have difficulty in reaping full benefits from their well-established global network.

References

Barkema, HG, H Bell and J Pennings (1996). Foreign entry, cultural barriers and learning. *Strategic Management Journal*, 17(2), 151–166.

Beamish, PW and HY Wang (1989). Investing in China via joint ventures. *Management International Review*, 29(1), 57–64.

Borde, SF, AM Whyte, KJ Wiant and LL Hoffman (1998). New evidence on factors that influence the wealth effects of international joint ventures. *Journal of Multinational Financial Management*, 8(1), 63–77.

Chen, H, MY Hu and JCP Shieh (1991). The wealth effect of international joint ventures: The case of U.S. investment in China. *Financial Management*, 20(4), 31–41.

Chung, IY, KJ Koford and I Lee (1993). Stock market views of corporate multinationalism: Some evidence from announcements of international joint ventures. *Quarterly Review of Economics and Finance*, 33(3), 275–293.

Crutchley, CE, E Guo and RS Hansen (1991). Stockholder benefits from Japanese and U.S. joint ventures. *Financial Management*, 20(4), 22–30.

Dunning, JH (1992). The global economy, domestic governance, strategies and transnational corporations: Interactions and policy implications. *Transnational Corporations*, 1(3), 7–45.

Dunning, JH (1988). The eclectic paradigm of international production: A restatement and some possible extensions. *Journal of International Business Studies*, 19(1), 1–31.

Dunning, JH (1980). Toward an eclectic theory of international productions: Some empirical tests. *Journal of International Business Studies*, 11(1), 9–31.

Dunning, JH (1979). Explaining changing patterns of international production: In defense of the eclectic theory. *Oxford Bulletin of Economics and Statistics*, 41(4), 269–295.

Erramilli, MK (1996). Nationality and subsidiary ownership patterns in multinational corporations. *Journal of International Business Studies*, 27(2), 225–248.

Finnerty, JE, JE Owers and RC Rogers (1986). The valuation impact of joint ventures. *Management International Review*, 26(2), 14–26.

Harris, RS and D Ravenscraft (1991). The role of acquisitions in foreign direct investment: Evidence from the U.S. stock market. *Journal of Finance*, 46(3), 825--844.

Hennart, JF and J Larimo (1998). The impact of culture on the strategy of multinational enterprises: Does national origin affect ownership decisions? *Journal of International Business Studies*, 29(3), 515–538.

Hofstede, G (1980). The cultural relativity of organizational practices and theories. *Journal of International Business Studies*, 14(2), 75–89.

Hu, MY, H Chen and JC Shieh (1992). Impact of U.S. and China joint ventures on stockholder's wealth by degree of international involvement. *Management International Review*, 32(2), 135–148.

Jensen, MC (1986). Agency costs of free cash flow, corporate finance, and takeovers. *American Economic Review*, 76(2), 323–329.

Kogut, B and H Singh (1988). The effect of national culture on the choice of entry mode. *Journal of International Business Studies*, 19(3), 411–432.

Lee, I and SB Wyatt (1990). The effects of international joint ventures on shareholder wealth. *The Financial Review*, 25(4), 641–649.

Lummer, SL and JJ McConnell (1990). Stock valuation effects of international joint ventures. In *Pacific-Basin Capital Markets Research*, Rhee, SG and RP Chang (eds.). Elsevier Science Publishers.

Makino, S and PW Beamish (1998). The performance and survival of joint ventures with non-conventional ownership structures. *Journal of International Business Studies*, 29(4), 797–818.

Meschi, PX (2004). Valuation effect of international joint ventures: does experience matter? *International Business Review,* 13(5), 595–612.

Min, JH and LJ Prather (2001). Tobin's q, agency conflicts, and differential wealth effects of international joint ventures. *Global Finance Journal,* 12(2), 267–283.

Norburn, D, S Birley, M Dunn and A Payne (1990). A four-nation study of the relationship between marketing effectiveness, corporate culture, corporate values, and market orientation. *Journal of International Business Studies.* 21(3), 451–468.

Osland, GE and ST Cavusgil (1996). Performance issues in U.S. and China joint ventures. *California Management Review,* 38(2), 106–130.

Pan, Y (1997). The formation of Japanese and U.S. equity joint ventures in China. *Strategic Management Journal,* 18(3), 247–254.

Pan, Y (1996). Influences on foreign equity ownership level in joint ventures in China. *Journal of International Business Studies,* 27(1), 1–26.

Pan, Y and PSK Chi (1999). Financial performance and survival of multinational corporations in China. *Strategic Management Journal,* 20(4), 359–374.

Pan, Y and X Li (2000). Joint ventures formation of very large multinational firms. *Journal of International Business Studies,* 31(1), 179–189.

Park, SH and GR Ungson (1997). The effect of national culture, organizational complementarity, and economic motivation on joint venture dissolution. *Academy of Management Journal,* 40(2), 279–307.

Parkhe, A (1991). Interfirm diversity, organizational learning, and longevity in global strategic alliances. *Journal of International Business Studies,* 22(4), 579–601.

Plummer, M and M Montes (1995). Direct investment in China: An introduction. In *Emerging Patterns of East Asia Investment in China: From Korea, Taiwan, Hong Kong,* LaCroix, S, M Plummer and K Lee (eds.). East Gate Books.

Porter, ME (1990). *The Competitive Advantage of Nations.* London: Macmillan.

Porter, ME (1987). From competitive strategy to cooperative strategy. *Harvard Business Review,* 65(3), 43–59.

Rugman, AM (1980). Internalization as a general theory of foreign direct investment: A reappraisal of the literature. *Weltwirtschaftliches Archiv,* 116(2), 365–379.

Schroath, FW, MY Hu and H Chen (1993). Country-of-origin effects of foreign investments in the People's Republic of China. *Journal of International Business Studies,* 24(2), 277–290.

Tse, DK, Y Pan and KY Au (1997). How MNCs choose entry modes and form alliances: The China experience. *Journal of International Business Studies,* 28(4), 779–805.

Ueng, CJ, SH Kim and CC Lee (2000). The impact of firm's ownership advantages and economic status of destination country on the wealth effects of international joint ventures. *International Review of Financial Analysis,* 9(1), 67–76.

6

Maturity Transformation Strategies and Interest Rate Risk of Financial Institutions: Evidence from the German Market

Hendrik Scholz, Stephan Simon and Marco Wilkens

1. Introduction

The liquidity preference theory by Hicks (1946) postulates that investors have a preference for short-term, fixed-income investments due to their lower risk compared to long-term investments, while borrowers are presumed to favor long-term loans to secure a steady source of debt capital.[1] On a macroeconomic level, this necessitates a maturity transformation between these two macroeconomic sectors. Filling this gap is one of the major macroeconomic functions of the banking sector (Harrington, 1987; Johnson, 1994) and of financial institutions in general (Niehans, 1978). As a result, a mainly negative interest rate sensitivity of the equity value of financial institutions has been postulated and attributed at least to a large extent to the maturity mismatch of nominal assets and liabilities of financial institutions, as stated independently by Samuelson (1945) and Hicks (1946). This idea was formalized further and more generally in the framework of the nominal contracting hypothesis by French *et al.* (1983).[2]

The resulting exposure to interest rate risk of financial institutions is of interest to all stakeholders and is currently especially in the focus of banking regulators (Basel Committee on Banking Supervision, 2004). It has been extensively investigated and generally confirmed in various empirical studies of many national financial markets.[3] Staikouras (2003) provides a broad overview of empirical studies of the interest rate sensitivity of financial institutions since the late 1970s, when Stone first suggested the principal regression approach to test for interest rate sensitivity in stock returns in the context of a two-factor model (market factor and interest rate factor) (Stone, 1974). However, all these approaches do not allow one to estimate the underlying maturity transformation conducted by financial institutions.

This study advances the conventionally used approaches, analyzing the interest rate sensitivity of stock returns by introducing *maturity transformation factors* to better capture the maturity mismatch of financial institutions' assets and liabilities.[4] Additionally, this allows the effective maturities of assets and liabilities of financial institutions to be estimated for the first time based on publicly available stock market and interest rate data.

In our empirical analysis, we study the interest rate sensitivity of several German financial services sector (sub)indices applying both the conventional approaches used in the literature and the maturity transformation factors introduced here. Our results for the financial services index can be interpreted as the maturity transformation provided by the listed German financial services firms as a whole. Furthermore, we take a look at the maturity transformation exposure and its contribution to total return and risk of financial institutions.

This chapter is organized as follows. Section 2 theoretically analyzes the effect of interest rate changes on the net present value of a position of mismatched nominal assets and liabilities. Subsequent to a review of commonly used regression approaches to estimate interest rate sensitivities of stock returns, we derive the maturity transformation factor as an innovative factor to explain stock returns. Section 3 presents data and results of our empirical analysis and examines the significance and explanatory power of maturity transformation factors in comparison to conventional interest rate factors. Finally, we analyze the estimated effective maturities of assets and liabilities of financial and non-financial institutions in the German market. Section 4 concludes.

2. Interest Rate Sensitivities and Empirical Tests

2.1. *Principal Regression Approach*

The equity value of a notional financial institution NPV_E can be interpreted as the difference between the net present values of its credit risk-free assets NPV_A and liabilities NPV_L. These values are defined as the cash flows from nominal assets and nominal liabilities of maturities $m = 1, \ldots, T$, discounted at the corresponding risk-free market spot rates $r_{rf,m}$ (e.g., Unal and Kane, 1988; Staikouras, 2003)[5]:

$$NPV_E = NPV_A - NPV_L = \sum_{m=1}^{T} \frac{A_m}{(1 + r_{rf,m})^m} - \sum_{m=1}^{T} \frac{L_m}{(1 + r_{rf,m})^m}. \tag{1}$$

If assets and liabilities of a financial institution are not exactly matched regarding their amounts and maturities, changes in the term structure of interest rates will differently affect the net present values of its assets and liabilities, resulting in a change of the financial institution's equity value. Assuming the average asset maturity to be larger than the average liability maturity, an increase in interest rates should result in a larger decrease in the assets' than in the liabilities' net present value, yielding a decreasing equity value of the financial institution. This relationship becomes obvious if changes in the net present values ΔNPV to parallel shifts of the term structure of interest rates Δr_{rf} are approximated by the modified duration of assets mD_A and liabilities mD_L (e.g., Bierwag, 1987), as first suggested in principle by Samuelson (1945) and Hicks (1946)[6]:

$$\Delta NPV_E = \Delta NPV_A - \Delta NPV_L = \Delta r_{rf}(-mD_A)NPV_A - \Delta r_{rf}(-mD_L)NPV_L. \tag{2a}$$

Defining $\rho = NPV_E/NPV_A$ as the equity-to-assets-ratio at market values one obtains:

$$\begin{aligned}\Delta NPV_E &= \Delta r_{rf}\,(-mD_E)\,NPV_E \\ &= \Delta r_{rf}\left(-\left(mD_A\frac{1}{\rho} - mD_L\frac{1-\rho}{\rho}\right)\right)NPV_E. \qquad (2b)\end{aligned}$$

The modified duration of the equity value mD_E is thus the market value-weighted, modified duration of assets mD_A and liabilities mD_L of the financial institution. A mainly negative interest rate sensitivity of the equity value of financial institutions can thus be postulated based on the established assumption of financial institutions conducting positive maturity transformation, i.e., mD_A being larger than mD_L.

Equation (2b) provides the basic idea underlying the principal regression approach employed to test for interest rate sensitivities in stock return time-series. Dividing (2b) by NPV_E yields the definition of stock or index returns on the left-hand side, leaving the change in an interest rate factor times its sensitivity on the right-hand side. In this way, Stone (1974) extended the market model by including an interest rate factor resulting in the principal regression equation used in this and other empirical time-series studies:

$$\tilde{R}_{i,t} = \beta_{0,i} + \beta_{M,i}\tilde{R}_{M,t} + \beta_{Z,i}\tilde{Z}_t + \tilde{e}_{i,t}, \qquad (3)$$

$\beta_{0,i}$ being the average return component of stock (index) i not explained by the model, $\beta_{M,i}$ the sensitivity of the stock (index) returns $\tilde{R}_{i,t}$ to the market factor $\tilde{R}_{M,t}$, $\beta_{Z,i}$ the corresponding sensitivity to the interest rate factor $\tilde{Z}_t$, and $\tilde{e}_{i,t}$ being a stationary error term in period t with an expected value of zero.

Three degrees of freedom have to be substantiated when actually employing the regression approach of Eq. (3): (i) the form of the interest rate factor $\tilde{Z}_t$, (ii) the maturity m of the interest rate considered and (iii) the treatment of multicollinearity in the explanatory factors. Concerning (i) two approaches are used in empirical studies: firstly, *holding period returns* $\tilde{R}_{rf,m,t}$ of risk-free fixed-income securities or indices of a given constant maturity m are applied (e.g., Fogler *et al.*, 1981; Flannery and James, 1984a, b; Unal and Kane, 1988).

In the following, zero coupon bond prices $P_{m,t}$ of maturity m are considered:

$$R_{rf,m,t} = \frac{P_{m-1,t} - P_{m,t-1}}{P_{m,t-1}}. \tag{4}$$

Secondly, *interest rate differentials* $\Delta\tilde{r}_{rf,m,t}$ for risk-free investments of maturity m are used, as, e.g., in Chance and Lane (1980).[7] Here the risk-free spot rates $r_{rf,m,t}$ are based on the corresponding zero coupon bond prices $P_{m,t}$:

$$\Delta r_{rf,m,t} = r_{rf,m,t} - r_{rf,m,t-1}. \tag{5}$$

The first approach allows for an easy replication of the interest rate factor using standard fixed-income securities. Moreover, it straightforwardly allows us to calculate an ex-post risk premium. Additionally, following Eq. (2b), holding period returns also incorporate non-linear effects of interest rate changes on stock returns in contrast to only direct linear effects being considered in interest rate differentials. On the other hand, sensitivities $\beta_{Z,i}$ resulting from interest rate differentials can immediately be interpreted as the modified duration of the financial institution's equity mD_E in Eq. (2b).

The second degree of freedom (ii) is the maturity m of the chosen interest rate factor. As there is no economic theory suggesting a specific maturity m to be considered in the interest rate factor, any single as well as any mix of empirically observable maturities can be found for the interest rate factor in empirical studies — with a slight trend towards longer maturities.

The treatment of empirical correlations between the returns of the market index and the interest rate factor, as the third degree of freedom (iii) in applying Eq. (3), is discussed, e.g., in Giliberto (1985).[8] From an econometric point of view, the sensitivity of the unorthogonalized variable will not be biased by either orthogonalizing $\tilde{R}_{M,t}$ by $\tilde{Z}_t$ or $\tilde{Z}_t$ by $\tilde{R}_{M,t}$ before using the respective time-series as explanatory variables in Eq. (3). However, orthogonalizing $\tilde{Z}_t$ by $\tilde{R}_{M,t}$ yields an interest rate factor that only contains the interest rate variability additional to the one already contained in the market factor. Thus, this approach captures the *extra-market interest rate sensitivity*. On the other hand, if one seeks to measure the whole interest rate exposure of financial institutions, orthogonalizing $\tilde{R}_{M,t}$ by $\tilde{Z}_t$ is the appropriate approach. Here the *total interest rate sensitivity* is captured via the unorthogonalized interest rate factor $\tilde{Z}_t$.

The third conceivable alternative is no orthogonalization at all and yields the same sensitivity for the interest rate factor as orthogonalizing $\tilde{Z}_t$ by $\tilde{R}_{M,t}$. Since in this study the interest factor is the primary focus, this alternative need not be investigated further. Additionally, it does not allow for a complete and unequivocal decomposition of the variance of the dependent variable because it fails to eliminate a potential correlation between the two explanatory variables (e.g., Bessler and Opfer, 2003).

2.2. *Derivation of the Maturity Transformation Factors*

The aforementioned forms of the interest rate factor implicitly assume stock prices react — at least approximately — only to interest rate changes in one maturity or to averaged changes across a spectrum of maturities. They do not account for the fact that all possible changes in the form of the term structure of interest rates will affect stock prices. Parametric models describing the static form of the term structure of interest rates for a given point in time (see, e.g., Nelson and Siegel, 1987), as well as its dynamic intertemporal behavior (see, e.g., Bühler *et al.*, 1999), require at least two factors to achieve an adequate and realistic description and modeling of the actual term structure. Moreover, by accepting average asset and liability maturities of financial institutions to differ at least partially and temporarily, in general a minimum of at least two maturities becomes relevant which have opposite effects on the equity value of financial institutions.

Both arguments suggest that more than one maturity should be considered in the empirical investigation of interest rate sensitivities of financial institutions. The most obvious consequence would be to consider at least two distinct interest rate factors of different underlying maturities within the principal regression approach (Lynge and Zumwalt, 1980; Fogler *et al.*, 1981; Oertmann *et al.*, 2000). This usually results in the problem of multicollinearity of these two factors. If orthogonalization of one of these two interest rate factors with respect to the other is chosen as a remedy, the orthogonalized interest rate factor can no longer be interpreted immediately nor compared directly to the unorthogonalized interest rate factor.

Based on Sec. 2.1 (deducing the interest rate sensitivity of financial institutions), our innovative approach is to calculate holding period returns of maturity transformation strategies as explanatory variables. We calculate these returns as the return of a constant equity share in a maturity transformation position of nominal assets and liabilities of mismatched maturities m and n. Subsequently, we employ these *maturity transformation factors* in place of *conventional interest rate factors* in the two-factor model proposed by Stone (1974).

Econometrically, this strategy has the advantage of circumventing multicollinearity between individual interest rate factors of differing underlying maturities. Additionally, from an economic perspective, maturity transformation factors more appropriately represent the behavior of the equity value of maturity transformation strategies than holding period returns of a simple unleveraged long position of fixed-income securities. Moreover, the explicitly stated asset (m) and liability maturities (n) of the maturity transformation factors allow for an economic interpretation. They enable us to identify average maturity transformation strategies that come closest to the real interest rate exposure of financial institutions. Finally, by using holding period returns in the maturity transformation factors, ex-post risk premia for bearing interest rate risk can be calculated easily.

The holding period returns of maturity transformation (MT) strategies $\tilde{R}_{MT,m,n,t}$ are calculated from holding period returns $\tilde{R}_{rf,m,t}$ and $\tilde{R}_{rf,n,t}$ of assets and liabilities with a constant maturity m and n, respectively. To calculate the holding period returns, we use zero coupon bond prices $P_{m,t}$ and $P_{n,t}$ as in Eq. (4). Assuming a constant equity-to-assets-ratio at market values $\rho = NPV_E/NPV_A$ one obtains[9]:

$$\tilde{R}_{MT,m,n,t} = \frac{(1+\tilde{R}_{rf,m,t}) - (1+\tilde{R}_{rf,n,t})(1-\rho)}{\rho} - 1. \quad (6)$$

Thus, holding period returns of maturity transformation strategies are basically value-weighted holding period returns of its assets and liabilities in relation to the equity value of this maturity transformation position.

3. Empirical Analysis

3.1. *Data*

The stock market data used in this study have been obtained from the academic time-series database for the German capital market provided by the University of Karlsruhe (the DAFOX market index and ten subindices (see Göppl and Schütz, 1995): one general financial services index and nine non-financial services indices) and Datastream (nine financial services subindices). To yield comparable results to existing empirical studies of the interest rate sensitivity of stock returns, a monthly sampling frequency is employed throughout the whole sample period from January 1973 to December 2003. Copeland and Weston (1992) and Campbell *et al.* (1997) suggest using (holding period) excess returns in empirical studies for economic and econometrical reasons. Throughout the chapter, we use monthly returns in excess of the one-month German interbank rate.[10] The respective total excess return (holding period)[11] time-series are $\tilde{R}_{i,t}$ and $\tilde{R}_{M,t}$. Table 1 contains the descriptive statistics of the stock indices examined.

To compute holding period returns of zero coupon bonds and interest rate differentials we use German (Deutsch Mark/Euro) risk-free spot rates for maturities m ranging from one year to ten years in yearly intervals. All interest rate data employed are available from the time series database of the German central bank (Deutsche Bundesbank). Table 2 shows the descriptive statistics for the respective monthly holding period returns in excess of the one-month interbank rate and monthly interest rate differentials according to Eqs. (4) and (5).

For the maturity transformation factor, all 100 maturity combinations, which can be created based on the aforementioned ten risk-free spot rates, have been considered. A constant equity-to-assets

Table 1. Descriptive statistics for monthly excess returns of stock indices, January 1973 to December 2003.

Index description	Basic descriptive statistics Mean (%)	Standard deviation (%)	Test for normal distribution[a] (%)
Market index	0.35	5.17	0.00
Financial services sector stock indices and subindices			
General Financial Services Index	0.49	6.47	0.00
General Bank Index	0.31	6.59	0.00
All large cap universal banks[b]	0.42	7.45	0.00
All other small cap banks[b]	0.17	4.18	0.00
All real estate banks[b]	0.28	4.23	0.00
General Insurance Index	0.66	7.58	0.00
Large cap composite insurance index	0.59	7.84	0.00
Small cap composite insurance index	0.59	5.88	0.00
Life insurance index	0.67	8.62	0.00
Reinsurance index	0.71	10.76	0.00
Non-financial services sector stock indices			
Automotive/mechanical engineering	0.55	6.56	0.00
Chemicals/pharmaceuticals	0.53	5.14	0.00
Construction/building materials	0.19	6.32	0.00
Consumer goods/entertainment	0.17	4.17	0.00
Electrical industry/electronics	0.52	8.00	0.00
Steel industry/metal industry	0.67	7.17	0.00
Transportation	0.70	8.40	0.00
Utilities	0.40	4.03	2.31
Other industries	0.24	6.42	0.00

[a]Probability of error when rejecting the null hypothesis that the time-series of monthly excess returns follows a normal distribution, based on the with two degrees of freedom χ^2-distributed *Jarque-Berra*-test-statistic.
[b]All banks in the respective segment available from the Datastream financial time-series database weighted according to their respective market values.

ratio of $\rho = 10\%$ has been set for the calculation of the maturity transformation strategies' returns $\tilde{R}_{MT,m,n,t}$ assuming a constant equity capital base at market values and,[12] therefore, implicitly respective monthly equity payments out of or into the maturity transformation portfolio. Table 3 summarizes the descriptive statistics for all maturity transformation strategies considered. We later restrict our sample to maturity transformation factors yielding positive regression coefficients $\beta_{MT,n,m,i}$ so as to consider only maturity transformation strategies with positive equity shares ρ.

Table 2. Descriptive statistics for monthly conventional interest rate factor time-series, January 1973 to December 2003.

	Panel A: Holding period excess returns[a]			Panel B: Interest rate differentials		
	Basic descriptive statistics			Basic descriptive statistics		
Maturity	Mean (%)	Standard deviation (%)	Test for normal distribution[b] (%)	Mean (%)	Standard deviation (%)	Test for normal distribution[b] (%)
1 year	0.03	0.33	0.00	−0.013	0.39	0.00
2 years	0.09	0.58	0.00	−0.015	0.34	0.00
3 years	0.12	0.79	0.00	−0.014	0.31	0.00
4 years	0.15	0.96	0.00	−0.013	0.29	0.00
5 years	0.16	1.10	0.00	−0.013	0.28	0.00
6 years	0.18	1.24	0.00	−0.012	0.27	0.00
7 years	0.19	1.36	0.00	−0.012	0.26	0.00
8 years	0.20	1.48	0.00	−0.012	0.26	0.00
9 years	0.20	1.59	0.00	−0.012	0.26	0.00
10 years	0.21	1.70	0.00	−0.011	0.26	0.00

[a]Holding period excess returns of a simple, unleveraged long position in a single zero bond of a given constant maturity m.
[b]Probability of error when rejecting the null hypothesis that the time-series of monthly excess returns/interest rate differentials follows a normal distribution, based on the with two degrees of freedom χ^2-distributed *Jarque-Berra*-test-statistic.

3.2. *Comparison of Interest Rate Factor*

Kane and Unal (1988), Bessler and Opfer (2003, 2005), and Reilly *et al.* (2005) find pronounced intertemporal variations in interest rate sensitivities of stock returns. Correspondingly, the approach pursued here focuses on investigating the interest rate sensitivity of financial institutions for monthly rolling 60-month subperiods across the whole sample period to capture variations in the significance and explanatory power of the interest rate factors. To compare the adequacy of the introduced maturity transformation factors with those of conventional forms of the interest rate factor, variations across all combinations of the three degrees of freedom have been estimated. Then, we proceed with the ones yielding minimal p-values[13] with respect to different maturities. The results are of particular interest to shareholders to better understand the interest

Table 3. Descriptive statistics for monthly excess returns of maturity transformation strategies, January 1973 to December 2003.

Maturity	Liabilities (%)									
assets	1 year	2 years	3 years	4 years	5 years	6 years	7 years	8 years	9 years	10 years
Panel A: Mean of monthly excess returns										
1 year	0.03	−0.51	−0.84	−1.06	−1.21	−1.33	−1.42	−1.50	−1.57	−1.63
2 years	0.62	0.09	−0.25	−0.47	−0.62	−0.74	−0.83	−0.91	−0.98	−1.04
3 years	0.99	0.45	0.12	−0.10	−0.25	−0.37	−0.46	−0.54	−0.61	−0.67
4 years	1.23	0.70	0.37	0.15	−0.01	−0.12	−0.22	−0.29	−0.36	−0.42
5 years	1.40	0.87	0.54	0.32	0.16	0.05	−0.05	−0.12	−0.19	−0.25
6 years	1.53	1.00	0.67	0.45	0.29	0.18	0.08	0.01	−0.06	−0.12
7 years	1.63	1.10	0.77	0.55	0.40	0.28	0.19	0.11	0.04	−0.02
8 years	1.72	1.19	0.86	0.64	0.48	0.37	0.27	0.20	0.13	0.07
9 years	1.79	1.26	0.93	0.71	0.56	0.44	0.35	0.27	0.20	0.14
10 years	1.86	1.33	1.00	0.78	0.63	0.51	0.42	0.34	0.27	0.21
Panel B: Standard deviation of monthly excess returns										
1 year	0.33	2.65	4.69	6.31	7.70	8.96	10.13	11.24	12.30	13.36
2 years	3.38	0.58	1.88	3.71	5.27	6.66	7.93	9.12	10.27	11.40
3 years	5.64	2.98	0.79	1.42	3.08	4.58	5.96	7.23	8.44	9.64
4 years	7.43	4.97	2.76	0.96	1.21	2.71	4.14	5.49	6.78	8.05
5 years	8.97	6.67	4.56	2.69	1.10	1.10	2.45	3.83	5.19	6.54
6 years	10.36	8.18	6.19	4.37	2.68	1.24	1.07	2.29	3.67	5.10
7 years	11.66	9.58	7.68	5.92	4.25	2.70	1.36	1.11	2.26	3.69
8 years	12.88	10.88	9.06	7.37	5.75	4.21	2.75	1.48	1.21	2.35
9 years	14.05	12.13	10.38	8.76	7.21	5.71	4.25	2.84	1.59	1.33
10 years	15.22	13.37	11.67	10.13	8.65	7.21	5.79	4.37	2.96	1.70

(Continued)

Table 3. (*Continued*)

Maturity assets	Liabilities (%)									
	1 year	2 years	3 years	4 years	5 years	6 years	7 years	8 years	9 years	10 years
Panel C: Test for normal distribution[a]										
1 year	0.00	0.00	0.00	0.16	0.02	0.00	0.00	0.00	0.00	0.00
2 years	0.00	0.00	1.25	0.09	0.01	0.00	0.00	0.00	0.00	0.00
3 years	0.00	0.10	0.00	0.04	0.10	0.13	0.11	0.08	0.10	0.23
4 years	0.03	0.02	0.00	0.00	15.46	25.66	8.29	3.41	2.39	3.12
5 years	0.00	0.00	0.00	0.00	0.00	0.03	45.18	16.69	9.83	8.80
6 years	0.00	0.00	0.00	0.00	0.00	0.00	0.00	4.67	6.68	2.33
7 years	0.00	0.00	0.00	0.00	0.00	0.00	0.00	0.00	0.00	0.00
8 years	0.00	0.00	0.00	0.00	0.00	0.00	0.00	0.00	0.00	0.00
9 years	0.00	0.00	0.00	0.00	0.01	0.01	0.01	0.00	0.00	0.00
10 years	0.00	0.00	0.00	0.02	0.08	0.15	0.10	0.02	0.00	0.00

[a]Probability of error when rejecting the null hypothesis that the time-series of monthly excess returns follows a normal distribution, based on the with two degrees of freedom χ^2-distributed *Jarque-Berra*-test-statistic.

rate maturities they are implicitly exposed to via stock holdings in financial institutions.

For each investigated financial services index, Table 4 contains the share of all rolling 60-month subperiods yielding a significant regression coefficient for the respective interest rate factors used: interest

Table 4. Significance of interest rate factors.

		Share of subperiods with significant sensitivities to interest rate factor[a]		
Index description	Orthogonalization	Interest rate differentials (%)	Holding period returns[b] (%)	Maturity transformation strategies[c] (%)
General Financial Services Index	Total interest rate sensitivity	**100.0**	**100.0**	**100.0**
	Extra-market interest rate sensitivity	66.0	65.3	**75.7**
General Bank Index	Total interest rate sensitivity	**99.4**	97.4	98.9
	Extra-market interest rate sensitivity	87.5	86.2	**91.0**
All large cap universal banks[d]	Total interest rate sensitivity	98.7	97.4	**100.0**
	Extra-market interest rate sensitivity	82.7	84.9	**86.8**
All other small cap banks[d]	Total interest rate sensitivity	95.5	93.3	**95.6**
	Extra-market interest rate sensitivity	68.6	63.5	**73.5**
All real estate banks[d]	Total interest rate sensitivity	63.1	55.4	**54.0**
	Extra-market interest rate sensitivity	50.6	42.9	**55.8**
General Insurance Index	Total interest rate sensitivity	**100.0**	99.7	**100.0**
	Extra-market interest rate sensitivity	61.2	59.0	**67.2**
Large cap composite insurance index	Total interest rate sensitivity	**100.0**	99.7	**100.0**
	Extra-market interest rate sensitivity	53.8	51.0	**70.1**
Small cap composite insurance index	Total interest rate sensitivity	**89.1**	75.0	81.7
	Extra-market interest rate sensitivity	47.8	44.6	**59.2**

(*Continued*)

Table 4. (*Continued*)

Index description	Orthogonalization	Share of subperiods with significant sensitivities to interest rate factor[a]		
		Interest rate differentials (%)	Holding period returns[b] (%)	Maturity transformation strategies[c] (%)
Life insurance index	Total interest rate sensitivity	**64.1**	52.2	**64.1**
	Extra-market interest rate sensitivity	34.9	28.5	**41.0**
Reinsurance index	Total interest rate sensitivity	**98.1**	97.2	**98.1**
	Extra-market interest rate sensitivity	26.2	24.3	**67.3**

[a]Significance assumed for p-values (probabilities of error) of less than 10%; for each subperiod t and for each interest rate factor the maturity m/maturity combination m, n yielding the lowest p-value has been considered; interest rate factor yielding highest share of subperiods with significant sensitivities marked in bold.
[b]Holding period excess returns of a simple, unleveraged long position in a single zero bond of a given constant maturity m.
[c]Holding period excess returns of a maturity transformation strategy of two zero bonds of given constant maturities m and n.
[d]All banks in the respective segment available from the Datastream financial time-series database weighted according to their respective market values.

rate differentials, holding period returns of zero coupon bonds, and holding period returns of maturity transformation strategies. Returns are in excess of the one-month interbank rate. Results for both orthogonalization options regarding the explanatory variables are shown: total interest rate sensitivity and extra-market interest rate sensitivity. The regression coefficient is assumed to be significantly different from zero at the 10% confidence level. The t-tests are based on error terms corrected for autocorrelation and heteroskedasticity according to Newey and West (1987).

Table 4 presents the portion of all rolling 60-month subperiods across the full sample period that yield p-values of less than 10% for the regression coefficients (sensitivities) with respect to interest rate factors. The maturity transformation factors are significant most frequently for almost all German financial services indices. In particular, they perform better than holding period returns of simple, unleveraged long positions in single zero coupon bonds.

The unambiguously higher proportions of subperiods showing significant sensitivities mostly close to unity for the total interest rate sensitivity (market returns are orthogonalized by regressing them on the interest rate factor) could be expected, given the fact that these interest rate factors hold all the interest rate variability otherwise already contained in the market factor. On the other hand, the results for the extra-market interest rate sensitivities (interest rate factors are orthogonalized by regressing them on the market factor) suggest that there are subperiods for which no significant extra-market interest rate sensitivity and thus extra-market interest rate risk is assumed by the financial services sector. Evidently, banks possess significant extra-market interest rate sensitivities more often than insurances. Additionally, the gain from using maturity transformation strategies with respect to this metric is higher for insurances.

For each investigated financial services index, Table 5 contains the averaged portion across all rolling 60-month subperiods of the stock indices' excess return variance explained by the variance of the respective interest rate factors used: interest rate differentials, holding period returns of zero coupon bonds, and holding period returns of maturity transformation strategies. Results for both

Table 5. Explanatory power of interest rate factors.

		Average portion of return variance explained by interest rate factor[a]		
Index description	Orthogonalization	Interest rate differentials (%)	Holding period returns[b] (%)	Maturity transformation strategies[c] (%)
General Financial Services Index	Total interest rate sensitivity	15.6	15.1	**15.8**
	Extra-market interest rate sensitivity	1.9	2.0	**2.0**
General Bank Index	Total interest rate sensitivity	17.2	17.7	**19.2**
	Extra-market interest rate sensitivity	3.0	3.0	**3.3**

(*Continued*)

Table 5. (*Continued*)

Index description	Orthogonalization	Average portion of return variance explained by interest rate factor[a]		
		Interest rate differentials (%)	Holding period returns[b] (%)	Maturity transformation strategies[c] (%)
All large cap universal banks[d]	Total interest rate sensitivity	17.8	18.2	**19.2**
	Extra-market interest rate sensitivity	3.4	**3.4**	3.4
All other small cap banks[d]	Total interest rate sensitivity	13.5	13.4	**15.1**
	Extra-market interest rate sensitivity	2.4	2.5	**3.1**
All real estate banks[d]	Total interest rate sensitivity	8.3	8.2	**8.4**
	Extra-market interest rate sensitivity	3.8	3.4	**4.1**
General Insurance Index	Total interest rate sensitivity	13.1	12.9	**14.3**
	Extra-market interest rate sensitivity	1.9	1.9	**2.1**
Large cap composite insurance index	Total interest rate sensitivity	13.1	12.8	**13.7**
	Extra-market interest rate sensitivity	2.0	1.8	**2.4**
Small cap composite insurance index	Total interest rate sensitivity	8.5	7.7	**8.8**
	Extra-market interest rate sensitivity	2.5	2.3	**3.5**
Life insurance index	Total interest rate sensitivity	6.7	6.2	**6.9**
	Extra-market interest rate sensitivity	2.1	1.9	**2.9**
Reinsurance index	Total interest rate sensitivity	7.7	7.0	**11.2**
	Extra-market interest rate sensitivity	2.0	1.8	**3.2**

[a] Interest rate factor yielding highest average explained portion of stock index excess return variance marked in bold; for each subperiod t the maturity m/maturity combination m, n yielding the lowest p-value has been considered in each interest rate factor.
[b] Holding period excess returns of a simple, unleveraged long position in a single zero bond of a given constant maturity m.
[c] Holding period excess returns of a maturity transformation strategy of two zero bonds of given constant maturities m and n.
[d] All banks in the respective segment available from the Datastream financial time-series database weighted according to their respective market values.

orthogonalization options regarding the explanatory variables are shown: total interest rate sensitivity and extra-market interest rate sensitivity.

Table 5 contains the proportion of return variance explained by the interest rate factor averaged across all rolling 60-month subperiods. A comparison between the maturity transformation factor and the two conventional forms of the interest rate factor yields even clearer results in favor of a higher explanatory power of maturity transformation factors than comparing the significance of factor sensitivities. The maturity transformation strategies de facto always possess the highest average explanatory power. This also supports the theoretic reasoning in favor of maturity transformation factors described in Sec. 2.2.

Also the postulated difference between the two orthogonalization alternatives is clearly reflected in the strongly differing explanatory power of the two alternative interest rate factor representations. Regardless of the orthogonalization alternative used, all forms of interest rate factors perform better for bank indices compared to insurance indices in terms of average explanatory power — indicating the peculiarity of banks among all financial institutions in bearing interest rate risk (Harrington, 1987; Johnson, 1994).

The intertemporal variations in the explanatory power of all three interest rate factors are illustrated in Fig. 1 for the General Bank and General Insurance Indices in both orthogonalization alternatives. These variations become more obvious when compared to the averages of the explanatory power presented in Table 5.

Most obvious are the periods of generally high versus low explanatory power of interest rate factors. Especially during periods of generally low explanatory power of these factors, meaningful differences between the explanatory power of the three factors can be observed — usually the maturity transformation strategies doing best or at least second best in terms of stock index variance explained. During periods of generally relative high interest rates, inverse term structures, and interest rate turbulences, such as in the late 1970s to early 1980s, the early 1990s, and — though to a lesser extent — also in the first few years of the 21st century, the explanatory power

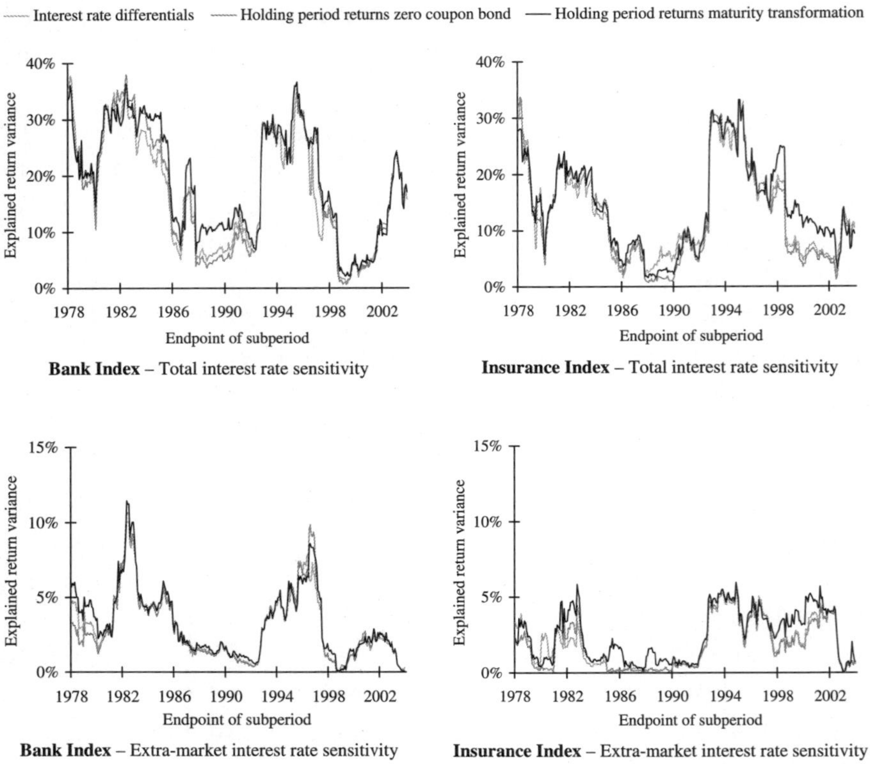

Figure 1. Explained return variance for General Bank Index and General Insurance Index.

of the interest rate factors drop, because no stable interest rate sensitivity can be identified throughout these periods. This could indicate adjustment behavior of the financial institutions as suggested by the findings of Hirtle (1997). Bessler and Opfer (2003) find similar patterns over time regarding the explanatory power of conventional interest rate factors for the German market.

Finally, despite the general big-picture patterns for both financial services, sector indices being similar, marked differences can be identified during certain periods. While the variance explained by the interest rate factors declines nearly to zero for the General Bank Index in the second half of the 1990s, these factors maintain a relatively stable explanatory power for the General Insurance Index. This difference might be explained by the different roles of these two financial services subsectors with respect to interest rate risk as mentioned before. In particular, banks seem to adjust strongly to interest rate risk, producing large swings of the explanatory power of interest rate factors as suggested also by Harrington (1987) and Johnson (1994).

3.3. *Capital Markets Based Maturity Estimates for Financial Institutions*

In Sec. 3.2, interest rate factor maturities yielding the lowest *p*-values for each rolling 60-month subperiod are identified. Regarding the maturity transformation factors, these are considered as estimates of the effective maturities of the underlying financial institutions' assets and liabilities from an external shareholder's perspective. Table 6 and

Table 6. Financial services sector stock indices and subindices: Maturities yielding minimal *p*-values by interest rate factors averaged across all subperiods.

		Maturities yielding min. *p*-values by interest rate factor averaged across all subperiods[a]			
Index description	Orthogonalization	Interest rate differentials	Holding period returns[b]	Maturity transformation strategies[c]	
General Financial Services index	Total interest rate sensitivity	4.7	6.2	5.5	2.9
	Extra-market interest rate sensitivity	3.9	3.9	4.9	3.1
General Bank Index	Total interest rate sensitivity	6.5	6.8	5.6	3.4
	Extra-market interest rate sensitivity	5.3	5.6	5.3	3.9
All large cap universal banks[d]	Total interest rate sensitivity	6.2	6.4	5.8	3.4
	Extra-market interest rate sensitivity	4.8	5.5	4.8	2.9
All other small cap banks[d]	Total interest rate sensitivity	4.3	6.1	5.3	3.3
	Extra-market interest rate sensitivity	3.1	3.1	5.1	3.2
All real estate banks[d]	Total interest rate sensitivity	2.8	2.9	5.4	3.9
	Extra-market interest rate sensitivity	2.3	2.8	5.6	6.2

(*Continued*)

Table 6. (*Continued*)

Index description	Orthogonalization	Maturities yielding min. p-values by interest rate factor averaged across all subperiods[a]			
		Interest rate differentials	Holding period returns[b]	Maturity transformation strategies[c]	
General Insurance Index	Total interest rate sensitivity	6.6	8.3	7.5	4.2
	Extra-market interest rate sensitivity	4.0	3.9	5.6	4.1
Large cap composite insurance index	Total interest rate sensitivity	7.0	8.5	7.8	4.6
	Extra-market interest rate sensitivity	3.6	3.6	5.8	4.1
Small cap composite insurance index	Total interest rate sensitivity	5.3	5.5	6.9	4.7
	Extra-market interest rate sensitivity	2.8	2.5	6.0	5.6
Life insurance index	Total interest rate sensitivity	2.4	2.6	5.4	4.1
	Extra-market interest rate sensitivity	1.9	1.9	4.5	5.3
Reinsurance index	Total interest rate sensitivity	7.8	8.1	8.0	5.8
	Extra-market interest rate sensitivity	2.6	2.4	8.3	6.5

[a]For each subperiod t and each interest rate factor the maturity m/maturity combination m, n yielding the lowest p-value has been considered.
[b]Holding period excess returns of a simple, unleveraged long position in one zero bond of a given constant maturity m.
[c]Holding period excess returns of a maturity transformation strategy of two zero bonds of given constant maturities m and n; first column: estimated average asset maturity m, second column: estimated average liability maturity n.
[d]All banks in the respective segment available from the Datastream financial time-series database weighted according to their respective market values.

Table 7 report these estimates for various German financial services and non-financial services indices averaged across all subperiods.

For each investigated financial (non-financial) services stock index, Table 6 (Table 7) lists the average across all rolling 60-month subperiods of maturities m (and maturity combinations m, n, respectively) which, during the individual 60-month subperiod, yield the minimal p-values for the respective interest rate factor used: interest

Table 7. Non-financial services sector stock indices: Maturities yielding minimal p-values by interest rate factors averaged across all subperiods.

		Maturities yielding min. p-values by interest rate factor averaged across all subperiods[a]			
Index description	Orthogonalization	Interest rate differentials	Holding period returns[b]		Maturity transformation strategies[c]
Automotive/ mech. engineering	Total interest rate sensitivity	6.5	8.3	8.3	4.6
	Extra-market interest rate sensitivity	2.4	2.8	3.3	5.3
Chemicals/ pharmaceuticals	Total interest rate sensitivity	4.9	5.9	7.4	4.3
	Extra-market interest rate sensitivity	1.1	1.3	4.4	4.9
Construction/ building materials	Total interest rate sensitivity	5.8	5.9	6.9	4.6
	Extra-market interest rate sensitivity	1.5	1.5	4.1	5.0
Consumer goods/ entertainment	Total interest rate sensitivity	5.5	5.9	7.1	4.7
	Extra-market interest rate sensitivity	2.9	2.8	4.0	5.9
Electrical industry/ electronics	Total interest rate sensitivity	6.0	6.8	7.8	5.6
	Extra-market interest rate sensitivity	1.1	1.2	4.3	4.5
Steel industry/ metal industry	Total interest rate sensitivity	5.3	6.4	6.9	4.9
	Extra-market interest rate sensitivity	2.4	2.4	2.5	3.9
Transportation	Total interest rate sensitivity	5.4	5.3	6.7	3.8
	Extra-market interest rate sensitivity	1.1	1.0	4.7	4.8
Utilities	Total interest rate sensitivity	6.2	6.6	6.8	4.2
	Extra-market interest rate sensitivity	1.0	1.1	5.0	4.2
Other industries	Total interest rate sensitivity	4.6	4.9	6.1	4.1
	Extra-market interest rate sensitivity	2.3	1.9	4.3	5.1

[a] For each subperiod t and each interest rate factor the maturity m/maturity combination m, n yielding the lowest p-value has been considered.
[b] Holding period excess returns of a simple, unleveraged long position in one zero bond of a given constant maturity m.
[c] Holding period excess returns of a maturity transformation strategy of two zero bonds of given constant maturities m and n; first column: estimated average asset maturity m, second column: estimated average liability maturity n.

rate differentials, holding period returns of zero coupon bonds, and holding period returns of maturity transformation strategies. Results for both orthogonalization options regarding the explanatory variables are shown: total interest rate sensitivity and extra-market interest rate sensitivity. The coefficient is assumed to be significantly different from zero at the 10% level. The *t*-tests are based on error terms corrected for autocorrelation and heteroskedasticity according to Newey and West (1987).

The results shown in Table 6 clearly confirm that financial institutions generally conduct positive maturity transformation — or at least their stock returns behave as if they did so. Even when investigating extra-market interest rate sensitivities, on average positive maturity transformation strategies are obtained for almost all financial services subsectors — with the exception of the real estate banking and life insurance subsector.[14] In other words, banks implicitly conduct positive maturity transformation in addition to the positive maturity transformation implicit in the market factor.

In contrast to the financial institutions, Table 7 shows that almost all non-financial services sectors implicitly conduct negative extra-market maturity transformation.[15] That confirms the special role of banks with regard to maturity transformation in the economy. The economic theory does not yet provide any specific predictions for the concrete maturity transformation of financial institutions that these results could be tested against. However, the actual values of the average asset and liability maturities of the financial services sector of about 5–10 years against three years appear plausible when roughly estimating the average maturities based on maturity data provided by Deutsche Bundesbank for German banks.

A substantial advantage of using maturity transformation factors is that these can be directly replicated by simple investment strategies in zero coupon bonds. As a consequence, the implicit ex-post contribution of the estimated maturity transformation strategies to total stock returns of the financial institutions can be approximated based on the excess returns of the maturity transformation strategies as shown in Table 3.

Table 6 shows an average total maturity transformation strategy for the General Bank Index of about six years against three years. Across the whole sample period, this strategy yields a mean monthly excess return of 67 basis points and a standard deviation of 6.19% (Table 3). Since the sensitivity of the General Bank Index to this maturity transformation strategy is 0.21, the ex-post contribution of the maturity transformation strategy to the stock returns of the General Bank Index is 14 basis points in terms of mean excess return and 1.3% in terms of standard deviation. An investor could have realized such a return by investing 0.21 of his/her wealth in the maturity transformation strategy "6 against 3" and the remainder risk-free. Compared to the ex-post mean excess return of the General Bank Index of 31 basis points (Table 1), almost half of its excess return can be attributed to maturity transformation. Moreover, compared to the index standard deviation of 6.6%, maturity transformation is clearly contributing disproportionately little to total risk.

Obviously, the financial services sector provides positive extra-market maturity transformation as expected. Therefore, from a macroeconomic perspective, the results concerning extra-market sensitivity support the assumption of financial institutions providing maturity transformation between investors on the one hand and borrowers on the other.

4. Conclusion

To the best of our knowledge, this study is the first one to simultaneously analyze the interest rate sensitivity and the average asset and liability maturities of exchange listed financial and non-financial companies from the perspective of an external shareholder. The innovative contribution of this chapter to the literature is the use of holding period returns of maturity transformation strategies as interest rate factors which offers three major advantages.

First, the maturity transformation factor can easily be replicated by actual investment strategies, which is not immediately possible, e.g., for interest rate differentials. Second, it allows for an easy calculation of at least ex-post excess returns and risk premia. Third, it reflects the actual economic balance sheet structure of financial institutions more closely by considering mismatched assets and liabilities in the explanatory factor. Thus from a theoretical point of view, this factor should perform better than conventional interest rate factors.

The empirical superiority of maturity transformation factors has been confirmed by the significance of the sensitivities and the explanatory power of these factors. The estimated average asset and liability maturities verify that financial institutions generally conduct positive maturity transformation — also in addition to the already positive maturity transformation implicitly contained in the market factor.

Endnotes

1. A more current discussion of the liquidity preference hypothesis and the liquidity premium hypothesis, linking the preferences of economic agents to the behavior of the term structure of interest rates, can be found in Campbell and Shiller (1984), Malkiel (1992), and Bühler and Uhrig-Homburg (2000).
2. Merton (1973) derives an equilibrium model of the capital market in continuous time, but also postulates an interest rate sensitivity of stock returns due to macroeconomic equilibrium considerations.
3. Most recently, Bessler and Booth (1994), Madura and Zarruk (1995), Dinenis and Staikouras (1998, 2000), Faff and Howard (1999), Elgeti and Maurer (2000), Oertmann *et al.* (2000), Fraser *et al.* (2002), Elyasiani and Mansur (2003, 2004), Bessler and Opfer (2003, 2005), Bessler and Murtagh (2004) and Brewer *et al.* (2006).
4. The maturities considered in the context of the maturity transformation discussed and investigated in this chapter refer exclusively to the fixed interest rate periods for nominal payment agreements, though the terms "maturity" and "maturity transformation" can also apply to capital commitment or lockup periods and therefore liquidity transformation.
5. Some of these assets and liabilities will formally be variable rate payment agreements, which do not have a defined legal maturity but rather an effective economic maturity. Applying the market interest rate concept (Copeland *et al.*, 1998) or estimating effective fixed interest rate periods for these assets and liabilities, respectively, a large portion of these assets and liabilities can essentially be considered risk-free nominal payment agreements with unequivocally defined maturities.
6. Bierwag (1987) provides an extensive discussion of the duration concept.
7. Few empirical studies (Aharony *et al.*, 1986, 1988; Scott and Peterson, 1986; Bae, 1990; Madura and Zarruk, 1995) employ relative interest rate differentials instead of simple interest rate differentials.
8. A general discussion of the problem of multicollinearity can be found, for example, in Greene (2003).

9. Equation (6) is derived from Eq. (1).
10. We use one-month FIBOR and one-month EURIBOR before and after the introduction of the Euro, respectively.
11. Mostly suppressed below for convenience.
12. A constant equity-to-assets-ratio is necessary to obtain statistically comparable returns for the maturity transformation strategies. A value of ten percent has been chosen for the equity-to-assets-ratio based on the average empirical equity-to-assets-ratio for German banks.
13. An alternative criterion for selecting the maturities is the explanatory power of the models (R^2). This yields identical results for nearly all stock indices as well as subperiods. Rare differences arise from *p*-values, which are corrected for occasional autocorrelation and heteroskedasticity according to Newey and West (1987). These corrections are not considered in the R^2. Theoretically though, *p*-values are the relevant statistic to determine whether the interest rate factor has a significant influence on the returns.
14. The average negative extra-market maturity transformation of life insurance companies can be attributed to the very long maturity of their liabilities, stemming especially from annuities, but they are somewhat restricted in matching these extremely long liability maturities with corresponding fixed-income assets (Brewer *et al.*, 1993).
15. The results for the utilities sector, the only non-financial sector with a positive extra-market maturity transformation, are postulated and confirmed by, for example, Haugen *et al.* (1978), Sweeny and Warga (1986) and O'Neal (1998).

References

Aharony, J, A Saunders and I Swary (1986). The effects of a shift in monetary policy regime on the profitability and risk of commercial banks. *Journal of Monetary Economics*, 17, 363–377.

Aharony, J, A Saunders and I Swary (1988). The effects of DIDMCA on bank stockholders' returns and risk. *Journal of Banking and Finance*, 12, 317–331.

Bae, SC (1990). Interest rate changes and common stock returns of financial institutions: revisited. *Journal of Financial Research*, 13, 71–79.

Basel Committee on Banking Supervision (2004). Principles for the management and supervision of interest rate risk. Basel: Bank for International Settlements.

Bessler, W and GG Booth (1994). Interest rate sensitivity of bank stock returns in a universal banking system. *Journal of International Financial Markets, Institutions and Money*, 3, 117–136.

Bessler, W and JP Murtagh (2004). Risk characteristics of banks and non-banks: An international comparison. In *Aktuelle Entwicklungen im Finanzdienstleistungsbereich*, S Geberl, H-R Kaufmann, MJ Menichetti and DF Wiesner (eds.). Heidelberg: Physica-Verlag.

Bessler, W and H Opfer (2003). Eine empirische Untersuchung zur Bedeutung makroökonomischer Einflussfaktoren auf Aktienrenditen am Deutschen Kapitalmarkt. *Financial Markets and Portfolio Management*, 17, 412–436.

Bessler, W and H Opfer (2005). Aktienrenditen und makroökonomische Risikoprämien: Eine empirische Untersuchung für den Deutschen kapitalmarkt. *Zeitschrift für Bankrecht und Bankwirtschaft*, 17, 73–82.

Bierwag, GO (1987). *Duration Analysis: Managing Interest Rate Risk*. Cambridge, Massachusetts: Ballinger.

Bühler, W, M Uhrig, U Walter and T Weber (1999). An empirical comparison of forward-rate and spot-rate models for valuing interest-rate options. *Journal of Finance*, 54, 269–305.

Bühler, W and M Uhrig-Homburg (2000). Rendite und Renditestruktur am Rentenmarkt. In *Geld-, Bank- und Börsenwesen — Handbuch des Finanzsystems*, J Hagen and JH von Stein (eds.). Stuttgart: Schäffer-Poeschel Verlag.

Brewer III, E, JM Carson, E Elyasiani, I Mansur, and WL Scott (2006). Interest rate sensitivity and equity values of life insurance companies: A GARCH-M model. *Journal of Risk and Insurance*, 74, 401–423.

Brewer III, E, TH Mondschean and PE Strahan (1993). Why the life insurance industry did not face an S&L type crisis. In *Economic Perspectives*. Chicago: Federal Reserve Bank of Chicago.

Campbell, JY, AW Lo and AC MacKinlay (1997). *The Econometrics of Financial Markets*. Princeton, New Jersey: Princeton University Press.

Campbell, JY, and RJ Shiller (1984). A simple account on the behavior of long-term interest rates. *American Economic Review*, 74, 25–44.

Chance, DM and WR Lane (1980). A re-examination of interest rate sensitivity in the common stocks of financial institutions. *Journal of Financial Research*, 3, 49–56.

Copeland, TE, T Koller and J Murrin (1998). *Valuation — Measuring and Managing the Value of Companies*, 2nd Ed. New York: Wiley.

Copeland, TE and JF Weston (1992). *Financial Theory and Corporate Policy*. Reading, Massachusetts: Addison-Wesley Publishing Company.

Dinenis, E and SK Staikouras (1998). Interest rate changes and common stock returns of financial institutions: Evidence from the UK. *European Journal of Finance*, 4, 113–127.

Dinenis, E and SK Staikouras (2000). The pricing of risk factors and the UK insurance stocks' returns: A nonlinear multivariate approach. *European Research Studies*, 3, 131–144.

Elgeti, R and R Maurer (2000). Zur Quantifizierung der Risikoprämien deutscher Versicherungsaktien im Kontext eines Multifaktorenmodells. *Zeitschrift für die gesamte Versicherungswissenschaft*, 89, 577–603.

Elyasiani, E and I Mansur (2003). International spillover of risk and return among major banking institutions: A bivariate GARCH model. *Journal of Accounting, Auditing, and Finance*, 18, 303–330.

Elyasiani, E and I Mansur (2004). Bank stock return sensitivities to the long-term and short-term interest rates: A multivariate GARCH approach. *Managerial Finance*, 30, 32–55.

Faff, RW and PF Howard (1999). Interest rate risk of Australian financial sector companies in a period of regulatory change. *Pacific-Basin Finance Journal*, 7, 83–101.

Flannery, MJ and CM James (1984a). The effect of interest changes on the common stock returns of financial institutions. *Journal of Finance*, 39, 1141–1153.

Flannery, MJ and CM James (1984b). Market evidence on the effective maturity of bank assets and liabilities. *Journal of Money, Credit, and Banking*, 16, 435–445.

Fogler, HR, K John and J Tipton (1981). Three factors, interest rate differentials and stock groups. *Journal of Finance*, 36, 323–334.

Fraser, DR, J Madura and RA Weigand (2002). Sources of bank interest rate risk. *Financial Review*, 37, 351–367.

French, KR, RC Ruback and GW Schwert (1983). Effects of nominal contracting on stock returns. *Journal of Political Economy*, 91, 70–96.

Giliberto, M (1985). Interest rate sensitivity in the common stocks of financial intermediaries: A methodological note. *Journal of Financial and Quantitative Analysis*, 20, 123–126.

Göppl, H and H Schütz (1995). Die Konzeption eines Deutschen Aktienindex für Forschungszwecke (DAFOX). Diskussionspapier Nr. 162, Universität Karlsruhe.

Greene, WH (2003). *Econometric Analysis*. Upper Saddle River, New Jersey: Prentice Hall.

Harrington, R (1987). Asset and liability management by banks. In *Trends in Banking Structure and Regulation in OECD Countries*. OECD, Paris.

Haugen, RA, AL Stroyny and DW Wichern (1978). Rate regulation, capital structure and the sharing of interest rate risk in the electricity utility industry. *Journal of Finance*, 33, 707–721.

Hicks, JR (1946). *Value and Capital: An Inquiry into Some Fundamental Principles of Economic Theory*, 2nd Ed. Oxford: Oxford University Press.

Hirtle, BJ (1997). Derivatives, portfolio composition, and bank holding company interest rate risk exposure. *Journal of Financial Services Research*, 12, 243–266.

Johnson, HJ (1994). *Bank Asset Liability Management — The Impact, Issues and Trends*. Chicago: Probus Publishing.

Kane, EJ and H Unal (1988). Change in market assessments of deposit-institution riskiness. NBER working paper No. 2530, New York: National Bureau of Economic Research.

Lynge, MJ and JK Zumwalt (1980). An empirical study of the interest rate sensitivity of commercial bank returns: A multi-index approach. *Journal of Financial and Quantitative Analysis*, 15, 731–742.

Madura, J and ER Zarruk (1995). Bank exposure to interest rate risk — A global perspective. *Journal of Financial Research*, 18, 1–13.

Malkiel, BG (1992). Term structure of interest rates. In *The New Palgrave Dictionary of Money and Finance* (Volume III N–Z), P Newman, M Milgate and J Eatwell (eds.). London: The Macmillan Press Limited.

Merton, RC (1973). An intertemporal capital asset pricing model. *Econometrica*, 41, 867–887.

Nelson, CR and AF Siegel (1987). Parsimonious modeling of yield curves. *Journal of Business*, 60, 473–489.

Newey, W and K West (1987). A simple positive semi-definite, heteroskedasticity and autocorrelation consistent covariance matrix. *Econometrica*, 55, 703–708.

Niehans, J (1978). *The Theory of Money*. Baltimore, Maryland: The Johns Hopkins University Press.

Oertmann, P, C Rendu and H Zimmermann (2000). Interest rate risk of european financial corporations. *European Financial Management*, 6, 459–478.

O'Neal, ES (1998). Why electric utility stocks are sensitive to interest rates. *The Financial Review*, 33, 147–162.

Reilly, FK, DJ Wright and RR Johnson (2005). An analysis of the interest rate sensitivity of common stocks. European Conference of the Financial Management Association International, Siena.

Samuelson, PA (1945). The effects of interest rate increases on the banking system. *American Economic Review*, 35, 16–27.

Scott, WL and RL Peterson (1986). Interest rate risk and equity values of hedged and unhedged financial intermediaries. *Journal of Financial Research*, 9, 325–329.

Staikouras, SK (2003). The interest rate risk exposure of financial intermediaries: A review of the theory and empirical evidence. *Financial Markets, Institutions & Instruments*, 12, 257–289.

Stone, BK (1974). Systematic interest-rate risk in a two-index model of returns. *Journal of Financial and Quantitative Analysis*, 9, 709–721.

Sweeny, RJ and AD Warga (1986). The pricing of interest-rate risk: Evidence from the stock market. *Journal of Finance*, 41, 393–410.

Unal, H and EJ Kane (1988). Two approaches to assessing the interest rate sensitivity of deposit institution equity returns. *Research in Finance*, 7, 113–137.

7

ASYMMETRIES IN THE MARKET PRICE OF RISK: EVIDENCE FROM LATIN AMERICA

Gökçe Soydemir, Rahul Verma and Jose Moreno

1. Introduction

Higher returns in emerging markets, despite a corresponding higher degree of volatility, still make them a viable option for international portfolio diversification. For example, in the past five years, average annualized return in Latin American markets was about 23.5%, while the world annualized return in the same period was 3.6%.[1] In fact, the annualized return over the same period in the U.S. was only 2.8%. As such, international fund managers benefit greatly from the existing gaps in risk premium between developed and emerging markets.

For instance, out of the top ten of U.S. international funds, nine specialized in Latin American stock markets.[2] Latin American stock markets therefore offer one of the most appealing alternatives to improve portfolio performance. Because of the great contribution of Latin American equity markets in internationally diversified portfolios, researchers and others have begun to pay increasing attention to factors affecting performance.

With this objective in mind, several studies examine return spillovers across national stock markets (Cha and Seykung, 2000; Pagán and Soydemir, 2001), while others examine volatility spillovers (Brandt and Kang, 2004). However, such studies omit basic finance theory that investors attempt to maximize reward to risk ratio, the Sharpe ratio, rather than solely maximizing return or minimizing risk. As such, a more comprehensive analysis would focus on the spillovers from the market price of risk, the application of the Sharpe ratio to the market index returns and risk. More appropriately, market price of risk is the ratio of market risk premium to the standard deviation of market returns. Thus, market price of risk measures the extra compensation investors require to take on a unit of market risk.

In this chapter, we examine the extent of asymmetric pricing of market risk in Latin American markets, as they respond to similar shocks originating in the U.S. It is important for the pricing of risk to signal accurate information to investors. If market risk is not correctly priced, it may lead to excessive risk taking on the part of investors, with potentially disastrous consequences on the financial market. For example, some business circles argue that the incorrect pricing of risk in the U.S. housing market led to the sub-prime mortgage problems.[3] Using daily data from six Latin American markets, we construct a six-variable vector autoregression (VAR) model, one for downturns in the market price of risk and the other for the upturns from Mexico, Brazil, Argentina, Chile and the U.S. We examine the period from 15 January 2003 to 15 August 2007.

As expected, our findings reveal that an upward movement in the market price of risk from the U.S. increases the market price of risk in Mexico, Brazil, Argentina and Chile. A similar downward movement also leads to a decrease in the above-mentioned markets. However, we find that the Latin American response to upward movements in the U.S. market price of risk is consistently greater than the response to downward movements pointing to asymmetric behavior. In conclusion, international investors penalize an increase in risk much more heavily than a decrease by requiring an uneven compensation from similar movements in the U.S. market. The remainder of this chapter is structured as follows. Section 2 reviews the literature. Section 3 describes data and the methodology. Section 4 reports empirical findings and Sec. 5 concludes with a summary.

2. Literature Review

Many studies have separately examined either return or volatility spillovers across national stock markets, but most do not control for the one or the other. Pagán and Soydemir (2001) study response asymmetries in Latin American countries. They have used four years of daily data from Mexico, Argentina, Brazil and Chile. They have constructed a VAR model and IRF's procedure to check magnitude and pattern of responses between two markets. They have found statistically significant asymmetries, in the impact and pattern, in the response of Argentina, Brazil and Chile to changes in the Mexican equity market.

VAR models have been used recently in other issues related with the equity markets including the relation between them. Cha and Sekyung (2000) study the relationship between developed equity markets and the Pacific Basin's emerging equity markets. They have used a trivariate VAR model with an ARCH extension in the methodology. The data used includes weekly returns from markets of U.S., Japan, Hong Kong, Korea, Singapore and Taiwan. Their evidence indicates that the links between developed markets and the Asian emerging markets began to increase after the crash of October 1987, and they have significantly intensified since the outbreak of the Asian financial crisis in July 1997.

Bekaert *et al.* (2002) study the interrelationship between capital flows, returns, dividend yields and world interest rates in 20 emerging markets. They have applied a VAR analysis adapted for structural breaks. They have used monthly data for series of capital flows, returns and dividends. They found that after liberalization, equity capital flows have increased by 1.4% of markets capitalization on an annual basis. However, three years post-liberalization, the equity flows decreased. They have used the fundamental non-stationarity in the data ignored by previous research to differentiate their work and found that the non-stationarity in data was not without consequences in the results presented.

One exception is the study by Brandt and Kang (2004) who analyzed return over risk in the U.S. and other developed markets. They examined closely the time series relationship between the conditional moments through a latent VAR model and monthly data. They have used a VAR model with one equation to the conditional mean and the other to the conditional volatility. This latent VAR implied that the conditional Sharpe ratio was log-normally distributed and that it followed a two-factor AR process. They found that the contemporaneous correlation between the conditional mean and volatility was negative and significant. Surprisingly, the unconditional contemporaneous correlation was large and positive.

Guidolin and Ono (2006) investigated the hypothesis of time-varying dynamic linkage across financial markets and the macro-economy in a highly flexible multivariate regime-switching framework captured by a VAR model. They have used monthly U.S. data for eight financial and economic variables. They developed a Markov-switching VAR process with heteroscedastic components and density specification tests to investigate their hypothesis. They found no evidence of time-variation in the structure of the predictability patterns linking financial markets and the economy at large.

Ferrus Agudo and Sarto Marzal (2004) analyzed the investment performance Sharpe's ratio strategy and the conceptual framework of utility theory in the presence of risk. They proposed an alternative variation of the Sharpe ratio when the risk-free rate was higher than the return of the portfolio. They have used two sets of data: the first set comprised 91 Spanish fixed-income funds and the second set was formed by 40 Spanish equity funds. Using this information, they set out the properties of the Sharpe ratio, as this measure does not require the validation or verification of any equilibrium model for financial assets as other measures such as the Treynor ratio or the Alpha's Jensen. They concluded that the classic Sharpe ratio may give rise to inconsistent rankings where the average returns on the portfolios considered are lower than the average returns on the risk-free asset taken as a reference. These differences are explained by a distinct treatment given to the risk-return combination, with a greater or lower compensation being required for return when there is an increase in risk.

Dowd (2000) analyzed the Sharpe ratio using the value-at-risk (VaR) approach. He proposed a new generalized rule for risk adjustment and performance evaluation. In addition, he proposed to use the VaR rather than the standard deviation. The theoretical methodology helped Dowd to conclude that the generalized Sharpe rule is straightforward to implement and can be easily programmed into packages for decision makers to use. He declared in his paper that the Sharpe ratio structure is better than other ratios to measure return over risk. However, correlations between portfolios can be a problem for the Sharpe ratio.

Our study differs from the extant literature in several unique ways. First, we focus on the market price of risk spillovers among a set of national markets. Second, we investigate whether there is any asymmetry between upturns and downturns in the market price of risk. Third, we focus on Latin American emerging markets and lastly, we use a more recent data sample with daily frequency.

3. Econometric Methodology

To test for the presence of response asymmetries in the pricing of Latin American equity market risk, we use two statistical approaches. Market price of risk i (R_i) is defined to have an asymmetric impact if an increase in the market price of risk (R_j) affects market price of risk i increases differently than a decrease of equal magnitude.[4] The statistical model takes the form[5]:

$$RI_{it} = \alpha_0 + \alpha_1 RI_{jt-1} + \alpha_2 RI_{it-1} + e_t, \tag{1}$$

$$RD_{it} = \gamma_0 + \gamma_1 RD_{jt-1} + \gamma_2 RD_{it-1} + \delta_t, \tag{2}$$

where α_0 is a constant term, e_t, and δ_t is a white noise error term and

$$R_t = (P_t - P_{t-1})/\sigma \tag{3}$$

$$RI_t,\ \text{if } (R_t - R_{t-1}) > 0 \text{ and } = 0 \text{ otherwise, and} \tag{4}$$

$$RD_t,\ \text{if } R_t - R_{t-1},\ \text{if } (P_t - P_{t-1}) < 0 \text{ and } = 0 \text{ otherwise,} \tag{5}$$

where R_t and R_{t-1} are expressed in logarithms so that returns R_i are continuously compounded returns. All RI_t are positive or zero and all RD_t are negative or zero. If, for example, the Chilean market price of risk responds symmetrically to U.S. market price of risk increases and decreases then one would expect to find $\alpha_2 = \gamma_1$. If the model is estimated using daily data then one-day lags may be sufficient to characterize the model dynamics and capture the return generating process. To obtain unbiased and efficient parameter estimates, we also assume that the intercept captures the average influence of factors that are not explained by changes in the Latin American markets.

To test the hypothesis that the market price of risk in Argentina, Brazil and Chile responds symmetrically to upturns and downturns in the U.S. market price of risk, we examine "magnitude" symmetry by testing the hypothesis $H_0 : \alpha_1 = \gamma_1$ using a Wald test (Greene, 2000). In addition to "magnitude" symmetry, we test for the presence of "pattern" asymmetry by estimating a VAR model:

$$Z_t = \lambda_0 + \sum_{s=1}^{m} \gamma_s Z_{t-s} + v_t, \tag{6}$$

where Z_t includes RI_t and RD_t for each market, λ_0 is the deterministic component, λ_s is the matrix of coefficients, m is the lag length and v_t is the vector of innovations. By construction, v_t is uncorrelated with the past Z_s.

The VAR model is essentially a dynamic simultaneous equation system with uniform sets of lagged dependent variable as regressors. The model does not impose *a priori* restrictions on the structure of the relationship among variables. Since no restrictions are imposed on the structure of the system, VARs can be viewed as a flexible approximation to the reduced form of the correctly specified but unknown model of the actual economic structure (Sims, 1980). The VAR specification is particularly useful when trying to understand empirical regularities embedded in time-series data when correct specification is difficult.

Impulse response functions (IRFs) are constructed from the VAR model to investigate the postulated response of the dependent variable to a one-standard deviation shock to another variable in the system and can be thought of as a type of dynamic multiplier. The "pure" effects of these shocks can then be captured using Choleski orthogonalization (Runkle, 1987). The statistical significance of the IRFs can be assessed by Monte Carlo methods to estimate confidence bands around the mean IRFs.

3.1. *Data and Descriptive Statistics*

Our sample consists of daily data covering the period from 15 January 2002 to 8 August 2006. The data includes the U.S. and the six Latin American countries: Argentina, Brazil, Chile, Colombia, Peru and Mexico. The data is obtained from Datastream and all prices are in U.S. dollars.[6] The returns are continuously compounded and the yield on the three-month U.S. T-bill is used as the risk-free rate.

Table 1 reports descriptive statistics for the markets considered in the study. The period studied includes daily data from 15 January 2003 to 30 August 2006. As we expect, Latin American market prices of risk exhibit higher volatility than the U.S. market and the world index. Brazil has the most volatile market price of risk in the sample with a standard deviation of 2.11 in upturns and 2.13 in downturns, while Peru has the lower standard deviation for Latin American countries with 1.40 in upturns and 1.34 in downturns. In most countries, the mean of upturns is higher than the mean of downturns. The volatility is higher for upturns in comparison with downturns in all Latin American countries. The skewness and kurtosis indexes suggest that

Table 1. Summary statistics of market prices of risk: Upturns and downturns (15 January 2003–30 August 2006).

Latin American countries	Mean	Std. dev.	Skewness	Kurtosis	Maximum	Minimum
Mexico (Up)	1.049658	1.795691	0.849237	3.632919	7.557653	−2.581381
Mexico (Down)	0.949721	1.660445	0.898986	3.750975	7.328014	−2.663953
Brazil (Up)	1.125997	2.110841	1.286425	5.932282	10.62602	−4.177936
Brazil (Down)	1.040194	2.130419	1.168072	5.862748	10.45643	−4.302001
Argentina (Up)	1.15403	1.617997	1.402579	4.829265	8.406958	−1.612305
Argentina (Down)	1.032745	1.520163	1.488486	5.239162	8.136248	−1.809397
Chile (Up)	0.637556	1.429217	0.231701	4.723039	5.599854	−3.956357
Chile (Down)	0.644926	1.391716	0.067513	5.017782	5.003536	−4.045481
Colombia (Up)	1.893109	2.063064	0.492866	1.699255	6.317539	0
Colombia (Down)	1.641155	1.988829	0.660667	1.835322	6.100294	0
Peru (Up)	1.106158	1.437196	0.888504	2.376383	5.167781	−0.80561
Peru (Down)	1.086503	1.418023	0.878104	2.354967	5.037825	−0.846276
U.S. Index						
U.S. (Up)	−0.053808	1.123422	−1.696904	7.034253	2.497367	−4.697533
U.S. (Down)	−0.179909	1.180619	−1.918457	7.170407	1.95748	−4.927536

the distribution of market prices of risk may be different from normal in the series of our sample.

Table 2 reports cross-correlations between markets for upturns whereas Table 3 reports correlations for downturns. Upturn correlations appear to be consistently higher than downturn correlations, with one exception between Chile and the U.S. where the downturn correlations are higher than the upturn correlations. Higher correlations imply higher risk. This finding of higher correlation for upturns is therefore consistent with the view that upturns in market price of risk makes such countries more vulnerable to such movements originating in other markets than downturns.

Table 4 reports ratio of the U.S. international transactions with Latin America from 2002 to 2006. Mexico has the strongest links with the U.S. registering close to 10% import and export figures. Argentina has the smallest percentage, registering less than 1% each year. Other countries considered in this study are included under the category "other", which excludes Venezuela according to the

Table 2. Cross-correlations of upturns of market price of risk.

	Mexico	Brazil	Argentina	Chile	Colombia	Peru	U.S.	World
Mexico	1.000							
Brazil	0.526	1.000						
Argentina	0.337	0.530	1.000					
Chile	0.365	0.398	0.295	1.000				
Colombia	0.223	0.201	0.192	0.179	1.000			
Peru	0.086	0.149	0.133	0.075	0.022	1.000		
U.S.	0.258	0.192	0.108	0.416	0.157	0.070	1.000	

Table 3. Cross-correlations of downturns of market price of risk.

	Mexico	Brazil	Argentina	Chile	Colombia	Peru	U.S.	World
Mexico	1.000							
Brazil	0.509	1.000						
Argentina	0.321	0.531	1.000					
Chile	0.363	0.384	0.292	1.000				
Colombia	0.183	0.147	0.129	0.128	1.000			
Peru	0.032	0.094	0.089	0.059	−0.004	1.000		
U.S.	0.169	0.139	0.050	0.424	0.128	0.062	1.000	

Table 4. International transactions.

	U.S. Exports (%)					U.S. Imports (%)				
	2002	2003	2004	2005	2006	2002	2003	2004	2005	2006
Argentina	0.21	0.37	0.41	0.43	0.43	0.26	0.24	0.23	0.24	0.20
Brazil	1.6	1.4	1.5	1.5	1.6	1.1	1.1	1.1	1.1	1.1
Mexico	9.5	9.1	8.7	8.4	7.9	9.4	9.0	8.5	8.0	8.1
Other*	3.1	3.0	2.9	2.9	2.8	2.2	2.1	2.2	2.3	2.2

*Excludes Venezuela.

classification provided by the Bureau of Economic Analysis. The ratio of this aggregated category registers about 3%. However, the per country effect is conjectured to be much smaller.

Lastly, test of unit roots and cointegration reveal that all market price of risk series are stationary and that there is no presence of cointegrating vectors among them especially amongst upturns and downturns.

4. Empirical Results

Our results show that the responses of downturns exhibit a different pattern than responses of upturns. In particular, the magnitude of upper movements on the market price of risk is persistently greater than in downturn responses for all emerging markets responding to the U.S. shocks. Further upturns are transmitted much more quickly and with much less lagged statistically significant responses, exhibiting little persistence to shocks coming from the U.S. market.

Figures 1(a) and 2(a) plot Mexican upward (MEXU) and downward (MEXD) responses corresponding shocks coming from U.S. market respectively. For example, the magnitude of Mexican upward response to the U.S. is greater than 0.11 closer to 0.15. However, downturn response is less than 0.08 closer to 0.06. Further, the upturn in the market price of risk is disseminated very quickly within one day to the Mexican market, with no persistent lag. In contrast, the downturn is transmitted after about two days lasting for about three days, and exhibiting persistence in the 30th and 50th days in the form of statistically significant response.

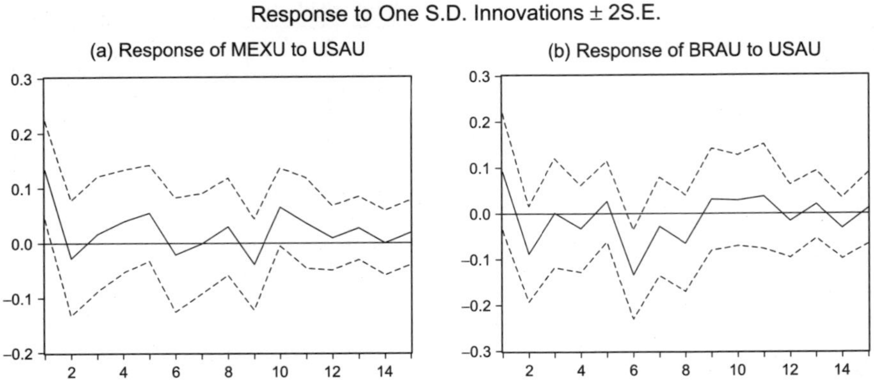

Figure 1. Upward impulse response functions for Mexico and Brazil.

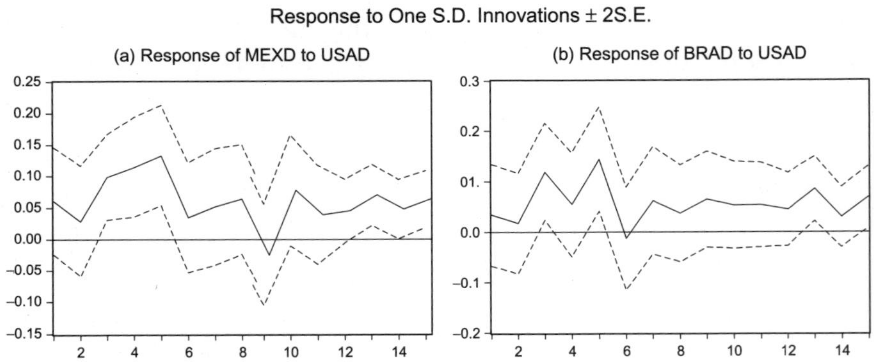

Figure 2. Downward impulse response functions for Mexico and Brazil.

Same pattern in the magnitude of shocks and the greater number of statistically significant responses of downturns appears to present itself in other markets as well. Figures 1(b) and 2(b) plot the Brazilian responses to shocks in the U.S. market. The magnitude of upturn response in the Brazilian market is near 0.10, while the downturn magnitude is lower than 0.05 near 0.02. Besides, the persistence in upturn response disappears in the second day, while in downturns we can observe statistically significant persistence until day 30 and 50 after the shock.

Figures 3(a) and 4(a) plot Argentinean responses to shocks from the U.S. market. The magnitude of upturn response to the U.S.

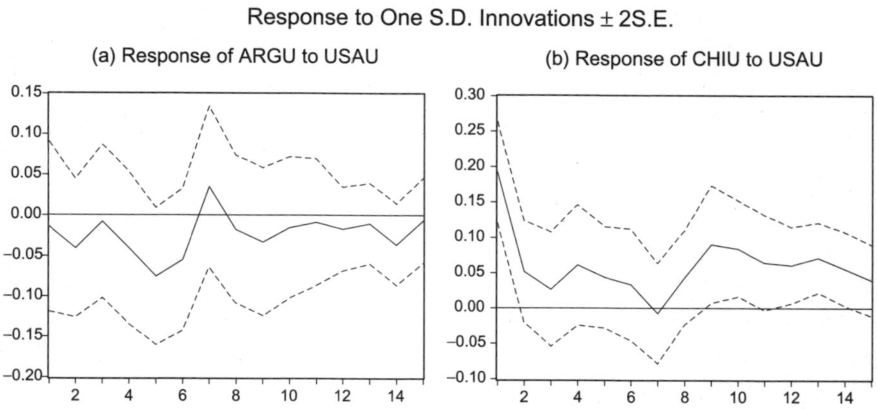

Figure 3. Upward impulse response functions for Argentina and Chile.

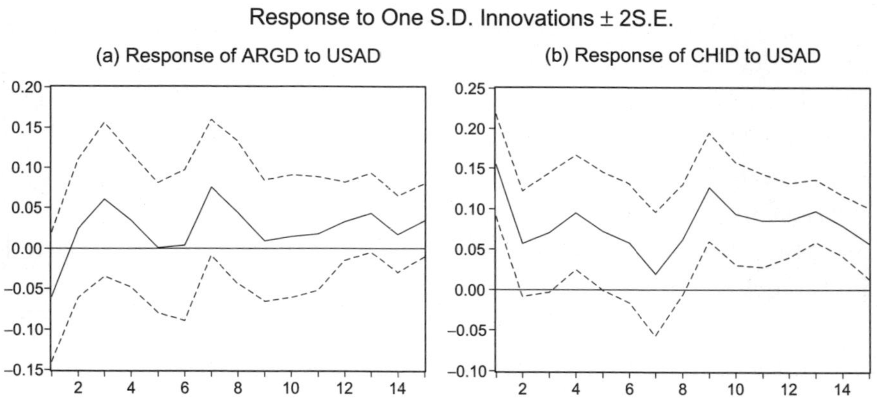

Figure 4. Downward impulse response functions for Argentina and Chile.

shock is negative and near −0.02. On the other hand, the downturn response is, as in other markets, lower than upturn response. Downturn response is lower than −0.04 near −0.06. Further, the upturn in the market price of risk is dispersed more quickly than the downturn response. However, both do not present statistical significance after the seventh day.

Figures 3(b) and 4(b) present Chilean upward and downward responses to shocks in U.S. market. Chilean market presents the higher magnitude responses (upward and downward) of our sample.

The magnitude of Chilean upturn response to the U.S. is near 0.2, while the downturn response is only around 0.16. However, upturn exhibits transmission no longer than two perhaps three days, whereas downturn shock causes transmission in periods between four and five days. Persistence is presented in both responses, but still in the fifth day, downturn response is more persistent than upturn response.

Figures 5(a) and 6(a) plot Colombian upward and downward response corresponding shocks coming from the U.S. market respectively. The magnitude of Colombian upward response to the U.S. shock is near 0.01, which is greater than the downward response (closer to −0.05). Transmission is similar in both responses that are between three to four days lasting. Persistence is higher in downturn response than in upturn response.

Figures 5(b) and 6(b) plot Peruvian market price of risk responses to a shock in the U.S. market price of risk. Similar characteristics to other markets are observed. The magnitude of upturn response is near 0.05 and higher than the downturn response which is negative lower to 0.01. However, transmission appears in longer periods in downturns in comparison with upturns. These results are also consistent with the closeness of trading partners reported in Table 4.

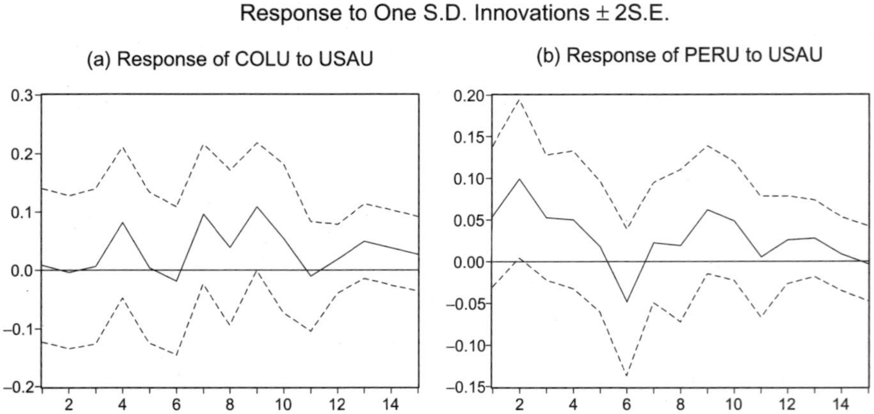

Figure 5. Upward impulse response functions for Colombia and Peru.

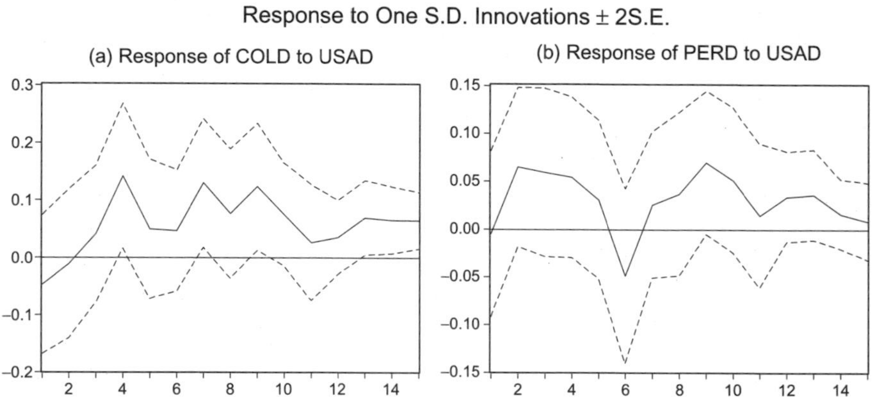

Figure 6. Downward impulse response functions for Colombia and Peru.

5. Concluding Remarks

In this chapter, we examined whether the pricing of Latin American market risk is asymmetric when responding to similar shocks coming from the U.S. market. We used a daily sample and estimated a VAR model to analyze the postulated asymmetries. Our findings showed that an upward movement in the U.S. market price of risk increases the market price of risk in Mexico, Brazil, Argentina and Chile. A similar downward movement also leads to a decrease in the above-mentioned markets. However, our findings also indicated that the response to the upward market price of risk movements originating in the U.S. market is consistently greater than the response to the downward movements pointing to asymmetric behavior.

Further, upturns of market price of risk are transmitted more quickly than downturns. Nevertheless, downturns appear to exhibit longer persistence than upturns and therefore longer lag effects. However, with the exception of one case, correlations of upturns appear to be greater than the correlations of downturns between markets, making these markets more vulnerable to each other during upturns than downturns. In conclusion, investors penalize an increase in risk much more heavily than a decrease in risk by requiring an uneven compensation.

Our results have practical implications for investors and policymakers. Investors, knowing about the presence of this asymmetry, can better distinguish the impact of the upward and downward movements on their international diversified portfolios. Policymakers can devise better strategies to alleviate the impact of such asymmetries on international and domestic capital flows and minimize detrimental effects on economic growth and international financial stability.

Endnotes

1. Returns presented here are based on the MSCI indexes that are measured in U.S. dollars.
2. These top ten international funds are based on returns. Data obtained from *Morningstar and Commodity Systems Inc.* (CSI); *USA Today*, 2006.
3. IMF chief sees hope in market reckoning. *Financial Times*, 10 September 2007.
4. Price-movement asymmetries have been found to exist in several commodity markets (Karrenbrock, 1991) as well as on real and underground output in New Zealand (Giles, 1999).
5. The statistical model presented here does not capture time varying parameters and is not based on an asset-pricing model but, rather, it attempts to capture contemporaneous relationships of daily equity returns between markets (for example, Karolyi and Stulz, 1996).
6. Because the returns are denominated in U.S. dollars, we assume that investors undertake unitary hedging in this study.

References

Bekaert, G, CR Harvey and RL Lumsdaine (2002). The dynamics of emerging market equity flows. *Journal of International Money and Finance*, 21, 295–350.

Brandt, MW and Q Kang (2004). On the relationship between the conditional mean and volatility of stock returns: A latent VAR approach. *Journal of Financial Economics*, 72, 217–257.

Cha, B and O Sekyung (2000). The relationship between developed equity markets and the Pacific Basin's emerging equity markets. *International Review of Economics and Finance*, 9, 299–322.

Dowd, K (2000). Adjusting for risk: An improved Sharpe ratio. *International Review of Economics and Finance*, 9, 209–222.

Ferruz Agudo, L and JL Sarto Marzal (2004). An analysis of Spanish investment fund performance: Some considerations concerning Sharpe's ratio. *Omega: The International Journal of Management Science*, 32, 273–284.

Giles, DEA (1999). The rise and fall of New Zealand underground economy: Are the responses symmetric? *Applied Economics Letters*, 6, 185–189.

Greene, WH (2000). *Econometric Analysis*. Upper Saddle River, NJ: Prentice-Hall.

Guidolin, M and S Ono (2006). Are the dynamic linkages between the macroeconomy and asset prices time-varying? *Journal of Economics and Business*, 58, 480–518.

Karolyi, AG and RM Stulz (1996). Why do markets move together? An investigation of U.S.–Japan stock return comovements. *Journal of Finance*, 51, 950–986.

Karrenbrock, JD (1991). The behavior of retail gasoline prices: Symmetric or not? *Federal Reserve Bank of St. Louis Bulletin*, 73, 19–29.

Pagán, JA and GA Soydemir (2001). Response asymmetries in the Latin American equity markets. *International Review of Financial Analysis*, 10, 175–185.

Runkle, DE (1987). Vector autoregressions and reality. *Journal of Business and Economics Statistics*, October, 437–442.

Sims, CA (1980). Macroeconomics and reality. *Econometrica*, 48, 1–49.

Part II

Corporate Finance and Investments

8

Corporate Governance Institutions as Signaling and Commitment Devices

Angelo Baglioni

1. Introduction[1]

Private benefits of control are a central issue in corporate finance.[2] Recent theoretical and empirical literature (surveyed in the next section) conveys a basic message: some governance institutions emerge as a way to limit the extraction of private benefits by the controlling party. For example, independent physicians are included in the board with the task of monitoring managerial decisions, which might not be congruent with firm value maximization. The institutional solutions differ across firms: the structure of the board of directors depends on firm size, complexity, industry etc. Then some cross-sectional relationships between corporate governance institutions and firm features are identified by theory and tested empirically.

The main contribution of this chapter relative to the existing literature on corporate boards is the following. Other works focus on the moral hazard problem generated by the ability of managers and executive directors to extract private benefits, hence the monitoring role of independent directors. My chapter adds to this moral hazard issue the lemon problem arising when different types of firms raise equity funds: investors are not able to distinguish between firms where the scope for the extraction of private benefits is high from those where it is low.[3] This is quite a realistic assumption. External investors can only have indirect indicators of the scope for the extraction of private benefits such as the amount of free cash flow and the size and complexity of firm organization. However, they do not have information as accurate as that available to insiders.

By analyzing a model where the moral hazard and the adverse selection issues interact, I am able to derive some interesting insights. First, the board structure is a *non-monotonic* function of private benefits. A governance institution — such as independent directors — limiting the extraction of private benefits by the controlling party will be exploited either as a signaling device by firms where private benefits are low, or as a commitment device by those where private benefits are potentially high. Firms with an intermediate level of private benefits will not apply such mechanism. This non-monotonic relationship is a distinctive feature of the model, since the theory of corporate boards generally points to a degree of board independence monotonically increasing in the scope for private benefits (with the relevant exception of Adams and Ferreira, 2007).[4]

Second, only those governance institutions providing a *credible* commitment to neglect private benefits are useful as a separating device. Take for example independent directors: only a few firms are ready to have "watch-dogs" in the board, while all of them are willing to have innocuous "lap-dogs". Third, the signaling role emerges only if the structure of the board is a market outcome (possibly self-regulated), and it is not imposed by the law.

While the literature on corporate boards is mainly concerned with managers' opportunistic behavior, in this chapter the focus is on the extraction of private benefits by a dominant shareholder. The divergence of interests between large and small shareholders is a common problem in countries where firms exhibit a high level of ownership concentration (continental Europe). The plan of the chapter is as follows. Section 2 provides a brief survey of the most recent literature on the structure of corporate boards. In Sec. 3, a basic model with both moral hazard and adverse selection is presented, where issuers differ in their ability to extract private benefits of control. Section 4 introduces a regulation, imposing a commitment to pursue the general interest of shareholders. In Sec. 5, the adoption of a governance institution, implying such a type of commitment, is left to the discretion of controlling shareholders: here our main results are derived. Finally, Sec. 6 discusses the empirical implications of my analysis. All proofs are in the Appendix.

2. Related Literature

2.1. *The Theory of Corporate Boards*

This chapter shares with other theoretical works the view that corporate governance mechanisms emerge as an optimizing response of agents to the fundamental issue of separation between ownership and control.[5] This idea goes back to Fama and Jensen (1983), who state that the agency problems arising from such separation are expected to be controlled by splitting "decision management" (i.e., initiation and implementation of decisions) from "decision control" (i.e., ratification and monitoring of decisions).

Following this approach, the theoretical literature has begun analyzing the determinants of the structure of corporate boards: their size and composition. Hermalin and Weisbach (1998) model the bargaining game between the CEO and the incumbent directors, reaching — among others — the conclusions that "the probability of independent directors being added to the board rises following poor firm performance" and that "board independence declines over the course of a CEO's tenure".[6]

More recently, the literature on boards has deepened our understanding of the interaction between the two basic functions of the board of directors: the advisory role and the monitoring role. The optimal structure of the board emerges by balancing the costs and benefits of such two tasks. For instance, Adams and Ferreira (2007) stress the following trade-off: on the one hand, a more independent board will monitor more intensively managers' decisions. On the other hand, managers will be reluctant to reveal firm-specific information to an independent board, since this information may be used both for advising and for interfering. Since the communication between managers and board is valuable, shareholders might prefer to appoint less independent directors (a "friendly board"). Moreover, a two-tier board structure might emerge as an optimal solution, by allocating the two tasks to different bodies: a management board (advising role) and a supervisory board (monitoring role); the CEO always reveals his/her information to the management board, since such information cannot be used to monitor him/her.

Similar results are reached by Harris and Raviv (2008). In their model, shareholders face a trade-off: an inside (executive) director is better informed than an outside (independent) director; but the former's objective function is distorted by private benefits, contrary to the latter. When the information available to insiders is critical, shareholders prefer a board dominated by them, as their advisory role is essential. To the contrary, when the agency costs — generated by the possibility to extract private benefits — are more relevant, a board dominated by outsiders is preferred, since their monitoring role becomes crucial.

Raheja (2005) builds up a model where the voting power of the two types of directors, insiders and outsiders, play a crucial role. Again, insiders are better informed than outsiders, but they might decide to support the CEO in selecting an inferior project, due to private benefits. Outsiders may use their CEO succession votes to induce the insiders — who compete with each other to become CEO — to reveal their superior information. The optimal board structure is designed in such a way that the majority votes against an inferior project, and it depends on a number of firm features. For example, as private benefits increase the size of the board and the proportion of outsiders increase as well.

While the above models focus on the agency problem between managers and dispersed shareholders, others point to the role of a dominant shareholder.[7] Graziano and Luporini (2005) analyze the properties of different board structures: they interpret the two-tier structure as a way through which a large shareholder can commit to limit his/her own interference with management; their prediction is that shareholders enjoying a high level of private benefits are not willing to commit, since they have much to loose. Similarly in Dahya *et al.* (2005) controlling shareholders with lower equity stakes wish to have fewer independent directors on the board, in order to be able to divert more resources. Both these papers reach opposite conclusions from mine, for the reason that they overlook the impact of the ability to extract private benefits on the equilibrium price of corporate liabilities (in particular, of equity).

2.2. *Empirical Evidence*

A number of recent empirical studies support the view that firms design their governance institutions in a way able to minimize the agency costs arising in their specific contracting environment. Cross-sectional evidence shows that the structure of boards depends on those firms' features affecting the costs and benefits of the monitoring and advising roles of directors.[8] Using a sample of 7,000 firms from 1990 to 2004, Linck *et al.* (2007) find, among others, the following results: board independence is increasing in the availability of managerial private benefits, measured by free cash flow; board independence is decreasing in insider incentive alignement, proxied by the CEO ownership stake in the firm. The strong relationships between board structure and firm features lead them to state that "any approach that mandates uniform requirements on board structure could be ill-conceived".

Similar results are obtained in other works. Lehn *et al.* (2003) find a direct relation between board independence and firm size, where the latter is interpreted as a proxy for the extent of agency conflicts between managers and owners. Boone *et al.* (2007) find that several measures of firm size and complexity are positively related to board size and independence, pointing to the need of monitoring and advising by specialized directors. Coles *et al.* (2005) find that insider representation in the board is increasing in the relevance of firm-specific knowledge, proxied by R&D intensity. Gillan *et al.* (2006) focus on the interplay between internal mechanisms for controlling agency problems (such as board structure and charter provisions) and external ones (such as the market for corporate control and the legal environment), finding that they act as substitutes in the design of corporate governance. Finally, Brickley *et al.* (1997) tackle the issue of separation between the titles of CEO and Chairman of the board; they find that achieving combined titles is not only the widespread practice of U.S. corporations but it is also efficient, concluding that a separation imposed by the regulator would be misguided.

3. A Basic Model with Moral Hazard and Adverse Selection

Let us consider a population of entrepreneurs.

Assumption 1. Each entrepreneur is the owner of a firm with value $V = Vmax - B$, where B denotes his/her private benefits of control. He/she sells an (exogenous) equity stake $(1-\alpha)$ to external dispersed investors (small shareholders), receiving a revenue denoted by R. He/she retains control over his/her own firm for any relevant values of his/her stake α (in particular, for α_h and α_l defined below).

Assumption 2. After issuing equity, entrepreneurs have to decide the value of B; this cannot be contracted ex-ante, due to the incompleteness of contracts.

Assumption 3. The population is made up of two types of entrepreneurs: good and bad ($t \in \{g, b\}$). The proportion of g-type over total is k.

Assumption 4 (good type). The utility function of g-type is: $\alpha V + R$.

Assumption 5 (bad type). The utility function of b-type is $u(B) + \alpha V + R$, where: $u(B)$ is strictly concave, $u(0) = 0$, $\exists \hat{B} > 0$ such that $u'(\hat{B}) = 1$ (see Fig. 1).

Assumption 6 (hidden information). Entrepreneurs know their own type. Investors do not observe each entrepreneur's type.

Assumption 7. External investors are risk neutral. Due to competition among them, investors demand an expected return equal to the riskless rate of interest, which is normalized to zero.

All the above assumptions are common knowledge. A few additional comments are in order. All entrepreneurs have to raise external funds in the form of *equity*: this enables us to focus on the conflict

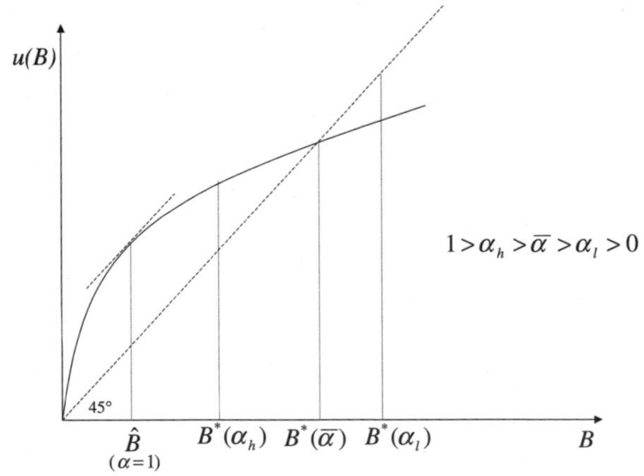

Figure 1. Utility of private benefits (bad type).

of interest between controlling and minority shareholders. All firms are assumed to be identical in all regards but one. While the goal of good entrepreneurs is to maximize the value of their firms, this goal is somewhat distorted for bad entrepreneurs: these are also interested in maximizing their own private benefits of control (e.g., perks, empire building, deals with related parties, diversion of funds), leading to a reduction of the firm value.

This framework is designed to capture the heterogeneity across firms: in some of them, the ability or willingness of the dominant shareholder to extract private benefits of control are higher than in others; for simplicity, the utility function of a good type completely rules out private benefits. The information regarding private benefits is typically not verifiable or simply too complex to describe in detail, so financial contracts cannot prescribe a specific level of B: this creates a moral hazard issue. On top of this, a "lemon problem" emerges from the inability of external investors to distinguish between the two types of issuers.

Let us focus first on the moral hazard issue, which is relevant only for a b-type issuer (the level of private benefits of a g-type is trivially zero, due to Assumption 4). Lemma 1 states, within our framework, the well-known result of Jensen and Meckling (1976): after selling equity, a b-type entrepreneur is induced to increase his/her own private benefits, as he/she is able to shift part of the cost to small shareholders, while retaining the full benefit. Let us denote B^* the equilibrium level of private benefits for a b-type. While a full owner ($\alpha = 1$) sets his/her private benefits to a level $\hat{B}$, an entrepreneur retaining a fraction of equity ($\alpha < 1$) extracts $B^* > \hat{B}$.

Lemma 1. *B^* is a decreasing function of α. In particular: $B^*(1) = \hat{B}$ and $B^*(\alpha) > \hat{B}$ for any $\alpha < 1$.*

We can now be more specific about the exogenous level of equity retained by each entrepreneur.

Assumption 8. The exogenous share of equity retained by an entrepreneur is either $\alpha_l \in (0, \overline{\alpha})$ or $\alpha_h \in (\overline{\alpha}, 1)$, where $\overline{\alpha}$ is defined by: $B^*(\overline{\alpha}) = u[B^*(\overline{\alpha})]$. Within each group of entrepreneurs — those retaining a stake α_l, and those retaining a stake α_h — the proportion of g-type is k.

Of course, the share of equity retained by an entrepreneur is public information. However, by observing α an investor is not able to infer his/her type (good or bad), since within each group of entrepreneurs — those retaining a high and those retaining a low fraction of equity — both types are present.[9] Assumption 8 enables us to state that: $B^*(\alpha_h) < B^*(\overline{\alpha}) < B^*(\alpha_l)$, $u[B^*(\alpha_h)] > B^*(\alpha_h)$, and $u[B^*(\alpha_l)] < B^*(\alpha_l)$ (see Fig. 1). The moral hazard issue may be further analyzed by momentarily removing Assumption 6 and assuming that each entrepreneur's type is public information: this situation is labeled "full information".

Lemma 2 shows that, if bad entrepreneurs were able to commit to $\hat{B}$ prior to issuing equity, they would do so; unfortunately, such a solution is precluded by the incompleteness of contracts. Investors anticipate the equilibrium level of private benefits $B^*(\alpha)$, which is incorporated into the selling price of equity: $R_b(\alpha) = (1 - \alpha)$ (Vmax $- B^*$). The bottom line is that bad entrepreneurs bear the full cost of the incentive distortion, created by the ability to extract private benefits (of course, it is crucial that the level of private benefits is set after issuing equity, when the selling price is taken as given).

Lemma 2. *In an equilibrium with full information, the bad entrepreneurs' utility level is* $Vmax + u[B^*(\alpha)] - B^*(\alpha)$, *for* $\alpha = \alpha_h, \alpha_l$. *If they were able to commit to a specific level of B prior to issuing equity, bad entrepreneurs' utility level would be* $Vmax + u(\hat{B}) - \hat{B}$. *It is* $Vmax + u[B^*(\alpha)] - B^*(\alpha) < Vmax + u(\hat{B}) - \hat{B}$.

Good entrepreneurs do not suffer the above problem, since they do not extract private benefits. Their revenue from the equity sale is $R_g(\alpha) = (1-\alpha)\text{Vmax}$, and in equilibrium their utility level is $\alpha\text{Vmax} + R_g(\alpha) = \text{Vmax}$.

Let us now introduce Assumption 6: hidden information. The consequence is that bad entrepreneurs are subsidized by good ones.

Proposition 1. *In the equilibrium with hidden information there is cross-subsidization. Good (bad) entrepreneurs have a lower (higher) utility level than in the equilibrium with full information.*

As in any "lemon problem", issuers know the true (fundamental) value of their shares, while external investors do not. Hence both types issue equity at the same price $R_{HI}(\alpha)$ (within each group: those with $\alpha = \alpha_h$ and those with $\alpha = \alpha_l$), leading to an under(over)-evaluation of the shares issued by good (bad) firms: $R_g(\alpha) > R_{HI}(\alpha) > R_b(\alpha)$. As a consequence, good entrepreneurs bear part of the cost due to the extraction of private benefits by bad ones.[10]

4. Governance Regulation as a Commitment Device

In recent years, an increasing role has been assigned to "independent" directors: they should act in the interest of all shareholders, avoiding that the private benefits of some stakeholders prevail over the maximization of the firm value. They also play a crucial role in (audit, compensation, nomination) committees within the board. In some countries, the board of directors has a two-tier structure, with a management board (MB) and a supervisory board (SB): controlling shareholders are supposed to be represented only in the SB, with the power of selecting the members of the MB and of taking some strategic decisions; the MB is entitled to run the firm.[11] These are examples of governance institutions enabling a dominant shareholder to commit to let the general interest of shareholders — namely the maximization of the firm value — prevail over his/her own private benefits. In this section, we consider a governance institution which is mandated by the corporate law (this assumption will be relaxed in the next section, where entrepreneurs are supposed to be free to apply a governance rule. Our main results will then be obtained).

Corporate governance rules are far from perfect. In particular, the focus here is on two kinds of imperfections. First, they cannot directly specify a particular value of B, since the level of private benefits is not verifiable: the incompleteness of contracts carries over to the corporate law.[12] The regulation can assign some relevant decisions to an agent different from the dominant shareholder, and introduce checks and balances into the governance structure, which should in principle avoid the extraction of private benefits by the controlling shareholder. Second, a governance institution does not necessarily imply full commitment.

Despite the presence of corporate rules and monitoring agents, a dominant shareholder might extract private benefits by affecting managerial decisions in several ways, such as his/her influence over the selection of independent directors, the power of dismissing managers, or the ability to collude with them. These features of the corporate regulation are formalized here by introducing the following assumption (modifying Assumption 2), where the parameter π measures the degree of commitment incorporated into the governance institution; in other words, π provides a measure of the effectiveness — and of the credibility — of the corporate regulation.[13]

Assumption 9 (regulation). After issuing equity, with probability π the level of B is decided by a third party, with utility function V; with probability $1 - \pi$ the level of B is decided by the large shareholder.

The regulation applies to all firms. However those firms, where the controlling shareholder is of type g, are unaffected: here the level of private benefits is zero in any case. The regulation is instead binding on those firms where the controlling shareholder is of type b: here private benefits are set to a level $B = 0$ with probability π, and $B = B^*(\alpha)$ otherwise. The following proposition shows how the regulation affects the equilibrium with hidden information.

Proposition 2. *The equilibrium with regulation still implies cross-subsidization. The regulation raises the utility level of a g-type, and it lowers the utility of a b-type retaining a stake* α_h*; the effect on a b-type retaining* α_l *is ambiguous.*

The regulation cannot avoid cross-subsidization, as the market price of equity $R_C(\alpha)$ (C stands for commitment) is the same for both types of firms (within each group: those with $\alpha = \alpha_h$ and those with $\alpha = \alpha_l$). However, the revenue from issuing equity is increased by the governance institution, and the increase is larger the more binding is its commitment power: $R_C(\alpha) > R_{HI}(\alpha)$, with $R_C(\alpha)$ increasing in π. The payoff of a good entrepreneur is increased accordingly. The effect on the payoff of a bad entrepreneur is not clear-cut, since the gain from the higher market price of equity has to be balanced with the cost of the constraint; the balance is negative for those retaining α_h, and it is ambiguous for those retaining α_l.

5. Self-Regulation as a Separating Tool

Several governance features are left to self-regulation, through best practice codes, and to private initiative. Other features are imposed by the corporate law. For example, the number of independent directors is largely left to the discretion of shareholders, as the regulation generally mandates only a minimum number. In some countries (France and Italy), the corporations are free to chose between a one-tier and a two-tier board structure, while in other countries one of the two structures is imposed by the regulation (one-tier in the U.S. and U.K., two-tier in Germany). Auditing is regulated, but several items are left to private decisions (such as the choice of the auditor). In general, the authorities have to decide the boundaries of regulatory imposition.

In this section, I analyze the impact of a discretionary governance institution: corporations are supposed to be free to apply it (for example, through charter provisions). For brevity, I label this situation as "self-regulation". In particular, I assume that a governance institution is available, and large shareholders have to decide whether to apply it or not.[14] It is reasonable to assume that such decision is taken *before* issuing equity, reflecting the fact that the adoption of governance rules is a long-run decision, that cannot easily be modified afterwards. By applying the governance institution, a large shareholder voluntarily commits to let the general interest of shareholders prevail over his/her own private benefits (if any). Formally, the following assumption — where the parameter π continues to measure the degree of commitment incorporated into the governance institution — replaces Assumption 9 (Fig. 2 shows the timing of events).

Assumption 10 (self-regulation). Before issuing equity, the large shareholder decides whether to apply (A) or not (NA) the governance institution, and this choice is public information. The consequences of his/her choice are as follows.

- If he/she plays A: after issuing equity, with probability π the level of B is decided by a third party, with utility function V; with probability $1-\pi$ the level of B is decided by the large shareholder himself/herself.
- If he/she plays NA: after issuing equity, he/she decides the value of B.

Assumption 10 implies that, in a firm where the controlling shareholder is of type b and he/she plays A, private benefits are set to a level $B = 0$ with probability π and $B = B^*(\alpha)$ otherwise; to the contrary, if he/she plays NA, it is $B = B^*(\alpha)$. Those firms, where the controlling shareholder is of type g, are not affected by the choice A, NA: the constraint possibly introduced through the governance institution is not binding for them.

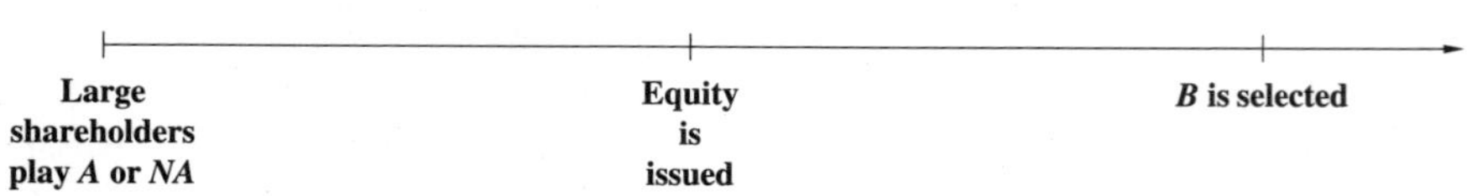

Figure 2. Self-regulation: Timing of events.

Proposition 3. *Let us define:*

$$\overline{\pi}(\alpha) \equiv \frac{B^*(\alpha) - \alpha B^*(\alpha)}{u[B^*(\alpha)] - \alpha B^*(\alpha)}, \quad \text{for } \alpha = \alpha_h, \alpha_l \tag{1}$$

The equilibrium with self-regulation is as follows.

(A) If $\pi \geq \overline{\pi}(\alpha_h)$:

(A.1) within the group of entrepreneurs retaining an equity stake α_h, a separating equilibrium obtains, where good ones play A and bad ones play NA; they have the same utility levels as with full information and

(A.2) within the group of entrepreneurs retaining an equity stake α_l, a pooling equilibrium obtains, where all play A and they have the same utility levels as with regulation.

(B) If $\pi < \overline{\pi}(\alpha_h)$: $\exists \overline{k} \in (0, 1)$ such that iff $k \geq \overline{k}$ a pooling equilibrium obtains in both groups (α_h and α_l), where all entrepreneurs play A and they have the same utility levels as with regulation.

Corollary 1. *Regulation is weakly Pareto-dominated by self-regulation.*

Proposition 3 shows our main point: a governance institution, preventing a dominant shareholder from pursuing his/her own private benefits, may be used as a separating tool; thus good entrepreneurs avoid subsidizing bad ones. The reason behind this result lies in the different cost of adopting such an institution: it is costly for a bad type (constrained to give up $u[B^*(\alpha_h)]$ with probability π) while it is costless for a good type.

Separation emerges within the group of entrepreneurs retaining a high equity stake (α_h), while it does not within those retaining a low equity stake (α_l). The different outcomes across the two groups deserve an explanation. As noted above (Sec. 3), a bad entrepreneur would commit to set $B = \hat{B}$, if he/she was able to do so: $\hat{B}$ is the first best level of private benefits (the one chosen by an owner retaining the whole equity, i.e., $\alpha = 1$). The governance institution provides a commitment device, but this is imperfect: in particular, it implies a constraint to set $B = 0$ (with probability π). Therefore, only those entrepreneurs, starting from a high level of private benefits ($B^*(\alpha_l)$), are willing to implement such a commitment device: the distortion due to private benefits ($B^*(\alpha_l) - \hat{B}$) is large, and the commitment enables them to avoid it. To the contrary, those facing a lower distortion $(B^*(\alpha_h) - \hat{B})$ are not willing to give up their private benefits altogether.[15]

The bottom line is that the governance institution is applied by those firms where controlling shareholders either do not have private benefits (g-type) or they start from a high level of private benefits, as they retain a small fraction of equity (b-type, α_l): the former apply it as a *separating* device (signaling their own type), the latter as a *commitment* tool (binding themselves to restrain from the extraction of private benefits). The governance mechanism is not applied by those firms where the controlling shareholder extract an intermediate level of private benefits, retaining a large share of equity (b-type, α_h), as neither motivation works in this case.

It is worth noting that the separation outcome can be reached only if the commitment power of the governance institution is strong enough ($\pi \geq \overline{\pi}(\alpha_h)$). Otherwise, the cost of the constraint to set $B = 0$ is too low for bad types, compared with the benefit of issuing equity at a higher price by "imitating" good types. In the latter case, a pooling equilibrium obtains (provided k is large enough), where all firms apply the governance institution. The larger the α_h, the weaker the condition $\pi \geq \bar{\pi}(\alpha_h)$, as a higher concentration of ownership makes the separating equilibrium more likely.[16]

Corollary 1 highlights that self-regulation is superior to regulation: issuers' payoffs are (weakly) larger with the former than with the latter. Intuitively, as far as the governance institution is useful as a commitment device, it is applied by firms without any need to be imposed by the law; in this regard, regulation is simply redundant. But it is only in a free market equilibrium that the governance mechanism may be useful as a separating device. This leads to a better outcome than under a regulation imposing a uniform governance structure across all firms.

To help the reader comparing the outcomes of the different equilibria obtained throughout the chapter, I summarize them in Table 1, where the payoffs of the issuers are indicated as follows: FI stands for the payoff in the equilibrium with full information and HI in that with hidden information, R stands for the payoff in the equilibrium under regulation and SR under self-regulation.

Table 1. Entrepreneurs' payoffs: Comparison among equilibria.

	$\pi \geq \overline{\pi}(\alpha_h)$	$\pi < \overline{\pi}(\alpha_h)$
g-type, α_h	FI = SR > R > HI	FI > R = SR > HI
g-type, α_l	FI > R = SR > HI	FI > R = SR > HI
b-type, α_h	HI > FI = SR > R	HI > R = SR > FI
b-type, α_l	HI $\geq$ *or* $\leq$ R = SR > FI	HI $\geq$ *or* $\leq$ R = SR > FI

6. Concluding Remarks: Empirical Implications

Let us conclude by drawing some implications from the above model. The main message is that the relationship between governance institutions and the ability to extract private benefits is in principle non-monotonic. As far as the scope for private benefits is observable — for example through a proxy such as free cash-flow — one should observe that firms more reliant on self-disciplining mechanisms such as independent directors are those with levels of free cash-flow in the lower and upper tails of the distribution, as opposed to those with an intermediate cash-flow level. The empirical evidence available so far (see Sec. 2.2) points to a monotonic direct relationship. This is consistent with the view that some governance institutions are used as a way to cope with the moral hazard issue related to private benefits of control.

The model tells us that some further empirical work may be needed to detect those firms using such institutions as a signaling device to cope with an adverse selection problem. The second prediction of the model is that the relationship between ownership concentration and the application of self-disciplining mechanisms is negative: where the incentives of the controlling party are more aligned to those of shareholders, the need to introduce such mechanisms is reduced. This is consistent with the empirical findings that the independence of the board is decreasing in the equity stake retained by the CEO.

Finally, a normative implication may be drawn. The adoption of governance institutions limiting the extraction of private benefits of control should be left to the free decisions of firms, rather than be imposed by the law. Only in a free market equilibrium some firms are able to distinguish themselves from others by structuring their governance in a way that signals their quality. This argument supports the view — developed in the literature referred to in Sec. 2 — that governance institutions emerge as optimizing responses to firm-specific features, thus the imposition of uniform rules would be detrimental.

Appendix

Proof of Lemma 1. After issuing equity, R is given. Hence, the decision problem of a b-type is:

$$\max_B u(B) + \alpha(\text{Vmax} - B) \tag{2}$$

and the FOC is:

$$u'(B^*) = \alpha, \tag{3}$$

which implicitly defines $B^*(\alpha)$ as a decreasing function. $B^*(1) = \hat{B}$ by definition (Assumption 5).

Proof of Lemma 2. Thanks to Assumption 7, the selling price of the equity share $(1 - \alpha)$ must equal the payoff that external investors expect from holding equity. The level of private benefits is fully anticipated by investors. Therefore, for any given level of B, a b-type earns a revenue from the equity sale equal to $R_b(\alpha) = (1 - \alpha)(\text{Vmax} - B)$, and their utility level is $u(B) + \alpha(\text{Vmax} - B) + R_b(\alpha) = \text{Vmax} + u(B) - B$. From Assumption 5, it follows that $\hat{B} = \text{argmax}[\text{Vmax} + u(B) - B]$; hence, $\hat{B}$ is the optimal level of private benefits under commitment. From Lemma 1, the equilibrium level of private benefits is $B^*(\alpha) > \hat{B}$, for $\alpha = \alpha_h, \alpha_l$; so the equilibrium level of utility is $\text{Vmax} + u[B^*(\alpha)] - B^*(\alpha) < \text{Vmax} + u(\hat{B}) - \hat{B}$.

Proof of Proposition 1. With hidden information, the revenue from the equity sale is the following for both types (t = g, b):

$$\begin{aligned} R_{HI}(\alpha) &= (1 - \alpha)[k\text{Vmax} + (1 - k)(\text{Vmax} - B^*(\alpha))] \\ &= (1 - \alpha)[\text{Vmax} - (1 - k)B^*(\alpha)] \end{aligned} \tag{4}$$

since with probability k $(1-k)$ an investor buys shares issued by a g-type (b-type). For $\alpha = \alpha_h, \alpha_l$, it is $R_g(\alpha) > R_{HI}(\alpha) > R_b(\alpha)$, and the equilibrium levels of entrepreneurs' utility are the following:

- g-type: $\alpha\text{Vmax} + R_{HI}(\alpha) = \text{Vmax} - (1-\alpha)(1-k)B^*(\alpha) < \text{Vmax}$ and
- b-type: $u[B^*(\alpha)] + \alpha(\text{Vmax} - B^*(\alpha)) + R_{HI}(\alpha) = \text{Vmax} + u[B^*(\alpha)] - [1-k(1-\alpha)]B^*(\alpha) > \text{Vmax} + u[B^*(\alpha)] - B^*(\alpha)$.

Proof of Proposition 2. For both types (t = g, b), the revenue from the equity sale is:

$$\begin{aligned} R_C(\alpha) &= (1-\alpha)\{k\text{Vmax} + (1-k)[\pi\text{Vmax} \\ &\quad + (1-\pi)(\text{Vmax} - B^*(\alpha))]\} \\ &= (1-\alpha)[\text{Vmax} - (1-k)(1-\pi)B^*(\alpha)] \end{aligned} \tag{5}$$

and $R_g(\alpha) > R_C(\alpha) > R_b(\alpha)$ (for $\alpha = \alpha_h, \alpha_l$). The equilibrium levels of utility are as follows:

- g-type: $\alpha\text{Vmax} + R_C(\alpha) = \text{Vmax} - (1-\alpha)(1-k)(1-\pi)B^*(\alpha) > \text{Vmax} - (1-\alpha)(1-k)B^*(\alpha)$, for $\alpha = \alpha_h, \alpha_l$ and
- b-type: $\pi\alpha\text{Vmax} + (1-\pi)\{u[B^*(\alpha)] + \alpha(\text{Vmax} - B^*(\alpha))\} + R_C(\alpha) = \text{Vmax} + (1-\pi)\{u[B^*(\alpha)] - [1-k(1-\alpha)]B^*(\alpha)\}$.
  $\text{Vmax} + (1-\pi)\{u[B^*(\alpha_h)] - [1-k(1-\alpha_h)]B^*(\alpha_h)\} < \text{Vmax} + \{u[B^*(\alpha_h)] - [1-k(1-\alpha_h)]B^*(\alpha_h)\}$, since the term in brackets is positive;
  $\text{Vmax} + (1-\pi)\{u[B^*(\alpha_l)] - [1-k(1-\alpha_l)]B^*(\alpha_l)\} \leq or \geq \text{Vmax} + \{u[B^*(\alpha_l)] - [1-k(1-\alpha_l)]B^*(\alpha_l)\}$, since the sign of the term in brackets is undetermined.

Proof of Proposition 3. (A.1) Let $\alpha = \alpha_h$. By playing A, good entrepreneurs signal their type to investors. Hence, a separating equilibrium obtains, where the revenue from the equity sale is $R_g(\alpha_h) = (1-\alpha_h)\text{Vmax}$ for a g-type and $R_b(\alpha_h) = (1-\alpha_h)[\text{Vmax} - B^*(\alpha_h)]$ for a b-type, and their utility levels are Vmax and $\text{Vmax} + u[B^*(\alpha_h)] - B^*(\alpha_h)$ respectively (as in the full information equilibrium of Sec. 3). We have to check that the incentive compatibility constraints (IC) for both types are met: a b-type does not have an incentive to "mimic" a g-type by playing A, and vice versa. By playing A, a b-type would get $\pi\alpha_h\text{Vmax} + (1-\pi)\{u[B^*(\alpha_h)] + \alpha_h(\text{Vmax} - B^*(\alpha_h))\} + R_g(\alpha_h) = \text{Vmax} + (1-\pi)\{u[B^*(\alpha_h)] - \alpha_h B^*(\alpha_h)\}$, hence IC for a b-type is: $\text{Vmax} + u[B^*(\alpha_h)] - B^*(\alpha_h) \geq \text{Vmax} + (1-\pi)\{u[B^*(\alpha_h)] - \alpha_h B^*(\alpha_h)\}$, which is equivalent to $\pi \geq \overline{\pi}(\alpha_h)$, which is true by assumption. By playing NA, a g-type would get $\alpha_h\text{Vmax} + R_b(\alpha_h) = \text{Vmax} - (1-\alpha_h)B^*(\alpha_h)$; hence, IC for a g-type is: $\text{Vmax} \geq \text{Vmax} - (1-\alpha_h)B^*(\alpha_h)$, which is trivially met.

(A.2) Let $\alpha = \alpha_l$. It is $\overline{\pi}(\alpha_l) > 1$, since $u[B^*(\alpha_l)] < B^*(\alpha_l)$; hence, $\pi < \overline{\pi}(\alpha_l)$, and the separating equilibrium cannot be sustained, as IC for a b-type is not met. A pooling equilibrium obtains, where the revenue from the equity sale is $R_C(\alpha_l)$ (see Eq. (5)) for both types, and utility levels are the following (see the proof of Proposition 2):

$$\text{Vmax} - (1-\alpha_l)(1-k)(1-\pi)B^*(\alpha_l) \text{ for a g-type,}$$
$$\text{Vmax} + (1-\pi)\{u[B^*(\alpha_l)] - [1-k(1-\alpha_l)]B^*(\alpha_l)\} \text{ for a b-type.}$$

As for the out-of-equilibrium beliefs of investors, it is reasonable to assume that they believe a deviating entrepreneur (playing NA) to be a b-type, since only a b-type bears some cost for playing A. Therefore, a g-type does not deviate, as he/she would get $\alpha_l\text{Vmax} + R_b(\alpha_l)$ instead of $\alpha_l\text{Vmax} + R_C(\alpha_l)$, where $R_b(\alpha_l) < R_C(\alpha_l)$. A b-type does not deviate if:

$$\begin{aligned}\text{Vmax} + (1-\pi)\{u[B^*(\alpha_l)] - [1-k(1-\alpha_l)]B^*(\alpha_l)\}\\ \geq \text{Vmax} + u[B^*(\alpha_l)] - B^*(\alpha_l),\end{aligned} \tag{6}$$

which holds for $k = 0$, and the LHS is increasing in k; hence, condition (6) holds for any $k \geq 0$ (and any π).

(B) For the group of entrepreneurs retaining an equity stake α_l, the proof is the same as in (A.2).

For the group of entrepreneurs retaining an equity stake α_h, the proof is the same as in (A.2) with α_h replacing α_l, except for the following:

- the separating equilibrium breaks down because by assumption, it is $\pi < \overline{\pi}(\alpha_h)$ and

- for $k = 0$ condition (6) fails to hold, while for $k = 1$ it holds with strict inequality[17]; hence, $\exists \bar{k} \in (0, 1)$ such that (6) is met iff $k \geq \bar{k}$.

Proof of Corollary 1. We only need to check that utility levels in (A.1) are higher than those achieved with regulation.

For a g-type: Vmax $>$ Vmax $- (1 - \alpha_h)(1 - k)(1 - \pi)B^*(\alpha_h)$
For a b-type: Vmax $+ u[B^*(\alpha_h)] - B^*(\alpha_h) \geq$ Vmax $+ (1 - \pi)$ $\{u[B^*(\alpha_h)] - [1 - k(1 - \alpha_h)]B^*(\alpha_h)\}$

This inequality is met for $k = 1$ (given $\pi \geq \bar{\pi}(\alpha_h)$), and the RHS is increasing in k, so it is met (with strict inequality) for any $k < 1$ as well.

Endnotes

1. Many thanks to A. Carmignani and audience at the Midwest Finance Association Conference 2008 for useful comments.
2. Empirical measures of the value of control have been provided — among others — by Dyck and Zingales (2004) and Nenova (2003). The first exploits the difference between the price paid in a control block transaction and the market price of shares while the second is based on the price difference between multiple and limited voting shares.
3. This extension implies some costs. In particular, the governance institution limiting the extraction of private benefits will be modeled in a very stylized way, abstracting from organizational details. Then issues such as the size and composition of the board of directors are not explicitly analyzed. However, the model bears some implications on such issues, that will become apparent below.
4. However, in Adams and Ferreira (2007), the relationship between board independence and managerial private benefits is non-monotonic for quite different reasons than in my model. In their approach, it is optimal for shareholders to appoint a "friendly board" for intermediate levels of private benefits, in order to induce the CEO to reveal his information. Otherwise, it is not optimal to do so, and a fully independent board is appointed. For low levels of private benefits the CEO shares his/her information with the board anyway; for high levels, it is too costly to induce him/her to share his/her information.
5. For a comprehensive survey of the theory of control rights in corporate finance see Tirole (2006).
6. Warther (1998) also focuses on the interplay between the CEO's power to select directors and the board power to dismiss the CEO, finding that the board typically swings from unanimous support to unanimous opposition to the CEO; so "a lack of routine dissent is nevertheless consistent with a significant disciplinary role". Maug (1997) stresses the role of independent directors in monitoring managers who may want to inefficiently oppose to a corporate restructuring process.

7. The issue of large shareholders' interference with managers has been raised by Burkart *et al.* (1997). In their framework the drawback of shareholders' interference is the adverse effect on managers' incentive to exert effort. The issue analyzed here is instead the extraction of private benefits by a dominant shareholder.
8. Hermalin and Weisbach (2003) provide a comprehensive survey of the empirical evidence on board structure.
9. Assuming that the proportion (k) of g-type is the same across the two groups simplifies the exposition, without altering any of the results obtained in the chapter.
10. Note that the hidden information problem affects the market price of shares, while it does not affect the equilibrium level of private benefits.
11. For a comparative analysis of the legal framework of corporate governance in different countries, see Kraakman *et al.* (2004) and Enriques and Volpin (2007).
12. The concept of incomplete law, and its implications for the regulation of financial markets, is analyzed in Pistor and Xu (2003).
13. Of course, full commitment is incorporated into the model as the particular case where $\pi = 1$.
14. We are of course abstracting from the specific ways through which a large shareholder can have a determinant influence over such decision (this kind of decisions are generally taken in the shareholders' meeting).
15. Note that a bad entrepreneur with a high share of equity (α_h) is not willing to commit, even though by committing he/she would be able to "mimic" a good type and sell shares at price $R_g(\alpha_h)$ instead of $R_b(\alpha_h)$.
16. By derivating (1), the reader can check that $\overline{\pi}(\alpha_h)$ is decreasing in α_h (in the limit, it is $\overline{\pi}(\overline{\alpha}) = 1$ and $\overline{\pi}(1) = 0$).
17. For $k = 1$, condition (6) boils down to $\pi \leq \overline{\pi}(\alpha_h)$, which is true by assumption.

References

Adams, R and D Ferreira (2007). A theory of friendly boards. *Journal of Finance*, 62(1), 217–250.

Boone, A, L Field, J Karpoff and C Raheja (2007). The determinants of corporate board size and composition: An empirical analysis. *Journal of Financial Economics*, 85, 66–101.

Brickley, J, J Coles and G Jarrell (1997). Leadership structure: Separating the CEO and chairman of the board. *Journal of Corporate Finance*, 3, 189–220.

Burkart, M, D Gromb and F Panunzi (1997). Large shareholders, monitoring, and the value of the firm. *Quarterly Journal of Economics*, 112, 693–728.

Coles, J, N Daniel and L Naveen (2005). Boards: Does one size fit all? Working Paper (http://ssrn.com/abstract=665746).

Dahya, J, O Dimitrov and J McConnell (2005). Dominant shareholders and allied directors: A simple model and evidence from 22 countries. ECGI, Finance Working Paper no. 99/2005.

Dyck, A and L Zingales (2004). Private benefits of control: An international comparison. *Journal of Finance*, 59, 537–600.

Enriques, L and P Volpin (2007). Corporate governance reforms in continental Europe. *Journal of Economic Perspectives*, 21, 117–140.

Fama, E and M Jensen (1983). Separation of ownership and control. *Journal of Law and Economics*, 26(2), 301–325.

Gillan, S, J Hartzell and L Starks (2006). Tradeoffs in corporate governance: Evidence from board structures and charter provisions. Working Paper (http://ssrn.com/abstract=917544).

Graziano, C and A Luporini (2005). Ownership concentration, monitoring and optimal board structure. Working Paper (http://ssrn.com/abstract=657165).

Harris, M and A Raviv (2008). A theory of board control and size. *Review of Financial Studies*, 21, 1797–1832.

Hermalin, B and M Weisbach (1998). Endogenously chosen boards of directors and their monitoring of the CEO. *American Economic Review*, 88, 96–118.

Hermalin, B and M Weisbach (2003). Boards of directors as an endogenously determined institution: A survey of the economic literature. *FRBNY Economic Policy Review*, April, 7–26.

Jensen, M and W Meckling (1976). Theory of the firm: Managerial behavior, agency costs and ownership structure. *Journal of Financial Economics*, 3, 305–360.

Kraakman, R *et al.* (2004). The anatomy of corporate law. *A Comparative and Functional Approach.* Oxford University Press.

Lehn, K, S Patro and M Zhao (2003). Determinants of the size and structure of corporate boards: 1935–2000. Working paper, University of Pittsburgh.

Linck, J, J Netter and T Yang (2007). The determinants of board structure. *Journal of Financial Economics*, 87, 308–328.

Maug, E (1997). Boards of directors and capital structure: Alternative forms of corporate restructuring. *Journal of Corporate Finance*, 3, 113–139.

Nenova, T (2003). The value of corporate voting rights and control: A cross-country analysis. *Journal of Financial Economics*, 68, 325–351.

Pistor, K and C Xu (2003). Incomplete law — A conceptual and analytical framework and its application to the evolution of financial market regulation. *Journal of International Law and Politics*, 35, 931–1013.

Raheja, C (2005). Determinants of board size and composition: A theory of corporate boards. *Journal of Financial and Quantitative Analysis*, 40(2), 283–306.

Tirole, J (2006). *The Theory of Corporate Finance.* Princeton University Press.

Warther, V (1998). Board effectiveness and board dissent. *Journal of Corporate Finance*, 4, 53–70.

9

Managing the Costs of Issuing Common Equity: The Role of Registration Choice

Jennifer E. Bethel and Laurie Krigman

1. Introduction

Issuing common equity is an expensive way to raise the capital. Costs include fees paid to underwriters, downwards price pressure from an increased supply of shares, time delays that uniquely arise from registering equity, and asymmetric information-related stock-price declines at issuance announcements. These costs can differ, however, depending on the type of equity that firms choose to raise and firm the characteristics. For example, Fama and French (2005) argue that some equity issuances, including employee stock options and equity used as currency in mergers, do not suffer from an asymmetric information problem and are therefore less costly than public equity issuances. Gomes and Phillips (2005) demonstrate that firms with high levels of information asymmetry are more likely to privately place equity than firms with low-information asymmetry. These findings suggest that firms choose low-cost methods to raise the capital.

In the United States, most firms have a choice of how to register and issue equity through seasoned equity offerings (SEOs). In this chapter, controlling for firm and offering characteristics, we test whether firms can lower the costs of raising equity by optimally choosing among Securities and Exchange Commission (SEC) requirements for registering and issuing SEOs. The traditional method requires firms to file registration statements that include detailed disclosure about the firm and the securities being offered for sale in advance of security offerings. This information-intensive procedure, which is designed to mitigate problems of asymmetric information between firms and investors, is time consuming and subject to delays.[1]

The second method is a deregulated streamlined process called "unallocated shelf registration"). Shelf registration permits firms to file a single all-encompassing registration statement once every two years rather than filing individual registration statements for every security offering. A shelf registration simultaneously registers many types of potential security offerings, including debt and common equity, which a firm may issue at its discretion over the succeeding two years. Firms register securities without specifying the amount of each security to be offered, the expected timing of offerings or, importantly, the expected use of the proceeds. Once registration statements are approved by the SEC, firms face no additional disclosure requirements or regulatory delays when issuing the securities. Compared to the traditional registration procedure, shelf registration contains few features to mitigate the information asymmetry between firms and investors. However, shelf registration offers users increased flexibility in the timing of securities sales and design. Accessing the market quickly allows firms to fulfill capital immediacy needs and take advantage of windows of opportunity in the market (Bayless and Chaplinsky, 1996). Proponents also argue that shelf registration promotes underwriter competition, lowering direct issuance costs, relative to traditional registration. The design of shelf registration trades off maximizing shareholder welfare in terms of asymmetric information and minimizing firm-specific issuance costs.

Using a sample of SEOs between 1992 and 2002, we examine the types of firms that choose each registration strategy and compare the costs that firms incur. Although all of the firms we examine are eligible to use both shelf and traditional registration, we find firms that choose shelf registration are larger, more highly levered, and more widely followed by analysts than firms that use traditional registration. After controlling for selection effects, we find firms that use shelf registration access the market significantly faster than firms that use traditional registration. The underwriting spread for shelf registration common equity issuances is significantly lower than for traditional SEOs. Thus, shelf registration lowers the cost of raising equity relative to traditional registration.

Despite these advantages, only 20% of the equity that is eligible for shelf registration is issued using it. Certain firms may experience potentially significant disadvantages using shelf relative to the traditional procedure. Because firms register up to two years of securities sales — sales that may or may not take place and that may or may not be common equity — instead of only the exact amount of their next equity offering, investors do not know how much capital ultimately will be raised, the use of the funds or the type of securities that will be offered. As such, the market may fear that common equity will be issued to fund unprofitable projects, and therefore discount equity share prices when shelf registrations are filed, well ahead of announcements of actual security offerings. Price drops that occur at this time are commonly referred to as "market overhang" (Bhagat *et al.*, 1985).[2]

We examine the severity of and determinants of market overhang when firms file shelf registrations, controlling for selection effects. Because market overhang is a response by the market to uncertainty about corporate actions, we test whether market overhang is related to firm-specific levels of information asymmetry. We conjecture that firms with high information asymmetry should incur more severe market overhang when registering common equity on shelf registrations than firms with low information asymmetry. On average, we find no statistically significant evidence of market overhang. However, when high information asymmetry firms register by means of shelf registrations, they experience large, statistically significant declines in share price, and we find that relatively few of these firms issue common equity using shelf registration. In contrast, firms with low information asymmetry experience no market overhang when registering by shelf registrations. Our results suggest that managers select registration procedures that lower costs and base their registration choices on information characteristics.

We also find that high information asymmetry firms that take equity off shelf registrations have significantly more negative price reactions than do high information asymmetry firms that use the traditional registration procedure. The cumulative abnormal return for registering and issuing equity using shelf for high information asymmetry firms averages −4.7%, compared to −1.9% for comparable firms that use the traditional procedure. The market deeply discounts the share prices of firms that are difficult to value, knowing that these firms have incentives to choose shelf registration over traditional registration when projects are unprofitable. The market's reaction is also more negative for high information asymmetry firms that use shelf registrations than for low information asymmetry firms that use shelf. Thus, although shelf registration lowers some issuance costs (including fees to underwriters and delays accessing the market) for all firms, price declines vary by information asymmetry, making shelf registration more valuable to some firms than others. The market imposes costs on high information asymmetry firms. These firms tend to use the traditional registration procedure with detailed disclosure to raise equity even though the SEC allows these firms to use shelf registration.

Finally, we explore why some high information asymmetry firms use shelf registration even though they experience high market overhang. We find these firms pay lower gross spreads and go to market faster than the same type of firm that chooses the traditional registration procedure. Thus the advantages of shelf registration may outweigh its disadvantage — market overhang — for some high information asymmetry firms.

The rest of the chapter proceeds as follows. In Sec. 2, we describe the details of securities registration. We discuss the costs of issuing equity using shelf registration relative to the traditional registration procedure. Section 3 describes our data set. In Sec. 4, we examine the types of firms that choose the registration strategies, and in Sec. 5 and 6, we compare their costs. Section 7 concludes.

2. Traditional Registration of Common Equity Offerings

The Securities Act of 1933 requires firms that offer securities to the public to register them with the SEC. Consistent with the SEC's mandate to protect investors through detailed information disclosure, the traditional procedure stipulates that firms file registration statements that include preliminary prospectuses (red herrings) that specify information about the firm, the securities being offered for sale, and the expected use of proceeds. The SEC's staff have the option of reviewing preliminary prospectuses for accuracy and completeness, and in some instances it requests changes. For example, according to the *Report of the Advisory Committee on Capital Raising Activity: July 24, 1996*, the SEC reviewed 14% of SEO filings during the period from January 1994 through December 1995.

Staff reviews can take weeks or even months to complete and may require several iterations with firms. According to the same report, the staff approved or declared effective firms registration statements 32 days after firms filed initial preliminary prospectuses. Once the staff declares registration statements effective, firms are free to price and sell securities, and they typically access the market as soon as possible thereafter. Following the sale of securities, the SEC requires firms to file pricing supplements within two days of sale to notify the market participants of the exact terms of offerings.

3. A Brief History of Shelf Registration

In 1969, Congress commissioned the Wheat Report to address the problems with the capital-raising process. The report criticized the traditional registration procedure as being unnecessarily burdensome and costly. The SEC responded in 1982 by adopting Rule 415, a reform that allows firms to raise the capital using allocated shelf registration. Allocated shelf registration permits firms to register a core prospectus that includes the maximum dollar amount of a single type of security that they "reasonably expect to be offered and sold within two years." For example, firms can register either debt or equity on an allocated shelf registration. After SEC review (which is typically negligible or non-existent), the SEC declares firms' shelf registration statements effective, and firms can then sell or take down securities with no further regulatory intervention or delay. Firms must notify the SEC of final offering details within two days following the completion of offerings. It is important to note that there is no implicit or explicit guarantee that firms actually raise the capital specified on shelf registrations. Thus, shelf registrants publicly declare they might raise capital, but they do not specify the actual amounts, timing of offerings or the expected use of proceeds.

Following the introduction of allocated shelf registration, firms quickly began registering debt securities on shelf registrations. By 1991, firms registered approximately 60% of all debt and preferred equity issued on allocated shelf registrations.[3] In contrast, less than 1% of common equity issued was registered on shelf registrations.[4] The SEC responded in 1992 to firms' reluctance to register common equity on allocated shelf registrations by permitting them to register multiple types of securities on a single-unallocated shelf registration statement. Under this process, firms do not need to specify the amount of each type of security that they plan to offer. Qualifying firms need only file a core prospectus specifying their potential financing needs over the subsequent two years and a list of the securities they might issue. As with allocated shelf registrations, firms publicly declare they might raise capital, but do not specify the amount to be raised. Unlike allocated shelf registrations, the types of securities that firms can choose to issue are also uncertain. We depict timelines for the traditional and unallocated shelf registration procedures below in Fig. 1.

In its Adopting Release 33-6964, the SEC expressed its hope that issuers would use this new, more flexible registration procedure for common equity. The purported advantages of issuing common equity using unallocated shelf are threefold. First, by registering common equity on unallocated shelf registrations, managers avoid SEC review of offerings at the time of sale and hence, regulatory uncertainty and the possibility of delay.

Thus, firms using unallocated shelf registrations should be able to fulfill their funding needs more quickly and with greater certainty of

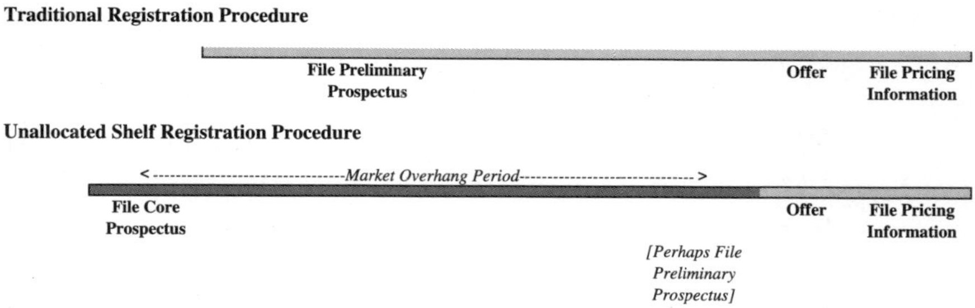

Figure 1. The sequence of events for filing registration statements and issuing securities using traditional and unallocated shelf registration procedures, In the unallocated shelf registration procedure, the filing of a prelimiary prospectus is optional.

timing than would firms using the traditional registration procedure. Second, because firms avoid possible regulatory delays, they should be able to better exploit short-term pricing opportunities in the market. Whether stock price movements arise from economy-wide or firm-specific sources, managers have incentives to issue common equity when stock prices are high. Graham and Harvey (2001), in a survey of CFOs, document that 67% of managers admit that[5] "the amount by which our stock is undervalued or overvalued by the market" is an important factor in their decision to issue common equity. Third, managers who register and take common equity off shelf registrations should encounter a more competitive underwriting market and have lower direct issuance costs.

Because firms that register core prospectuses typically have no immediate capital-raising needs, underwriters have less bargaining power over fees than they do when firms want to go to market quickly. When common equity is taken down, because many of the regulatory hurdles have already been met, due diligence is generally shorter and fees are lower. Consistent with this argument, Bhagat *et al.* (1985) and Blackwell *et al.* (1990) document lower issuance costs for common equity offerings from allocated shelf registrations in the early and mid-1980s. Denis (1993) finds a selection bias in the type of firm that chose to use allocated equity shelf registrations in the 1980s. The study documents the differences previously found in underwriter fees are based on issuer characteristics rather than registration choice.[6]

Offsetting these advantages is a potential disadvantage — market overhang. As discussed above, managers avoided registering common equity on allocated equity shelf registrations because they feared that doing so would result in high levels of prolonged market overhang.[7] Models of asymmetric information such as Ambarish *et al.* (1987), Myers and Majluf (1984), and Cooney and Kalay (1993) demonstrate that the cost of raising equity capital is positively related to asymmetric information. Extending this line of reasoning, we conjecture that the cost of shelf registration should be increasing in firm-specific information asymmetry; stock-price drops surrounding shelf registrations are likely to vary across the firms and should be positively related to information asymmetry.

Because shelf registration allows firms to raise the capital without specifying the amount, timing or use of proceeds in advance of offerings, firms with high information asymmetry will likely incur more severe market overhang when registering common equity on shelf registrations than low information asymmetry firms. For high information asymmetry firms, it is difficult for the market to evaluate the need for and the potential use of proceeds. For firms with low information asymmetry, uncertainty should be minimal and firms should experience little, if any, market overhang.

In related work, Denis (1991) examines allocated-equity shelf registrations in the early 1980s to test whether market overhang is more severe for shelf registration firms that need underwriter certification of firm value than for those that do not need certification. The results show that announcement-period returns are more negative for shelf registration issuers than other issuers, and that firms with low certification needs are more likely to use shelf registration.[8] Extending Denis (1991, 1993), we perform a comprehensive study of the unallocated shelf registration choice and simultaneously examine all of the purported shelf costs and benefits controlling for selection effects. We find that although some costs of equity issuance, including underwriter fees and delays in accessing the market, depend on registration choice and are lower for shelf registration issuers, other costs such as market overhang depend on firms' characteristics. Thus shelf registration is a low-cost choice for some, but not all firms.

To date, there is limited research examining the managers' choice of registration strategy. Previous studies show, however, that managers actively manage the security offering process in numerous other ways. For example, Booth and Smith (1986) show that managers choose high-quality underwriters as certification agents to mitigate the adverse impact of issuing common equity. Managers issue debt when interest rates are low and common equity when stock prices are high. Bayless and Chaplinsky (1996) document that firms are sensitive to information asymmetry in the market when raising the capital, because it affects the contracting costs due to adverse selection. Following this line of research, we investigate whether managers choose registration strategies that lower the costs of raising common equity.

4. The Data

We examine the characteristics of firms that filed common equity on unallocated shelf registrations between the date of unallocated shelf registration adoption, 29 October 1992, and 31 December 2001. Only firms eligible to register securities on Form S-3 can register securities on unallocated shelf registrations. Eligibility for Form S-3 is restricted to firms that meet the following requirements:

1. The aggregate market value of voting shares held by non-affiliates must be at least $75 million.
2. The firm must not have defaulted on debt, preferred stock, or rental payments.
3. The firm must meet all SEC disclosure requirements for the last 12 months.
4. The firm's debt must be investment grade.

Because the financial information for REITS and financial services firms differs from that of other firms, we eliminate these firms from the sample. We also remove ADRs from the sample, because their filing requirements differ from those of domestic firms.[9]

We identify common equity takedowns from these shelf registrations for the two-year period following their registration. (We note that given the adoption date of 29 October 1992, issuers had only 71 days in 1992 during which to file shelf registrations. None took common equity off shelf registrations during this period.) We compare the characteristics of these firms with those of all firms that were eligible to use unallocated shelf registration, but whose managers chose instead to use the traditional registration procedure to issue the common equity.

Using information on unallocated shelf registrations and takedowns from SEC filings and Securities Data Corporation New Issues Database, we find that during the period we study, 402 issuers registered $641 billion of securities on 670 unallocated shelf registrations that included common equity. Table 1 contains details of the sample. Firms registered $600 million of securities per unallocated shelf registration. In addition to common equity, 97% of the shelf

Table 1. Unallocated shelf registration.

				Other securities included on shelf				
Year	# Shelves filed	Median shelf amount ($MM)	Total shelf amount ($MM)	Debt (%)	Preferred equity (%)	Convertible debt (%)	Other equity %	Other debt %
1992	2	350.0	700.0	100.0	100.0	0.0	100.0	50.0
1993	37	500.0	18,528.0	94.5	73.0	5.4	24.3	24.3
1994	56	400.0	27,655.0	100.0	83.9	1.7	25.0	21.4
1995	48	394.0	25,497.0	100.0	87.5	2.1	25.0	25.0
1996	56	409.5	28,682.0	98.2	67.8	8.9	32.1	26.7
1997	76	600.0	66,203.0	96.1	77.6	3.9	71.1	48.6
1998	99	500.0	88,949.2	96.9	80.8	2.0	67.6	43.4
1999	102	775.0	105,464.7	96.1	78.4	1.0	72.5	42.1
2000	83	1,000.0	122,639.6	97.5	86.7	1.2	80.7	48.2
2001	111	999.0	156,953.0	96.3	83.7	4.5	77.5	50.4
Full sample	670	600.0	641,271.4	97.2	80.5	3.1	60.1	40.0

The table shows the characteristics by year of 670 unallocated shelf registrations that occurred between 1992 and 2001. "#Shelf registrations Filed" is the total number of unallocated shelf registrations filed that included equity, "Median shelf amount" is the amount of capital registered on the median unallocated shelf, "Total shelf amount" is the amount of capital registered on unallocated shelf registrations each year, and "Other securities included on shelf" is the percentage of unallocated shelf registrations that included the indicated security as well as common equity. "Other equity" includes dual class shares, common stock warrants, rights, and depository shares. "Other debt" includes debt guarantees, equipment trust certificates, debt warrants, etc.

registrations included straight debt, 80% included preferred equity, 3% included convertible debt, 60% included other equity, and 40% included other types of debt. The table indicates that over time, firms have increasingly registered unallocated shelf registrations that include common equity, and that the size of unallocated shelf registrations has increased.

Table 2 presents information on takedowns from shelf registrations that included common equity and SEOs that used the traditional registration procedure. From the 670 unallocated shelf registrations, 217 firms took common equity off 262 times. An additional 37 shelf registrations had no securities taken down. A total of 185 firms that registered common equity on unallocated shelf registrations never issued common equity off their shelf registrations.

Of the unallocated shelf registrations that had securities taken down, firms raised $66 billion in common equity, $165 billion in straight debt in 291 offerings, and $7 billion in preferred equity in 29 offerings. They raised $204 billion in 445 offerings of other classes of securities. Issuers that were eligible to issue common equity from unallocated shelf registrations registered $287 billion in common equity in 2,148 traditional registration offerings. The average size of these offerings is $134 million, compared to an average common equity takedown from shelf registrations of $251 million.

5. Who Uses Shelf Registrations?

To investigate the types of firms that adopt the different registration strategies, we use financial information from Compustat and the Center for Research in Security Prices (CRSP), trade and quote data from the New York Stock Exchange's TAQ database, and analyst forecast data from the I/B/E/S database. Table 3 shows that shelf registrants have greater market capitalizations and more total assets than firms that choose the traditional registration procedure. Shelf registration users are nearly twice as financially leveraged as are firms that use traditional registration. We find stock-return volatility (Volatility) measured as the standard deviation of daily stock returns calculated over the previous calendar year is higher for firms that

Table 2. Unallocated shelf takedowns and traditional SEO filings.

	Securities taken off unallocated shelf								Traditional SEO registration	
Year*	# Common equity TDs	$ Common equity TD ($MM)	# Debt TDs	$ Debt TD ($MM)	# Preferred equity TDs	$ Preferred equity TD ($MM)	# Other TDs	$ Other TD ($MM)	#SEOs Filed	$ SEO ($MM)
1993	10	$144.8	7	$292.3	7	$145.8	13	$167.4	226	$79.4
1994	13	$136.4	14	$299.7	4	$157.5	8	$278.1	146	$74.7
1995	13	$85.3	16	$472.9	2	$161.6	18	$361.8	255	$105.6
1996	13	$187.4	22	$321.1	3	$352.5	18	$253.4	301	$103.8
1997	20	$197.8	36	$611.7	3	$178.3	38	$553.7	292	$101.7
1998	35	$241.1	51	$464.7	6	$190.8	69	$420.6	179	$120.7
1999	46	$250.1	37	$549.9	2	$162.5	76	$423.1	202	$192.2
2000	42	$418.1	28	$586.7	1	$200.0	64	$490.0	222	$229.8
2001	51	$288.9	63	$813.8	1	$1,400.0	105	$560.5	131	$162.2
2002	19	$143.4	17	$600.2	0	$0.0	36	$389.7	194	$196.9
Full sample	262	$250.7	291	$567.4	29	$231.8	445	$458.5	2,148	$133.8

The table shows the characteristics by year of 1,027 unallocated shelf takedowns and 2,148 nonshelf SEOs that occurred between 1992 and 2002. "# Common Equity TDs" is the number of common equity issuances from unallocated shelf registrations. "$ Common Equity TD" is the mean amount of common equity taken off unallocated shelf registrations. "# Debt TDs" is the number of debt issuances from unallocated shelf registrations. "$ Debt TD" is the mean amount of debt taken off unallocated shelf registrations. "# Preferred Equity TDs" is the number of preferred equity issuances from unallocated shelf registrations. "$ Preferred Equity TD" is the mean amount of preferred equity taken off unallocated shelf registrations. "# Other TDs" is the number of issuances of convertible debt, other equity, and other debt from unallocated shelf registrations. "$ Other TD" is the mean amount of other securities taken off unallocated shelf registrations. "# SEOs Filed" is the number of SEOs using traditional registration procedures. "$ SEO" is the mean amount of equity issued using traditional registration procedures.

Table 3. Firm characteristics and registration strategies.

	Shelf registration		Traditional SEO		Test of differences	
	Mean	Median	Mean	Median	*t*-test *p*-value	Kruskal–Wallis *p*-value
Market capitalization ($MM)	12,407.8	3,209.2	2,491.8	637.5	(0.0001)	(0.0001)
Total assets ($MM)	7,154.9	2,941.5	1,328.9	158.6	(0.0001)	(0.0001)
Long-term debt-to-assets	30.9%	28.3%	18.7%	11.2%	(0.0001)	(0.0001)
Volatility	2.6%	2.2%	3.6%	3.5%	(0.0001)	(0.0001)
Market-to-book ratio	3.29	1.69	10.50	3.93	(0.0001)	(0.0001)
Free cash flow-to-assets	−17.6%	−10.4%	−39.4%	−30.1%	(0.0001)	(0.0001)
Return on equity	4.33%	10.83%	−5.82%	9.62%	(0.3312)	(0.0118)
Percentage bid–ask spread	0.75%	0.56%	1.92%	1.50%	(0.0001)	(0.0001)
Number of analysts	10.32	13.00	3.04	3.00	(0.0001)	(0.0001)
Analyst forecast dispersion	26.56%	19.20%	26.63%	17.40%	(0.9621)	(0.8457)
Share turnover	6.30%	4.19%	10.44%	6.24%	(0.0001)	(0.0001)
% Listed on NYSE	80.29%		31.37%		(0.0001)	(0.0001)
Observations	670		2,148			

The table shows the mean and median characteristics of our sample of shelf and traditional SEO issuers between 1992 and 2001. "Market capitalization" is the market value of common equity and "Total assets" is the book value of total assets. "Long-term debt-to-assets" is the book value of long-term debt divided by total assets and "Volatility" is the standard deviation of daily stock returns over the prior calendar year. "Market-to-book ratio" is the [market value of common equity + total assets − book value of common equity] divided by total assets. "Free cash flow-to-assets" is measured as [operating income after tax + nonoperating income after tax − change in net working capital — net capx — interest expense — common stock dividends — preferred stock dividends] divided by total assets; and "Return on equity" is net income divided by shareholders' equity. "Percentage bid–ask spread" is the percentage bid–ask spread scaled by the midpoint of the two quotes that define the spread, using the average of the percentage bid–ask spreads across all quotes from day −30 to the shelf registration filing day. "Number of analysts" is the number of analysts issuing forecasts as reported by IBES. "Analyst forecast dispersion" is the absolute value of the range of analyst forecasts divided by the mean estimate. "Share turnover" is defined as trading volume as a percent of shares outstanding measured over the 60 trading days preceding the filing of a registration statement. *p*-values are shown in parentheses.

choose the traditional registration procedure to issue common equity than shelf registrants.

We also compare the investment opportunities and need for capital (financial slack) between shelf and non-shelf equity issuers. Jensen (1986) argues that the market should respond positively to common equity issuances if firms have valuable investment opportunities and limited free cash flow. We proxy investment opportunities with the market-to-book ratio and financial slack by the free cash flow ratio. We define market-to-book as [market value of common equity + total assets − book value of common equity] divided by total assets. We define free cash flow as [operating income after tax + non-operating income after tax − change in net working capital − net capx − interest expense − common stock dividends − preferred stock dividends] divided by total assets. Firms using the traditional registration procedure have stronger investment opportunities and less financial slack than firms using shelf. On average, shelf registrants are no more profitable than the traditional firms based on return on equity.

There are many empirical proxies used in the literature to capture information asymmetry. Based on the work of Copeland and Galai (1983), Glosten and Milgrom (1985), Corwin (2003), and Wu (2004), we employ several measures suggested by the literature to assure robustness. In the microstructure literature, percentage bid–ask spread is used as a measure of asymmetric information, order processing, and inventory-holding costs. We use percentage bid–ask spread measured over the calendar month before the event day, as our first proxy for information asymmetry.[10]

To control for the order processing and inventory components of bid–ask spreads, we include in our multivariate analyses a measure of liquidity, share turnover, defined as daily trading volume as a percentage of shares outstanding measured over the 60 trading days preceding the filing of a registration statement, and exchange listing. Second, we use the log of the number of analysts covering a firm during the calendar year prior to the offering as a proxy. The number of analysts covering a firm has a complex relationship with information asymmetry. The value of analyst coverage should be greatest for firms that have high information asymmetry. However, as more analysts cover a firm, the level of information asymmetry is likely to diminish and the marginal value of analyst coverage should decline.

As a result, the univariate relationship between information asymmetry and the number of analysts is difficult to interpret. To correct for this, we include analyst forecast dispersion as our third measure of information asymmetry. We measure analyst forecast dispersion as the absolute value of the range of analyst forecasts divided by the mean estimate. Information asymmetry should be increasing in the dispersion among analyst forecasts, holding the number of analysts constant. Firm size has also been used in the literature as a proxy for asymmetric information with larger firms assumed to have lower information asymmetry. We include it measured as the log of total assets as a control variable in all estimations. Because firm size has been used to proxy many other firm characteristics, we focus our discussion in this chapter on the other proxies.

Table 3 shows that shelf firms have significantly less information asymmetry than do traditional registration firms. Shelf firms have an average percentage bid–ask spread of 0.75% and 10 analysts following them compared to a percentage bid–ask spread of 1.92% and three analysts for firms that raise equity using the traditional procedure. On a univariate level, we find no difference in analyst forecast dispersion between shelf and traditional registration firms.

The univariate results in Table 3 indicate that the characteristics of firms that use shelf differ significantly from those that use traditional registration. Here in a multivariate setting, we further explore the types of firms that use shelf. We estimate a probit model, where the dependent variable, Shelf Registration, is an indicator variable equal to one if a firm files an unallocated shelf that includes equity and zero if it raises common equity using the traditional registration procedure. We test whether the firms that are likely to achieve the greatest benefits and the lowest costs from using shelf are likely to use it. Thus, the independent variables of interest are our proxies for information asymmetry and stock-return volatility. Firms with low levels of information asymmetry should have a low cost to using shelf in terms of market overhang and firms with high stock-return volatility should benefit from the market-timing option offered by shelf.

The control variables in the analysis include investment opportunities (as measured by the market-to-book ratio), free cash flow, liquidity (as measured by share turnover), and exchange listing. To control for the impact of differences in asset size on the probability of shelf usage, we include firm size, as measured by the log of assets.

We also control for firm leverage, which we measure by total debt divided by total assets. This variable captures the ability of firms to raise debt rather than having to resort to common equity (Galai and Masulis, 1976). We control for one-digit SICs and calendar years using indicator variables. In addition to coefficients, we estimate marginal probabilities. The results are presented in Table 4.

We find the likelihood that firms register common equity on unallocated shelf registrations is strongly related to information asymmetry. In Model 1 of Table 4, we find that firms with low information asymmetry, as measured by percentage bid–ask spread, are significantly more likely to register common equity on unallocated shelf registrations than use the traditional registration procedure. In Model 2, we measure information asymmetry using the number of analysts following firms, and find a statistically significant and positive relation between analyst following and the likelihood of shelf usage.

Combining the two measures in Model 3, we find a negative (positive) relation between percentage bid–ask spread (number of analysts) and shelf usage. In Models 4 and 5, we include analyst forecast dispersion as an additional measure of information asymmetry and find that greater forecast dispersion is related to a lower likelihood of shelf usage. Note that we lose a significant number of observations in these final two estimations, because the construction of the forecast-dispersion measure eliminates the firms with fewer than two analyst forecasts from the sample. To control for this data loss, we create an indicator variable "Low Coverage Indicator" equal to one if analyst forecast dispersion is not measurable (and zero otherwise) and display the results in Models 6 and 7. As can be seen, the results are robust to this specification. Greater forecast dispersion is related to a lower likelihood of shelf registration usage and more analyst coverage is related to increased shelf usage. Overall, the results show that the choice of shelf registration is strongly related to each of our measures of information asymmetry.

Our results show that shelf registration use is not related to stock-return volatility. After controlling for firm characteristics, the firms we anticipate would benefit the most from the market-timing option are no more likely to use shelf registration than the traditional

Table 4. Choice of registration strategy.

	Model 1	Model 2	Model 3	Model 4	Model 5	Model 6	Model 7
Intercept	−4.560	−4.671	−4.447	−4.540	−4.565	−6.104	−5.749
	(0.0001)	(0.0001)	(0.0001)	(0.0001)	(0.0001)	(0.0001)	(0.0001)
Percentage Bid–ask Spread	−14.824		−9.836		−2.077		−15.632
	[−3.460]		[−1.813]		[−0.675]		[−1.832]
	(0.0080)		(0.0710)		(0.7460)		(0.1111)
Log (Number of Analysts)		0.407	0.392	0.448	0.437	0.812	0.793
		[0.077]	[0.072]	[0.147]	[0.142]	[0.085]	[0.085]
		(0.0001)	(0.0001)	(0.0001)	(0.0001)	(0.0001)	(0.0001)
Low Coverage Indicator						0.062	0.089
						[0.011]	[0.143]
						(0.6650)	(0.7360)
Analyst Forecast Dispersion				−0.005	−0.005	−0.008	−0.008
				[−0.002]	[−0.002]	[−0.008]	[−0.001]
				(0.0020)	(0.0002)	(0.0030)	(0.0030)
Exchange Listing	0.119		0.084		0.274		0.088
	[0.028]		[0.016]		[0.089]		[0.017]
	(0.3190)		(0.4610)		(0.0410)		(0.6770)
Share Turnover	−0.160		−0.149		0.152		0.029
	[−0.037]		[−0.027]		[0.049]		[−0.037]
	(0.6990)		(0.7190)		(0.7440)		(0.9610)
Investment Opportunities	−0.008	−0.010	−0.011	−0.009	−0.009	−0.020	−0.023
	[−0.002]	[−0.002]	[−0.002]	[−0.003]	[−0.003]	[−0.002]	[−0.002]
	(0.1150)	(0.0300)	(0.0230)	(0.1220)	(0.1410)	(0.0360)	(0.0630)

(Continued)

Table 4. (*Continued*)

	Model 1	Model 2	Model 3	Model 4	Model 5	Model 6	Model 7
Free Cash Flow	−0.559	−0.474	−0.478	−0.517	−0.537	−0.660	−0.648
	[−0.128]	[−0.090]	[−0.088]	[−0.169]	[−0.174]	[−0.184]	[−0.083]
	(0.0010)	(0.0020)	(0.0020)	(0.0006)	(0.0040)	(0.0250)	(0.0560)
Log (Assets)	0.562	0.471	0.434	0.492	0.460	0.828	0.773
	[0.129]	[−0.090]	[0.080]	[0.161]	[0.149]	[0.088]	[0.078]
	(0.0001)	(0.0001)	(0.0001)	(0.0001)	(0.0001)	(0.0001)	(0.0001)
Leverage	0.420	0.675	0.716	0.614	0.611	1.193	1.262
	[0.096]	[0.128]	[0.132]	[0.201]	[0.199]	[0.129]	[0.133]
	(0.0001)	(0.0001)	(0.0001)	(0.0050)	(0.0050)	(0.0001)	(0.0001)
Volatility	4.211	−3.550	−0.525	−6.902	−2.971	−12.288	−8.547
	[1.060]	[−0.675]	[−0.097]	[−2.260]	[−0.966]	[−0.964]	[−0.334]
	(0.2830)	(0.2820)	(0.8890)	(0.0830)	(0.5120)	(0.0490)	(0.2640)
Pseudo R-squared	44.8%	47.3%	47.5%	43.3%	43.5%	47.7%	48.0%
observations	2,818	2,818	2,818	1,680	1,680	2,818	2,818

In this table, we estimate probit models of registration choice. The dependent variable in each model equals one if a firm registers a shelf that includes common equity, and zero otherwise. Independent variables include three measures of "Information Asymmetry"; (1) the percentage bid–ask spread in the month prior to the filing of the core shelf prospectus, (2) "Log(Number of Analysts)" is the log of the number of analysts issuing forecasts, and (3) "Analyst Forecast Dispersion" is the absolute value of the range of analyst forecasts divided by the mean estimate. "Exchange Listing" is an indicator variable equal to one if the firm is NYSE listed, and zero otherwise; "Share Turnover", defined as trading volume as a percentage of shares outstanding; "Investment Opportunities", defined as market-to-book; "Free Cash Flow", defined as free cash flow divided by total assets; "Log(Assets)", measured as the log of total assets; "Leverage", measured as total debt divided by total assets; and "Volatility" is the standard deviation of daily stock returns over the prior calendar year. We also control for industry effects and calendar years. Marginal probabilities are shown in brackets and coefficient p-values are shown in parentheses.

registration procedure. We find that investment opportunities are also not related to shelf registration usage. Shelf registration use, however, is negatively related to free cash flow. When financial resources are tight, the market may interpret common equity issuances positively, and thus firms are willing to use shelf. Our results also indicate that firm size and leverage are positively related to shelf use. Firms that are relatively large and therefore likely to be known are more likely to use unallocated shelf registrations than are smaller firms. Similarly, firms with high financial leverage are more likely to use shelf registration. It appears they may do so, at least in part, because they have few options for additional debt issuance, and so the specter of issuing equity may not send a negative signal to the market.

6. Costs of Issuing Equity

We now examine whether the costs of using shelf registration are lower than the costs of using traditional registration, and whether capital-raising costs differ by firm characteristics. We present results for each of the four costs of issuing equity: underwriting fees, share price discounts, delays in registration, and asymmetric information-related stock-price declines. The results in Table 5 indicate that shelf registration issuers pay lower underwriting fees than firms using the traditional registration procedure. The average gross spread for common equity takedowns from shelf registrations is 3.88%, but the gross spread for issuances using the traditional registration procedure is 4.91%. Although the gross spreads of shelf registrants do not include the fees paid when they register core prospectuses, interviews with investment bankers and shelf registrants indicate these expenses are generally negligible, and thus gross spreads are a reasonable estimate of total fees.

A second cost of issuing equity is the price discount required to place offerings. Higher discounts are indicative of placement difficulty. We measure SEO Discount as the offer price relative to the closing price on the day before the offering. When firms issue common equity off shelf registrations, we find the average offering is priced 2.09% below the previous day's closing price, whereas the

Table 5. Cost of issuing equity using unallocated shelf and traditional registration.

	Shelf		Traditional SEO		Test of differences	
	Mean	Median	Mean	Median	*t*-test *p*-value	Kruskal–Wallis *p*-value
Gross spread	3.88%	4.00%	4.91%	5.00%	(0.0001)	(0.0001)
SEO discount	2.09%	1.07%	2.55%	1.66%	(0.0193)	(0.0041)
Days in registration	10.1	8.0	44.1	29.0	(0.0001)	(0.0001)
Price percentile	58.4	66.0	59.2	63.0	(0.6437)	(0.7663)
Overnight offerings	39.8%		0.0%			
Shelf registration CAR	−0.246% (0.1800)	−0.160% (0.1608)				
Equity takedown CAR	−1.402% (0.0003)	−1.217% (0.0001)				
Total SEO CAR	−2.073% (0.0001)	−1.638% (0.0001)	−2.300% (0.0001)	−2.519% (0.0001)	(0.7114)	(0.0736)

In this table, we compare the costs of issuing common equity using unallocated shelf registration and the traditional registration procedure. We compare the gross spreads paid by issuers, the SEO discount (measured relative to the closing price on the day before the offering), the number of days between the initial filing of preliminary prospectuses with the SEC and issuing common equity, the price percentile received from issuing equity, and the market reactions to equity issuance filings and announcements. For firms that issued common equity using unallocated shelf registration, "Price percentile" is measured as the price percentile at which equity was issued using daily closing prices in the two-year period surrounding the equity issuance. The market reactions to equity issuance filings and announcements are measured as the mean and median cumulative abnormal returns (CARS) from Day −1 to Day 2 for firms filing common equity on unallocated shelf registrations ("Shelf registration CAR") and for firms issuing common equity off unallocated shelf registration statements ("Equity takedown CAR"). "Total SEO CAR" is defined as the sum of the CAR at the filing of unallocated shelf registrations and first indications of common equity takedowns off shelf registrations for shelf issuers and the abnormal return at the earlier of an announcement or filing of a preliminary prospectus for traditional issuers. *p*-values are shown in parentheses.

average traditionally registered SEO is priced 2.55% below. Shelf registration issuers appear to be able to place their share more readily and thus do not need to discount the price as much as traditional SEO issuers.

The traditional registration procedure can delay firms' equity issuances. As shown in Table 5, firms that use the traditional registration procedure spend 44 days in equity registration. In contrast, shelf registrants take only ten days to access the market. This difference is not surprising as the SEC designed shelf to accelerate offerings. In fact, nearly 40% of shelf equity offerings are issued overnight without the filing of any preliminary prospectuses.

One benefit to firms of avoiding unanticipated regulatory delays is that managers should be able to exploit short-term pricing opportunities. We therefore anticipate that shelf registration offerings are sold for higher prices than traditional SEOs. To measure managers' ability to time offerings, we form an empirical distribution of daily closing prices over a two-year window and measure where the actual offering price lies within the distribution ("Price percentile"). For firms that use shelf registration, we record daily closing prices beginning with the date when they file the core prospectus and ending when the shelf expires two years later.[11] We measure the timing ability using price percentile rather than price run-up or pre-offer return, because price percentile implicitly controls for cross-sectional variation in stock-price volatility. By normalizing each firm's price level by its own distribution, we compare timing ability across firms and market conditions.[12]

We anticipate that if managers can take common equity off shelf registrations for two years, they will try to exploit pricing opportunities over that period. For firms that use the traditional registration procedure, we subtract 267 days from the date that firms file their first preliminary prospectus. We select 267 days, because that is the average length of time between core prospectus filings and common equity issuances off shelf registrations. We then measure the price percentile at which firms issue common equity over the next two years. The idea is that managers anticipate exploiting the pricing opportunities over some time horizon. To compare pricing of the two registration regimes, we hold duration constant.

Table 5 shows that managers profit from pricing opportunities regardless of which registration procedure they choose. Shelf registration users issue equity at a price in the 58th percentile, whereas firms that use the traditional registration procedure price in the 59th percentile. We find no statistical evidence that firms using shelf registration exploit market-timing opportunities any more aggressively than do firms that use the traditional registration procedure. Consistent with these results, Heron and Lie (2004) find little evidence of market-timing ability for shelf issuers. They conclude that shelf registrations are used to fulfill the capital immediacy needs, rather than exploiting the temporary pricing opportunities.[13]

A significant cost of issuing equity is an asymmetric information-related stock-price decline when an issuance is announced. Firms that use shelf registration face potential market overhang when core prospectuses are filed and downwards pressure on share prices when equity issuances are announced. Firms that use the traditional registration procedure incur price declines when share issuances are disclosed. To compare the cost of using unallocated shelf registration with that of using the traditional registration procedure, we compare the Cumulative Abnormal Returns (CARs) around shelf registration and common equity takedown dates with the CARs around traditional equity registration dates.

We measure Shelf Registration CAR on Day −1 through Day +2 around the earlier of the filing of unallocated shelf registrations and filing announcements.[14] Because firms can file pricing supplements for takedowns at the time of or after offerings, the market may have little or no advance notice of offerings. Therefore, the market's reaction to shelf registration takedowns may occur after filing events rather than at the time of or before events. The four-day window captures the market's reaction to both more marketed offerings that are slower and quick offerings that do not have preliminary prospectuses. The Equity Takedown CAR captures the market reaction on Day −1 through Day +2 around the first indication that a firm has taken equity off a shelf — either at the filing of the first preliminary prospectus, the filing of a pricing supplement following an overnight offering, or the announcement of an equity issuance.

The Total SEO CAR is the sum of the CAR at the first indication of a filing of an unallocated shelf and the CAR at the first indication of a common equity takedown off the shelf. For firms that use the traditional registration procedure, we define the event day as the earlier of when they first file a preliminary prospectus or announce an offering. We measure CARs as returns in excess of the CRSP NYSE/NASDAQ/Amex value-weighted index.

As can be seen in Table 5, the CAR when firms file shelf registrations is not statistically different from zero. Overall, we find no evidence of market overhang. We next examine the market's reaction when firms issue common equity. We find that the mean CAR when firms take common equity off shelf registrations is −1.4%. When we combine the CARs for firms that file shelf registrations and take down common equity, we find the mean CAR is −2.1%. When firms use the traditional registration procedure, they experience a mean abnormal return of −2.3%. The combined CAR for firms that file shelf registrations and take down common equity is statistically indistinguishable from the CAR when firms use the traditional registration procedure.

Overall, the results show that for the average firm, using shelf registration is no more or less costly in terms of market reaction than is the traditional registration procedure. This finding runs counter to the argument conveyed by Heron and Lie (2004), who argue that shelf registrations convey less unfavorable information than traditional offerings, and thus the market should react less negatively.[15] The univariate results in Table 5 demonstrate that shelf issuers pay lower fees, offer smaller price discounts, and access the market faster than traditional equity issuers.

Additionally, these firms incur no greater cost in terms of negative market reaction to the announcement and raising of equity. The question is then, why would firms ever choose to use the traditional registration procedure rather than shelf registration? The results in Sec. 4 indicate that shelf registration and traditional equity issuers have different characteristics. Here, we explore differences in the costs of issuing equity, not only by registration strategy, but also by firm characteristics. These costs include underwriting fees, share price discounts, delays in registration, and asymmetric information-related stock-price declines.

We examine the gross spreads paid by issuers by estimating a Heckman two-stage model to control for the potential selection bias in the type of firm that chooses to use shelf. The first-stage probit estimation, which includes both shelf registration and traditional-registration issuances, is estimated as Model 3 in Table 4. Column 1 of Table 6 shows estimates of the second stage of the Heckman model. We control for Information Asymmetry, Exchange Listing, Share Turnover, the Log of Offering Proceeds, Dilution, Industry, and Calendar Year. Finally, we include Lambda, the inverse Mills Ratio calculated from the first stage probit model, which is the predicted probability that a firm uses shelf. We expect that firms using shelf registration will incur lower underwriting fees and therefore expect the coefficient on lambda to be negative.

The results indicate Gross Spread is related to both of our proxies for information asymmetry. Firms with high levels of information asymmetry, as measured by either a high percentage bid–ask spread or by having low analyst coverage, incur large underwriting fees. Gross Spread is negatively related to the log of Proceeds Raised, evidence of at least some fixed costs in the underwriting business. Importantly, Gross Spread is also determined by registration choice. The coefficient on Lambda is negative and significant at the 1% level. Thus, even after controlling for firm characteristics and information about offerings, firms that choose to use shelf incur significantly lower underwriter fees than firms that use the traditional registration procedure. When the SEC adopted shelf, it hoped to confer this benefit to shelf registration issuers.

Our univariate analysis shows that the price discount for shelf registration issuers is significantly lower than for traditional issuers. In column 2 of Table 6, we control for firm and offering characteristics and use OLS to test whether the price discount required to place offerings is lower for shelf registrants than traditional equity issuers. The dependent variable is SEO Discount and the independent variables are Information Asymmetry, Exchange Listing, Share Turnover, Volatility, Industry, and Calendar Year. We include the Log of Proceeds Raised, Dilution, the Log of the Number of Days in Registration, and an indicator variable, "Overnight" which is equal to one for offerings for which no preliminary prospectus was filed with the SEC.

To compare the price discounts of the registration choices, we use an indicator variable, Choice, which equals one if a firm issues common equity from an unallocated shelf registration, and zero if it uses the traditional registration procedure.[16]

Table 6. Costs of issuing equity using unallocated shelf and traditional registration procedure multivariate analyses.

	Gross spread Heckman (1)		SEO discount OLS model (2)		Days in tobit model (3)		Price percentile OLS model (4)	
Intercept	5.453	(0.0001)	−0.025	(0.0015)	34.841	(0.0060)	−0.286	(0.9802)
Percentage Bid–ask Spread	13.737	(0.0001)	−0.224	(0.0005)	65.214	(0.6207)	121.577	(0.0156)
Log (Number of Analysts)	−0.244	(0.0001)	0.004	(0.0005)	−1.522	(0.4505)	−2.050	(0.0161)
Exchange Listing	−0.543	(0.0001)	−0.002	(0.4187)	17.987	(0.0001)	−1.523	(0.4127)
Share Turnover	−0.009	(0.9442)	−0.023	(0.0005)	−7.675	(0.5820)	14.887	(0.0025)
Log (Proceeds Raised)	−0.002	(0.0001)	0.005	(0.0001)	−1.481	(0.4376)	6.523	(0.0001)
Dilution	0.000	(0.0001)	0.000	(0.1102)			0.000	(0.3591)
Volatility			−0.174	(0.0132)	190.531	(0.1687)	124.546	(0.0239)
Log (Days in Registration)			−0.005	(0.0001)			−3.155	(0.0014)
Overnight			−0.014	(0.0476)			2.566	(0.6662)
S&P 500 Price Percentile							0.015	(0.0001)
Lambda	−0.093	(0.0058)						

(*Continued*)

Table 6. (*Continued*)

	Gross spread Heckman (1)		SEO discount OLS model (2)		Days in tobit model (3)		Price percentile OLS model (4)	
Choice			−0.005	(0.1547)	−48.960	(0.0001)	−8.608	(0.0016)
Adjusted *R*-squared	54.6%		10.9%				12.6%	

In this table, we compare the costs of issuing equity using unallocated shelf registration and the traditional registration procedure. We estimate a Heckman two-stage model of gross spreads. The first stage is probit Model 3 presented in Table 4. It examines which firms choose unallocated shelf registration. The second stage, shown in Column 1 of this table, examines gross spreads, controlling for firm and offering characteristics. In Columns 2 and 4, we use OLS estimations to compare shelf and traditional SEO discounts and price percentiles. In Column 3, we use a tobit estimation to compare the number of days in registration for the registration procedures. "Gross Spread" is the percentage fee paid to underwriters. "SEO Discount" is measured relative to the closing price on the day before the offering. "Log(Days in Registration)" is the natural log of the number of days between the initial filing of preliminary prospectuses with the SEC and issuing common equity. "Price Percentile" is measured as the price percentile at which equity was issued using daily closing prices over a two-year period. Information asymmetry is measured as the percentage bid–ask spread in the month prior to the filing of the core shelf prospectus and the log of the number of analysts; "Exchange Listing" is an indicator variable equal to one if the firm is NYSE listed, and zero otherwise; "Share Turnover" is defined as trading volume as a percentage of shares outstanding; "Volatility" is measured as the standard deviation of daily stock-return for the previous year; "S&P 500 Price Percentile" is the percentile at which the S&P 500 traded over the same period as the offering's Price Percentile; "Proceeds Raised" is the dollar amount of common equity raised in $ millions; "Dilution" is the number of shares issued as a percentage of shares outstanding; "Overnight" is equal to one if offerings take less than one day, and zero otherwise; "Lambda" is the inverse Mills ratio calculated from the first stage probit model; and "Choice" equals one if a firm issues common equity from an unallocated shelf, and zero if it uses the traditional registration procedure. Coefficient *p*-values are shown in parentheses.

We find that SEO Discount is significantly related to Information Asymmetry, Volatility, and Speed to Market, as captured by both Days in Registration and Overnight. Uncertainty about firm value and volatile prices cause managers to offer price concessions. Placement difficulty is also positively related to SEO Discount; i.e., large or quick-to-market offerings increase price discounts. That said, counter to the univariate results, we find no difference in SEO discounts between shelf registrations and traditional equity issuances once we control for firm and offering characteristics. Thus, unlike gross spread, SEO Discount cannot be lowered through the use of shelf registration.

In Column 3 of Table 6, we examine the time spent in SEC registration. We use a Tobit specification to model the dependent variable, Days in Registration, because it is censored at zero. The independent variables include Information Asymmetry, Exchange Listing, Share Turnover, Volatility, Industry, and Calendar Year. We control for Proceeds Raised and include an indicator variable of registration choice. The findings in Column 3 indicate that firm and offering characteristics do not affect the time spent in registration. Instead, we find registration choice determines registration duration. Shelf registration issuers register offerings faster than firms that use the traditional registration procedure. This result, although not surprising, substantiates the ability of firms to access this benefit of shelf registration.

Finally, we examine whether shelf registration filers are able to exploit short-term pricing opportunities better than traditional equity issuers. We use OLS to model the pricing benefits of shelf registration. The dependent variable is Price Percentile and the independent variables are Information Asymmetry, Exchange Listing, Share Turnover, Volatility, Industry, and Calendar Year. We include the S&P 500 Price Percentile, calculated for each offering as the percentile at which the S&P 500 traded over the same period as the offering's Price Percentile. We also include Dilution, Days in Registration, whether offerings are offered overnight, and an indicator variable of registration choice.

We anticipate the S&P 500 Price Percentile will be positively related to Price Percentile; i.e., the level of the market should influence managers' issuance timing, and that issuers will focus on dilution, as it should affect the final price achieved. It is difficult to predict the relation between Price Percentile and Overnight, as managers who issue equity overnight may be taking advantage of a temporarily high stock price or just seeking funding immediacy. The indicator variable of registration choice allows us to compare firms' relative abilities to time issuances for high prices based on their registration choices.

The results in Column 4 of Table 6 show that shelf registration issuers are significantly worse at exploiting pricing opportunities in the market relative to traditional equity issuers. However, when offerings are done by firms with higher levels of information asymmetry and with higher stock-return volatility, they extract significantly higher prices. When firms spend more time in the registration process, the price percentile of offerings is low. Thus, although shelf registration users do not appear to take advantage of the timing option afforded to them, speed to market is a significant determinant of pricing ability.

We find Price Percentile is also positively related to the S&P 500 Price Percentile. When the market is high, managers receive a higher price than when it is low. Taken together, we find that timing and pricing benefits are related to firm and offering characteristics, as well as registration choice. The benefits that the SEC sought to confer with shelf registration — lower underwriting fees and faster time to market — are in fact realized by shelf registration issuers.

A major cost of raising equity is the downward pressure on share price when managers file shelf registrations and announce equity issuances. We now examine market reaction using a two-stage Heckman model to correct for the potential selection bias in the type of firm that uses shelf registration. We start by examining market overhang — the market's reaction to unallocated shelf registrations. The first stage estimation is probit Model 3 of firm registration choice that is presented in Table 4. Table 7 contains the second stage results. In Column 1, we explore the impact of information asymmetry on

Table 7. Cost of issuing equity: Market's reaction to shelf registration and equity issuance.

	Shelf registration CAR (1)		Total SEO CAR (2)	
Intercept	0.0007	(0.9658)	0.3538	(0.6397)
Percentage Bid–ask Spread	−0.7557	(0.0294)	4.2294	(0.3130)
Log (Number of Analysts)	0.0054	(0.0545)	0.0612	(0.3848)
Exchange Listing	−0.0020	(0.7458)	0.1699	(0.2761)
Share Turnover	−0.0965	(0.0039)	−0.0719	(0.8634)
Investment Opportunities	0.0011	(0.0004)	0.0004	(0.7296)
Free Cash Flow	0.0001	(0.9869)	−0.4199	(0.0124)
Volatility	0.1918	(0.3130)	−1.4954	(0.7416)
Shelf Amount	0.0000	(0.0319)		
Equityness	−0.0199	(0.2532)		
Leverage			0.6747	(0.0154)
Log (assets)			−0.1329	(0.0573)
Proceeds Raised			0.0008	(0.0168)
Gross Spread			−0.2572	(0.0020)
Log (Days in Registration)			0.2445	(0.0005)
Price Percentile			0.0033	(0.0932)
Lambda	0.0081	(0.1414)	0.5390	(0.0001)
Adjusted R-squared	3.51%		4.61%	

In this table, we estimate two Heckman models of the market's reaction to shelf registration and common equity issuance using shelf registration and the traditional registration procedure. "Shelf Registration CAR" is the mean CAR (Day −1 to Day 2) for firms filing common equity on unallocated shelf registrations. "Total SEO CAR" is defined as the sum of the CAR at the filing of unallocated shelf registrations and first indications of common equity takedowns off shelf registrations for shelf issuers and the abnormal return at the earlier of an announcement or filing of a preliminary prospectus for traditional issuers. The first stage is the probit model presented in Table 4. Independent variables include: information asymmetry as measured by the percentage bid–ask spread and the log of the number of analysts; "Exchange Listing" is an indicator variable equal to one if the firm is NYSE listed, and zero otherwise; "Share Turnover", defined as trading volume as a percentage of shares outstanding; "Investment Opportunities", defined as market-to-book; "Free Cash Flow", defined as free cash flow divided by total assets; and "Volatility", measured as the standard deviation of daily stock return for the previous year. "Shelf Amount" is the dollar amount of securities registered on core prospectuses and "Equityness" is the percentage of securities registered on shelf registrations that can dilute common equity; "Leverage", measured as total debt divided by total assets; "Log(Assets)", measured as the log of total assets; "Proceeds Raised" is the dollar amount of common equity raised. "Gross Spread" is the percentage fee paid to underwriters. "Log Days in Registration" is log of the number of days between the filing of preliminary prospectuses with the SEC and issuing common equity. "Price Percentile" is measured as the price percentile at which equity was issued using daily closing prices over a two-year period, and "Lambda" is the inverse Mills ratio calculated from the first stage probit model. Coefficient p-values are shown in parentheses.

market overhang, controlling for selection bias and firm-specific characteristics.

The dependent variable is Shelf Registration CAR and the independent variables are as follows: Information Asymmetry proxied by both percentage bid–ask spread and the log of the number of analysts following the firm; Exchange Listing; Share Turnover; Investment Opportunities; Free Cash Flow; and Volatility. Following Krasker (1986), we also control for shelf registration size. Issuances of new shares can create permanent price pressure if demand curves are downward sloping or temporary price pressure if issuances cause liquidity shocks. We measure shelf registration size (Shelf Amount) as the total dollar amount of securities registered on shelf registrations. We control for the percentage of securities registered on shelf registrations that can dilute common equity (Equityness).

We anticipate that the market will react negatively to unallocated shelf registrations that contain a high proportion of potentially dilutive securities. We include Lambda, which is the predicted probability that a firm files a shelf registration that was estimated in the first stage. Consistent with the univariate findings, we find the market reaction to the filing of shelf registrations is related to information asymmetry. When the bid–ask spread is wider or analyst coverage is thin, consistent with higher information asymmetry, the market revises its estimate of a shelf registrant's value downwards. Also, when a firm has greater investment opportunities, the market is more positive in its reaction to the filing of a shelf registration. Firms' free cash flow and financial slack do not affect the market's reaction to the filing of shelf registrations. Once we control for the level of information asymmetry and other firm characteristics, the market response is unrelated to firms' choice of registration strategy.

The second-stage estimation in Column 2 examines the market return for both traditional seasoned equity issuances and the combined return for shelf registration users at the filing of shelf registrations and equity takedowns. The independent variables include information that the market can observe when core prospectuses are filed: Information Asymmetry as proxied by the percentage bid–ask spread and the log of the number of analysts, Exchange Listing,

Share Turnover, Investment Opportunities, Free Cash Flow, Volatility, Leverage, and Size. We also include independent variables reflecting information about specific common equity offerings. These variables are Proceeds Raised, Gross Spread, Log of Days in Registration, and Price Percentile. We include Lambda, which is the predicted probability that a firm files a shelf that was estimated in the first stage.

We anticipate that the CAR is negatively related to Proceeds Raised and Gross Spread. Large offerings tend to exert downward pressure on share prices, and in this setting, gross spread reflects the difficulty of underwriting an issue, because investment banks charge more for facilitating the difficult offerings. The expected relation between the market's reaction and Log of Days in Registration is ambiguous. Slow offerings provide market participants time to assimilate the information, potentially mitigating the adverse market response.

Managers are also less likely to be able to exploit short-term pricing opportunities in slow, rather than fast offerings. In either case, the market should respond less favorably to quick offerings from shelf registrations than slow offerings. On the other hand, long marketing periods can indicate that offerings are difficult to sell. If this effect dominates, the market will respond less favorably to slow offerings than quick ones. Finally, we include the Price Percentile of the actual offering to capture managers' timing ability. If managers aggressively exploit pricing opportunities, the market should respond negatively.

We find that the market's reaction is not related to our proxies for information asymmetry or investment opportunities. Consistent with the prediction of the free cash flow model (Jensen, 1986), the market responds negatively when firms have financial slack. As anticipated, the results show the combined CAR is negatively related to Gross Spread. Market reaction is, however, positively related to the Log of Days in Registration. When the market has more time to digest information, the reaction to an equity issuance is less negative. The market reaction is significantly related to Lambda. Conditional on a firm choosing to raise equity using a shelf registration, the CAR when equity is taken down is significantly less negative for shelf issuers than for traditional SEO issuers.

7. Why Do Some High Information Asymmetry Firms Choose Shelf Registration?

The results of the multivariate analyses show that firms benefit from choosing shelf registration in terms of underwriter fees and time to market. When asymmetric information-related price declines related to shelf are small, firms have clear incentives to choose it. When price declines are large, however, firms may instead choose the traditional registration procedure. In this section, we investigate whether firms that choose shelf registration have low information asymmetry and whether firms that choose the traditional registration procedure have high information asymmetry.

We then explore why firms might choose the opposing strategy. To do so, in Table 8 we divide firms into quartiles based on their information asymmetry using both percentage bid–ask spread and analyst coverage. Because spreads have declined over time, we define new quartile breaks each calendar year for percentage bid–ask spread. We also partition calendar year 1997 into two periods around the date when the minimum tick size changed from eighths to sixteenths. We find that 56% of shelf registration issuers are in the lowest quartile of information asymmetry. If firms were randomly distributed, we would expect 25%. In contrast, only 6.4% of shelf registration issuers are in the highest quartile of information asymmetry. We find a very different pattern for users of traditional registration: 14.4% are in the lowest quartile of information asymmetry and 31% are in the highest quartile.

Regardless of whether we partition firms by percentage bid–ask spread or analyst coverage, shelf registration issuers across all quartiles pay lower gross spreads than the same type of firm that chooses the traditional registration procedure. The average gross spread when high information asymmetry firms issue equity using shelf is 4.4%, whereas it is 5.13% for similar firms that use the traditional registration procedure. When low information asymmetry firms issue equity using shelf registration, the average gross spread 3.48%, in contrast to low information asymmetry firms that use the traditional registration procedure that pay an average gross spread 4.71%. When

Table 8. Information asymmetry and issuance costs.

	Gross spread			SEO discount			Days in registration			Price percentile		
	TD	SEO	*p*-value	TD	SEO	*p*-value	TD	SEO	*p*-value	TD	SEO	*p*-value
Panel A: Percentage bid–ask spread information asymmetry analysis												
Top quartile (wide spreads)												
Mean	4.39%	5.13%	(0.0001)	2.60%	2.62%	(0.9642)	6.8	45.3	(0.0125)	69.6	62.2	(0.1346)
Median	4.38%	5.22%	(0.0001)	1.15%	1.84%	(0.4902)	7.0	28.0	(0.0001)	82.5	66.0	(0.0438)
Quartiles 2 and 3												
Mean	4.02%	4.95%	(0.0001)	1.68%	2.56%	(0.0044)	11.9	44.4	(0.0001)	60.2	61.8	(0.5488)
Median	4.23%	5.00%	(0.0001)	1.07%	1.72%	(0.0030)	8.0	29.0	(0.0001)	67.0	65.0	(0.7594)
Bottom quartile (narrow spreads)												
Mean	3.48%	4.71%	(0.0001)	2.28%	2.69%	(0.2401)	7.6	44.8	(0.0001)	58.1	60.9	(0.2472)
Median	3.50%	5.00%	(0.0001)	0.95%	1.54%	(0.0372)	0.0	29.0	(0.0001)	65.0	66.0	(0.6947)
Test of differences (top quartile versus bottom quartile)												
Kruskal–Wallis *p*-value	(0.0002)	(0.0001)		(0.5180)	(0.0803)		(0.1626)	(0.8297)		(0.0874)	(0.5022)	

(*Continued*)

Table 8. (*Continued*)

	Gross spread			SEO discount			Days in registration			Price percentile		
	TD	SEO	p-value	TD	SEO	p-value	TD	SEO	p-value	TD	SEO	p-value
Panel B: Number of analysts information asymmetry analysis												
Top quartile (few analysts)												
Mean	4.27%	5.13%	(0.0001)	2.68%	3.06%	(0.5021)	8.3	43.5	(0.0001)	68.6	60.9	(0.1131)
Median	4.94%	5.24%	(0.0001)	1.61%	2.13%	(0.8000)	7.0	31.0	(0.0001)	75.7	65.0	(0.7583)
Quartiles 2 and 3												
Mean	4.48%	4.95%	(0.0001)	2.10%	2.44%	(0.4033)	14.1	46.3	(0.0001)	58.6	58.4	(0.9576)
Median	4.58%	5.00%	(0.0001)	1.18%	1.64%	(0.4382)	10.0	28.0	(0.0001)	65.0	61.0	(0.2838)
Bottom quartile (many analysts)												
Mean	3.34%	3.93%	(0.0001)	1.60%	1.33%	(0.2696)	8.3	40.5	(0.0001)	55.1	54.4	(0.8295)
Median	3.26%	4.00%	(0.0001)	0.71%	0.48%	(0.3162)	7.0	26.0	(0.0001)	59.5	57.0	(0.5157)
Test of Differences (top quartile versus bottom quartile)												
Kruskal–Wallis p-value	(0.0001)	(0.0001)		(0.0286)	(0.0001)		(0.0061)	(0.0001)		(0.5715)	(0.0755)	

In this table, we compare four costs of issuing common equity using unallocated shelf registration and the traditional registration procedures. We compare the gross spreads paid by issuers, the SEO discount, the number of days between the initial filing of preliminary prospectuses with the SEC and issuing common equity, and the price percentile received from issuing equity. "SEO Discount" is measured relative to the closing price on the day before the offering. "Price Percentile" is measured as the price percentile at which equity was issued using daily closing prices over a two-year period surrounding the equity issuance. Firms are divided into top quartile, interquartile, and bottom quartile based on two measures of information asymmetry; percentage bid–ask spreads and number of analysts. p-values are shown in parentheses.

we perform the same analysis based on the number of analysts, the results are qualitatively the same.

Firms that use shelf registrations go to market faster than firms that use the traditional registration procedure, regardless of their information asymmetry quartile. High information asymmetry shelf issuers go to market in 6.8 days, whereas similar firms that use the traditional registration procedure take 45.3 days. Low information asymmetry shelf registration issuers go to market in 7.6 days, but similar firms that use the traditional registration procedure take 44.8 days to sell equity.

Again measuring information asymmetry based on analyst coverage produces similar results. Overall our findings indicate that shelf registration confers advantages to firms, regardless of information asymmetry, in terms of underwriter fees and speed to market.

SEO Discount and Price Percentile are not strongly related to registration choice. Whether we measure information asymmetry as percentage bid–ask spread or analyst coverage, we find no difference within quartiles between shelf registration firms and firms that use the traditional registration procedure. When we measure information asymmetry as the number of analysts, however, the results show that low information asymmetry issuers, regardless of whether they use shelf registration or the traditional registration procedure, discount shares less to place them. Thus firm characteristics and not registration choice appear to determine SEO Discount.

Given the advantages of shelf registration, the question then is why don't all firms use it? In Table 9, we examine the market reaction to raising equity, again partitioned by information asymmetry quartiles using both percentage bid–ask spread and analyst coverage. We find that market overhang is strongly related to firm-specific information asymmetry. For high information asymmetry firms that file unallocated shelf registrations, market overhang is severe: The average CAR when firms file shelf registrations is −2.2%. In contrast, the average CAR when low information asymmetry firms file shelf registrations is not statistically different from zero. The Kruskal–Wallis test indicates that the abnormal return for high information asymmetry firms is significantly more negative than the return for low

Table 9. Information asymmetry and issuance costs: Market's reaction to shelf registration and equity issuance.

	Shelf registration CAR		Combined shelf registration & equity TD CAR		Traditional SEO CAR		Combined versus SEO
	CAR	*p*-value	CAR	*p*-value	CAR	*p*-value	*p*-value
Panel A: Percentage bid–ask spread information asymmetry analysis							
Top quartile (wide spreads)							
Mean	−2.214%	(0.0525)	−4.677%	(0.0173)	−1.916%	(0.0001)	(0.0356)
Median	−1.856%	(0.0715)	−4.979%	(0.0158)	−2.633%	(0.0001)	(0.0523)
Quartiles 2 and 3							
Mean	0.004%	(0.9919)	−2.488%	(0.0006)	−2.604%	(0.0001)	(0.8191)
Median	0.000%	(0.8975)	−1.857%	(0.0005)	−2.839%	(0.0001)	(0.0576)
Bottom quartile (narrow spreads)							
Mean	−0.187%	(0.2987)	−0.897%	(0.2096)	−1.478%	(0.0001)	(0.3317)
Median	−0.160%	(0.2559)	−0.234%	(0.3709)	−1.291%	(0.0001)	(0.0727)
Test of differences across quartiles							
Kruskal–Wallis *p*-value	(0.0019)		(0.0185)		(0.8381)		
Panel B: Number of analysts information asymmetry analysis							
Top quartile (few analysts)							
Mean	−1.68%	(0.0288)	−2.03%	(0.2025)	−2.38%	(0.0001)	(0.7871)
Median	−1.83%		−1.03%		−2.68%		
Interquartile range							
Mean	0.07%	(0.8530)	−1.93%	(0.0238)	−1.80%	(0.0001)	(0.8608)
Median	−0.12%		−1.85%		−2.54%		
Bottom quartile (many analysts)							
Mean	−0.15%	(0.3905)	−1.57%	(0.0007)	−1.76%	(0.0001)	(0.6982)
Median	−0.02%		−1.43%		−1.55%		
Test of differences across quartiles							
Kruskal–Wallis *p*-value		(0.0072)		(0.7257)		(0.1684)	

The table shows the mean and median four-day (Day −1 to Day 2) CAR for firms filing common equity on unallocated shelf registrations ("Shelf registration CAR"), for firms issuing common equity off unallocated shelf registration statements ("Equity TD CAR"), and for firms using traditional registration procedures to register SEOs ("Traditional SEO CAR"). "Combined shelf registration & equity TD CAR" is defined as the sum of the four-day CAR at the filing of unallocated shelf registrations and first indications of common equity takedowns off shelf registrations. Firms are divided into top quartile, interquartile, and bottom quartile based on two measures of information asymmetry; percentage bid–ask spreads and number of analysts. *p*-values are shown in parentheses.

information asymmetry firms. When we perform the same analysis based on the number of analysts, the results are qualitatively the same.

High information asymmetry firms that choose to take common equity off shelf registrations are further discounted by the market. The average combined CAR at shelf registration filing and takedown is −4.7%, which is statistically different from zero. When information asymmetry is low, the average combined CAR at shelf registration filing and takedown of −0.90%, which is not statistically significant. Again, we find a negative relation between combined market reaction and information asymmetry.

By comparison, the CAR for traditional SEOs in the high information asymmetry group is −1.9%, which is both economically and statistically higher than −4.7%. The CAR for low information asymmetry firms using the traditional registration procedure is −1.5%. It is more negative than the combined CAR for low information asymmetry firms at shelf filing and takedown of −0.90%. Thus, for firms with low information asymmetry, unallocated shelf registration imposes lower costs than does the traditional registration procedure, but for firms with high information asymmetry, shelf is significantly more costly in terms of market reaction.

High information asymmetry firms' use of shelf registration rather than the traditional registration procedure suggests that lower fees, increased flexibility, and speed to market can outweigh the cost of market overhang.

Contrary to our findings for shelf registration issuers, an examination of firms that use the traditional registration procedure reveals that the market's reaction is not related to information asymmetry. One interpretation is that traditional registration, by design, mitigates information asymmetry by requiring detailed advance information. Shelf registration, on the other hand, was not intended to resolve information asymmetry, but rather to provide a quick, low-cost means of raising capital.

We show that low information asymmetry shelf registrants pay lower gross spreads and go to market faster than the same type of firm that uses the traditional registration procedure. Many low information asymmetry firms, however, select the traditional registration procedure. The only obvious benefit to doing so is avoidance of possible market overhang (although low information asymmetry firms in our sample experience no market overhang on average). Choosing the traditional registration procedure may be a risk-minimizing rather than cost-minimizing strategy for these firms.

8. Conclusion

Our evidence shows that unallocated shelf registration lowers certain costs of raising equity for all firms. Shelf registration firms pay lower gross spreads and access the market faster than similar firms that issue equity using the traditional registration procedure. Price declines related to asymmetric information, however, can be either higher or lower for shelf registration issuers than for firms that use traditional registration. The market response when firms with low information asymmetry take equity off shelf registrations is minimal. In contrast, high information asymmetry firms that choose to register and issue common equity off shelf registrations incur severe market overhang and significantly negative abnormal returns when issuing equity off shelf registrations.

Fama and French (2005) demonstrate that firms can issue common equity with little adverse market impact. High information asymmetry firms, however, must choose issuance venues, where inside information cannot be exploited. Here, we document high information asymmetry firms do not incur greater costs than low information asymmetry firms if they issue SEOs using the traditional registration procedure, which requires detailed disclosure and slower access to the market.

The SEC's congressionally legislated mandate is to protect investors. It took nearly 25 years to deregulate the equity registration system in a way that issuers were willing to use. Both the proposing and adopting releases for the shelf registration rules query whether investors can get timely and accurate information about issuers and their offerings under the deregulated registration system. After much deliberation and several iterations, the SEC settled on its eligibility requirements. In hindsight, it need not have been so concerned.

Our study suggests that the market is a harsher judge and jury than the SEC: Firms with high information asymmetry, even if they are eligible for shelf registration, experience large stock price declines if they use this process. Market forces dictate that high information asymmetry firms choose a registration strategy that compels them to provide detailed advance disclosure and to access the market slowly. Low information asymmetry firms, on the other hand, benefit from the deregulation and can lower their cost of raising equity by using shelf registration.

Endnotes

1. Leone *et al.* (2007) find that detailed disclosures regarding expected use of proceeds in IPO prospectuses result in lower underpricing and lower costs of capital.
2. Market overhang should not be too severe if investors anticipate that debt rather than equity will be issued (Heron and Lie, 2004).
3. See U.S. Securities and Exchange Commission Proposing Release No. 33-6943, 22 July 1992; 1991 SEC *Annual Report*; and Denis (1991) for further discussion.
4. Autore *et al.* (2005) find the use of equity shelf registration began increasing in the late 1990s. They do not distinguish between allocated and unallocated shelf registrations in their sample. Analysis shows, however, that most of the shelf registrations are allocated shelf registrations. Here we focus on unallocated shelf registration.
5. Kidwell *et al.* (1987) find no evidence of timing ability in debt offerings, although Thatcher and Thatcher (1988) and Kadapakkam and Kon (1989) document some benefit.
6. Kidwell *et al.* (1984, 1987) find lower costs for issuing debt from allocated shelf registrations. Hansen (1986) argues firms with low costs under the traditional procedure may have preferentially used allocated shelf registration and continued to have lower costs. Consistent with this, Allen *et al.* (1990) fail to find cost savings after accounting for differences in the types of firms using allocated shelf registrations for debt offerings.
7. Most empirical studies of allocated shelf registration common equity offerings in the early 1980s find little or no evidence of market overhang. See Bhagat *et al.* (1985), Jensen *et al.* (1995), Moore *et al.* (1986), and Heron and Lie (2004). Denis (1991), however, finds evidence that market overhang is more severe for shelf offerings than non-shelf offerings.
8. Sherman (1999) develops a model of underwriter certification for shelf registration.
9. We also eliminate 68 firms that had missing data on TAQ or CRSP.
10. We ran all tests using dollar bid–ask spread. All results are qualitatively the same and are available upon request.

11. We adjust prices after equity takedowns by adding back price drops that occur when firms announce equity issuances. This procedure controls for any biases in price levels created by the announcements.
12. When managers file a core prospectus, they do not know where within a future price distribution a particular price will fall. What they do know is that the core prospectus is good for up to two years of issuances. Thus, they enter into a game of guessing when to issue equity during the two-year window. If they guess right, they issue equity at a high price percentile. If they guess wrong, they either miss issuing equity at a previous high price that is no longer available or the opportunity to issue equity at a later high price. It is important that we use a measure that implicitly controls for cross-section variation in return volatility, because return volatility determines the price levels at which managers can issue equity, and not all firms have the ability to issue at the same price levels. The variable, price percentile, controls for cross-section variation in return volatility by measuring how well a manager does relative to how well he or she could have priced equity, given that particular firm's price path, over the period. Price run-up on the other hand, only measures timing ability relative to historic price levels.
13. Autore *et al.* (2005) find that allocated shelf registration issuers have superior timing ability based on pre-offering price run-ups. Based on the same metric, we find that unallocated shelf issuers have worse market-timing ability.
14. Press announcements were collected from the *New York Times* and *Wall Street Journal.*
15. Heron and Lie (2004) examine 256 allocated and unallocated shelf registrations over the period 1980 through 1998.
16. We use OLS rather than a Heckman model, because the independent variable is a choice variable rather than dictated by market forces and the result of a selection bias, as is the case with gross spreads or abnormal returns.

Acknowledgments

The authors thank Reena Aggarwal, Anup Agrawal, Vladimir Atanasov, Bill Atkinson, Helen Bowers, Dan Bradley, Sharon Brown-Hruska, Ying Duan, Katrina Ellis, Wayne Ferson, Stuart Gillan, Michael Goldstein, Kathy Hevert, Julie Hoffman, Gang Hu, Anita Klein, Karthik Krishnan, Mike Lemmon, Patricia Miller, Cathy Niden, Tim Opler, Erik Sirri, Li-Anne Woo, Sheridan Titman, and seminar participants at the 2005 Frontiers of Finance Conference, Babson College, Boston College, Boston University, Brandeis University, Notre Dame, the University of Alabama, the University of Delaware, the University of Mississippi, the University of Texas at Dallas, and the U.S. Securities and Exchange Commission for helpful comments and suggestions. We gratefully acknowledge valuable research assistance from Tom Dowling, Vera Goncalves, Ming Hui, Edwin Jean, Andrea

Mendonca, and John Sundborg. We thank Robert Van Ness for generously supplying data. Krigman recognizes the generous research support provided by the Peter Black Senior Term Chair. All errors are our own.

References

Allen, D, R Lamy and GR Thompson (1990). The shelf registration of debt and self selection bias, *Journal of Finance*, 45, 275–287.

Ambarish, R, K John and J Williams (1987). Efficient signaling with dividends and investments. *Journal of Finance*, 42, 321–344.

Autore, DM, R Kumar and DK Shome (2008). The revival of shelf-registered corporate equity offerings. *Journal of Corporate Finance*, 14(1), 32–50.

Bayless, M and S Chaplinsky (1996). Is there a window of opportunity for seasoned equity issuance? *Journal of Finance*, 51, 253–278.

Bhagat, S, MW Marr and GR Thompson (1985). The rule 415 experiment: Equity markets. *Journal of Finance*, 40, 1385–1401.

Blackwell, D, MW Marr and M Spivey (1990). Shelf registration and the reduced due diligence argument: Implications of the underwriter certification and the implicit insurance hypothesis. *Journal of Financial and Quantitative Analysis*, 25, 245–259.

Booth, J and R Smith (1986). Capital raising, underwriting, and the certification hypothesis. *Journal of Financial Economics*, 15, 261–281.

Cooney, J and A Kalay (1993). Positive information from equity issue announcements. *Journal of Financial Economics*, 33, 149–172.

Copeland, T and D Galai (1983). Information effects on the bid–ask spread. *Journal of Finance*, 38, 1457–1469.

Corwin, S (2003). The determinants of underpricing for seasoned equity offers. *Journal of Finance*, 58, 2249–2279.

Denis, D (1991). Shelf registration and the market for seasoned equity offerings. *Journal of Financial Research*, 16, 189–212.

Denis, D (1993). The costs of equity issues since Rule 415: A closer look. *Journal of Business*, 64, 77–88.

Fama, E and K French (2005). Financing decisions: Who issues stock? *Journal of Financial Economics*, 3, 549–582.

Galai, D and R Masulis (1976). The option pricing model and the risk factor of stock. *Journal of Financial Economics*, 3, 53–81.

Glosten, L and P Milgrom (1985). Bid, ask and transaction prices in a specialist market with heterogeneously informed traders. *Journal of Financial Economics*, 14, 71–100.

Gomes, AR and GM Phillips (2007). Why do public firms issue private and public securities? (16 February 2007). *AFA 2008 New Orleans Meetings Paper.* Available at SSRN: http://ssrn.com/abstract=972723.

Graham, J and C Harvey (2001). The theory and practice of corporate finance: Evidence from the field. *Journal of Financial Economics*, 60, 187–243.

Hansen, R (1986). Evaluating the costs of a new equity issue. *Midland Corporate Finance Journal*, 4, 42–55.

Heron, R and E Lie (2004). A comparison of the motivations for and the information content of different types of equity offerings. *Journal of Business*, 73, 605–632.

Jensen, M (1986). Agency costs of free cash flow, corporate finance, and takeovers. *American Economic Review*, 76, 323–329.

Jensen, M, C Hudson and M Sullivan (1995). Should managers shelf register secondary offerings? *Quarterly Journal of Business and Economics*, 36, 25–38.

Kadapakkam, P and S Kon (1989). The value of shelf registration for new debt issues. *Journal of Business*, 62, 271–292.

Kidwell, D, MW Marr and GR Thompson (1984). SEC Rule 415: The ultimate competitive bid. *Journal of Financial and Quantitative Analysis*, 19, 183–195.

Kidwell, D, MW Marr and GR Thompson (1987). Shelf registration: Competition and market flexibility. *Journal of Law and Economics*, 30, 181–206.

Krasker, W (1986). Stock price movements in response to stock issues under asymmetric information. *Journal of Finance*, 41, 93–105.

Leone, AJ, S Rock and M Willenborg (2007). Disclosure of intended use of proceeds and underpricing in initial public offerings. *Journal of Accounting Research*, 45, 111–153.

Moore, N, D Peterson and P Peterson (1986). Shelf registrations and shareholder wealth: A comparison of shelf and traditional equity offerings. *Journal of Finance*, 41, 451–463.

Myers, S and N Majluf (1984). Corporate financing and investment decisions when firms have information that investors do not have. *Journal of Financial Economics*, 13, 187–221.

Sherman, A (1999). Underwriter certification and the effect of shelf registration on due diligence. *Financial Management*, 28, 5–19.

Thatcher, J and J Thatcher (1988). Timing performance and the flotation of shelf-registered bonds. *Financial Management*, 17, 16–26.

Wu, Y (2004). The choice of equity-selling mechanisms. *Journal of Financial Economics*, 74, 93–119.

10

The Impact of Arrangers and Buyout Sponsors on Loan Pricing in LBOs: A Cross Border Study

Kenneth Daniels and Irwin Morgan

1. Introduction

Since the mid-1980s, there have been three significant trends in the debt capital markets. The first significant trend, loan syndication, has grown from a low of $9 billion in 1985 to over $1.3 trillion in 2002 (Gadanecz, 2004). This market began as a mechanism to service sovereign debt, but has become a primary source for corporate capital. Syndicated loans have become major sectors in the debt capital markets representing over 50% of U.S. corporate finance originated in 2002 (Sufi, 2007). One reason for this growth in loan syndication is because individual loans to borrowers have increased in size therefore necessitating increased risk sharing by lenders. In addition, globalization by borrowers has increased syndication.

A second trend is the resurgence in Leveraged Buyout (LBO) activity. The market for LBOs has grown from $9.8 billion in 1986 to $64 billion in 2002. LBO activity has been cyclical fueled by financial innovations. In the late 1980s heyday, LBO activity reached a peak of over $231 billion fueled by the junk bond market while achieving the visibility with major buyouts like the RJR-Nabisco transaction led by private equity specialists Kohlberg, Kravis, and Roberts (KKR).

LBO activity slowed to a low of only $4.8 billion during 1992. This market has rebounded to nearly $64 billion in 2002 fueled by another financial innovation, loan syndication. One reason for this growth in LBOs (as noted by Thomas and Wang, 2004) is that syndicated lending often provided a bridging vehicle in corporate mergers and acquisitions as syndicated loans provided financing for leveraged buyouts.

The third trend is the growth in participation of private equity or buyout specialists in LBO activity. Buyout specialists' participation in LBO deals included in the Dealogic Loanware database has grown from 28.9% in 1988 to over 91% in 2002 (Table 2). Private equity or buyout specialists contribute several factors to an LBO transaction: equity, monitoring and active participation. These new organizations LBOs (Jensen, 1989) use private debt and equity along with public debt to modify standard agency issues faced by publicly held corporations with dispersed ownership. Because bank debt through loan syndication has become a primary capital source to fund many LBOs, it is a vital research and public policy issue for practitioners, academics and regulators. Our focus is the intersection of loan syndication, LBOs and buyout sponsors and its impact on loan pricing.

Our objective is to investigate the impact of arrangers and buyout sponsors on loan pricing, deal size and type of syndicate loans for LBOs in the U.S. and European markets. We investigate whether arrangers play useful roles in reducing information asymmetries between borrowers and syndicate loan participants.[1] Consistent with the monitoring role suggested for arrangers, as suggested by Sufi (2007), we examine if multiple arrangers loan syndicates result in reduced agency cost and hence lower loan spreads for borrowers. Sufi (2007) uses the number of lenders to proxy for syndication and finds a positive relation between firm information levels and the structure and concentration of the syndicate.

We also study whether using a buyout sponsor provides benefits to borrowers. Buyout sponsors, usually private equity companies, participate in LBO transactions by investing equity and other instruments in the company and take partial or full control of the acquired entity. Unsponsored LBOs are syndicated deals that are only brought to market by the arranger. Sponsored LBOs are syndicated deals brought to the market by arrangers and buyout sponsors and may reveal the role of the buyout sponsor in the LBO market.

Specifically, we examine if all in drawn spreads (AIS) are lower for LBO-syndicated-loan issues based upon the monitoring of the arranger and the participation of a buyout sponsor. Limited prior research has examined the benefits for borrowers and market participants for issues that have used the services of a buyout sponsor. However, our results using a large sample of 2,280 LBO-syndicated loans for the period 1986–2002 show that buyout sponsors play significant roles in LBO-syndicated lending. We find that syndicated loans with buyout sponsors are larger deal sizes, have higher AIS spreads, and are significantly more leverage than syndicated loans without buyout sponsors.

Our results also suggest a strong correlation between buyout sponsors and private highly leveraged transactions, which tend to be smaller LBOs. Smaller LBOs tend to be more informationally problematic than larger LBO transactions. However, our results also indicate that buyout sponsors are associated with relatively larger public LBOs, which tend to be complex and highly leveraged. We also find buyout sponsors are more closely aligned with single arranger deals. This indicates that buyout sponsors are able to add value to single arranger deals and bring more complex LBO deals to the market. On the other hand, buyout sponsors are negatively associated with club deals as borrowers seek to protect their ownership structure.

More importantly, we find the presence of buyout sponsors results in higher AIS spreads of approximately 29 basis points, which are statistically and economically significant, even after controlling for the contract terms of the syndicated loan and syndicate structure imposed by the arrangers and providers. This suggests that buyout sponsors play an important role and help bring opaque LBO transactions to the market, which are significantly riskier transactions. We also find the lender-to-borrower relationship associated with single arrangers and multiple providers result in reduced agency cost and greater monitoring such that the AIS spread is smaller. On the other hand, multiple arranger loans are larger in size with higher risk characteristics.

We examine these issues separately for U.S. and European LBO loans, given the distinct differential characteristics of these types of issues. As documented in Carey and Nini (2007), European LBO loans have smaller loan spreads than U.S. LBO loans. Carey and Nini (2007), Nini (2004) and to some extent Sufi (2005) argue and find that different types of arrangers and borrowers from different market locations tend to price loans differently, i.e., a home bias. Borrowers are partitioned into groups based on their market location (Europe vs. U.S.) and whether the LBO borrower is from the same market location as the arranger and the provider. Within these classifications, we examine if differences exist across groupings based on whether the issue is supported by a buyout sponsor.

The rest of the paper is organized as follows. Section 2 summarizes the existing literature. Section 3 formulates the hypothesis. Section 4 describes the data and descriptive statistics for the study. Section 5 details the methodology and our multivariate tests. We end our discussions with some policy recommendations.

2. Literature Review

A syndicated loan in an LBO is a loan that is originated by one or more arrangers for a borrower, where either internal management or outsiders acquire the equity or assets of a corporation or its division by using a combination of equity and debt. Syndicated loans are a hybrid between relationship banking, where a bank provides a multitude of services to a client/borrower and public debt, where a bank simply represents the sale and distribution of the bonds for a fee. Syndicated loan arrangers, who are selected by the borrower, originate and negotiate contract terms, loan placement on a best effort, or firm commitment of underwriting to other lenders called participants.

Subsequently, these lead arrangers have the responsibility to screen, monitor and coordinate activities on behalf of loan participants. Arrangers are responsible for loan documentation, collateral administration and covenant enforcement. For these services, arrangers earn additional fees some of which they share with lenders that become co-arrangers. Funding for syndicated loans may be supplied by one or more participants. Arrangers function as liquidity insurers in situations of unexpected deterioration (Elsas and Krahnen, 1998; Hallak, 2003) and lead negotiator if borrowers become financially distressed. These requirements are best fulfilled by well-capitalized lenders who have strong reputations.

Mullineaux (2004) finds that despite entry by new syndication participants, the market has become more concentrated in the recent years as a result of consolidation among major banks. The top three U.S. banks controlled 68% of dollar volume in first half of 2002, while the top three European banks controlled only 27.9%. If arrangers in a syndicate are less competitive structurally, then they must compete more heavily through pricing concessions. Fridson (2005) confirms this industry dynamic referencing that intermediaries are getting squeezed and must sacrifice spreads or terms and conditions or risk a reduction in league-table position. For example, competition for loans has intensified to the point, where London Interbank Offered Rate (LIBOR) spreads on leveraged loans have reached a mere 139--225 basis points, a three-year low, according to the Loan Pricing Corporation Gold Sheet's broadly syndicated-loan grid (Roche and Szuch, 1997).

Gadanecz (2004) showed that the syndication loan market allows a more efficient geographical and institutional risk sharing. The syndicated-loan structure cultivates additional business opportunities for financial institutions and provides a mechanism for funding more highly leveraged transactions — as lenders are only expected to assume a portion of the credit risk. The higher the perceived credit risk, the more likely a syndicated-loan package will include additional protection in the form of collateral and financial covenants. Syndicated-loans act as a risk-management tool for financial firms allowing lenders to engage in portions of credit relationships while avoiding excess risk to capital loss. Angbazo *et al.* (1998) supported by Dennis *et al.* (2001) show that credit spreads on syndicated highly leveraged transactions (HLTs)[2] have lower yield spreads than other

HLT loans, providing evidence in favor of the hypothesis that better risk diversification among a pool of borrowers reduce the cost of credit. Many leveraged buyouts by their nature are considered HLTs.

According to Cebenoyan and Strahan (2004), banks manage their risks by both buying and selling loans appear to benefit. These institutions are able to operate with less capital and hold fewer liquid assets on their balance sheet, and they can engage in more risky lending without unduly increasing their risk. Armstrong (2003) concurs with Cebenoyan and Strahan (2004) citing that agent banks can tailor the degree of credit risk and interest-rate risk they wish to retain by parceling pieces of the loan through the syndication process. Armstrong (2003) discusses the credit-risk transfer capability related to the syndicated-loan process. Credit-risk transfer instruments have been around for years in the form of credit guarantees and credit insurance. However, over the past decade, loan syndication has become more prominent (Kiff and Morrow, 2000). Markets in credit-risk transfer can help to better efficiently allocate credit risk in the economy. Syndications effectively represent a "pooling" of financing resources, which offers the potential for a broader dispersion of credit risk, including transfer to institutional investors such as insurance companies and investment funds. If banks hold more diversified credit portfolios, they will be less vulnerable to the performance of individual borrowers or industries (Armstrong, 2003). Risk reduction through diversification should result in a lower cost of funds unless syndications attract higher risk loans.

For syndicated loans, monitoring becomes a key role, particularly in the case of LBOs, where the post-LBO entity becomes private. Bolten and Scharfstein's (1996) model predicts that firms with high credit risk will borrow from fewer lenders which are empirically tested by Lee and Mullineaux (2004) and Sufi (2007). Dennis and Mullineaux (2000) find that loans are more likely to be syndicated as information about borrowers becomes more transparent. They also find that longer-term loans are more likely to be syndicated than shorter-term loans. Casolaro *et al.* (2003) in their study of syndicated loans in over 80 countries also conclude that arrangers mitigate informational asymmetries by retaining a larger share of the loan.

They show that this certification effect by the arranger results in lower interest rates and is greater for smaller, more opaque loans, where monitoring is more important.

In addition, Lee and Mullineaux (2004) find that syndicates are smaller and more concentrated when there is little information about the borrower, when credit risk is relatively high, and when a loan is secured suggesting that syndicates are structured to enhance the monitoring efforts and renegotiations in the event of financial distress. Sufi (2007) confirms both Lee and Mullineaux (2004) and Casolaro *et al.* (2003) in that when borrowers require more intense investigation and monitoring, the lead arranger retains a larger portion of the loan, forms a more concentrated syndicate and adds that arrangers choose participants in the syndicate that are closer to the borrower (both geographically and in terms of previous relationships).

The syndicated-loan structure cultivates additional business opportunities for financial institutions and provides a mechanism for funding more highly leveraged transactions — as lenders are only expected to assume a portion of the credit risk. The higher the perceived credit risk, the more likely a syndicated-loan package will include additional protection in the form of collateral and financial covenants. For transactions with greater required traditional and cash-flow leverage, the structural elements of the loan package will naturally be more stringent. Moreover, the loan agreement will include higher compensation to the lenders in return for the additional credit risk undertaken. The additional cost of capital is warranted and accepted by the borrower since the loan-syndicate structure provides client access to capital despite an inherently higher degree of credit risk.

We find that the syndicate-loan structure also uses the services of a buyout sponsor to sometimes complement the deal. To our knowledge, there has been limited prior research on the impact of services of buyout sponsor on syndicated-loan deals. Prior research (Kaplan and Stein, 1993; Cotter and Peck, 2001; Cumming *et al.*, 2007 are exceptions) has examined the benefits for borrowers and market participants for issues that have used the services of a buyout sponsor.

Cotter and Peck (2001) using a sample of 64 previously public LBOs between 1984 and 1989 found that when buyout specialists hold the majority of post-LBO equity, the deal is financed with less short-term and senior debt.

3. Hypothesis Development

The syndicated-loan structure allows for more highly leveraged transaction to consummate since the syndication facilitates asset diversification and the ability to utilize the secondary market. However, it does not necessarily ensure the supply of financial institutions seeking arranger appointment will increase and reduce the market share earned by the leading arranger firms. The required institutional knowledge and adequate capital structure act as barriers to entry on the largest scale thus allowing leverage buyout organizations (LBOs) and buyout sponsors to innovate and propose substitutive transactional structures to syndicated-loan arrangers. Since arranger firms underwriting the syndicates must convince other traditional lenders to participate, the arranger's structural flexibility to remove standard covenants and default provisions is more limited than non-traditional financiers.

The ordinary syndicated participants operate in a highly regulated industry and must adhere to more traditional underwriting standards such as lending against "hard" security assets and governing the credit exposure through a standard covenant package. The competitive landscape forces arrangers to compete and has a natural effect on proposed credit spreads. If arrangers in a syndicate are less competitive structurally, then they must compete more heavily through pricing concessions. Additionally, arrangers and buyout sponsors also help complete the market and bring complex informational opaque deals to completion. If the required credit risk is too great for traditional syndicated-loan underwriting, borrowers must turn to the venture-capital industry.

Private equity (buyout sponsors) transactions allow for even greater credit risk since investors seek and require the opportunity to consult in the operating direction of the funded entity. As such, the combination of the syndicated-loan market and private equity funding has increased the access to business capital and fostered greater product and service development for our underlying economy. Private-equity investors are more nimble and less regulated thus allowing for easier execution of flexible terms and conditions. By early 2004, these "active investors"[3] were persuading investment bankers to forgo material adverse change clauses in the loan agreement (Fridson, 2005).

From a practitioner's standpoint, the growth in private equity firms plays a highly important role in the functioning of our overall economy. However, despite the growth in the syndicated structure and the access to a well-functioning secondary loan market, traditional underwriting institutions are unlikely to move credit standards aggressively enough to eliminate the need for buyout sponsors. This is largely attributable to the functional dynamic of two distinct roles within traditional financiers: the loan originators and the loan underwriters. While these two positions play very distinctive roles within an organization, many traditional lenders are unable to allow these roles to operate mutually exclusive of one another. The loan originators must maintain some role in the overall analysis of the proposed credit exposure since these individuals are closer to the prospective client and able to measure the intangible, qualitative aspects of the borrower.

Since two distinctive roles are blended into a single operating principle focused on funding non-speculative assets, overall credit origination is likely to remain more conservative than if an organization was solely focused on asset growth — which more closely defines the operating strategy of buyout sponsors. In this environment, single arranger syndicated LBO deals are more likely to use the services of a buyout sponsor than multiple arranger syndicated LBO deals. Multiple arrangers are able to combine their expertise in the LBO market along with their information-processing capabilities to complete a significant amount of LBO deals without the need for buyout sponsors. On the contrary, single arrangers may lack the necessary expertise to complete the LBO transaction without the complementary services of the buyout sponsor.

H1: LBO deals with a buyout sponsor are more likely to be single arranger loan syndicates rather than multiple arranger syndicates.

H2: LBO deals with a buyout sponsor are relatively more informationally complex deals that warrant less favorable loan pricing to bring the syndicate loan to market.

Extant research shows that the type of lender, its size, and its ability to more efficiently monitor the borrower's are important determinants of credit quantity, quality and pricing, especially for the corporate credit market. Thus, we more specifically investigate LBO practices by analyzing arrangers and buyout sponsors based on their potential information capabilities. We use several classifications of syndicate structures to capture different levels of informational sensitivities. Extant literature hypothesized that banks are unique in monitoring. As shown by Hughes *et al.* (2003), banks are able to gain an information advantage over other type of lenders through checking accounts that in turn are used to monitor accounts receivables and inventories.

Similarly, Dell'Ariccia and Marquez (2005) argue that private information obtained by banks generates lender–client specificity. Further, Berger and Udell (2002) find evidence consistent with the idea that small banks lend to riskier, more "opaque" small firms that require more monitoring and that large banks focus on relatively safer, more "transparent" small firms. Rajan (1992) and Diamond (1993) also cite the benefits of bank financing and monitoring for small firms that have high levels of information asymmetry. Thus, we use the number of arrangers (one vs. multiple) to reflect efficiencies in the process of information handling and monitoring. Detragiache *et al.* (2000) derive and test a model, which shows that multiple banking relationships may minimize project underfunding due to bank liquidity.

Multiple arrangers may result from these prior relationships with the borrower or sponsors in the LBO transactions. We also use whether the arranger is the sole lender to capture expertise in coping with information problems. If the arranger is the sole lender, we expect the due diligence performed by the syndicate will be more information-intense as the arranger attempts to signal the soundness of the borrowers' financial condition by playing a larger role in the informational gathering and lending process. One extreme example of this is the syndicated club deal, where the borrower is the arranger and the borrower may receive more lenient loan and pricing arrangements because it is willing to share more information with participant lenders seeking a relationship.

Therefore, single arranger deals should increase the flexibility of contract terms for the arranger and borrower. The arranger has a competitive advantage against other providers since it constantly interacts with the core contacts of the borrower and is more efficiently able to position products and services. Moreover, Casolero *et al.* (2003) find when the lead arranger underwrites a larger percentage of the credit facility it results in lower interest rates to the borrowers. In these situations, the lead arrangers provide a certification role for the borrower.

H3: LBO deals which are club deals or single arranger loan syndicates are more likely to have favorable loan pricing.

In addition, the international nature of our sample allows us to investigate the "home bias" policy issue as documented in Carey and Nini (2007). We investigate whether the geographical location on the borrower, arranger or provider matters for LBO-syndicated loan pricing.

H4: LBO deals where the borrower and the arranger are from the same location will have less favorable loan pricing ("home bias"). In addition, LBO deals where the borrower and the provider are from the same location will have less favorable loan pricing.

Our large sample size permits us to explore these issues further. We test for these expectations and analyze these issues using large samples of both single and multiple arranger LBO issues, along with whether the LBO-syndicated loan has a buyout sponsor. The next section describes the data and some preliminary results obtained in our analysis.

4. Data and Preliminary Results

Our sample consists of syndicated loans on leverage buyouts (LBOs) issued between 1986 and 2002. LBO loan data are obtained from Loanware, a database of syndicated loans constructed by Dealogic Capital Data. Carey and Nini (2007) discuss the intricate details of the Loanware database that covers a significant fraction of the dollar amount of outstanding consumer and industrial loans. In addition, Loanware provides information about borrowers, arrangers, and providers of LBO loans. In many instances, a single LBO loan or deal is comprised of several facilities; therefore, our analysis is at the tranche level since many LBO transactions include multiple loans from the participant lenders to the same company.

We also use term and revolving loans in our analysis. Although, revolving lines of credits are the most common type of loan (Strahan, 1999) that is not the case for LBO borrowers. Several prior studies have used the Loanware database in corporate credit market research such as Casolaro *et al.* (2003) and Carey and Nini (2007). Our final sample has 2,280 syndicated facilities for which data for all variables necessary for our analyses were available in the Loanware database. Table 1 gives a full description of the variables used in the study.

4.1. *Descriptive Statistics and Univariate Results*

The distribution of the LBO-syndicated loans is shown in Table 2 and illustrates the composition of the LBO-syndicated loan market over time. Our LBO-syndicated loan market started with 10 loans in 1986 with over $9.8 billion in LBO deals with mean AIS of 291 basis points. The market experienced significant growth as seen by the 191 loans in 2002 with over $64 billion dollars of transactions completed.

The average syndicated loan size for LBOs is $414 million with average AIS of 264 basis points. The percentage of deals with a buyout sponsor grew considerably over time from 0% in 1986 to over 91% in 2002. Single-arranger transactions started at very high percentages in the 1980s but have trended downward to 29.8% in 2002.

Table 3A illustrates the impact of the single arranger relative to the multiple arrangers while controlling for the impact of the buyout

Table 1. Description of variables.

Variable	Description
AIS :	The drawn all-in-spread. It measures the cost of the DIP loan. AIS is as reported in Loanware database, which is the sum of coupon spread, annual fee, and upfront fee measured as a mark-up over LIBOR.
DINV :	a dummy variable coded 1 indicating that the syndicated loan is investment grade, 0 otherwise.
DSEC :	a dummy variable coded 1 indicating that DIP loan is secured (as reported in DealScan database); 0 otherwise.
INDEX :	is the average yield spread above the federal funds rate on the total commercial and industrial loans as reported by the Federal Reserve Board Index
LOGAMT :	is the log of the facility size.
LOGMAT :	is the log of the maturity of the DIP loan.
DLEV :	is a dummy variable coded 1 indicating the loan is a highly leverage transaction.
NUMPROV :	is an ordinal number indicating the number of providers as reported in Loanware.
NUMARR:	is an ordinal number indicating the number of arrangers as reported in Loanware.
RATING :	is an ordinal number indicating the crediting by S&P and Moody's, 1 indicates AAA etc.
ONEPROV :	is a dummy variable coded 1 if there is one provider, 0 otherwise.
ONEARR :	is a dummy variable coded 1 if there is one arranger, 0 otherwise.
SAMENATP :	is a dummy variable coded 1 if the borrower and provider are from the same region, 0 otherwise.
SAMENATA :	is a dummy variable coded 1 if the arranger and borrower are from the same region, 0 otherwise.
DCLUB :	is a dummy variable coded 1 indicating the syndicated loan is a club deal, 0 otherwise.
DPRIVATE :	is a dummy variable coded 1 indicating the borrower is a private firm, 0 otherwise.
DTERM :	is a dummy variable coded 1 indicating that the loan was a term loan; 0 otherwise.
IMR :	is the inverse Mills ratio calculated from the respective first stage logit regression. The IMR is calculated based upon the dummy variables DSPONSOR.
DSPONSOR :	is a dummy variable coded 1 indicating the syndicated loan has a sponsor, 0 otherwise.
D1-D40 :	is a dummy variable coded 1 indicating the borrower respective industry, 0 otherwise.
86-Y02 :	are respective dummy variables indicating the year of the loan (1986–2002), respectively.

sponsor. The average loan size for LBOs with a single arranger is $295 million, significantly smaller than $549 million for multiple arranger loans. Table 3 also illustrates that deals with the sponsor tend to be smaller on average for single and multiple arrangers. However,

Table 2. Loan characteristics of LBOs 1986–2002.

	No. of loans	% Sponsored	% Single arranger	Dollar volume (millions $) Mean	Median	Total	% Total ($)	All in drawn spread (bps) Mean	Median
1986	10	0.0	90.0	980.6	820	9,805.6	1.0	291	277
1987	22	0.0	59.1	1,309.4	550	28,807.8	3.0	220	250
1988	90	28.9	80.0	739.1	283	66,521.1	7.0	241	250
1989	157	17.2	86.0	1,471.9	248	231,095.3	24.4	231	246
1990	64	29.7	67.2	468.0	173	29,952.7	3.2	220	230
1991	38	36.8	73.7	201.7	127	7,664.1	0.8	262	250
1992	36	36.1	83.3	135.3	75	4,871.4	0.5	270	278
1993	81	61.7	74.1	167.4	130	13,561.6	1.4	278	275
1994	128	33.6	73.4	177.8	90	22,756.4	2.4	261	250
1995	109	32.1	67.9	218.4	135	23,804.6	2.5	262	275
1996	106	68.9	36.8	435.4	325	46,148.3	4.9	259	250
1997	125	68.8	42.4	337.0	195	42,125.4	4.5	235	238
1998	277	91.7	51.6	277.2	158	76,791.1	8.1	242	231
1999	299	96.7	45.2	294.5	180	88,050.8	9.3	281	285
2000	304	88.8	38.2	348.1	213	105,830.8	11.2	278	275
2001	243	92.6	43.2	344.7	200	83,766.8	8.9	274	275
2002	191	91.6	29.8	335.8	212	64,136.5	6.8	307	285
Total	**2,280**	**70.1**	**52.9**	**414.8**	**185**	**945,690.4**	**100.0**	**264**	**250**

these results based on means only are misleading as the median deal sizes for single and multiple arrangers with sponsor relative to single arranger and multiple arrangers without a sponsor is larger. Thus we conclude LBO-syndicated loans with a sponsor are not necessarily smaller LBO transactions. However, the presence of the sponsor allows these deals to receive larger amounts of funding. The average AIS for single arranger loans with a sponsor are 260 basis points as against 236 basis points for single arranger loans without sponsors. Correspondingly, the average AIS for LBOs with a multiple arranger with a sponsor are 284 basis points, higher than 256 basis points for LBO-syndicated loans with multiple arrangers and sponsors.

A clear and interesting pattern emerges from the descriptive statistics of Tables 2 and 3A, indicating that syndicated loans for LBOs with a sponsor tend to be larger loans with higher AIS. Even after we control for the impact of the type of arranger (single or multiple), LBO-syndicated loans with a sponsor tend to have a higher

Table 3A. Descriptive statistics — Single vs. multiarranger LBO loans.

		Single arranger			Multiple arrangers		
	Total	ALL	w/sponsors	w/o sponsors	All	w/sponsors	w/o sponsors
Facility size	415	295	260	356	549	525	634
	(185)	(131)	(141)	(110)	(270)	(274)	(245)
All in drawn	264	251	260	236	278	284	256
Spread	(250)	(250)	(250)	(250)	(275)	(275)	(250)
Maturity	77	77	79	73	78	79	74
	(84)	(84)	(84)	(78)	(84)	(84)	(82)
Ordinal rating	28	28	29	28	27	27	27
Highly leveraged	29%	18%	21%	13%	41%	46%	22%
Club deals	4%	4%	3%	5%	5%	4%	9%
% Secured	24%	17%	15%	21%	32%	32%	35%
% Sponsored	70%	64%	100%	0%	78%	100%	0%
Term loans	64%	62%	65%	57%	66%	68%	60%
Revolving loans	36%	38%	35%	43%	34%	32%	40%
Investment grade	2%	1%	1%	2%	4%	4%	3%
Private firms	73%	72%	83%	53%	73%	76%	64%
% US	56%	51%	46%	61%	60%	61%	58%
% Europe	41%	47%	52%	36%	36%	36%	35%
Samenata	67%	68%	64%	77%	64%	64%	67%
No. of arrangers	1.9	1.0	1.0	1.0	2.8	2.9	2.7
	(1.0)	(1.0)					
No. of providers	8.0	6.3	6.5	6.0	9.9	9.3	11.9
	(5.0)	(4.0)					
No. of Loans	2280	1206	766	440	1074	833	241

This table presents the mean and median (in parenthesis) for several key loan variables for U.S. and European LBOs based upon borrower's home nation and presence of buyout sponsor. These are LBO loans between 1 January 1986 and 31 December 2002 using Dealogic's Loanware database. The tranche size is in millions of dollars. The all in drawn spread are in basis points over LIBOR. Maturity is expressed in months. Ordinal Rating is conversion of the Moody's or S&P rating on a scale from 1 to 31 (non rated loans are 31). The percent of loans where the arranger and borrower are in the same region are represented by (Samenata).

AIS. This would suggest that sponsors are on average associated with much more complex deals that are riskier on average, which we examine next.

Table 3A presents the key facility variables by the category of the deal. Examining data for discrete variables and for the full sample, 24% of LBO-syndicated loans are secured with the predominant type of loan being a term loan at 64%, as compared to 36% for revolving lines of credit. A total of 29% of the LBO credit facilities are categorized as highly leveraged with a very small amount identified as investment grade at 2%. Private-syndicated LBOs are very prominent at 73% of the sample. The LBO deals have more US geographical influence relative to Europe at 56% and 41%, respectively. Sponsorship is heavily involved among the deals at 70% respectively and the average-syndicated LBO has 1.9 arrangers along with 8.0 providers.

Given that prior literature documents (e.g., Mullineaux, 2004; Sufi, 2007), significant interest cost savings for credit facilities with a competitive syndicate structure, it is important to control for the number of arrangers and providers in the analysis. Prior research has ignored the role of the sponsor (Cotter and Peck (2001) are an exception for a small sample of 64 public U.S. firms) and has not documented the role played by the sponsor or the expected impact on the cost of capital for borrowers. We highlight some of these sponsor issues while controlling for the impact of the arranger.

A large percentage of LBO-syndicated loans with single and multiple arrangers are private firms (72% and 73%, respectively). This percentage increases to 83% for single arrangers with a sponsor and may help explain the smaller facility size for deals with a sponsor. Also, there is a smaller percentage of secured LBO-syndicated loans (15%) with a single arranger and sponsor in comparison to the 32% of secured loans for multiple arrangers with a sponsor. In addition, multiple arranger deals with a sponsor are overwhelmingly, highly leveraged transactions when compared to single arranger LBO deals.

Our sample also shows that a significant percentage of the borrowers and arrangers come from the same location (SAMENATA) at 67% indicating the potential for a home bias in loan pricing. This allows controlling for the regional effect of the borrower and arranger and examining its impact on LBO loan pricing. An examination of discrete variables also reveals that highly leveraged transactions usually involve the use of a sponsor as shown by the respective percentages of 21%, and 46% for single arranger and multiple arrangers with sponsorship, respectively. These results tend to suggest that sponsors migrate to larger highly leveraged transactions and are able to charge significantly higher AIS relative to the rest of the LBO-syndicated-loan market.

We divide our descriptive statistics into two subpanels for U.S. and European LBOs based on the home nation of the LBO target. Results are shown in Table 3B. We have 1,269 U.S. and 1,011 European loan facilities, respectively. We find some key differences between the borrowing patterns of U.S. versus European LBOs. U.S. LBOs have larger tranche sizes (143 vs. 94 m USD). However, U.S. LBO targets are financed with an average of three tranches compared to European deals that have a mean of four tranches per facility.

Consistent with the findings of Carey and Nini (2007), the all in drawn spread for European LBOs is approximately 50 bps lower than U.S. LBOs. This lower spread is partly due to a larger percentage of HLTs (50% vs. 2%) in U.S. LBOs. Because U.S. deals are more levered, they have a higher percentage of secured transactions (31% vs. 16%) when compared to their European counterparts. The lower AIS for European LBOs are despite the fact that financing for European LBOs are on average 11 months longer in maturity (83 vs. 73 months).

Our sample includes zero investment grade tranches for the European LBOs while 4% of the U.S. tranches were investment grade. Over 85% of European LBOs were private firms, whereas 62% of the U.S. are private firms prior to the buyout. There are no significant differences in the number of arrangers between the U.S. and European LBOs, however, European LBOs have nearly 1.4 more providers (8.8 vs. 7.4) than U.S. LBOs in their transactions.

Sponsorship for both U.S. (68%) and European (73%) LBOs are similar. For U.S. LBOs, deals with sponsors have smaller tranches (126 m vs. 178 m); incur a higher all in drawn spread (300 vs. 266 bps); and are more likely to be highly leveraged (61% vs. 27%). European LBOs with sponsors also have smaller tranches (88 m vs. 109 m); incur higher AIS (241 bps vs. 208 bps); have longer maturity (85 months vs. 77 months); are more likely to be highly leveraged (3% vs. 0%) and

Table 3B. Descriptive statistics — U.S. vs. European LBOs.

	Total LBOs	US LBOs			European LBOs		
	All	All	w/sponsor	w/o sponsor	All	w/sponsor	w/o sponsor
Tranche amount	121 (55)	143 (60)	126 (60)	178 (65)	94 (49)	88 (50)	109 (48)
Number of tranches	4 (3)	3 (3)	3 (3)	3 (3)	4 (4)	4 (4)	3 (3)
All in drawn spread	264 (250)	289 (275)	300 (300)	266 (257)	232 (225)	241 (225)	208 (200)
Maturity	77 (84)	73 (72)	73 (72)	71 (72)	83 (84)	85 (84)	77 (84)
Ordinal rating	28	26	26	26	30	30	30
Highly leveraged	29%	50%	61%	27%	2%	3%	0%
Club deals	4%	0%	0%	1%	9%	7%	15%
% Secured	24%	31%	34%	25%	16%	11%	28%
% Sponsored	70%	68%	100%	0%	73%	100%	0%
Term loans	64%	60%	63%	55%	69%	71%	63%
Revolving loans	36%	40%	37%	45%	31%	29%	37%
Investment grade	2%	4%	4%	3%	0%	0%	0%
Private firms	73%	62%	66%	55%	85%	95%	59%
Samenatp	48%	55%	57%	53%	40%	39%	41%
Samenata	67%	80%	78%	82%	50%	46%	61%
No. of arrangers	1.9 (1.0)	1.8 (2.0)	2.0 (2.0)	1.5 (1.0)	1.9 (1.0)	2.0 (1.0)	1.7 (1.0)
No. of providers	8.0 (5.0)	7.4 (4.0)	7.2 (3.0)	7.8 (4.0)	8.8 (6.0)	8.9 (7.0)	8.4 (6.0)
No. of loans	2280	1269	862	407	1011	737	274

This table presents the mean and median (in parentheses) for several key loan variables for U.S. and European LBOs based upon borrower's home nation and presence of buyout sponsor. These are LBO loans between 1 January 1986 and 31 December 2002 using Dealogic's Loanware database. The tranche size is in millions of dollars. The all in drawn spreads are in basis points over LIBOR. Maturity is expressed in months. Ordinal Rating is conversion of the Moody's or S&P rating on a scale from 1 to 31 (non-rated loans are 31). The percent of loans where the arranger and borrower are in the same region are represented by Samenata.

are overwhelmingly private firms (95% vs. 59%). However, European LBOs with sponsors are less likely to be club deals (7% vs. 15%) and have a smaller percentage secured (11% vs. 28%).

To understand these distinctions concerning loans with and without sponsors, we also estimate probit regressions using as the dependent variable a dummy variable coded 1 if the issue had a sponsor (DSPONS) and 0 otherwise. The results are presented in Table 4. The descriptive test results discussed in this section suggest that borrowers using the services of a sponsor should be aware of the costs of these services. However, these results need to be interpreted with caution, as they do not control for other factors that could affect these differences. Multivariate tests and results discussed in the next section are more useful and appropriate for further tests of the hypotheses.

Table 4. Probit regression of sponsor choice.

		All loans		US LBOs		European LBOs	
Variables		Coefficient	*t*-value	Coefficient	*t*-value	Coefficient	*t*-value
Constant		−4.04	11.88*	−10.03		−12.30	
contract characteristics							
Log of maturity	LOGMAT	−0.01	1.44	−0.06	−1.16	−0.03	−0.23
Fraction secured	DSEC	−0.17	1.85	−0.25	−1.95	0.10	0.40
Log of amount	LOGAMT	0.36	8.68*	0.36	5.95*	0.31	3.22*
Information variables							
Investment grade	DINV	0.18	0.71	−0.04	−0.12	0.16	0.08
Highly leveraged	DLEV	0.44	2.66*	−0.05	−0.25	1.99	3.26*
Private	DPRIV	−0.16	1.54	−0.27	−2.04*	0.15	0.40
Number of arrangers	NUMARR	−0.14	5.14*	−0.09	−1.27	−0.12	−2.92*
Year dummies		Yes		Yes		Yes	
Industry dummies		Yes		Yes		Yes	
Fraction of correct predictions		85%					
Pseudo R^2		0.43		0.42		0.71	
Observations		2280		1269		1011	

This table presents the determinants of sponsor choice for the full sample. The dependent variable, DSPONSOR, is a dummy variable for whether there is a sponsor or not a sponsor. Fixed effects for each year and industry were included in the regression but are not reported to save space. See Table 1 for a full description of each variable.

Note: * indicates significance at the 5% level or better.

5. Multivariate Tests and Results

5.1. *Model and Control Variables*

Arrangers and borrowers choose to use the services of a sponsor if the perceived benefits exceed the costs. Benefits accrue to the borrower by receiving the necessary capital in an LBO. The use of a sponsor is not exogenous but is endogenously determined by several factors. If there is a correlation between factors such as loan size, number of arrangers and the use of a sponsor, the coefficient on the sponsor variable (DSPONSOR) in an ordinary least squares estimation with AIS as the dependent variable may be biased. This selectivity bias may also be generated by other loan-specific characteristics such as rating, and secured collateral features. Moreover, this selectivity bias may also be enhanced by borrower-specific characteristics. Hence, using ordinary least squares estimation under these conditions may not be appropriate. To avoid this selectivity bias problem, we estimate the following two-equation model:

$$s_i^* = \gamma' z_i + \varepsilon_i \quad \text{(sponsorship choice model)}$$

$$c_i = \beta' x_i + \delta f_i + \mu_i \quad \text{(cost of capital model)}$$

with $s_i = 1$ if $s_i^* > 0$ and $s_i = 0$ otherwise, s_i^* as the borrower's unobservable benefits from choosing a sponsor, s_i as the borrower's observed sponsor choice, z_i as vector of variables determining the decision to choose a sponsor, c_i the observed component of the borrower's cost of capital, x_i as vector of exogenous variables determining this component, ε_i and μ_i as normally distributed disturbances.[4]

The first equation specifies a probit regression and models the borrower's decision to choose a sponsor, and is intended to control for self-selection. The second equation captures the linkages between the borrower's cost of capital, its decision to use a sponsor or not, and other loan and borrower characteristics. This specification takes into account that the choice of usage of a sponsor is endogenous and provides a measure of the marginal effect of the decision to use a sponsor.

Given that the disturbances in the two regressions are correlated, a simple OLS estimation produces biased coefficients. To overcome this, we include in the second equation an additional term to account for the selectivity bias. This term is the inverse Mills ratio, which can be obtained from the probit estimation of the first equation. Including this term in the cost of capital model leads to consistent parameter estimates using OLS. We estimate the two equations using a general procedure based on Trost and Lee (1984). We interpret the inverse Mills ratio as an unexpected surprise from sponsorship to the cost of capital for the firm. The functional form of the probit equation we estimate first is

$$\begin{aligned} DSPONSOR = {} & \alpha_0 + \beta_1(LOGSIZE) + \beta_2(LOGMAT) + \beta_3(DTERM) \\ & + \beta_4(DPRIVATE) + \beta_5(DINV) + \beta_6(DSEC) \\ & + \beta_7(DLEV) + \beta_8(NUMARR) + \beta_{9-22}(Y89 - Y02) \\ & + e_i. \end{aligned} \tag{1}$$

DINV is coded 1 if the loan is rated as investment grade by either Standard and Poor's or Moody's, 0 otherwise. We use the DINV to proxy the borrower's firm and credit characteristic because the financial data are not publicly available for many of our samples. In addition, DLEV is coded 1 if the loan is a highly leveraged transaction loan and 0 otherwise. Buyout sponsor tend to be associated with highly leveraged transactions and we expect a positive relationship between DLEV and sponsorship. NUMARR is an ordinal variable indicating the number arranger in the LBO deal and is expected to be negatively correlated with sponsorship as indicated in *H1*.[5] All other variables are as defined in Table 1. This model specifies that the choice of the sponsor is endogenous and is influenced by loan-specific and borrower-specific characteristics in (1) above.

Overall, the models for sponsor choice are significant ($p < 0.000$), and have reasonable explanatory power. They show that LBO-syndicated loans with high leverage and larger facility sizes are more likely to have sponsors, while LBO-syndicated loans with a larger number of arrangers are less likely to have a sponsor. The results are achieved while controlling for year and industry effects of the sample. The results reported in Table 5A are consistent with our descriptive results. More importantly, they support our main hypothesis. Multiple arranger deals are less likely to be associated with buyout sponsor as they take advantage of the expanded skills of the arranger pool, which allows them transact larger and more complex deals without the use of a buyout sponsor.

However, this does suggest that buyout sponsors are able to concentrate on LBO-syndicated deals with single arrangers which may not have the expertise to bring the LBO deal to market without the services of a buyout sponsor. This is important because it illustrates the segmentation of the market and allows for the buyout sponsor to play an important functional systematic role that brings new additional information, labor and capital to the LBO market. Similarly, DLEV illustrates how buyout sponsor are attracted to highly leveraged transactions.

We then estimate the following model using ordinary least squares regression, with AIS, as the dependent variables, respectively:

$$\begin{aligned} AIS = {} & \alpha_0 + \beta_1(LOGMAT) + \beta_2(LOGMAT) + \beta_3(DTERM) \\ & + \beta_4(DPRIVATE) + \beta_5(RATING) + \beta_6(INDEX) + \beta_7(DSEC) \\ & + \beta_8(DCLUB) + \beta_9(DSAMENATP) + \beta_{10}(DSAMENATA) \\ & + \beta_{11}(ONEARR) + \beta_{12}(ONEPROV) + \beta_{21-29}(D1 - D40) \\ & + \beta_{21-29}(Y91 - Y99) + \beta_{30}(DSPONSOR) \\ & + \beta_{31}(IMR) + e_i. \end{aligned} \tag{2}$$

where IMR is the inverse Mills ratio obtained from the probit estimation of (1), and all other variables are as defined in Table 1. The statistical significance (or lack thereof) of the coefficient of IMR is an indication of whether selectivity bias exists or not. It also captures the unexpected impact of sponsorship on the cost of capital to the firm.

The variable of particular interest to us is DSPONSOR. We expect that the coefficient of this variable would be positive, as indicated by *H2*, in our estimation using Eq. (2) above, indicating a higher AIS to borrowers using the services of a sponsor. We use several control variables based on prior research (e.g., Carey *et al.*, 1998; Sufi, 2005) to control for factors that have been shown to influence AIS. We expect AIS to be positively related to INDEX[6] and positively related to better credit quality as represented by the Standard and Poor's or Moody's bond ratings (RATING). We expect that LOGMAT to be negatively related to AIS reflecting economies of scale for the arranger and we also expect that the variable ONEARR and DCLUB will be negatively associated with AIS.

H3 recognizes that the one arranger and club deals may be relationship deals with greater transparency and therefore, have a negative relationship AIS indicating favorable loan pricing. ONEPROV also captures the competitive distribution process among the providers and is expected to have a positive relationship with AIS. DTERM and DSEC should be positively associated with AIS reflecting greater return uncertainty due to maturity and collateral risk. Borrower-specific factors represented by DPRIV, DSAMENATP and DSAMENATA represent the informational problems associated with being a private firm that is usually small and the informational barriers associated with borrower not being in the same region as the provider and arranger, respectively.

H4 recognizes the informational barrier posed by the "home bias problem" and we expected a positive relationship with AIS and the geographical barrier variables. Finally, we include a series of dummy variables for the industry (year) of the loan to control for industry (year)-specific effects.

5.2. *Regression Results*

Table 5A shows estimation results of our models for LBO loan pricing. Prior research (e.g., Carey *et al.*, 1998) argues that credit quality is the most important factor to be considered for pricing private corporate debt. In our analysis, we control for the credit quality of the borrower by the Moody's and Standard and Poor's credit rating along with a

Table 5A. OLS regression of LBO loan pricing.

Variables		Panel A: full sample for LBO-syndicated loans		Panel B: one arranger only for LBO-syndicated loans		Panel C: multiple arrangers only for LBO-syndicated loans	
		Coefficient	*t*-value	Coefficient	*t*-value	Coefficient	*t*-value
Constant		312.19	18.66*	297.86	14.44*	251.3	9.30*
contract characteristics							
Log of maturity	LOGMAT	−0.01	0.98	0.015	1.35	−0.02	3.22*
Fraction secured	DSEC	17.66	3.68*	2.76	0.69	16.51	1.87
Log of amount	LOGAMT	−6.81	4.92*	−16.7	8.10*	0.72	0.3
Term loans	DTL	24.19	9.51*	27.29	7.34*	21.19	5.94*
Information variables							
Ordinal credit rating	Rating	1.71	4.94*	1.35	2.44*	1.91	3.85*
Private	DPRIV	21.9	3.95*	3.81	0.4	30.48	4.92*
Club loan	DCLUB	25.84	4.21*	29.69	3.74*	11.29	1.53
One provider	ONEPROV	18.73	3.78*	−4.61	0.36	24.09	5.65*
One arranger	ONEARR	23.65	5.31*				
Provider and borrower from same region	SAMENATP	5.91	2.32*	5.84	1.29	8.26	1.78
Arranger and borrower from same region	SAMENATA	5.09	1.63	3.69	0.73	10.09	2.35*
Sponsorship	DSPONSOR	29.64	3.95*	73.16	9.15*	5.47	0.76
Inverse Mills ratio	IMR	−8.6	3.09*	41.15	7.04*	10.64	2.22*
Control variables							
Loan index	Index	0.38	4.21*	0.02	1.81	0.14	1.27
Year dummies		Yes		Yes		Yes	
Industry dummies		Yes		Yes		Yes	
Adjusted R^2		0.43		0.2		0.15	
Observations		2,280		1,080		1,200	

This table presents the determinants of LBO Loan Pricing. The dependent variable is the drawn AIS. IMR is the inverse Mills ratio and controls for the propensity of a sponsor in the sample. Fixed effects for each year and industry were included in the regression but are not reported to save space. See Table 1 for a full description of each variable.
Note: *indicates significance at 5% or better.

rich array of informational variables. More importantly, we find that the role of the sponsor is still a critical factor even after controlling for contract terms, informational variables, market, industry and year effects.

Panel A of Table 5A reports second-stage OLS estimation results for full sample of LBO loan pricing using AIS as the dependent variable. Panel B reports the results of loan pricing model using the one arranger sample only, while Panel C reports the results of the loan pricing model for the multiple arranger sample only. All estimation results for LBO loan pricing appear well-specified and the overall model is all significant at $p < 0.0001$. The adjusted R-square for the full sample is robust being 0.43 for the full sample.

The variable of interest to us is DSPONSOR. The coefficient of this variable is positive and significant at $p < 0.05$ for the full sample. These results indicate that borrowers pay significantly higher borrowing costs, approximately 29 more basis points, for LBO-syndicated loans by using the services of a sponsor. In theory, borrowers of syndicated loans should benefit by using the services of a sponsor. Sponsors provide both monitoring and information asymmetry reduction services and should be able to lower the borrowing costs of the borrower. They also assist not only in the selection of arranger, but also represent the interests of the borrower in negotiations with the arranger once the arranger has been selected. They have a significant role during the negotiation process in making certain that information asymmetries that exist between the arranger and borrower are reduced as far as possible such that the borrowers' interests are protected.

As such, sponsors can significantly influence the availability and cost of borrowing. Hence, the significant and positive coefficient on the sponsor dummy variable (DSPONSOR) reflects the ability of sponsors to facilitate the availability of capital to riskier borrowers albeit with a significantly higher rate. The risk associated with the complex deals they bring to the market after controlling several factors (including leverage, ratings and contract characteristics) is ironic, but it conveys that sponsorship is a significant market factor. This result confirms the inference of H2.

The results also show that the coefficients of most of our contract characteristics such as DSEC, LOGAMT and DTL are of the predicted sign and significant at $p < 0.01$ (two-tailed test) in models estimated using the full sample. In addition, most of our informational variables such as RATING, DPRIV, DCLUB, ONEPROV, ONEARR and SAME-NATP are of the predicted sign and significant at the $p < 0.01$ (two-tailed test) in models estimated using the full sample. Most importantly, we find support for *H3*. As expected, DCLUB and ONEARR have negative and significant coefficients reflecting the information-intensive relationship between borrower and lender. DPRIV exhibits the positive relationship with the AIS documenting the informational problematic nature a smaller private firms. ONEPROV is also positive with AIS reflecting that larger syndicates are able to offer lower AIS due to the sharing of risk and additional monitoring.

We use the RATING to proxy the borrower's firm and credit characteristic because the financial data are not publicly available for many of our samples and it has the expected sign for our analysis. Assuming, the credit rating is a good proxy for the firm's financial condition any additional cost incurred due to locational or lender characteristics has an impact on the firm's cost of capital. For example, the coefficient of SAMENATP is positive and significant indicating that borrowing costs are more for borrower and providers that come from the same region. *H4* supports the "home bias" problem as borrowers and providers from the same region should be more transparent deals that command lower AIS. The coefficient of the IMR variable is negative, and significant at $p < 0.01$ for the full sample estimation.

The significance of the coefficient of the IMR variable confirms the importance of controlling for selectivity bias. In addition, it also underscores the relevance of considering the role of the sponsor in examining the cost of the borrower in syndicated LBO loan transactions and shows the possibility of a significant unexpected component derived from sponsorship. Finally, the INDEX which controls for the overall market condition is positive and significant as expected. As market conditions worsen or improve, the AIS is adjusted accordingly. Industry and year effects are significant justifying the use of the dummy variable approach.

Panels B and C provide additional indirect support for *H1* and *H2*. The primary source of unfavorable loan pricing comes from the single arranger deals as the coefficient on DSPONSOR is positive and significant at the 5% level. On the other hand, sponsorship has no impact on pricing for the multiple arranger deals.

5.2.1. *U.S. vs. European LBOs*

We then divided our sample into U.S. and European LBOs (Table 5B, Panels D and E) to determine if there were significant differences in behavior due to region and find that the presence of a buyout sponsor

Table 5B. OLS regression of LBO loan pricing.

		Panel D: U.S. LBOs		Panel E: European LBOs	
Variables		Coefficient	*t*-value	Coefficient	*t*-value
Constant contract characteristics		320.40	12.03*	299.12	9.45*
Log of maturity	LOGMAT	0.50	0.28	3.07	1.20
Fraction secured	DSEC	13.36	3.04*	14.98	2.76*
Log of amount	LOGAMT	4.13	1.58	0.59	0.29
Term loans	DTL	28.19	8.11*	25.70	7.29*
Information variables					
Ordinal credit rating	Rating	0.44	0.90	−2.47	−2.80*
Private	DPRIV	2.51	0.29	29.96	2.23*
Club loan	DCLUB	31.34	−1.00	−1.31	−0.21
One provider	ONEPROV	5.29	1.04	8.61	1.70
One arranger	ONEARR	4.62	0.97	−12.95	−3.16*
Provider and borrower from same region	SAMENATP	2.30	0.56	−1.20	−0.30
Arranger and borrower from same region	SAMENATA	4.21	0.84	−9.83	−2.55*
Sponsorship	DSPONSOR	18.22	3.83*	−10.70	−1.55
Inverse Mills ratio	IMR	8.10	0.95	4.99	1.60
Control variables					
Loan index	Index	−0.49	−0.15	−7.91	−3.24*
Year dummies		Yes		Yes	
Industry dummies		Yes		Yes	
Adjusted R^2		0.35		0.31	
Observations		1,269		1,011	

This table presents the determinants of LBO Loan Pricing. The dependent variable is the drawn AIS. IMR is the inverse Mills ratio and controls for the propensity of a sponsor in the sample. Fixed effects for each year and industry were included in the regression but are not reported to save space. See Table 1 for a full description of each variable.

in U.S. deals raised the AISD spread by 18 bps (t-stat 3.83) and was very significant, while the presence of buyout sponsors in European LBOs did not significantly affect pricing. This latter finding could be a function of the overwhelmingly private transactions for the European subsample. DPRIV for European LBOs was economically (30 bps) and statistically significant ($t = 2.23$). 95% of the sponsored deals in Europe involved private firms. For European deals one arranger transaction reduced the AISD pricing by −13 bps ($t = -3.16$), whereas an additional reduction of −10 bps ($t = -2.55$) was incurred for those borrowers from the same nation as the arranger. These support a monitoring hypothesis. Term loans incurred higher AISD pricing for both U.S. (28 bps; $t = 8.11$) and European (26 bps, $t = 7.29$) LBO deals. Secured loans incurred similar premia for U.S. (13 bps, $t = 3.04$) and Europeans (15 bps, $t = 2.76$) LBO loans, which reflect the additional risk associated with secured loans.

5.2.2. *Number of Arrangers*

Following Lee and Mullineaux (2004), we estimate the number of arrangers using a Poisson distribution because the distribution is left censored count variables and skewed. As shown in Table 3A, the average number of arrangers for all loans is 1.86, which is consistent with earlier studies. Independent variables that increased the number of arrangers and are significant at the 0.05 level are loan size, secured, club deals and highly leveraged. If the loan was a special purpose one, had a sponsor or was financed by a European lender reduced the number of arrangers and were significant at the 0.05 level.

Only the size of the loan was significant for rated loans, while secured, club special purpose, highly leveraged, sponsor and European lenders maintained their sign and significance for unrated loans. Our sample has 1,844 unrated and 436 rated loans. These coefficients indicate support for the risk diversification hypothesis, where larger and riskier loans use more arrangers. Significant and positive at the 0.05 level for unrated and all loans is the club dummy variable. Syndication for club deals is primarily used to improve

Table 6. Estimated number of loan arrangers.

	All loans			Rated loans			Unrated loans		
	Coefficient	*Z*-stat.	Sig.	Coefficient	*Z*-stat.	Sig.	Coefficient	*Z*-stat.	Sig.
spvdum	−0.42	−2.82	*	−0.61	−0.81		−0.42	−2.71	*
clubdum	0.21	2.63	*	−0.30	−0.57		0.24	2.82	*
secdum	0.13	3.18	*	0.11	1.13		0.16	3.27	*
rating_num	0.00	0.36		−0.04	−2.51	*	Dropped		
lmat	0.02	0.96		−0.03	−0.54		0.03	1.32	
aisd	0.00	1.26		0.00	−0.63		0.00	1.73	
lamt	0.27	15.41	*	0.20	3.40	*	0.28	13.62	*
dspons	−0.18	−3.77	*	−0.19	−1.50		−0.17	−3.15	*
samenata	−0.07	−1.84		−0.10	−0.87		−0.07	−1.64	
samenatp	−0.06	−1.52		−0.09	−0.85		−0.06	−1.40	
eurolender	−0.09	−2.22	*	−0.03	−0.25		−0.12	−2.67	*
dtl	0.01	0.18		−0.01	−0.17		0.02	0.42	
dHTL	0.15	3.43	*	0.06	0.57		0.19	3.64	*
dpriv	0.00	−0.01		Dropped			−0.08	−0.75	
constant	−1.23	−4.58	*	0.01	0.02		−1.18	−3.34	*
Control variables									
Year dummies	Yes			Yes			Yes		
Industry dummies	Yes			Yes			Yes		
NOB	2,280			436			1,844		
Pseudo R^2	0.09			0.2			0.10		
Log likelihood	3,229.19			−592.81			−2,598.5		
LR chi^2 (71, 62, 69)	649.98			161.18			556.73		
Prob > chi^2	0.000			0.000			0.000		

This table estimates the number of arrangers assuming a Poisson distribution comparing the impact. Independent variables are spvdum 1/0 for ****; clubdum (1/0) for deals that are club deals; secdum (1/0) if the loan is secured; rating_num ranges from 1 to 28; AAA = 1; 30 and 31 = no rating; lmat is the natural log of maturity measured in months; spread = ***; lamt is the natural log of the facility size in millions of dollars; dspons (1/0) if a sponsor is present in the deal; samenata (1/0) if the borrower and arranger are same nationality; samenatp (1/0) if the borrower and a provider have the same nationality; eurolender (1/0) if the lender is headquartered in Europe; d80–d02 are year dummies. The dependent variable is numarr which are the number of arrangers for each facility. *indicates 0.05 significance or better.

distribution for riskier unrated loans. Using the club deal avenue does not supplant, but complements the arranger network.

There were three exogenous variables that reduced the number of arrangers in the syndication and were significant at the 0.05 level: spvdum and dspons. The strongest influence in reducing the number of arrangers is the presence of buyout sponsors, with −0.18, −0.19, and −0.17 for all loans, rated loans and unrated loans, respectively.

These results support a monitoring hypothesis. The special purpose vehicle dummy is negative and significant at 0.05 for unrated, −0.42, and all loans, but is not significant in rated loans. For unrated loans, Eurolender was negative (−0.12) and significant at the 0.05 level.

Finally, we included year dummies (not reported) to detect time trends for syndication in general and found that unrated loans used increasingly more arrangers from 1990 to 2002. Coefficients for every year except 1991 and 1992 (0.10 level) are positive and significant at the 0.05 or 0.01 level. The year dummies get increasingly stronger and more significant. This effect is incremental to the positive effect that loan size has on number of arrangers and reflects increasing active participation in loan syndication by lenders. This confirms other research findings of increased syndication activity at the arranger level. Rated loans show similar positive and significant activity from 1997 to 2002. Our Poisson results support our notion that sponsorship is heavily engaged with single arrangers as a complement.

6. Conclusion

The LBO lending market provides us with an excellent opportunity to study the determinants of lending practices and loan pricing in corporate debt markets. We find significant borrower and lender effects wherein single arrangers lend to smaller firms while multiple arrangers lend to larger firms. This may be the result of lender specialization based on information technologies. Smaller firms are more informational opaque and costlier to monitor.

Sponsors also tend to be associated with larger deal sizes that are highly leveraged. We use an arranger classification along with a sponsor type to evaluate how differential information among intermediaries affects pricing and competition in credit markets. Our results show that sponsors provide their services at a significant cost and tend to be associated with LBOs, where the pricing on AIS is significantly higher even after controlling for contract terms, default risk and the structure of arranger services. Buyout sponsors tend to complement the single arranger and bring more LBO deals to market while some borrowers shun the buyout structure and use the club loan deal to protect their ownership structure while seeking more favorable loan terms. Our analysis also confirms a "home bias" from providers, but also shows that sponsorship still matters even after controlling for this effect.

Several public policy issues arise from our analysis. One is that lender regulation should consider the role of the buyout sponsors in syndicated lending markets and not narrowly focus on traditional lenders. We provide evidence that suggests the information and monitoring abilities of lenders and buyout sponsors play an important role in determining the lending specialization, structure and pricing of corporate loans. Second, regulators need to evaluate the syndicate structure and impact on the availability and pricing of corporate debt. As the market structure for the corporate debt evolves, so will the availability of corporate debt. Finally, the syndicated lending market and the impact on LBO transaction has a significant macroeconomic impact on the restructuring of the economy and the overall growth aspects of the nation and deserves further attention and research from policy makers. An interesting future research question is whether the additional (AIS) incurred by borrowers when sponsors are present in LBOs results in early dividend distribution to the limited partnerships of the buyout sponsor funds.

Endnotes

1. Syndicate lenders are called "participants" that fund a tranche of the loan contract which the arranger allocates based on a best effort or firm commitment of underwriting.
2. HLTs are defined as leverage rates greater than 50% or post-transaction doubling of the borrower's liabilities and where the leverage ratio is increased by more than 75%.
3. Jensen (1989) defined the term "active investor" in a statement before the House Ways and Means Committee (1 February 1989) as an investor who actually monitors management, sits on boards, is sometimes involved in dismissing management, is often intimately involved in the strategic direction of the company, and on occasion even managers.
4. The approach described herein is being increasingly used to examine a variety of problems, where selection bias is an issue. For specific applications, see Leuz and Verrecchia (2000) and Covitz *et al.* (2004).

5. In a previous version of the paper, we included the club deal dummy variable and found it inversely related to sponsorship. We present the simpler model for ease of exposition.
6. Index is the average yield spread above the federal funds rate on the total commercial and industrial loans as reported by the Federal Reserve Board Index and is used to control for market-wide interest rate effects.

References

Angbazo, LA, J Mei and A Saunders (1998). Credit spreads in the market for highly leveraged transaction loans. *Journal of Banking and Finance*, 22, 1249–1282.

Armstrong, J (2003). The syndicated loan market: Developments in the North American context, Bank of Canada Working Paper 2003–15, June 2003.

Berger, AN and GF Udell (1995). Relationship lending and lines of credit in small firm finance. *Journal of Business*, 68, 351–381.

Bolton, P and D Scharfstein (1996). Optimal debt structure and the number of creditors. *Journal of Political Economy*, 104, 1–25.

Carey, M and G Nini (2007). Is the corporate loan market globally integrated? A pricing puzzle. *Journal of Finance*, 62(6), 2969–3007.

Carey, M, M Post and SA Sharpe (1998). Does corporate lending by banks and finance companies differ? Evidence on specialization in private debt contracting. *Journal of Finance*, 53, 845–878.

Casolaro, L, D Focarelli and AF Pozzolo (2003). The pricing effect of certification on bank loans: Evidence from the syndicated credit market. Economics & Statistics Discussion Paper No. 10–03, University of Molise, Italy.

Cebenoyan, AS and PE Strahan (2004). Risk management, capital structure and lending at banks. *Journal of Banking and Finance*, 28(1), 19–43.

Cotter, JF and SW Peck (2001). The structure of debt and active equity investors: The case of the buyout specialist. *Journal of Financial Economics*, 59, 101–147.

Covitz, DM, D Hancock and ML Kwast (2004). A reconsideration of the risk sensitivity of U.S. banking organization subordinated debt spreads: A sample selection approach. *Economic Policy Review*, 10(2), 73–92.

Cumming, D, DS Siegel and M Wright (2007). Private equity, leveraged buyouts and governance. *Journal of Corporate Finance*, 13(7), 439–460.

Dell' Ariccia, G and R Marquez (2005). Lending booms and lending standards, CEPR Discussion Papers 5095, C.E.P.R., London.

Dennis, S, D Nandy and IG Sharpe (2001). The determinants of contract terms in bank revolving credit agreements. *Journal of Financial and Quantitative Analysis*, 35(1), 87–110.

Dennis, S and D Mullineaux (2000). Syndicated loans. *Journal of Financial Intermediation*, 9, 404–426.

Detragiache, E, P Garella and L Guiso (2000). Multiple versus single banking relationships: Theory and evidence. *Journal of Finance*, 55(3), 1133–1161.

Diamond, D (1993). Seniority and the maturity of debt contracts. *Journal of Financial Economics*, 53, 341–368.

Elsas, R and JP Krahnen (1998). Is relationship lending special? Evidence from credit-file data in Germany. *Journal of Banking and Finance*, 22, 1283–1316.

Fridson, M (2005). It's good to be the issuer. *Leverage World*, 18 February, 1–3.

Gadanecz, B (2004). The syndicated loan market: Structure, development and implications. *The BIS Quarterly Review*, December, 75–89.

Hallak, I (2003). Why borrowers pay premiums to larger lenders: Empirical evidence from sovereign syndicated loans. European University Institute and Center for Financial Studies, Goethe University, Working Paper, June 2003.

Hughes, JP, WW Lang, LJ Mester, CG Moon and MS Pagano (2003). Do bankers sacrifice value to build empires? Managerial incentives, industry consolidation, and financial performance. *Journal of Banking & Finance*, 27(3), 417–435.

Jensen, MC (1989). Active investors, LBOs, and the privatization of bankruptcy. Statement before the House Ways and Means Committee (1 February 1989). Reprinted in *Journal of Applied Corporate Finance*, 2(1), 35–44.

Kaplan, SN and JC Stein (1993). The evolution of buyout pricing and financial structure in the 1980s. *The Quarterly Journal of Economics*, 108(2), 313–357.

Kiff, J and R Morrow (2000). Credit derivatives. *Bank of Canada Review*, Autumn, 3–11.

Lee, SW and D Mullineaux (2004). Monitoring, financial distress, and the structure of commercial lending syndicates. *Financial Management*, 33(3), 107–130.

Leuz, C and RE Verrecchia (2000). The economic consequences of increased disclosure. *Journal of Accounting Research*, 38 (Supplement), 91–124.

Mullineaux, D (2004). Tying and subsidized loans: Is there a problem? *Commercial Lending Review*, 19(1), 16–25.

Nini, G (2004). The value of financial intermediaries: Empirical evidence from syndicated loans to emerging market borrowers. Federal Reserve Board, Working Paper.

Rajan, R (1992). Insiders and outsiders: The choice between informed and Arm's length debt. *Journal of Finance*, 47, 1367–1406.

Roche, J and R Szuch (1997). Sponsors role in leveraged debt financings. *Fitch Research — Structured Finance*, 16 October, 1–5.

Sufi, A (2005). Agency and renegotiation in corporate finance: Evidence from syndication loans, MIT Working Paper.

Sufi, A (2007). Information asymmetry and financing arrangements: Evidence from syndicated loans. *Journal of Finance*, 62(2), 629–668.

Strahan, PE (1999). Borrower risk and the price and nonprice terms of bank loans. Working Paper, Federal Reserve Bank of New York.

Thomas, H and Z Wang (2004). The integration of bank syndicated loan and junk bond markets. *Journal of Banking and Finance*, 28, 299–329.

Trost, PR and LF Lee (1984). Technical training and earnings: A polychotomous choice model with selectivity. *Review of Economics and Statistics*, 66(1), 151–156.

11

Ownership Control and Valuation Changes for Earning Announcements around U.S. Cross-Listings by Canadian Firms

Lawrence Kryzanowski and Arturo Rubalcava

1. Introduction

The increasing volume of literature on the advantages of firms cross-listing on international stock markets has occurred primarily during the last ten years. Cross-listing on a major U.S. trade venue (such as NYSE or NASDAQ) is usually perceived as being more advantageous than cross-listing in non-U.S. markets. Significant positive market price and liquidity reactions are associated with firms that announce their intentions to cross-list in the U.S. (Miller, 1999; Errunza and Miller, 2000; Foerster and Karolyi, 1999; King and Segal, 2003; Hail and Leuz, 2008). This is mainly reflected in increased firm value, either by decreasing the cost of the announcing firm's capital or by increasing the firm's expected future cash flows (e.g., Lins *et al.*, 2005; Lee, 2005).

Various theoretical and empirical studies address the identification of the determinants of increases in firm values when firms cross-list in the U.S. These determinants, which include ownership structure, are summarized in the Appendix A to this chapter. Thus, studies on whether ownership structure plays an important role as a determinant of changes in firm values are an important research venue for determining the benefits of cross-listing in the U.S. The purpose of this chapter is to determine the extent to which changes in ownership diffuseness (or shares held by noncorporate insiders) influence the valuations of Canadian firms after cross-listing in the U.S. relative to their valuations prior to cross-listing.

Additionally, we examine whether share float (i.e., shares that are not held by insiders and that are available for trade), when used as a proxy for ownership control and liquidity, is an important determinant of the changes in firm values as measured by the abnormal returns around the announcement dates of earnings after controlling for other relevant variables. Our study is the first to address whether significant changes in firm values occur from the pre- to the post-cross-listing period, and on whether the changes are influenced by share float conditioned on the sign of surprises in earnings (SUEs). The surprises are positive (negative) when actual earnings are above (below) analysts' expectations.

This chapter has three main findings. First, share float is not a significant determinant of the changes in firm values either for the pre- or the post-cross-listing periods when share float is not conditioned on the sign of SUEs. This finding is similar to those of Himmelberg *et al.* (1999) and Demsetz and Villalonga (2001), who find that ownership structure does not have an effect on firm value as measured by Tobin's Q. SUEs are positively associated with market price reactions during the post-cross-listing period only.

Second, when share float and other control variables are conditioned on the sign of SUEs, share float is significant for negative SUEs only for the overall period. This implies that share float has an asymmetric effect on the market reaction. Specifically, CAR is decreasing for increasing changes in float only when conditioned on negative earnings surprises for the overall period. On the other hand, SUEs are significantly and positively associated with changes in firm values, during the same overall period.

Third, the cumulative abnormal return (CAR) around the earnings announcement is associated with share float conditioned on the sign of SUEs for the post-cross-listing period only. This result is consistent with DeFond *et al.* (2007) who find that the quality of the information content of earnings announcements is higher in countries with strong enforcement of insider trading laws. In turn, this results in a stronger market reaction. A similar result is found by Leuz *et al.* (2003) in the sense that higher quality of reported firms' earnings (less earnings management) is increasing in investor protection.

The remainder of the chapter is organized as follows. Section 2 examines the sample and data. The model for the abnormal returns of earnings announcements and the empirical results are presented in Sec. 3. The hypothesis, the model for the determinants of abnormal returns, descriptive statistics, and the empirical results are presented in Sec. 4. Finally, Sec. 5 concludes the chapter.

2. Sample and Data

The initial sample consists of 87 firms in the S&P/TSX (Standard & Poor's/Toronto Stock Exchange) composite index that cross-listed on the NYSE or NASDAQ during the period 1990–1999, since data on share float are available for these firms from the Toronto Stock Exchange (TSE). After removing primarily announcements for firms that did not have data on I/B/E/S, or for which share float data or trade data were not available during the pre-cross-listing period, the sample is reduced to 835 quarterly earnings announcements (325 for the pre- and 510 for the post-cross-listing period) for 55 TSX-listed firms that cross-listed on the NYSE or NASDAQ. The earnings announcement dates are originally obtained from Bloomberg, and are modified if an earlier date is found in Lexis-Nexis. The cross-listing dates are obtained from Lexis-Nexis. Quarterly earnings per share and latest consensus earnings forecasts (including those revised by earnings warnings) are obtained from the I/B/E/S detail tape for all earnings announcements.

Daily stocks returns, closing prices, trading volumes, closing bid and ask quotes, number of trades, the S&P/TSX composite index and the monthly number of shares outstanding for the firm shares executed on the TSX are obtained from the Canadian Financial

Markets Research Centre (CFMRC) database. Data are adjusted for stock splits. The monthly Canadian T-bill rate (risk-free proxy) and the share float data are obtained from CANSIM and a TSX database, respectively.

3. Abnormal Returns around the Announcements of Quarterly Earnings

The abnormal returns for each earnings announcement date during the pre- and post-cross-listing periods are computed using the following regression:

$$R_{it} = a_i + b_i R_{mt}^{\mathrm{TSX}} + c_i R_{mt}^{\mathrm{TSX}} * Dum1 + \gamma_{1i} DumCARPreAD_t + \gamma_{2i} DumAD_t + \gamma_{3i} DumCARPostAD_t + \varepsilon_{it} \quad (1)$$

In Eq. (1), R_{it} is the continuously compounded daily excess return for the closing trade executed on the TSX for firm i on trading day t and is equal to the stock return for firm i minus the Canadian risk-free rate. a_i is the intercept for firm i, and b_i is the coefficient that measures the TSX market risk or beta. R_{mt}^{TSX} is the continuously compounded daily excess return for the S&P/TSX composite index, which is used as a proxy for the market portfolio. The dummy *Dum*1 is included to account for the possibility that the market beta is changed by the earnings announcement, and it takes the value of one for each day in the period from 1 to 44 days after the announcement day (AD). The dummy variable $DumCARPreAD_t$, controls for abnormal performance (price run-up) prior to the announcement date, and takes on values of one for days −15 through −2 relative to the earnings announcement day, i.e., [AD − 15, AD − 2], and is zero otherwise. $DumAD_t$ is a dummy variable that is used to fully capture the market's response to the quarterly earnings announcement, and equals one for each day in the three-day announcement window [AD − 1, AD + 1], and is zero otherwise. The dummy variable $DumCARPostAD_t$ controls for abnormal performance after the announcement date due to slowness in the price discovery process, and takes the value of one for the period from 2 through 15 days after the announcement day, i.e., [AD + 2, AD + 15], and is zero otherwise.

The parameters γ_{1i}, γ_{2i}, and γ_{3i} are the daily average abnormal returns or AAR generated for the trading days in each of the three event windows for firm i. Therefore, $3\hat{\gamma}_{2i}$ is the three-day CAR for firm i for the earnings announcement window [AD − 1, AD + 1], and $14\hat{\gamma}_{1i}$ and $14\hat{\gamma}_{3i}$ are the *CARs* for firm i for the pre-AD window [AD − 15, AD + 2] and post-AD window [AD + 2, AD + 15], respectively.

The abnormal returns for the announcement and other windows are estimated simultaneously using the 45 trading days prior to the announcement day and ending 45 trading days after the announcement day. This period ensures that prior and subsequent announcement dates are not included in any estimation to obtain the *CAR*. The *CAR* for each event window are averaged across all of the earnings announcements, and the resulting average cumulative abnormal returns (ACAR) are tested for significance using Z-statistics. ACAR or parameter estimates that are significant at the 0.01, 0.05 or 0.10 levels are referred to hereafter as being highly significant, significant or marginally significant, respectively. The rationale for the aggregation of the event windows across time is examined in the next section.

3.1. *Empirical Results*

Table 1 tests the net effect of earnings announcements regardless of whether the announcements convey positive or negative information across firms and across time for the overall, pre- and post-cross-listing period, respectively. This allows for an examination of whether positive or negative earnings announcements, on average, dominate in terms of their influence across securities and across different time periods. Preliminary implications of these results are examined at the end of this section.

Table 1 reports the ACAR for the three event windows based on 835 quarterly earnings announcements for 55 Canadian firms during the period, 1990–1999. Panel A of Table 1 reports the ACAR for the overall period (pre- and post-cross-listing). The mean coefficient ACAR estimate for the pre-announcement window ($DumCARPreAD_t$) of 0.05% is not significant (Z-value of 0.44), and suggests that the content of the announcement is not anticipated or leaked to the market. The mean coefficient ACAR estimate for the announcement

Table 1. ACAR for quarterly earnings announcements by U.S. cross-listed Canadian firms.

Variable	Coefficient	Event window	Coefficient (Z-values)
Panel A: Overall period			
Constant	a		−0.0002 (0.60)
R_{mt}^{TSX}	b		0.7774 (65.83)***
$R_{mt}^{TSX} * Dum1$	d		−0.0036 (5.78)***
$DumCARPreAD_t$	$14\gamma_1$	[AD − 15, AD − 2]	0.0005 (0.44)
$DumAD_t$	$3\gamma_2$	[AD − 1, AD + 1]	0.0002 (1.88)*
$DumCARPostAD_t$	$14\gamma_5$	[AD + 2, AD + 15]	−0.009 (−0.65)
Panel B: Pre-cross-listing period (325 quarterly earnings announcements)			
Constant	a		−0.0001 (1.41)
R_{mt}^{TSX}	b		0.8211 (37.58)***
$R_{mt}^{TSX} * Dum1$	d		0.0178 (0.1019)
$DumCARPreAD_t$	$14\gamma_1$	[AD − 15, AD − 2]	−0.0011 (−0.9219)
$DumAD_t$	$3\gamma_2$	[AD − 1, AD + 1]	−0.0002 (−0.0403)
$DumCARPostAD_t$	$14\gamma_5$	[AD + 2, AD + 15]	−0.0185 (−2.94)***
Panel C: Post-cross-listing period (510 quarterly earnings announcements)			
Constant	a		−0.0003 (−0.3381)
R_{mt}^{TSX}	b		0.7513 (54.15)***
$R_{mt}^{TSX} * Dum1$	d		−0.0301 (0.0864)
$DumCARPreAD_t$	$14\gamma_1$	[AD − 15, AD − 2]	0.0015 (0.4799)
$DumAD_t$	$3\gamma_2$	[AD − 1, AD + 1]	0.0037 (2.40)**
$DumCARPostAD_t$	$14\gamma_5$	[AD + 2, AD + 15]	−0.0078 (−0.5678)

Note: This table reports the ACAR for different event windows around the announcement dates of quarterly earnings of Canadian firms listed on the TSX and are cross-listed on the NYSE and NASDAQ during the period from 1990 to 1999. The statistical significances of the coefficients are given in the parentheses by their Z-values. ***, ** and * denote significance at the 0.01, 0.05, and 0.10 levels, respectively.

window ($DumAD_t$) of 0.02% is significant at the 10% level (Z-value of 1.88), which suggests that the earnings announcements contain positive news. The mean estimated beta coefficient for the sample of 0.7774 is highly significant, and indicates lower average risk than for the market. The mean beta shift coefficient estimate of –0.0036 is not significant, and indicates that the betas of firms announcing quarterly earnings remain unchanged post-announcement.

Panel B of Table 1 reports the ACAR for the three event windows for the pre-cross-listing period (325 quarterly earnings announcements). The mean coefficient ACAR estimate for the announcement window ($DumAD_t$) of −0.02% is not significant (Z-value of −0.0403), which suggests that the earnings announcements do not contain new information. The mean ACAR for the post-announcement window ($DumCARPostAD_t$) is a significant −1.85%, which suggests some slowness in the price discovery process. The mean estimated beta coefficient for the sample of 0.8211 is also highly significant and slightly higher than the estimated beta coefficient for the overall period.

Finally, Panel C of Table 1 displays the ACAR for the post-cross-listing period (510 announcements). The mean ACAR for the pre- and post-announcement window periods are not significant. On the other hand, the mean coefficient ACAR estimate for $DumAD_t$ of 0.0037% is significant (Z-value of 2.40), which indicates that the positive new information is fully reflected around the time of the announcement only. The mean estimated beta coefficient for the sample of 0.7513 is highly significant and not significantly smaller than the estimated beta coefficient for the pre-cross-listing period. For the three sample periods, the mean estimated constant coefficient is not significant indicating that the model is well specified.

The results reported in Panels A, B and C of Table 1 suggest that the ACAR are positive and marginally significant for the overall period, and that they are mostly due to the positive and significant ACAR for the post-cross-listing period. This is a preliminary indication that the information content of the earnings announcements by Canadian cross-listed firms may be enhanced after cross-listing on the NYSE and NASDAQ. These results appear to be consistent with Leuz *et al.* (2003) and DeFond *et al.* (2007), for example, who find that the information content of earnings announcements is superior on major U.S. stock markets due to better investor protection. The examination of the empirical results reported in Sec. 4 provides important and significant evidence that corroborates these preliminary findings.

4. Determinants of Firm Value Changes around Earnings Announcements

4.1. *Hypotheses*

Since earnings announcements are highly relevant information events in the stock price formation process (Ball and Brown, 1968; Beaver, 1968; Landsman and Maydew, 2002; DeFond *et al.*, 2007), they provide a good information event for examining the impact of stock ownership. Thus, the following two null hypotheses are tested in this section:

> H_0^1: *The market reaction to earnings announcements of Canadian firms cross-listing on U.S. major exchanges as captured by their ARs is significantly different from the pre- to post-cross-listing periods.*
>
> H_0^2: *Ownership structure, as proxied by shares float, is a significant determinant of any market price reaction to earnings announcements after controlling for other variables. Share float and the other variables are conditioned on the sign of SUEs on the announcement dates. This also allows for a test of any asymmetric effects on abnormal returns of signed ownership.*

4.2. *Methodology*

The pooled least squares regression approach on cross-sectional and time-series data is used to examine the relationship between cumulative abnormal returns (*CAR*) for the announcement window and share float (*FLOAT*) after controlling for other potential determinants. The specific model used is

$$
\begin{aligned}
CAR_i = {} & a_0 + (a_1 + \delta_{1\Delta FLOAT} DumPRE)\Delta FLOAT_i \\
& + (a_2 + \delta_{2\Delta FLOAT} DumPRE) DumSUE^{(+)} * \Delta FLOAT_i \\
& + (a_3 + \delta_{3SUE} DumPRE) SUE_i + (a_4 + \delta_{4\Delta SIZE} DumPRE)\Delta SIZE_i \\
& + (a_5 + \delta_{5\Delta SIZE} DumPRE) DumSUE^{(+)} * \Delta SIZE_i \\
& + \cdots + (a_{14} + \delta_{14\Delta TRADES} DumPRE)\Delta TRADES_i \\
& + (a_{15} + \delta_{15\Delta TRADES} DumPRE) DumSUE^{(+)} * \Delta TRADES_i \\
& + a_{16} DumYEAR_{\tau=1990} + \cdots + a_{25} DumYEAR_{\tau=1999} + \xi_i. \qquad (2)
\end{aligned}
$$

The independent variables in regression model (2) are based on previous empirical studies and economic intuition. The expected signs of the independent variables when they take on positive values and are conditioned on positive SUEs or $DumSUE^{(+)}$ are provided in the brackets preceding the names of the independent variables. Although not shown, the expected sign is reversed when each independent variable takes on a negative value and is signed on negative SUEs or $DumSUE^{(-)}$.

The dependent and each independent variable are now described.

CAR_i is equal to the abnormal returns for the earnings announcement window [AD − 1, AD + 1] and is equal to $3\hat{\gamma}_{2i}$ from model (1).

[+] $FLOAT_i$ proxies for ownership control or stock diffuseness, and is measured by the ratio of the number of shares available for trade divided by the number of shares outstanding pre-announcement.

Δ as a prefix is the change in the mean value of each of the independent variables (except SUE) between the period $[(AD_{Q-2}+3)-(AD_{Q-1}-3), (AD_{Q-1}+3)-(AD_Q-3)]$. The period $[(AD_{Q-1}+3)-(AD_Q-3)]$ corresponds to the mean value that begins three days after the prior quarter's announcement day $[AD_{Q-1}+3]$ through the three days before the current quarter's announcement day $[AD_Q-3]$, where the subscript Q refers to the current quarter's announcement day. For example, *ΔFLOAT* is the change in the mean value of *FLOAT* between the period $[(AD_{Q-2}+3)-(AD_{Q-1}-3), (AD_{Q-1}+3)-(AD_Q-3)]$. Specifically, it is equal to the difference between its mean value during the period $[(AD_{Q-1}+3)-(AD_Q-3)]$ and its corresponding mean value for the period $[(AD_{Q-2}+3)-(AD_{Q-1}-3)]$.[2]

DumPER is a dummy variable that equals one during the period before the cross-listing date (*DumPRE*) and is equal to zero otherwise. Alternatively, *DumPER* is equal to one during the post-cross-listing date (*DumPOST*) and is equal to zero otherwise. This dummy variable is used to test our hypotheses by assessing whether the relationship between *CAR* and changes in *FLOAT* and the other control variables are significantly different from the pre- to post-cross-listing periods.

DumSUE$^{(+)}$ is a dummy variable that is equal to 1 if the surprise in earnings (*SUE*) is zero or positive, and is zero otherwise. The rationale for using this signing variable is as follows. Since a surprise in earnings (i.e., the difference between actual earnings and the consensus estimates of analysts) can be positive, zero, or negative, *FLOAT* and the other variables need to be conditioned on the direction of *SUE* to determine if there is an asymmetric impact of *FLOAT* on *CAR*. Thus, [+] indicates that *CAR* is expected to be increasing for positively signed *FLOAT* or $FLOAT|SUE^{(+)}$. Similarly, [−] indicates that *CAR* is expected to be decreasing for negatively signed *FLOAT* or $FLOAT|SUE^{(-)}$.[3]

[+] SUE_i is equal to the deviation of actual quarterly earnings from expectations, and is adjusted by the stock price three days before the announcement date.

[+] $SIZE_i$ proxies for firm size and is measured by market capitalization (i.e., the number of shares outstanding multiplied by the share price pre-announcement). Firm size may also proxy for other variables not included, such as the number of investment analysts, number of institutional investors, and number of firm news.

[+] STD_i is a proxy for equity risk and is equal to the standard deviation of daily stock excess returns (i.e., daily stock return minus the daily 30-day Canadian T-bill rate) during the period $[AD_{Q-1} + 3, AD_Q - 3]$. The standard deviation of excess returns reflects a better estimate of risk for the stock than the standard deviation of daily stock returns alone. This variable also may proxy for leverage (Ogden *et al.*, 2003) or cash flow instability (Fields and Mais, 1994).

[+] *PreCAR* represents the cumulative *CAR*, and is less likely to be contaminated by post-firm, information-related effects from a firm's previous quarterly earnings announcement. $PreCAR_i$ is the cumulative daily differences in the returns for firm i and the S&P/TSX composite index, in the spirit of Korajczyk *et al.* (1990). This variable measures the market's anticipation of the firm's earnings announcement.

[−] $SPREAD_i$ is the quoted bid–ask spread as a proportion of the quote mid-point. It is a proxy for the partial anticipation of the spread by the market maker. It is equal to the difference between ask and bid quotes divided by the average of the ask and bid quotes.

[−] *TRADES* is a proxy for firm-information-related volatility, and is given by the average of the daily number of transactions (Jiang and Kryzanowski, 1998). *TRADES* and *PreCAR* are variables that proxy for pre-disclosure firm information.

[−] $PRICE_i$ is used to control for share price, and is the price of the firm's stock three days prior to the earnings announcement date [AD−3].

$DumYEAR_\tau$ are dummy variables that are included to control for yearly economic conditions during the period from 1990 to 1999, inclusive.

Regression model (2) has three important advantages. First, it avoids the problem of identification of causality between changes in firm values and ownership structure (*FLOAT*) (Brous and Kini, 1994). The change in price is a reaction (effect) of the firm's earnings announcement relative to the analysts' forecast. Second, this model deals with the problem of endogeneity between ownership structure and firm values by including variables that are assumed (theoretically) to affect the level of insider ownership (such as firm size) and the standard deviation of returns, which is a proxy for cash instability (Fields and Mais, 1994). Endogeneity is not a problem if the inclusion or omission of these variables does not change the relationship between insider ownership and (changes in) firm values significantly. Finally, regression model (2) is a parsimonious model that incorporates the ownership control diffuseness effect from signed earnings surprises (asymmetric effects) simultaneously for the pre- and post-cross-listing time periods.

4.3. *Descriptive Statistics*

The mean values of *CAR*, *FLOAT*, *SUE* and other expected determinants of *CAR* for the overall, the pre- and the post-cross-listing periods are reported in Table 2. The number of announcements for the pre- and post-cross-listing periods are 325 and 510, respectively. *p*-values

Table 2. Cumulative abnormal returns and their determinants.

Variable	Overall	Pre-cross-listing	Post-cross-listing	Post-minus pre-cross-listing, *p*-value
CAR (%, daily)	0.1957	−0.0318	0.3406	0.2431
SUE (%)	−0.3522	−0.3665	−0.3432	0.9247
FLOAT (ratio)	0.8762	0.9012	0.8603	0.0314**
SIZE (millions of Cdn $)	3,448.8	2,394.4	4,120.7	0.0000***
STD (%, daily)	1.8791	1.6375	2.0332	0.0000***
PreCAR (%)	−1.118	−0.2262	−1.6863	0.1786
PRICE	$25.01	21.99	26.93	0.0000***

Note: This table reports the mean values of *CAR* and the expected determinants for the overall, pre- and post-cross-listing periods for the Canadian firms that are cross-listed in the NYSE and NASDAQ during the period of 1990 to 1999. *, ** and *** correspond to 0.10, 0.05, and 0.01 levels of significance, respectively.

for the *t*-tests for the differences of means values between the pre- and post-cross-listing periods are reported in the last row.

The statistical significance of unreported tests of the differences of median values between the two periods do not differ materially from those reported using the mean values. The mean values of *CAR* and *SUE* for the overall period are 0.1957% and −0.3222%, respectively, and are not significantly different between the pre- and post-cross-listing time periods. FLOAT decreases significantly from 0.9012 to 0.8603 for the post-cross-listing period.[4] This implies that, unexpectedly, insider ownership is augmented after Canadian firms cross-list in the U.S.

Firm size increases very significantly from $2,394.4 million to $4,120.7 million from the pre- to post-cross-listing period. This is highly expected since a major reason for cross-listing is to obtain additional financial resources in the deeper and more liquid U.S. stock markets. Daily return volatility increases significantly from the pre- (1.63%) to the post-cross-listing period (2.03%). The increase in volatility indicates increased firm-specific risk since the systematic risk or beta decreases between the two periods as reported earlier in Panels B and C of Table 1. The mean value of the proportional bid–ask spread decreases very significantly from 1.10% to 0.88% from the pre- to the post-cross-listing period. The decreased bid–ask spread suggests increased inter market competition for order flow between the TSX and the NYSE/NASDAQ trade venues. Finally, the number of trades increases over 100% from the pre- to the post-cross-listing period. This indicates increasing information volatility from the pre- to the post-cross-listing period.

4.4. *Determinants of Changes in Firm Values*

This section examines the results from the pooled least squares regressions of *CAR* on *SUE* and changes in *FLOAT* and other possible determinants with(out) conditioning on *SUE* for the pre- and post-cross-listing periods as reported in Table 3. The *CAR* at the announcement dates are regressed on the *changes* in proportional float ($\Delta FLOAT$) and on *SUE* and other control variables. Δ as a prefix is the change in the mean value of each of the independent variables between the period $[(AD_{Q-2} + 3) - (AD_{Q-1} - 3), [(AD_{Q-1} + 3) - (AD_Q - 3]$. For example, $\Delta FLOAT$ is the change in the mean value of *FLOAT* between the period $[(AD_{Q-2} + 3 \text{ days}) - (AD_{Q-1} - 3 \text{ days}), (AD_{Q-1} + 3 \text{ days}) - (AD_Q - 3 \text{ days})]$, where AD is the announcement day and Q is the quarter. *FLOAT* is a proxy for ownership control and stock liquidity. The table reports the results for the entire period with and without dummies for the pre- and post-cross-listing periods. The dummy variable *DumPER* is equal to *DumPER* [*DumPOST*] if the $\Delta FLOAT$, *SUE* and the other control variables correspond to the pre- [post]-cross-listing period. *DumSUE* is equal to *DumNegSUE* [*DumPosSUE*] when conditioned on negative [positive] *SUE*. The cells report the mean coefficients and the *p*-values in parentheses. Adjusted R^2 values and *F*-statistic probabilities also are reported.

The relevant findings are given major emphasis. Only the coefficient constraints associated with each of the expected determinants (e.g., control variables) that are statistically significant are examined to save valuable publication space. Column 1 of Table 3 reports the regression coefficient estimates without conditioning on signed *SUE* (*p*-values are in parentheses). The estimated coefficients of $\Delta FLOAT$ and the sensitivity shift of $\Delta FLOAT$ for the pre-cross-listing period are not significant. In an untabulated regression, the estimated

Table 3. Regressions of *CAR* on possible determinants with(out) conditioning on signs of earnings surprises from pre- to post-cross-listing periods.

	Conditioning			
	None	Positive surprises	Positive surprises	Negative surprises
Period	Pre-cross-listing	Full (pre & post)	Pre-cross-listing	Post-cross-listing
Variable	(1)	(2)	(3)	(4)
Constant	0.0084	0.0247	0.0101	0.0101
	(0.6433)	(0.1650)	(0.5923)	(0.5923)
Δ*FLOAT*	−0.0849	−0.1540	−0.1942	0.0347
	(0.1032)	(0.0073)***	(0.0074)***	(0.8626)
Δ*FLOAT* * *DumPER*	0.0404		0.0974	−0.0111
	(0.6932)		(0.4319)	(0.9587)
Δ*FLOAT* * *DumSUE*		0.2052	0.2177	−0.1314
		(0.0270)**	(0.0437)**	(0.5596)
Δ*FLOAT* * *DumSUE* * *DumPER*			−0.0863	−0.0863
			(0.7281)	(0.7281)
SUE	0.6505	0.4387	0.6681	0.0413
	(0.0000)***	(0.0002)***	(0.0000)***	(0.8125)
SUE * *DumPER*	−0.6300		−0.6267	0.6267
	(0.0025)***		(0.0030)***	(0.0030)***
Δ*SIZE*	−0.00973	−0.9370	−0.5220	−0.5060
	(0.9729)	(0.0276)**	(0.2905)	(0.7407)
Δ*SIZE* * *DumPER*	−1.24		−1.1700	0.9160
	(0.1743)		(0.3242)	(0.5586)
Δ*SIZE* * *DumSUE*		0.1260	0.9330	−1.1900
		(0.0226)**	(0.1299)	(0.5049)
Δ*SIZE* * *DumSUE* * *DumPER*			0.2530	0.2530
			(0.8926)	(0.8926)
Δ*STD*	−0.1787	−0.0306	−0.1032	0.5316
	(0.2193)	(0.8695)	(0.6617)	(0.2992)
Δ*STD* * *DumPER*	0.4826		0.3479	−0.7242
	(0.1119)		(0.3822)	(0.1852)
Δ*STD* * *DumSUE*		−0.1027	−0.0893	−0.2869
		(0.6908)	(0.7725)	(0.6354)
Δ*STD* * *DumSUE* * *DumPER*			0.3763	0.3763
			(0.5780)	(0.5780)
Δ*PreCAR*	−0.0100	−0.0137	−0.0069	−0.0307
	(0.3483)	(0.2882)	(0.6538)	(0.2550)
Δ*PreCAR* * *DumPER*	−0.0198		−0.0308	0.0162
	(0.3386)		(0.2844)	(0.6013)
Δ*PreCAR* * *DumSUE*		−0.0040	−0.0074	−0.0070
		(0.8324)	(0.7377)	(0.8468)
Δ*PreCAR* * *DumSUE* * *DumPER*			0.0145	0.0145
			(0.7330)	(0.7330)

(*Continued*)

Table 3. (*Continued*)

	Conditioning			
	None	Positive surprises	Positive surprises	Negative surprises
Period	Pre-cross-listing	Full (pre & post)	Pre-cross-listing	Post-cross-listing
Variable	(1)	(2)	(3)	(4)
Δ*PRICE*	−0.0006	−0.0001	−0.0011	0.0014
	(0.1659)	(0.8073)	(0.2017)	(0.5188)
Δ*PRICE* * *DumPER*	0.0023		0.0030	−0.0018
	(0.0373)**		(0.0423)**	(0.4257)
Δ*PRICE* * *DumSUE*		−0.0001	0.0007	0.0004
		(0.8478)	(0.4892)	(0.8506)
Δ*PRICE* * *DumSUE* * *DumPER*			−0.0012	−0.0012
			(0.6459)	(0.6459)
Δ*SPREAD*	0.3480	−1.8877	−1.1952	−1.4288
	(0.6491)	(0.0142)**	(0.2220)	(0.4611)
Δ*SPREAD* * *DumPER*	−3.0910		−2.2732	3.6043
	(0.0184)**		(0.1668)	(0.1074)
Δ*SPREAD* * *DumSUE*		2.8076	3.3707	−2.0396
		(0.0224)**	(0.0219)**	(0.3803)
Δ*SPREAD* * *DumSUE* * *DumPER*			−1.3310	−1.3310
			(0.6283)	(0.6283)
Δ*TRADES*	0.3450	0.2700	0.3780	0.2410
	(0.0538)*	(0.2629)	(0.1438)	(0.7533)
Δ*TRADES* * *DumPER*	−0.3490	0.0703	−0.7160	0.0974
	(0.5459)	(0.8378)	(0.3994)	(0.9044)
Δ*TRADES* * *DumSUE*			−0.0389	−0.5800
			(0.9151)	(0.6072)
Δ*TRADES* * *DumSUE* * *DumPER*			0.6190	0.6190
			(0.6017)	(0.6017)
R^2 Adj.	0.034	0.026	0.042	0.042
F (Prob.)	0.0364	0.0765	0.0236	0.0236

Note: This table reports the pooled least squares regression results for a sample of Canadian firms that made quarterly earnings per share announcements and were cross-listed in the U.S. stock market during the time period from 1990 to 1999. *, ** and *** indicate significance at the 0.10, 0.05, and 0.01 levels, respectively.

coefficients of *FLOAT* and the sensitivity shift of Δ*FLOAT* for the post-cross-listing period are also not significant. These results indicate that Δ*FLOAT* is not significant for both the pre- and post-cross-listing periods.

This finding is similar to Himmelberg *et al.* (1999) and Demsetz and Villalonga (2001), who find that ownership structure does not influence firm value as measured by Tobin's Q. The estimated coefficient of *SUE* is positive (0.6505) and highly significant but the sensitivity shift of *SUE* for the pre-cross-listing period is negative (−0.6300) and also highly significant. In an untabulated regression, the estimated coefficient of *SUE* is positive (0.0204 = 0.6505–0.6300, *p*-value of 0.9056) but not significant. However, the sensitivity shift of *SUE* (0.6300) for the post-cross-listing period is positive and highly significant (*p*-value of 0.0025), which indicates that *SUE* is positive (0.6505) and significant (*p*-value of 0.0000) for the post-cross-listing time period only.[5]

Δ*SPREAD* is the other variable that is also significant and negative for the pre-cross-listing period. Thus, the higher the increase in the average spread from one quarter to the other prior to the earnings announcement, the lower the *CAR*. Column 2 of Table 3 report the results when the variables are conditioned on positive signed *SUE* for the overall period. The estimated coefficient of Δ*FLOAT* is −0.1540 and is highly significant (*p*-value of 0.0073), and the sensitivity shift of Δ*FLOAT* is 0.2052 and is significant (*p*-value of 0.0270). In an untabulated regression of *CAR* on negative signed *SUE* on Δ*FLOAT* and the other variables, the estimated coefficient of Δ*FLOAT* of 0.0512 is not significant (*p*-value of 0.4795). This indicates that Δ*FLOAT* is not significant when conditioned with positive *SUE*. For the same untabulated regression, the sensitivity shift of Δ*FLOAT*, which is conditioned on negative signed *SUE*, is −0.2052 and is significant (*p*-value of 0.0270). This indicates that Δ*FLOAT* is significant when conditioned on negative *SUE*. This is also corroborated by the negative mean value of Δ*FLOAT* of −0.1540, which is highly significant (*p*-value of 0.0073), as is reported in Column 2 of Table 2. This result implies that Δ*FLOAT* has an asymmetric effect on *CAR*. That is, *CAR* is decreasing for increasing changes in float only when conditioned on negative earnings surprises for the overall period (pre- and post-cross-listing).

The coefficient estimate for *SUE* is positive (0.4387) and highly significant (*p*-value of 0.0002). In other words, positive (negative)

SUEs are positively (negatively) associated with *CAR*. In contrast, the coefficient estimate of Δ*SPREAD* is negative (−1.8877) and significant (*p*-value of 0.0142). However, the sensitivity shift of Δ*SPREAD* when conditioned on positive *SUE* is positive (2.8076) and significant (*p*-value of 0.0224). This reveals that Δ*SPREAD* is not significant when conditioned on positive *SUE* as is obtained in an untabulated regression, where the expected determinants are conditioned on negative *SUE*. Specifically, in this case, the coefficient estimate of Δ*SPREAD* is 0.9198 and not significant (*p*-value of 0.3572), and the sensitivity shift is −2.8076 and significant (*p*-value of 0.0224). These results imply that Δ*SPREAD* also has an asymmetric effect on *CAR*. Specifically, *CAR* decreases for increasing changes in spreads when conditioned on negative SUEs only.

Column 3 of Table 3 reports the regression results when the determinants are conditioned on positive-signed *SUE* for the pre-cross-listing period as indicated by the dummy variable *DumPER*. Emphasis is again given mainly to the examination of the coefficient estimates for the Δ*FLOAT* and other variables on signed positive *SUE* simultaneously for the pre- and the post-cross-listing periods, respectively. The coefficient estimate of Δ*FLOAT* conditioned on positive *SUE* is positive (0.2177) and significant (*p*-value of 0.0437). The coefficient of Δ*FLOAT* conditioned on positive *SUE* for the pre-cross-listing period (as reflected by the sensitivity shift *DumPER*) is negative (−0.0863) and not significant (*p*-value of 0.7281). In order to determine the significance of Δ*FLOAT* conditioned on positive *SUE* for the pre-cross-listing period, an untabulated regression indicates that Δ*FLOAT* when signed with positive *SUE* is not a significant determinant of *CAR* during the pre-cross-listing period, the coefficient estimate of Δ*FLOAT* conditioned on positive *SUE* is positive (0.1314) and not significant (*p*-value of 0.5596), and the coefficient estimate of Δ*FLOAT* conditioned on positive *SUE* for the post-cross-listing period is positive (0.0863) and not significant (*p*-value of 0.7281).

The insignificant *p*-value for Δ*FLOAT* indicates that it is not a significant determinant of *CAR* when conditioned on positive *SUE* during the pre-cross-listing time period. By following a similar analysis, we obtain a *p*-value of 0.0437 for the coefficient estimate of Δ*FLOAT* when conditioned on positive *SUE* during the pre-cross-listing period. This represents the significance of Δ*FLOAT* when conditioned on positive *SUE* for the post-cross-listing period. This implies that *CAR* is increasing in Δ*FLOAT* when conditioned on positive *SUE* for the post-cross-listing period only.

Based on Column 3 of Table 3, the coefficient estimate of *SUE* is positive (0.6681) and highly significant (*p*-value of 0.0000), and the sensitivity shift *DumPER* for the pre-cross-listing period is negative (−0.6267) and also highly significant (*p*-value of 0.0030). However, based on an untabulated regression, the coefficient of *SUE* of 0.0413 for the pre-cross-listing period is not significant (*p*-value of 0.8125). The positive and significant value of the coefficient estimate of *SUE* (0.6681, *p*-value of 0.0000) implies that *SUE* is positively associated with *CAR* for the post-cross-listing period only. On the other hand, the coefficient estimate of Δ*SPREAD* conditioned on positive *SUE* is positive (3.3707) and significant (*p*-value of 0.0219), but the sensitivity shift of Δ*SPREAD* conditioned on positive signed *SUE* is −1.3310 and not significant (*p*-value of 0.6283) for the pre-cross-listing period. Based on an untabulated regression, the *p*-value of the coefficient estimate of Δ*SPREAD* signed on positive *SUE* for the pre-cross-listing period has a nonsignificant value of 0.3803. This indicates that *CAR* is increasing on increasing Δ*SPREAD* for positive SUEs for the post-cross-listing period only. No other expected determinants (including the year dummies) are significant for the pre- and post-cross-listing periods.

Column 4 of Table 3 reports the regression results when the determinants are conditioned on negative signed *SUE* for the post-cross-listing period. The coefficient estimate (−0.1314) and nonsignificant *p*-value (0.5596) for Δ*FLOAT* conditioned on negative *SUE* indicates that Δ*FLOAT* is not a significant determinant of *CAR* for negative SUEs for the pre-cross-listing period. Although the coefficient of Δ*FLOAT* conditioned on negative *SUE* is negative (−0.1314) and not significant (*p*-value of 0.5596) and the sensitivity shift for the post-cross-listing period is also negative (−0.0863) and not significant (*p*-value of 0.7281), the coefficient of Δ*FLOAT* when conditioned on negative *SUE* is negative (−0.2177 = −0.1314 − 0.0863) and significant (0.0437) for the post-cross-listing period. This indicates that *CAR* decreases with increasing Δ*FLOAT* when conditioned on negative *SUE* for the post-cross-listing period only. As reported in Column 3 of Table 3, *SUE* is positively associated with *CAR* for the post-cross-listing period only.

The other determinant that is significant is Δ*SPREAD* when conditioned on positive (negative) *SUE* for the post-cross-listing period only. This indicates that *CAR* is increasing (decreasing) with increasing (increasing) Δ*SPREAD* for positive (negative) earnings announcements for the post-cross-listing period only. This finding suggests that market makers fail to anticipate the market reaction of earnings announcements. Therefore, they increase the bid–ask spread as protection for possible unfavorable market outcomes. The four regressions are run also without *SIZE* and *STD* and the change in the coefficient estimates and the significance of Δ*FLOAT* is not material. This indicates that Δ*FLOAT* and changes in firm value are not endogenous, as suggested by Fields and Mais (1994). For all four regressions, no dummy variable for each year is significant at the 5% level.

The three main findings of this section can be summarized as follows. First, when there is no conditioning on the SUEs, changes in ownership structure or changes in ownership diffuseness as proxied by Δ*FLOAT* are not a significant determinant of changes in firm values as determined by the *CAR* around the earnings announcements for firms for either the pre- or post-cross-listing periods. SUEs are positively associated with *CAR* for the post-cross-listing periods only. That is, the market reaction is positive and significant around the announcements of firms' earnings above analysts' expectations and only for the post-cross-listing period. Second, *CAR* is negative and significantly associated with changes in ownership diffuseness when conditioned on negative SUEs only for the overall period. On the other hand, as expected, *CAR* is significantly and positively associated with SUEs. Thus, earnings above (below) analysts' expectations are associated with positive (negative) market reactions. Third, *CAR* is positively (negatively) associated with ownership diffuseness conditioned on positive (negative) SUEs for the post-cross-listing periods only. Similarly, *CAR* is positively associated with the SUEs only for the post-cross-listing periods. Consistent with the first finding, *SUE* is positively associated with *CAR* for the post-cross-listing periods only.

These findings fail to reject the hypothesis that ownership diffuseness conditioned on signed SUEs has a differential impact on changes in firm values from the pre- to the post-cross-listing period. These results are consistent with those reported by DeFond *et al.* (2007), who find that the information content of earnings announcements is superior in the U.S. than in Canada due to stricter insider trading laws in the U.S. This is also corroborated by the significant and stronger market reactions around the earnings announcement dates that occur for the post- vs. pre-cross-listing periods, as reported in Panels B and C of Table 1.

5. Concluding Remarks

Positive market reactions typically occur when non-U.S. firms announce cross-listings on major U.S. stock exchanges. This chapter extends this cross-listing literature by examining the impact of ownership structure with(out) conditioning on the sign of SUEs on changes in firm values, after controlling for other expected determinants of value for Canadian firms that cross-list on the NYSE and NASDAQ. The chapter finds that changes in ownership structure or diffuseness as measured by share float without conditioning on SUEs is not a significant determinant of changes in firm values as measured by the market reaction during the overall, pre- and post-cross-listing periods.

This finding is consistent with that reported by Himmelberg *et al.* (1999) and Demsetz and Villalonga (2001). The chapter also finds a positive (negative) market reaction or cumulative abnormal return that is associated with changes in ownership diffuseness conditioned on positive (negative) SUEs for the post-cross-listing period only. When it is the sole independent variable, SUEs are positively associated with *CAR* for the post-cross-listing period only. *CAR* increases (decreases) with increasing changes in the quoted spread conditioned on positive (negative) SUEs. This suggests that market makers increase the bid–ask spread prior to the earnings announcements as a protective measure because they are unable to anticipate the market impact of earnings announcements. But again, this is only during the post-cross-listing period.

These results are consistent with those reported by DeFond *et al.* (2007), who find that the quality of the information content of earnings announcements is superior in the U.S. than in Canada due to stricter insider trading laws in the U.S. This should result in more significant market reaction during the post-relative to the pre-cross-listing periods, as is found in this chapter. However, these results are also consistent with other possible explanations that are presented in Appendix A for the results reported herein.

Appendix A: Benefits for Non-U.S. Firms from U.S. Cross-Listings

Decreased market segmentation (decreased investment barriers). Investors require less compensation for risk or less expected return, reducing the cost of capital of cross-listing firms (Alexander *et al.*, 1987, 1998; Foerster and Karolyi, 1999; Doukas and Switzer, 2000).

Decreased financial constraints (improved access to U.S. capital markets). Investors update upward the expected cash flows of announcing firms, which is reflected in a positive market reaction mostly for firms with growth opportunities (Lins *et al.*, 2005; Lee, 2005).

Increased investor base (recognition, visibility). Stocks generally command lower expected returns when their risks can be shared globally rather than locally (Foerster and Karolyi, 1999; Baker *et al.*, 2002).

Increased analyst coverage and superior earnings forecasts. This results in an increased amount and quality of information by financial intermediaries and more corporate transparency (Baker *et al.*, 2002; Lang *et al.*, 2003; Licht, 2003) and changes in the breadth and depth of investor cognizance as proxied by the number of analysts following each firm and the superiority of earnings forecasts by analysts, respectively (Chung and Kryzanowski, 2001).

Decreased overall and systematic risk. Increased diversification leads to decreased standard deviations of returns for firms (Kwok and Reeb, 2000).

Increased stock liquidity (lower bid–ask spreads, increased trading volume). Intermarket competition and lower order processing costs in the U.S. trade venue can increase the liquidity of the listed shares in both the foreign and domestic markets relative to the liquidity before the cross-listing (Domowitz *et al.*, 1998; Foerster and Karolyi, 1999; Bris *et al.*, 2007).

Increased disclosure (decreased information asymmetry). Since a U.S. cross-listing provides more disclosure and a stronger commitment to disclose continuously, it becomes less costly for investors to monitor management. In turn, this leads to more favorable terms and conditions of financing (Karolyi, 2006; Bailey *et al.*, 2006).

Improved corporate governance and increased investor protection (Bonding Hypothesis). Cross-listing in the U.S. provides a means to get insiders from countries with weak governance structures to credibly commit not to expropriate outside investors. Such bonding is particularly valuable to firms with large growth opportunities and external financing needs. Investors perceive the cross-listing decision as a way to secure their money for the long-run (Coffee, 1999, 2001, 2002; Cantale, 1998; Fuerst, 2000; Stulz, 1999; Doidge *et al.*, 2004; Hail and Leuz, 2008; Fresard and Salva, 2007).

Ownership structure. Additional support for legal bonding is provided by focusing on the role of ownership structure before a U.S. cross-listing and changes in ownership around the listing event (King and Segal, 2004; Doidge, 2004; Ayyagari, 2004; Doidge *et al.*, 2006).

Endnotes

1. Financial support from the Concordia University Research Chair in Finance, IFM2, SSHRC, SSHRC-President's Fund, and SSQRC-CIRPÉE are gratefully

acknowledged. This paper has benefited from helpful comments by workshop participants from the Faculty of Business Administration at the University of Regina. Amr Addas and Jong-Ho Choi provided valuable research assistance.

2. Changes in the mean values of the control variables strengthen the significance of the estimated coefficients relative to the use of only the mean values for the period $[(AD_{Q-1} + 3) - (AD_Q - 3)]$.
3. The results are virtually unchanged when the dummy variable for SUE is set equal to zero.
4. The large proportional mean values of *FLOAT* are due to the fact that the firms with available share float data correspond to the larger Canadian publicly listed firms, which usually are widely held.
5. The coefficient estimate of *SUE* and its significance for the post-cross-listing period is given directly by the coefficient estimate of *SUE* in Column 1 of Table 3 (i.e., 0.6505 with a *p*-value of 0.0000).

References

Alexander, GJ, CS Eun and S Janakiramanan (1987). Asset pricing and dual listing on foreign capital markets: A note. *Journal of Finance*, 42(1), 151–158.

Alexander, GJ, CS Eun and S Janakiramanan (1988). International listings and stock returns: Some empirical evidence. *Journal of Financial and Quantitative Analysis*, 23(2), 135–151.

Ayyagari, M (2004). Does cross-listing lead to functional convergence? *Empirical evidence*, World Bank Policy Research Working Paper, 3264.

Bailey, W, G Karolyi and C Salva (2006). The economic consequences of increased disclosure: Evidence from international cross-listings. *Journal of Financial Economics*, 81(1), 175–213.

Baker, HK, JR Nofsinger and DG Weaver (2002). International cross-listing and visibility. *Journal of Financial and Quantitative Analysis*, 37(3), 495–522.

Ball, R and P Brown (1968). An empirical evaluation of accounting income numbers. *Journal of Accounting Research*, 6, 159–178.

Beaver, W (1968). The information content of annual earnings announcements. *Journal of Accounting Research*, 6, 67–92.

Bris, A, S Cantale and G Nishiotis (2007). A breakdown of the valuation effects of international cross-listing. *European Financial Management*, 13(3), 498–530.

Brous, PA and O Kini (1994). The valuation effects of equity issues and the level of institutional ownership: Evidence from analysts' earnings forecasts. *Financial Management*, 23, 33–46.

Cantale, S (1998). The choice of a foreign market as a signal. Working Paper, Tulane University.

Chung, R and L Kryzanowski (2001). Tests of investor cognizance using earnings forecasts of North American analysts. *International Review of Economics and Finance*, 10, 187–204.

Coffee, JC (1999). The future as history: The prospects for global convergence in corporate governance and its implications. *Northwestern University Law Review*, 93, 641–708.

Coffee, JC (2001). The rise of dispersed ownership: The role of law in the separation of ownership and control. *Yale Law Journal*, 111, 1–82.

Coffee, JC (2002). Racing towards the top? The impact of cross-listing and stock market competition on international corporate governance. *Columbia Law Review*, 102(7), 1757–1831.

DeFond, M, M Hung and R Trezevant (2007). Investor protection and the information content of annual earnings announcements: International evidence. *Journal of Accounting and Economics*, 43(1), 33–67.

Demsetz, H and B Villalonga (2001). Ownership structure and corporate performance. *Journal of Corporate Finance*, 7(3), 209–233.

Doidge, C (2004). U.S. cross-listing and the private benefits of control: Evidence from dual-class firms. *Journal of Financial Economics*, 72, 519–553.

Doidge, C, GA Karolyi and RM Stulz (2004). Why are foreign firms listed in the U.S. worth more? *Journal of Financial Economics*, 71, 205–238.

Doidge, C, A Karolyi, K Lins, DP Miller and RM Stulz (2006). Private benefits of control, ownership, and the cross-listing decision. Working Paper, University of Toronto, Ohio State University, University of Utah, Indiana University, Ohio State University.

Domowitz, I, J Glenn and A Madhavan (1998). International cross-listing and order flow migration: Evidence from an emerging market. *Journal of Finance*, 53(6), 2001–2027.

Doukas, J and LN Switzer (2000). Common stock returns and international listing announcements: Conditional tests of the mild segmentation hypothesis. *Journal of Banking & Finance*, 24, 471–502.

Errunza, V and D Miller (2000). Market segmentation and the cost of capital in international equity markets. *Journal of Financial and Quantitative Analysis*, 35, 577–600.

Fields, LP and EL Mais (1994). Managerial voting rights and seasoned public equity issues. *Journal of Financial and Quantitative Analysis*, 19(3), 445–457.

Foerster, S and A Karolyi (1999). The effects of market segmentation and investor recognition on asset prices: Evidence from foreign stocks listing in the U.S. *Journal of Finance*, 54, 981–1013.

Fresard, L and C Salva (2007). Does cross-listing in the U.S. really improve corporate governance? Evidence from the value of corporate liquidity. Working Paper, University of Bern.

Fuerst, O (2000). A theoretical analysis of the investor protection regulations argument for global listings of stocks. Working Paper, Yale School of Management.

Hail, L and C Leuz (2008). Cost of capital effects and changes in growth expectations around U.S. cross-listings. Finance Working Paper, Wharton School and University of Chicago.

Himmelberg, CP, RG Hubbard and D Palia (1999). Understanding the determinants of managerial ownership and the link between ownership and performance. *Journal of Financial Economics*, 53, 353–384.

Jiang, L and L Kryzanowski (1998). Trading activity, quoted liquidity and stock volatility. *Multinational Finance Journal*, 1(3), 199–227.

Karolyi, GA (2006). The world of cross-listings and cross-listings of the world: Challenging conventional wisdom. *Review of Finance*, 10, 99–152.

King, MR and D Segal (2003). Corporate governance, international cross-listing and home bias. *Canadian Investment Review*, Winter, 8–18.

King, MR and D Segal (2004). International cross-listing and the bonding hypothesis. Working Paper, Bank of Canada.

Kwok, CCY and DM Reeb (2000). Internalization and firm risk: An upstream-downstream hypothesis. *Journal of International Business Studies*, 31, 611–629.

Korajczyk, RA, D Lucas and RL McDonald (1990). Understanding stock price behavior around the time of equity issues. In *Asymmetric Information, Corporate Finance, and Investment*, RG Hubbard (ed.). Chicago: University of Chicago Press.

Landsman, W and E Maydew (2002). Has the information content of quarterly earnings announcements declined in the past three decades? *Journal of Accounting Research*, 40, 797–808.

Lang, MH, KV Lins and D Miller (2003). ADRs, analysts, and accuracy: Does cross-listing in the U.S. improve a firm's information environment and increase market value? *Journal of Accounting Research*, 41(2), 317–345.

Lee, DW (2005). Why does shareholder wealth increase when non-U.S. firms announce their listing in the U.S.? Working Paper, University of Kentucky.

Leuz, C, D Nanda and PD Wysocki (2003). Earnings management and investor protection: An international comparison. *Journal of Financial Economics*, 69, 505–527.

Lins, K, D Strickland and M Zenner (2005). Do non-U.S. firms issue equity on U.S. stock exchanges to relax capital constraints? *Journal of Financial and Quantitative Analysis*, 40(1), 109–133.

Licht, AN (2003). Cross-listing and corporate governance: Bonding or avoiding? *Chicago Journal of International Law*, 4, 122–141.

Miller, DP (1999). The market reaction to international cross-listings: Evidence from depository receipts. *Journal of Financial Economics*, 51, 103–123.

Ogden, JP, FC Jen and PF O'Connor (2003). *Advanced corporate finance: Policies and strategies*. Prentice Hall, Upper Saddle River, NJ.

Stulz, R (1999). Globalization, corporate finance, and the cost of capital. *Journal of Applied Corporate Finance*, 26, 3–28.

12

Analysis of the Investment Potential and Inflation-Hedging Ability of Precious Metals

James R. McCown and John R. Zimmerman

1. Introduction

Precious metals have been used as media of exchange and stores of value for millennia. In recent times, their use as media of exchange has declined but they are still kept as stores of value, as many investors have investments in gold or silver in various forms in their portfolios. This research examines the investment performance of the metals using the traditional asset pricing models used to evaluate securities, and also examines their usefulness as hedges against inflation and as indicators of expected future inflation.

Several researchers have previously examined the investment value of the precious metals. Jaffe (1989) finds that gold and silver have positive but very low betas when measured against U.S. stocks using monthly data for 1971–1987. Using daily returns from 1976 to 2004, Hillier *et al.* (2006) find that gold and silver have negative betas that are very small in absolute value but statistically significant when measured against U.S. stocks, thus providing hedging of an investor's stock portfolio. They also find that the betas are positive and small, but also statistically significant, when measured against foreign stocks.

Researchers have also examined the inflation-hedging ability of gold and silver. Jaffe (1989) using monthly data finds that gold has a positive relation with inflation but that the *R*-squares are so low that he concludes there is "little relation between gold and consumer prices". However, Levin *et al.* (2004) find that cointegration techniques using monthly data from 1976 to 1999 show that gold can be regarded as a good long-term inflation hedge.

We test for the correlation between each of the metals and the U.S. CPI inflation rate from 1970 to 2007 using time horizons varying from one month to five years. We find that the correlation is very small at the one-month horizon but becomes larger as the horizon is lengthened. These results confirm the findings of Jaffe (1989), and Levin *et al.* (2004) that the metals prices are unrelated with inflation at short-time horizons and positively correlated with inflation at long-time horizons.

We estimate the CAPM for gold and silver for the period from 1970 to 2007, against both U.S. and world stock portfolios, and also find that the betas are close to zero when short-time horizons are examined but that they become negative and increase in absolute value and statistical significance as the time horizon is expanded. Subperiod analysis shows that the negative betas are confined to the high-inflation 1970s. During the period from 1980 to 2007 the betas are positive even for the longer time horizons. This shows that the ability of the metals to hedge against fluctuations in stock prices is primarily due to their ability to hedge against inflation.

Former Federal Reserve Board Chairman Alan Greenspan (1993) mentioned that he used gold prices as an indicator of expected future inflation. We test the ability of the metals prices to track expected inflation as computed from the yield spread between nominal U.S. treasury securities and the U.S. treasury inflation protected securities (TIPS). We find that the prices of both metals show a large positive correlation with the expected future inflation rate, and that the correlation is highest for the time horizon over 10 years. However, there were large increases in the metals prices beginning in September 2005 that were not matched by corresponding increases in expected inflation.

Section 2 examines the data. Section 3 looks at basic statistics for the metals prices, inflation and stock returns. In Sec. 4, we estimate the CAPM model for gold and silver. Section 5 examines the relation between the metals prices and expected future inflation. Section 6 concludes.

2. Data

There are several ways that an investor may take a position in gold or silver. They may purchase gold or silver bullion in the form of ingots or coins. If purchased in sufficient quantity, such items may be bought and sold for a small transaction cost. There are several companies that will store the ingots or coins for an investor and sell them when the owner desires. Exchange-traded funds that invest in bullion are also available, with low transactions and management fees.

Investors can purchase mining stocks, whose earnings will usually rise and fall with the metals prices and perhaps provide leverage, but the profits earned by these companies are also dependent on management practices and other issues that are not directly related to the metals prices. Derivatives based on the metals prices are available in many different varieties. The primary advantages of derivatives for an investor are to enable him to make leveraged bets on the metals or even to bet that their price might decline. Throughout this research, we will assume an investor is purchasing gold or silver bullion and assume no transactions costs, since they would not be significantly higher than transactions costs for securities.

The precious metals data consist of the month-end spot prices for gold and silver. These were obtained from DataStream and various issues of the *Wall Street Journal* and begin with 1970. The continuously compounded returns for each time horizon are computed by taking the change of the log spot prices from the beginning to the end of the period. For comparison purposes and for use in the asset pricing models, the following data are utilized:

- U.S. inflation: Log change of the CPI-U, from the Federal Reserve Bank of St. Louis.
- Interest rates on U.S. treasury bills: 30-day-maturity, from various issues of the *Wall Street Journal*.
- Returns on U.S. MSCI stock portfolio, including dividends, from MSCI Barra.

- Returns on World MSCI stock portfolio, U.S. dollar-denominated, including dividends, from MSCI Barra. This shows the returns a U.S. investor earns if he/she does not hedge his/her foreign exchange risk.
- Returns on World MSCI stock portfolio, local currency — denominated, including dividends, from MSCI Barra. This shows the returns an investor living anywhere in the world earns if he/she completely hedges the foreign exchange risk.

3. Basic Statistics

Table 1A shows summary statistics for the monthly log returns on the spot prices of gold and silver for 1970–2007. Both of the metals have returns inferior to the MSCI U.S. and World stock indexes, and higher volatility. Gold has a return that is over 2% less than that of stocks, and about 2.6% higher than that of U.S. treasury bills over the

Table 1A. Summary statistics.

	Mean annualized return	Standard deviation	First-order autocorrelation
Monthly Data: 1970–2007			
Gold	8.38%	5.93%	0.032
Silver	5.39	9.52	−0.010
U.S. inflation†	4.52	0.35	0.579
U.S. TBills*	5.74	2.81	0.973
U.S. stocks‡	10.39	4.34	0.022
World stocks — U.S.$ denominated‡	10.41	4.08	0.077
World stocks — local currency denominated‡	9.52	3.91	0.095
Subperiod: January 1970–January 1980			
Gold	29.26%	8.11%	0.092
Silver	29.14	9.99	0.099
U.S. inflation†	7.22	0.35	0.461
U.S. T-Bills*	6.17	1.98	0.951
U.S. stocks‡	5.05	4.56	0.019
World stocks — U.S.$ denominated‡	7.26	4.06	0.156
World stocks — local currency denominated‡	5.94	3.89	0.146

*Ask yield on 30-day U.S. treasury bills.

†Log change of the monthly CPI-U index.

‡Continuously compounded returns on the MSCI portfolios, including dividends.

Table 1B. Summary statistics.

	Mean annualized return	Standard deviation	First-order autocorrelation
Subperiod: February 1980–August 1999			
Gold	−4.78%	4.90%	−0.094
Silver	−9.89	10.10	−0.062
U.S. inflation†	3.90	0.29	0.351
U.S. TBills*	6.59	2.93	0.965
U.S. stocks‡	16.04	4.31	−0.006
World stocks — U.S.$ denominated‡	13.99	4.15	0.026
World stocks — local currency denominated‡	13.46	3.95	0.054
Subperiod: September 1999–December 2007			
Gold	14.25%	4.31%	−0.137
Silver	12.81	6.75	−0.211
U.S. inflation†	2.74	0.35	0.367
U.S. TBills*	3.22	1.72	0.980
U.S. stocks‡	2.59	4.08	0.002
World stocks — U.S.$ denominated‡	5.02	3.93	0.069
World stocks — local currency denominated‡	3.79	3.83	0.087

*Ask yield on 30-day U.S. treasury bills.
†Log change of the monthly CPI-U index.
‡Continuously compounded returns on the MSCI portfolios, including dividends.

same period. According to Jaffe (1989), the reason why gold has a lower return than other risky assets is due to non-pecuniary benefits.

First, gold has liquidity value. It is the most liquid asset in times of catastrophe, and thus investors are willing to pay a premium price for it. Secondly, gold has consumption value as it is used in jewelry. An owner of gold jewelry receives utility that an owner of stocks or bonds does not. Finally, gold has a convenience value in production. A producer of gold jewelry holds gold to avoid stockouts, receiving a convenience yield. Silver has a return that is lower than treasury bills. The low return on silver may be due to the same reasons stated by Jaffe for gold. As we shall show in this analysis, another reason for the low returns on the metals may be due to their value in hedging a portfolio.

We also looked at subperiods in Tables 1A and 1B. Examination of the graph of the time series of gold and silver spot prices in

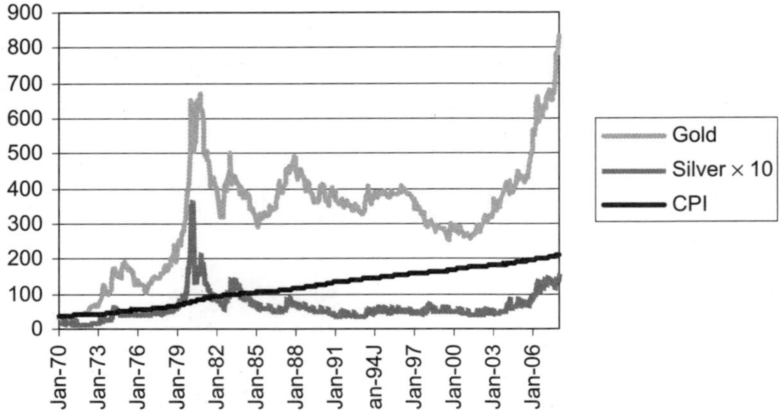

Figure 1. Gold and silver prices compared with the consumer price index 1970–2007. *Note*: CPI-U with index 1982–1984 = 100.

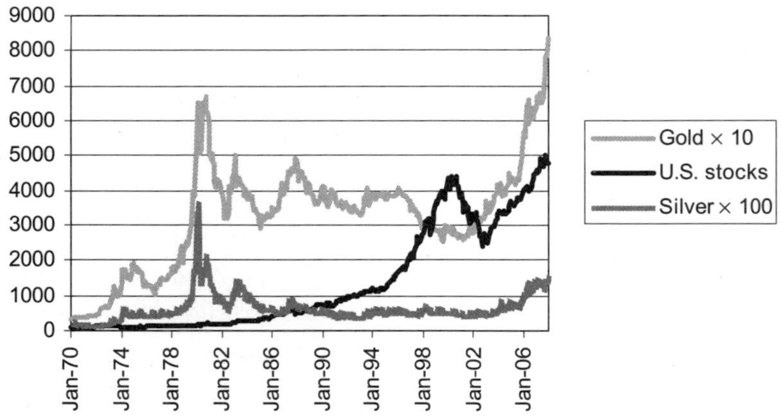

Figure 2. Gold and silver prices compared with U.S. stocks 1970–2007. *Note*: U.S. stocks are the MSCI U.S. index which assumes all dividends are reinvested.

Figs. 1 and 2 shows that the metals had large increases in prices throughout the 1970s, reaching a maximum in January 1980. The prices slowly decreased over the 1980s and 1990s, with a few reversals, reaching a minimum in August 1999. This was followed by increasing prices beginning September 1999 to the end of the sample. We have therefore conducted the analyses for three subperiods: (1) January

1970 to January 1980, (2) February 1980 to August 1999 and (3) September 1999 to December 2007.

For the first subperiod from January 1970 to January 1980, gold and silver had average annualized returns of over 29%, far in excess of stocks and inflation. During the second subperiod from February 1980 to August 1999, both metals had negative returns as compared with the large positive returns enjoyed by stocks. For the third subperiod from September 1999 to December 2007, gold and silver once again had positive returns, far in excess of inflation and the meager returns to stocks during the period.

The summary statistics, as well as Fig. 2, suggest a negative correlation between stocks and the metals, for which we test in Table 2. We compute the correlation of the returns on the metals with each other and with inflation and each of the stock market portfolios. The correlations of the metals with the stock portfolios are close to zero for the short-time horizon of one month, but as we examine larger and larger time horizons the correlation becomes increasingly negative,

Table 2. Correlations of returns on metals with inflation and stock returns 1970–2007.

Time horizon	Silver	Inflation	U.S. stocks*	World stocks — U.S.$ denominated*	World stocks — Local currency denominated*
Correlations of Gold with					
One month	0.666	0.119	−0.027	0.120	0.022
Two months	0.692	0.131	−0.091	0.078	−0.025
Three months	0.614	0.173	−0.079	0.073	−0.045
Six months	0.634	0.213	−0.197	0.028	−0.136
One year	0.763	0.417	−0.343	−0.161	−0.280
Two years	0.858	0.596	−0.471	−0.238	−0.369
Five years	0.926	0.711	−0.643	−0.411	−0.598
Correlations of Silver with					
One month	0.666	0.036	0.111	0.202	0.158
Two months	0.692	0.022	0.097	0.194	0.165
Three months	0.614	0.017	0.100	0.148	0.106
Six months	0.634	0.037	0.067	0.116	0.067
One year	0.763	0.212	−0.111	−0.047	−0.074
Two years	0.858	0.517	−0.281	−0.098	−0.193
Five years	0.926	0.530	−0.532	−0.458	−0.582

*Returns on MSCI indexes, including dividends.

reaching as much as −0.643 for the correlation between gold and the U.S. stock portfolio, for the five-year time horizon. The short-term movements between the metals and the stock prices appear to be independent, but over the long term, we find strong evidence of an inverse correlation. This shows the possibility of using the metals to hedge an investment in stocks, which we examine further in the next section.

Also in Table 2, the correlations between the returns on the metals and the U.S. CPI inflation rate show considerable differences when different time horizons are examined. For a monthly time horizon, both gold and silver returns are virtually uncorrelated with inflation. Increasing the time horizon, we see higher and higher correlations, culminating in a positive correlation between gold and inflation of 0.711 and between silver and inflation of 0.530, for the five-year horizon. Both metals show strong evidence of an ability to hedge inflation risk over the long term. These results confirm the findings of Jaffe (1989), who finds virtually no relation between gold prices and goods prices in the short term, and Levin *et al.* (2004) who find that gold is a good long-term inflation hedge.

4. Estimates of the Capital Asset Pricing Model

In order to estimate the Capital Asset Pricing Model of Sharpe (1964) and Lintner (1965) for the precious metals, the following ordinary least squares regression is estimated:

$$\mathrm{R}_{i,t} - \mathrm{R}_{f,t} = \alpha_i + \beta_i(\mathrm{R}_{m,t} - \mathrm{R}_{f,t}) + \varepsilon_t, \tag{1}$$

where $\mathrm{R}_{i,t}$ is the return on metal i, $\mathrm{R}_{f,t}$ is the risk-free rate (Yield on 30-day U.S. Treasury Bills), and $\mathrm{R}_{m,t}$ is the return on the market portfolio. We use three different proxies for the market portfolio: MSCI U.S. index, MSCI World local currency — denominated index, and MSCI World U.S. dollar — denominated index.

The results for gold and silver from 1970 to 2007 are in Table 3. The length of the time horizon can have a significant effect on the estimated beta coefficient. Using the one-month time horizon, the estimated betas are positive and less than one (except for gold with

Table 3. Estimates of the CAPM for gold and silver 1970–2007.

$$R_{i,t} - R_{f,t} = \alpha_i + \beta_i(R_{m,t} - R_{f,t}) + \varepsilon_t$$

Time horizon	U.S. stocks	World stocks — U.S.$ denominated	World stocks — Local currency denominated
Gold: Beta of risk premium against market proxy			
One month	−0.026	0.186	0.045
	(−0.317)	(2.080)	(0.516)
Two months	−0.108	0.134	−0.017
	(−0.168)	(1.404)	(−0.159)
Three months	−0.078	0.118	−0.037
	(−0.705)	(1.267)	(−0.387)
Six months	−0.255	0.093	−0.172
	(−1.015)	(0.371)	(−0.753)
One year	−0.464	−0.178	−0.377
	(−1.498)	(−0.528)	(−1.237)
Two years	−0.678	−0.331	−0.562
	(−2.020)	(−0.785)	(−1.457)
Five years	−1.628	−1.616	−2.086
	(−3.812)	(−2.632)	(−3.234)
Silver			
One month	0.260	0.487	0.404
	(1.763)	(2.599)	(2.325)
Two months	0.255	0.491	0.448
	(1.655)	(2.824)	(2.542)
Three months	0.227	0.329	0.249
	(1.623)	(2.164)	(1.917)
Six months	0.217	0.350	0.229
	(0.696)	(1.069)	(0.810)
One year	−0.164	−0.002	−0.079
	(−0.556)	(−0.008)	(−0.256)
Two years	−0.367	−0.101	−0.256
	(−1.081)	(−0.247)	(−0.629)
Five years	−1.309	−1.713	−1.965
	(−3.472)	(−2.810)	(−2.946)

Note: $R_{i,t} - R_{f,t}$ = log return on metal minus the 30-day treasury bill yield. $R_{m,t} - R_{f,t}$ = return on the MSCI index, including dividends, minus the 30-day treasury bill yield. Robust *t*-statistics in parentheses were computed using the method of Newey and West (1987).

the U.S. stock portfolio which has a negative beta that is close to zero). This result confirms the findings of Jaffe (1989) and Hillier *et al.* (2006) who find very small betas for gold and silver when measured against both U.S. and foreign stocks. Going to longer time horizons, the betas become increasingly negative, to as much as −2.086 for gold when using the World-local currency portfolio.

We also ran the CAPM regressions for the three subperiods and the results are shown in Tables 4, 5 and 6. We examined time horizons ranging from one month to one year. It is not practical to run the regressions for the longer time horizons of two or five years, because the samples are too small. From Table 4, we see the negative betas for both gold and silver for the high-inflation 1970s. The betas generally become more negative as the horizon is increased. However in Tables 5 and 6 for the subperiods from 1980 to 1999, and from 2000 to 2007, the betas are positive. The negative betas for the entire sample from 1970 to 2007 are primarily the result of the 1970s, a period of high inflation and poor stock returns. We conclude it is the

Table 4. Estimates of the CAPM for gold and silver subperiod analysis: 1970–1979.

$$R_{i,t} - R_{f,t} = \alpha_i + \beta_i(R_{m,t} - R_{f,t}) + \varepsilon_t$$

Time horizon	U.S. stocks	World stocks — U.S.$ denominated	World stocks — Local currency denominated
Gold: Beta of Risk Premium against market proxy			
One month	−0.130	0.202	0.012
	(−0.701)	(1.038)	(0.060)
Two months	−0.390	−0.098	−0.251
	(−2.165)	(−0.550)	(−1.185)
Three months	−0.100	0.094	−0.052
	(−0.486)	(0.648)	(−0.258)
Six months	−0.773	−0.563	−0.762
	(−3.941)	(−2.340)	(−3.479)
One year	−0.934	−0.972	−0.916
	(−2.839)	(−2.717)	(−2.503)
Silver			
One month	0.092	0.396	0.305
	(0.489)	(1.844)	(1.357)
Two months	0.068	0.318	0.278
	(0.271)	(1.070)	(0.934)
Three months	0.215	0.333	0.256
	(0.868)	(1.052)	(0.921)
Six months	−0.351	−0.434	−0.391
	(−2.203)	(−1.935)	(−2.033)
One year	−0.451	−0.687	−0.510
	(−1.143)	(−2.100)	(−1.470)

Note: $R_{i,t} - R_{f,t}$ = log return on metal minus the 30-day treasury bill yield. $R_{m,t} - R_{f,t}$ = return on the MSCI index, including dividends, minus the 30-day treasury bill yield. Robust *t*-statistics in parentheses were computed using the method of Newey and West (1987).

Table 5. Estimates of the CAPM for gold and silver subperiod analysis: 1980–1999.

$$R_{i,t} - R_{f,t} = \alpha_i + \beta_i(R_{m,t} - R_{f,t}) + \varepsilon_t$$

Time horizon	U.S. stocks	World stocks — U.S.$ denominated	World stocks — Local currency denominated
Gold: Beta of risk premium against market proxy			
One month	0.088	0.246	0.131
	(0.762)	(1.960)	(1.050)
Two months	0.135	0.308	0.169
	(0.861)	(2.104)	(0.999)
Three months	0.032	0.234	0.039
	(0.188)	(1.398)	(0.251)
Six months	0.295	0.582	0.265
	(0.948)	(2.375)	(0.969)
One year	0.376	0.590	0.277
	(0.870)	(1.929)	(0.867)
Silver			
One month	0.440	0.631	0.577
	(1.656)	(1.970)	(1.890)
Two months	0.489	0.665	0.654
	(1.705)	(2.227)	(2.004)
Three months	0.384	0.410	0.319
	(1.840)	(1.940)	(1.732)
Six months	0.968	0.938	0.754
	(2.312)	(2.372)	(2.092)
One year	0.754	0.658	0.543
	(1.633)	(2.336)	(1.492)

Note: $R_{i,t} - R_{f,t}$ = log return on metal minus the 30-day treasury bill yield. $R_{m,t} - R_{f,t}$ = return on the MSCI index, including dividends, minus the 30-day treasury bill yield. Robust *t*-statistics in parentheses were computed using the method of Newey and West (1987).

inflation-hedging ability of gold and silver that is behind the stock-hedging ability seen in Table 3.

We conducted an analysis (not shown) of the returns on gold and silver using the multiple-factor Arbitrage Pricing Model of Ross (1976). This provides a framework with which to evaluate an asset's exposure to multiple sources of risk simultaneously. We selected the macroeconomic factors following Chen (1991) and Chen *et al.* (1986) to include the market portfolio, default spread, term spread, change in U.S. industrial production, and change in the CPI inflation rate. The results were not informative except for the coefficients on the change in the inflation rate, which became more

Table 6. Estimates of the CAPM for gold and silver subperiod analysis: 2000–2007.

$$R_{i,t} - R_{f,t} = \alpha_i + \beta_i(R_{m,t} - R_{f,t}) + \varepsilon_t$$

Time horizon	U.S. stocks	World stocks — U.S.$ denominated	World stocks — Local currency denominated
Gold: beta of risk premium against market proxy			
One month	−0.006	0.131	0.015
	(0.055)	(1.108)	(0.128)
Two months	0.101	0.262	0.165
	(0.796)	(1.848)	(1.192)
Three months	0.093	0.161	0.085
	(0.753)	(1.280)	(0.653)
Six months	0.229	0.330	0.193
	(0.831)	(1.557)	(0.752)
One year	0.269	0.296	0.228
	(1.102)	(1.388)	(1.033)
Silver			
One month	0.222	0.357	0.243
	(1.717)	(2.316)	(1.586)
Two months	0.445	0.613	0.579
	(2.154)	(2.633)	(2.580)
Three months	0.308	0.412	0.362
	(1.957)	(2.555)	(1.939)
Six months	0.704	0.776	0.712
	(2.438)	(3.974)	(2.806)
One year	0.756	0.719	0.746
	(2.895)	(3.469)	(3.171)

Note: $R_{i,t} - R_{f,t}$ = log return on metal minus the 30-day treasury bill yield. $R_{m,t} - R_{f,t}$ = return on the MSCI index, including dividends, minus the 30-day treasury bill yield. Robust t-statistics in parentheses were computed using the method of Newey and West (1987).

positive and statistically significant as the investment horizon was increased.

5. How Do Prices of the Metals Correlate with Expected Future Inflation?

Former U.S. Federal Reserve Board Chairman Greenspan (1993) mentioned the price of gold as an indicator of expected inflation. Moreover, *inflation* expectations, at least by some measures, appear to have tilted upward this year, possibly contributing to price pressures. The University of Michigan survey of consumer attitudes, for example, reported an increase in the *inflation* rate expected to prevail over the next 12 months from about 3.75% in the fourth quarter of last year to nearly 4.5% in the second quarter of this year. Preliminary data imply some easing of such expectations earlier this month, but the sample from which those data are derived is too small to be persuasive. Moreover, the price of *gold*, which can be broadly reflective of inflationary expectations, has risen sharply in recent months.

In 1993, there was no available method to directly measure expected inflation. The introduction of the U.S. TIPS beginning in 1997 gives us a method of estimating investors' expectations of future inflation by comparing the yield on a TIPS bond with that of a nominal bond of comparable maturity. The Fisher equation can then be used to estimate the expected inflation rate:

$$\pi^e_{tk} = i_{tk} - r_{tk}, \tag{2}$$

where π^e_{tk} is the inflation rate that investors expect to prevail over the period $t + k$ as of time t, i_{tk} is the yield on a nominal bond with maturity k as of time t, and r_{tk} is the yield on a TIPS bond with maturity k as of time t.

We obtained the yields of all 22 TIPS bonds from the *Wall Street Journal* as of the last business day in each month from January 1997 when the first bond was issued up through the end of 2007. We also obtained the yield of a nominal bond with a maturity closest to the TIPS maturity to correspond with each of the TIPS bonds. The expected inflation rate was then computed from Eq. (2). The TIPS have been issued in maturities of 5, 10, 20 and 30 years. As each bond ages, it gives us an estimate of expected inflation for a steadily decreasing time horizon. We broke down the available maturities for each month into two categories: 5 to 10 years, and greater than 10 years. There was at least one TIPS bond outstanding with a maturity from five to ten years for the entire 1997–2007 period. There were TIPS bonds outstanding with maturities greater than 10 years from April 1998 to December 2007.

The expected inflation rates extracted from the TIPS spreads are shown in Figs. 3 and 4 alongside the corresponding end of month metals prices. Inspection of the graphs reveals co-movements between the metals prices and expected inflation from 1997 up

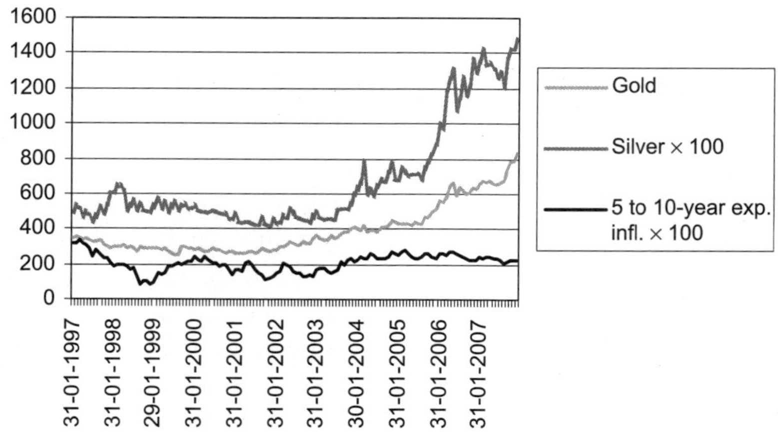

Figure 3. Metals prices and 5–10-year expected inflation from TIPS yields 1997–2007.

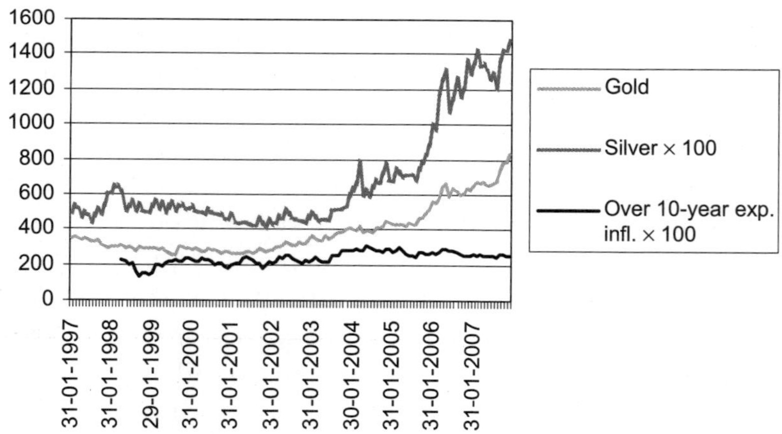

Figure 4. Metals prices and greater than 10-year expected inflation from TIPS yields 1997–2007.

until September 2005 when the price of both metals increased rapidly without any corresponding increase in expected inflation. We computed the simple correlation between the metals prices and the expected inflation for both of the time horizons. The results are shown in Table 7. The correlations are positive and higher for gold, especially for the time horizon greater than 10 years, for which we obtained a correlation coefficient of 0.583.

Table 7. Correlations between metal prices and expected future inflation from TIPS spreads.

From beginning of sample to 31 December 2007		
	5–10 years*	Over 10 years†
Correlation with expected inflation for time horizon		
Gold	0.575	0.583
Silver	0.556	0.492
From beginning of sample to 31 August 2005		
Correlation with expected inflation for time horizon		
Gold	0.520	0.776
Silver	0.458	0.621

*January 1997 to end of period.
†April 1998 to end of period.

We also computed the correlations for the period ending 31 August 2005, which was just before the metals prices increased significantly beginning in September 2005. The correlations were higher for the period ending 31 August 2005 for the over 10-year horizon, but lower for the 5 to 10-year horizon. As Greenspan (1993) discussed, policymakers can use the price of gold (and silver) as a secondary indicator for expected future inflation. Gold has a generally higher correlation with expected inflation than silver and is most useful for indicating long-term expectations.

6. Conclusions

Gold and silver show evidence of ability to hedge a stock portfolio. Estimates of the CAPM result in negative betas for both metals. The negative betas are greater in absolute value at longer time horizons. Both metals also show ability to hedge inflation, which increases in effectiveness at longer time horizons. Subperiod analysis reveals that the negative betas are confined to the high-inflation 1970s, leading to the conclusion that it is the metals' abilities to hedge inflation that is the cause of the negative betas. Confirming Greenspan's (1993) claim that the price of gold is a useful indicator of expected inflation, the prices of both gold and silver show high correlation with expected inflation as measured by the spread between nominal U.S. treasury securities and TIPS yields.

References

Chen, N (1991). Financial investment opportunities and the macroeconomy. *Journal of Finance*, 66, 529–554.

Chen, N, R Roll and S Ross (1986). Economic forces and the stock market. *Journal of Business*, 59, 383–403.

Greenspan, A (1993). The Fed aims for price stability. *Challenge*, 36(5), 4–10.

Hillier, D, P Draper and R Faff (2006). Do precious metals shine? An investment perspective. *Financial Analysts Journal*, 62, 98–106.

Jaffe, J (1989). Gold and gold stocks as investments for institutional portfolios. *Financial Analysts Journal*, March–April, 53–59.

Levin, E, P MacMillan, R Wright and D Ghosh (2004). Gold as an inflation hedge? *Studies in Economics and Finance*, 22, 1–25.

Lintner, J (1965). The valuations of risk assets and the selection of risky investments in stock portfolios and capital budgets. *Review of Economics and Statistics*, 47, 221–245.

Newey, W and K West (1987). A simple, positive semi-definite heteroskedasticity and autocorrelation consistent covariance matrix. *Econometrica*, 55, 703–708.

Ross, S, (1976). The arbitrage theory of capital asset pricing. *Journal of Economic Theory*, 13, 341–360.

Sharpe, W (1964). Capital asset prices: A theory of market equilibrium under conditions of risk. *Journal of Finance*, 19, 425–442.

13

Corporate Governance and Ownership Structure in Emerging Markets: Evidence from Latin America

Diego Cueto

1. Introduction

In this research, I study the role of ownership structure as a corporate governance mechanism in emerging economies. Corporate governance affects firm value, market liquidity, and the organization of industries and markets in a context of weak shareholders' protection. The ownership structures predominant in the Latin-American markets provide a rich environment to explore corporate governance practices in a regional setting.

I find that in the context of low protection for minority shareholders, and large ownership concentration, market participants impose a discount on the value of firms in which the voting rights of dominant shareholders exceed the cash-flow rights. However, investors prefer a dominant shareholder that is a corporation or a family group member rather than an institutional investor or a government agency. Such preference may obey to managerial expertise and efficiency and enhanced access to product markets. The evidence suggests that the stock market discount is lower when other corporations and family groups assume monitoring roles similar to that of creditors. On the other hand, institutional investors and government agencies are not perceived as efficient corporate monitors. Collusion between blockholders and dominant shareholders for the purpose of extracting private benefits of control, to the detriment of investors, is not evident.

According to a traditional finance paradigm, the ownership of public corporations is widely dispersed among atomistic investors. This paradigm is not applicable in many countries, particularly those in which families, business groups or governments control most of the publicly traded firms (Faccio and Lang, 2002; Claessens *et al.*, 2002; Lins, 2003). Even in the U.S., controlling shareholders govern a large number of firms. Concentrated ownership structures give rise to a new form of conflict of interests: between dominant shareholders and minority shareholders (Dahya *et al.*, 2008). The conflict of interests is characterized as the potential for asset diversion from the firms to dominant shareholders, thus perhaps reducing overall shareholders' value.

In some cases, blockholders could deter excessive private consumption by dominant shareholders. Some blockholders, such as pension funds, have the potential to prevent asset diversion increasing shareholders' value. However, others may negotiate with dominant shareholders to obtain a portion of the private benefits of control. Blockholders' identity, the stake in the firm and the value of the stake with respect to the total value of the portfolio determine the behavior of the blockholder. To the extent that blockholders collude with dominant shareholders, the monitoring incentives vanish. Moreover, when the voting rights exceed the cash-flow rights, the incentives for asset diversion are magnified.

The discrepancy between voting rights and cash-flow rights is created and amplified by three mechanisms: aggregation of voting rights through business groups, use of multiple class shares, and indirect ownership through pyramidal structures. In the latter, firms at the top are endowed with disproportionate voting rights over the cash flows generated by firms at the base, inducing asset diversion from the base up (Claessens *et al.*, 2002). On the other hand, the temptation for asset diversion may be curtailed when external financial markets are underdeveloped and relatively costly sources of funds. When the investment requirements of growing business opportunities exceed internally generated funds, equity represents the preferred source of funding. In this case, dominant shareholders avoid expropriating minority shareholders. Moreover, dominant shareholders may hold into significant cash-flow rights to signal its commitment not to expropriate minority shareholders.[1]

This research characterizes the ownership structure in Latin-American markets from a new perspective. In markets recognized by their weak protection for minority shareholders, dominant shareholders and their close collaborators assume managerial functions; alternatively, dominant shareholders closely monitor the firm's management. Blockholders may also strive to gain a seat on the board, file a law suit and/or obtain other benefits. Therefore, I assume that the management behaves in the interest of dominant shareholders and that blockholders are active monitors rather than passive investors (Bennedsen and Wolfenzon, 2000).[2]

To examine the argument of conflict of interests between shareholders, I develop a number of effective measures of share ownership. I use these measures to study the effect on firm value of ownership concentration and the discrepancy between voting rights and cash-flow rights for dominant shareholders. The role of blockholders is of particular interest. Depending on their ownership stakes and identity, blockholders may serve to either boost or depress investor confidence (McConnell and Servaes, 1990; Morck *et al.*, 1988; Demsetz and Villalonga, 2001; Bennedsen and Wolfenzon, 2000; Lins, 2003). La Porta *et al.* (1999) analyze the problem of monitoring families. My

[1]This approach diverges from La Porta *et al.* (1999) argument of bank-centered financial systems, where firms rely on debt finance and the controlling shareholder rarely has to issue equity to raise the funds.

[2]This framework questions the role of managers as independent decision makers and departs from Lins' (2003) approach, which studies management-controlled firms. I posit that the interests of managers are aligned with the dominant shareholder's interests. If the manager does not "belong" to the dominant shareholder's business group, he/she will have to compose with the dominant shareholder. For example, in 2005 at Ferreyros S.A.A., the largest holders of voting shares are two local pension funds (13.6% and 10.87%) and an insurance company (11.08%) and it is still managed by the founding family. The management has extensive power in operative and routine business decisions, but for strategic decisions, the institutional investors will be consulted.

approach extends this analysis, and focuses on the parties, whose role is to monitor the dominant shareholders. The results of this research project shed light on the motivations of investors to take large positions in firms in which there is potential for asset diversion.

There are a number of published academic works that study corporate governance mechanisms in individual countries (US: Agrawal and Knoeber, 1996; Canada: Switzer and Kelly, 2006) as well as multicountry or regional studies (East Asia: Claessens *et al.*, 2002; Western Europe: Faccio and Lang, 2002; Cross-country: Lins, 2003). Some studies focus on developed countries while others focus on emerging or transition economies. This investigation focuses on the Latin-American markets from a corporate governance perspective.

Figure 1 portrays the ownership concentration and interconnectedness of firms in the Latin-American sample. It represents a subsample of the firms and shareholders on the ownership database. Minimum holdings of 5% voting shares are represented by the ties (arrows) between firms and shareholders. Firms are represented by the circles originating from the arrows forming the remote semiellipse. Shareholders are represented by the circles receiving the head of the arrows, forming the nearest semiellipse. We should

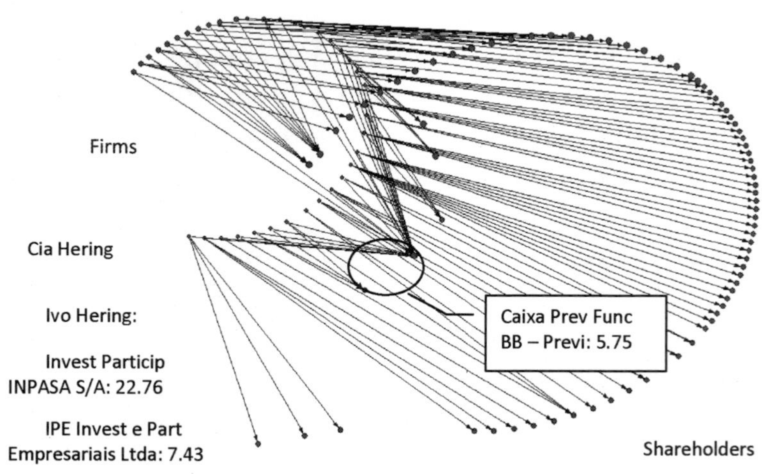

Figure 1. Ownership concentration and interconnectedness. Sub-network of firms and shareholders linked directly (or indirectly) to "Caixa Prev Func BB-Previ" through a minimum of 5% ownership of voting shares.

focus on the number of ties (arrows) each firm originates and each shareholder receives. Most of the firms in the subsample have in common "Caixa Prev Func BB-Previ" (center) as shareholder, or have another shareholder in common with a firm, where "Caixa Prev Func BB-Previ" has a stake. The ownership structure in Fig. 1 motivates the analysis in a regional setting. In this case, "Caixa Prev Func BB-Previ" is a large local pension fund. Its holdings of more than 5% of voting rights in many firms suggest its potential for a central role in the governance of a number of firms. It may as well be a passive investor and expend no resources in monitoring, but it would be difficult to justify that abdicating its monitoring role is consistent with its fiduciary duty toward investors and clients. Other shareholders important in the region (with many ties) are also present by the center of the figure. For an example, I have labeled Cia Hering, which has four shareholders with more than 5% of voting shares: Invest Particip INPASA S/A with 22.76%, Ivo Hering with 15.82%, IPE Invest e Part Empresariais Ltda. with 7.43% and Caixa Prev Func BB-Previ with 5.75%.

2. Empirical Approach: Aggregation of Voting Rights and Cash-Flow Rights

My analysis is based on a unique database that provides detailed ownership information for publicly traded firms from Brazil, Chile, Colombia, Peru, and Venezuela. Most of these firms are part of their respective country exchange index and hence may have liquidity advantages, relative to non-index firms.[3] The ownership database Economatica is matched to Bloomberg. The research focuses on the period 2000–2006, a period of relative stability and sustained growth.

From the ownership database, I obtain the names of 2,261 different shareholders holding voting and/or no voting shares, from the initial sample of 329 firms. The maximum number of shareholders per firm is 18 (three observations), with 62 observations indicating

[3]However, Nenova (2003) warns against survivorship bias by suggesting that firms where private benefits of control are higher could eventually delist, and Claessens *et al.* (2002) argue that covering only listed firms would create a bias in terms of ownership and firm valuation.

17 shareholders, and 318 observations with a solitary shareholder.[4] A given shareholder may occupy the dominant voting position in one firm, and be a marginal voting shareholder or just a non-voting shareholder in another firm or year. Additionally, a voting shareholder is frequently also a non-voting shareholder for the same firm-year, narrowing the discrepancy between voting rights and cash-flow rights.

I also obtain the percentage of voting and non-voting shares for each shareholder,[5] and the percentage of voting and non-voting shares owned by unnamed atomistic shareholders (floating shares) as well as the total number of voting and non-voting shares of the firm. Voting rights are numerically equal to the percentage of voting shares, assuming that all voting shares entitle the owner to one vote. Then, I calculate the cash-flow rights of each shareholder as the percentage of voting shares times the total number of voting shares of the firm plus the percentage of non-voting shares times the total number of non-voting shares. The sum is divided by the sum of total voting and non-voting shares. Cash-flow rights represent claims on future dividends.

When the shareholder is a corporation with an observable ownership structure, it (the management) is entitled only to the portion of cash-flow rights corresponding to its dominant shareholder, but to all the voting rights. I adjust the measure of cash-flow rights accordingly. Since voting rights are maintained intact while the cash-flow rights

[4]Bennedsen and Wolfenzon (2000) find that optimal ownership structures will have a single large shareholder or few large shareholders of similar size.

[5]Lins (2003) finds that managers of Latin-American firms frequently use shares with superior voting rights to increase the voting rights associated with their cash-flow rights. He reports a mean (median) of 45% (51%) of non-voting shares in the equity capital structure in Peru and Brazil. Nenova (2003) reports that dual-class shares are frequent in Brazil, but less so in Chile. Lefort and Walker (1999) also indicate that dual class shares are rare in Chile (7.5% of listed firms) while cross-holdings are forbidden by law. Valadares and Leal (2000) estate that in Brazil non-voting shares are frequently more liquid than the corresponding common shares. They note that Brazilian law allows the issuance of up to two non-voting shares for each voting share. Thus, in the extreme case the control of a Brazilian company could be obtained with 50% of the voting shares that represent only 16.7% of the total capital (control can be guaranteed with just 1/6 of its total capital). However, only 27% of Brazilian firms are close to the limit of non-voting shares. They find that 54% of equity is voting capital, but only 11% of Brazilian listed firms do not have non-voting shares.

are reassigned, these necessary recalculations likely weaken the cash-flow rights of corporation-shareholders and ultimately increase the discrepancy between voting rights and cash-flow rights. The resulting measures of voting rights and cash-flow rights are on the line the measures of ownership and control in Faccio and Lang (2002). The procedure designed with two nested steps takes care of pyramidal structures, of cross-ownership, and of diversion from the one-share-one-vote rule through the use of preferred stocks.[6]

One contribution of this study is to establish the identity of the shareholders. This identification facilitates an analysis of voting behavior by shareholders in business groups. A business group is an ad-hoc grouping, where distinct shareholders have ties such that during the shareholder's general meeting (or their representatives during the board of directors meeting) they will vote in the same direction in all matters, including actions that could expropriate other shareholders not members of coalition.

Being part of a business group may protect blockholders against expropriation by dominant shareholders. Since blockholders incur additional risk costs by holding undiversified portfolios, they may strengthen bargaining positions, and increase their predisposition to participate in expropriating minority shareholders. Moreover, otherwise unrelated, firms dominated by members of a business group may benefit from intrafirm financial transfers that are not necessarily market based, as in Claessens *et al.* (2002). Similarly, Lefort and Walker (1999) suggest that business groups may function as investment vehicles partially substituting for capital markets.

First, I identify each named shareholder as member of an intertemporal, cross-firm, business group or as a stand-alone investor.

[6]The aggregation procedure is integral, and is closer to the method of Lins (2003) than to Faccio and Lang's (2002) or Claessens *et al.* (2000), that use the "weakest link along the control chain" as a measure of voting rights, and the product as a measure of control rights. With the weakest link approach, a portion of voting rights are left unexercised. Lefort and Walker (1999) find that Chilean groups use relatively simple pyramid structures where four layers are rare. They point to large differences between personal tax rates and company tax rates to explain the wide use of holding companies. Valadares and Leal (2000) find that relatively flat pyramiding structures although common for Brazilian firms are not important means to separate ownership and control but to keep the control of the firm within the same family.

Grouping shareholder in business groups assures that all the siblings in a family (along with spouses, cousins, parents, and children) vote together (Claessens *et al.*, 2000). For example in 2005, Lucila, Barbara, Jaime, Carolina, Eduardo, Marian, Salvador, Silvia, and Patricia Gubbins G. own each one 7.99% of voting shares of Soc. Minera Corona. The Succession Reynaldo Gubbins Granger owns an additional 6.5%. With a cutoff level of 10%, it would be a publicly held firm; however, it is closely held at 78.41%. In the same way, the votes of all the shares owned by a mutual fund through different financial products or by a bank through different branches are cast in the same direction.[7] Thus, the voting rights of all members of a business group are aggregated.

Similarly, the cash-flow rights are aggregated. Cash-flow rights of voting shareholders are diluted, with respect to the simple percentage of voting shares, as cash-flow rights of other non-voting shareholders are taken into account. As a consequence, failing to aggregate voting and non-voting shares across members of a business group would result in a narrower (wider) voting rights/cash-flow rights discrepancy, if the unaccounted percentage of voting shares were larger (smaller) than the unaccounted percentage of non-voting shares.

Then, I reorganize the newly aggregated shareholders according to the level of voting rights and establish a direct correspondence between voting rights and cash-flow rights for each shareholder. Aggregating voting rights may consolidate the position of dominant shareholders, but previously dominant shareholders can also be overthrown by grouping siblings that become more powerful after aggregation. Finally, as treasury stocks are controlled by the firm's management, I assign any treasury stocks' voting rights and cash-flow rights to dominant shareholders.

[7] A mutual fund may offer a capital-preserving fund, a capital-growth fund, and an aggressive-growth fund to his clients. Such products designed to accommodate different risk-aversion profiles may invest different proportions of the capital in given markets and companies. Moreover, they may have independent flags for increasing and reducing exposure to idiosyncratic risk, but when converging as shareholders in a firm, their votes are aggregated. Such cases indeed occur in the database.

In some cases, by looking just at shareholders' names, it would not be evident why they should vote together, thus a detailed analysis is necessary to realize their tied relationships.[8] Members of a coalition have common family names, have similar firm names likely to be copyright, or have multifirm relationships (meeting at many firms). Group membership was double checked and members' voting rights are effectively aggregated when they meet on the same firm-year. Thus, "over grouping" would not have major effects; "under grouping" will more likely occur, due to limitations in finding the reasonable links between shareholders.

I group 793 shareholders in 225 business groups. The most populated business group has 24 members, the second most populated group has 17 different members, and there are 114 groups with just two members. A given shareholder may appear in the database in multiple opportunities, holding shares in different firms and years, but no shareholder will appear as member of two groups, nor as a group member and individually.

Figure 2 shows, on the inclined coordinate plane, the percentage of voting rights (from right to left) and cash-flow rights (from front to back) for dominant shareholders of firms in the sample (all years). Observations off the main diagonal indicate more voting rights than cash-flow rights for dominant shareholders, and thus incentives for asset diversion. In addition, Fig. 2 also gives a perception of the ownership concentration in these markets. Dominant shareholders concentrate most voting rights, leaving little room for other blockholders, when they exist at all. Floating shares are scarce, and voting shares float less than non-voting shares. Dominant shareholders frequently choose holding voting rights that exceed cash-flow rights reducing the own portion of the costs of asset diversion.

The vertical axis indicates Tobin's Q ratios for the firm-year observation. Market participants seem to valuate higher those firms

---

[8]Corporate documentation, analyst reports, and previous work were reviewed to confirm group membership. As any matching procedure, this will also be imperfect. The debate should center on whether it introduces bias to the sample or just noise to the ownership measures (Lins, 2003).

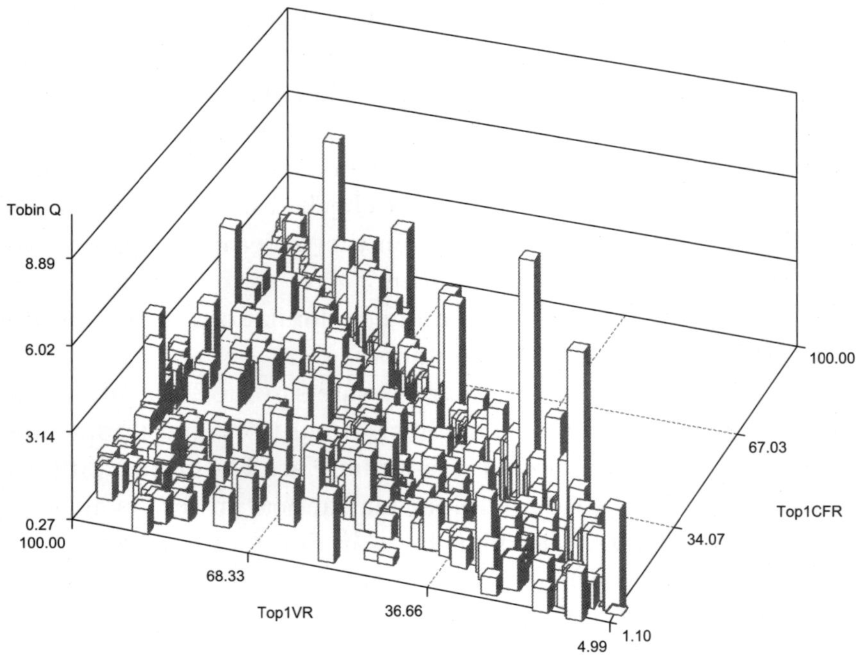

Figure 2. Ownership of dominant shareholders and firm value.

in which the discrepancy between voting rights and cash-flow rights is lower. However, having a balance between voting rights and cash-flow rights is not enough to guarantee high firm value. The variation on firm valuation along and near the main diagonal of zero discrepancy represents differentials on management ability, firm characteristics, market conditions, risks associated with industry effects and country-specific environments. Additional variability on firm valuation off-diagonal represents dominant shareholders' pre-commitment not to expropriate minority shareholders. The populated off-diagonal zone shows the necessity and willingness to finance the firm's activity beyond the availability of debt financing. Since the evidence shows similar market valuation at difference positions on the plane, some governance mechanisms should be in place to help protect minority shareholders. The identity of dominant shareholders plays an important role to credibly signal the degree of potential asset diversion.

Extending Faccio and Lang (2002), Claessens *et al.* (2002), and Lins (2003), the 793 shareholders members of the business groups and the 1,468 standalone investors are further classified into five categories. The purpose of the classification is to predict their behavior (the direction of their votes) in cases of imminent conflict of interests between dominant and minority shareholders. These excluding categories are Family, Institutional Investor, Corporation, Other, and Government. All members of a business group are in the same category. For example, a family-controlled corporation that appears as a shareholder in another firm is assigned to a family business group and behaves as a family member. Similarly, a government-controlled bank behaves as a government agency when it appears as a shareholder in another firm. The shareholder categories represent a first level of monitoring by blockholders as they can influence each other, dominant shareholders and managers. *A priori*, a specific behavior may be expected from the different categories of investors:

Family business group's members as well as individual investors (families of just one member) may favor expropriating minority shareholders and colluding with other shareholders to do so. However, for reputational reasons, they may refrain from consuming excessive private benefits of control.

Members of the Institutional Investor category such as banks, investment banks, mutual funds, pension funds, insurance companies, stock brokers, and stock exchanges[9] are legally obligated and functionally oriented to increasing the value of the firms in which they have interests. They presumably have the expertise and the resources to monitor, and meaningfully influence corporate actions and elect capable board members. Furthermore, most of these investors comply with their own strict governance codes and are likely to impose governance standards on the firms they control or influence, thus asset diversion and minority shareholders' expropriation are less likely.

In general, institutional investors will be against expropriation, will not collude with other shareholders, and will likely block expropriation attempts. Moreover, the mere presence of institutional

[9]In Peru, stock brokers include such denomination on their legal names.

investor shareholders may dissuade the dominant shareholder from engaging in expropriation activity to avoid waking up monitoring activity. Even if individually institutional investors look weak or distant, a large number of them may get organized and join voting rights when dominant shareholders excessively consume private benefits of control. Additionally, very well-known corporations that are cross-listed on international stock exchanges are included as institutional investors because they have strict governance mechanisms on their own, which are likely exported along with their capital to the firms they invest in. In fact, they would likely block expropriation attempts by dominant shareholders. They would also not compromise strategic alliances that may be key to enter emerging markets. This assumption does not preclude engaging in anticompetitive behavior in product markets.

Corporations in general are likely to engage in expropriation practices, but may also have the ability to block them. Moreover, belonging to a powerful business group may reduce the chances of being the victims of expropriation and may increase the chances of being "invited" to join forces and consume a portion of the private benefits as in Bennedsen and Wolfenzon (2000). However, Claessens *et al.* (2002) claim that managers of firms controlled by both widely held corporations and institutional investors have less opportunity to efficiently divert assets.

The few distinct shareholders under the classification "Others" are institutions of different kinds, such as fiduciaries (income trusts), foundations, cooperatives, religious organizations, active and retired employee associations, social security networks, fraternities, cultural foundations, universities, and educational foundations. When they are not related to any business group, and if properly run, they would behave as corporations. They are however few, and relatively powerless, and for subsequent analysis and reporting, they are subsumed into the Corporation category.

Shareholders classified as "Government" are federal, provincial, or municipal governments or government agencies, banks, development agencies, and firms owned by governments, such as utilities or natural resources companies. They may be part of a business group, meaning in this case that their representatives, when they meet at the boardroom, would vote in the same direction, probably following the most influential of them. This assumption makes sense if most government representatives have partisan allegiances, are disciplined and likely to rotate from one position to another and even in and out of political appointments. Governments would behave much as institutional investors blocking the asset diversion. However, some authors have suggested that politicians would appropriate private benefits or collude with management (or dominant shareholders) to do so. Government-controlled firms may also obtain preferential subsidies, which could be of benefit. On the other hand, they may be subject to greater pressure from unions.

3. Literature Review

The theoretical model of Bennedsen and Wolfenzon (2000) for closely held corporations shows that the founder of the firm can use control dilution as a mechanism to reduce the asset diversion, which would be harmful for him. In their model, some shareholders are large enough not to surrender control to the manager, but none is large enough to obtain control by himself. Diverting assets from the firm requires the consent of a coalition of large blockholders, and the winning coalition minimizes its cash-flow rights.

La Porta *et al.* (1999) find that families or the state typically controls most large corporations in 27 wealthy economies, in 1995. Additionally, the power of the controlling shareholder exceeds his cash-flow rights, and dispersed ownership is more of an exception in countries with poor shareholder protection, which tend to have civil law tradition.[10] They suggest that a mandatory rule of one-share-one-vote will have little impact as long as pyramids remain the principal vehicle to separate ownership and control.

McConnell and Servaes (1990) investigate the cross-sectional relationship between firm value and equity ownership for a sample of U.S. firms for years 1976 and 1986. They find that firm value first increases with insider ownership (alignment effects), and then it declines (entrenchment effects). Their sample average of inside

---

[10]All the countries in the Latin-American sample have civil law tradition (La Porta *et al.*, 1998).

ownership is about 13.9% and 11.84% for each period, and the inflexion point is close to 37%. In addition, they find no support for the hypothesis that blockholders have an independent effect on corporate value, but cannot reject the conjecture that large blockholders and insider ownership operate in conjunction. Their results, however, do suggest that institutional ownership reinforce the positive effects of insider ownership on corporate value (efficient monitoring hypothesis). They also outline the potential endogenous problem (managers and founders can be more inclined to retain a large fraction of successful firms/managers of successful firms are more likely to be rewarded with additional stocks).

Claessens *et al.* (2002) find that firm value increases with the cash-flow ownership of the largest shareholder, consistent with a positive incentive effect, for their sample of 1,301 publicly trade firms in eight East Asian economies in 1996. However, firm value falls when control rights exceeded cash-flow rights for the dominant shareholder (entrenchment effect). Finally, they find that the separation of ownership and control in general, and not any mechanism in particular (pyramidal structures, dual-class shares, cross-holdings), is responsible for value discount.

Faccio and Lang (2002) analyze the ultimate ownership and control of 5,232 corporations in 13 Western European countries, from 1996 to 1999. They find that firms are typically widely held (36.93%) or family controlled (44.29%) with financial and large firms more likely to be widely held, while non-financial and small firms are more likely to be family-controlled. In some countries, widely held financial institutions or the government may be important controlling shareholders, but widely held corporations control few firms. Although dual class shares, multiple control chains, cross-holdings and pyramidal structures are used to enhance the control of the largest shareholders; on average, the discrepancies between ownership (38.48%) and control (34.64%) are significant just in few countries. Closely controlled firms often have a sole control shareholder at the 10% cutoff level (53.99%).[11]

[11]Miller *et al.* (2007) distinguish between lone founder business and true family business, and find that only the former outperform public firms in the U.S., for the period 1996–2000.

In Lins (2003), management groups own on average 30% of firms and are the largest blockholders in 2/3 of their sample, while non-management blockholders own 20% of voting rights. He uses a cross-sectional sample of 1,433 public firms from 18 emerging markets for the year 1995, which predates my sample. For the robustness test, he uses a two simultaneous equations model to account for endogeneity between ownership and firm value (firm value is lower as a result of expected costly agency problems/if a manager expects lower cash-flow he would tend to increase the discrepancy between his voting rights and his cash-flow rights). He finds support for the managerial entrenchment hypothesis and concludes that the costs of the private benefits of control are capitalized into share prices in emerging markets. Additionally, he finds evidence that large non-management blockholders can reduce the valuation discount associated with expected managerial agency problems acting as a partial substitute for missing institutional governance mechanisms. He also shows that firm value declines as the separation of management group control and cash-flow rights gets larger. Finally, he suggests that future research should study why Latin-American firms use non-voting equity structures with such frequency.

Nenova (2003) analyzes a sample of 661 dual-class firms in 18 countries for the year 1997, developing an approach where a shareholder competing for control is willing to pay minority vote-owners a price up to his expected value of private benefits of control. Therefore, vote value can be identified as a lower bound of control benefits. She finds that control-block votes are value at more than a quarter of company market capitalization in Brazil and Chile.

Lefort and Walker (1999) describe the ownership of non-financial Chilean conglomerates. They consolidate the balance sheet of firms in defined economic groups to analyze the level of firm assets that are financed by minority shareholders' equity and debt. They indicate that pyramids are often used to separate ownership and control, and that controllers of Chilean conglomerates hold more shares than necessary to maintain control, suggesting potential large private benefits of controlling the cash-flow form subsidiaries. In addition, they find that board members are exclusively appointed within firms associated to their economic groups, indicating that economic groups do not collaborate with each other. Finally, pension funds and cross-listed shares (ADRs) constitute significant equity minorities.

Valadares and Leal (2000) show a high degree of ownership concentration for Brazilian public firms. The biggest shareholders have, on average, 41% of the equity capital, while the five biggest have 61% for their sample of 325 firms in 1996. In 62% of the companies, a single shareholder owns more than 50% of the voting shares. They outline that corporations are the main direct investors, while individuals are the more important indirect owners (through pyramiding or cross-holdings).

4. Description of the Data

Descriptive statistics[12] for the sample are shown in Table 1. When I filter the data imposing that Tobin's Q ratios — defined as total liabilities and market value of equity divided by total assets — are between 0 and 10, I accept 1,179 valid observations.[13] The average firm in the sample has a Tobin's Q value of 1.19. The average (median) firm has a leverage ratio of 0.54 (0.52), defined as total liabilities divided by total assets. In terms of total assets, the average (median) size of the firms in the sample is 3,955 millions of US$ (891 millions of US$), comparable to the size of the firms in Lins (2003). Nenova (2003) conjectures that large firms are subject to greater scrutiny, which would make it costlier for them to extract private benefits. Claessens *et al.* (2002) suggest that larger and older firms also have better disclosure, are more diversified, their stocks are more liquid, and are followed by more analysts, but have fewer growth opportunities.

Table 2, Panel A provides the geographical distribution of the sample. Brazilian (582 observations) and Chilean firms (269 observations) are the largest, and also outnumber firms in other

[12]Most variables are collected at the firm level. Security-specific volatility provides a measure of non-diversifiable risk. With multiple class shares, volatility is calculated for the most recently traded security.

[13]McConnell and Servaes (1990) delete firms with Q ratios larger than 6.0. Lins (2003) censors Q at the 1st and 99th percentiles.

Table 1. Statistics summary.

Variable	*N*	Mean	Std. dev.	Min	Max	Count
Tobin's Q	1,179	1.19	0.66	0.27	8.89	1,179
Largest Shareholder						
Top1VR	1,179	55.78	25.5	4.99	100	1,179
GAP1	1,179	16.29	21.59	−7.78	87.04	694
RAT1	1,179	0.73	0.3	0.03	1.11	694
cfcon1	1,179	0.77	0.42	0	1	905
Blockholders						
TOP2_3	1,179	8.98	9.94	0	50	781
BHS	1,179	17.02	17.59	0	76.03	834
BHD	1,179	0.72	0.45	0	1	854
INSOWN	1,179	5.6	9.57	0	58.05	462
GOVOWN	1,179	1.65	5.45	0	42.27	167
CIGOWN	1,179	7.1	10.68	0	58.05	563
Firm characteristics						
Size	1,179	3,955	11,468	4.4	138,763	1,179
Lsize	1,179	6.88	1.62	1.48	11.84	1,179
Leverage	1,179	0.54	0.23	0.02	3.11	1,179
Volatility	1,179	0.47	0.25	0	2.56	1,177

Note: Tobin's Q = (Total liabilities + market value of equity)/(total assets). TOP1VR, the percentage of voting rights held by the dominant shareholder. GAP1, the difference of the percentage of voting rights and the percentage of cash-flow rights held by the dominant shareholder. RAT1, the ratio of the percentage of cash-flow rights to the percentage of voting rights held by the dominant shareholder. TOP2_3, the percentage of voting rights held by the second largest shareholder provided that it is not an institutional investor or government (if the second largest shareholder is an institutional investor or government, I take the percentage voting rights held by the third largest shareholder provided that it is not an institutional investor or government). BHS, the sum of the percentage of voting rights held by all large blockholders (Family + Corp + Other) excluding dominant shareholders. BHD, an indicator variable equal to 1 if an aggregated blockholder exists, as defined in BHS, 0 otherwise. INSOWN, the percentage of voting rights held by institutional investors excluding dominant shareholders. GOVOWN, the percentage of voting rights held by governments excluding dominant shareholders. CIGOWN = INSOWN + GOVOWN, the percentage of voting rights held by combined institutional investors and governments excluding dominant shareholders. Cfcon1, a dummy variable that takes the value of 1 if the dominant shareholder is a corporation or member of a family group, and 0 otherwise. Size = total assets in USD$ MM. Lsize = log(size). Leverage = total liabilities/total assets. Volatility = standard deviation of monthly stock price returns for the past 24 months. The column count indicates how many observations are not 0 for those variables (not 1 for Rat1). 670 obs. are > 0 for GAP1.

countries. Table 2, Panel B presents the number of observations by country and year. There are 126 observations in 2006, 186 observations in 2005, 182 observations in 2004, 170 observations in 2003, 168 observations in 2002, 174 observations in 2001, and 173 observations in year 2000.

Table 2. Data set characteristics: time and geographic distribution by investor type.

Panel A. Number of observations by country and shareholder type for the dominant shareholder.

Country	Family	Corporation	Institutional	Government	Total
Brazil	72	401	50	59	582
Chile	16	165	75	13	269
Colombia	5	93	10	3	111
Peru	36	87	40	8	171
Venezuela	4	26	16	0	46
Total	133	772	191	83	1,179

Panel B. Number of observations by country and year.

Country	2000	2001	2002	2003	2004	2005	2006	Total
Brazil	80	82	81	75	81	97	86	582
Chile	40	38	38	41	41	39	32	269
Colombia	18	17	18	20	20	18	0	111
Peru	24	28	31	24	31	27	6	171
Venezuela	11	9	0	10	9	5	2	46
Total	173	174	168	170	182	186	126	1,179

Dominant shareholders depending on their identities and the levels of discrepancy between voting right and cash-flow rights may be tempted to expropriate minority shareholders. Table 3 shows the data statistics for voting rights and cash-flow rights by shareholder classification. On average, for non-floating shares, the range of voting rights (cash-flow rights) is from 5.68% (2.25%) to 100% (100%), with a mean of 63.91% (48.6%). Voting rights also exceed cash-flow rights for non-floating shares when averaging across all the shareholders of a given category. For example, institutional investors have on average 33.39% of voting rights but only 27.98% of cash-flow rights. On the other hand, for floating shares owned by unnamed atomistic investors, the range of voting rights (cash-flow rights) is from 0.01% (0.15%) to 94.32% (94.32%) with a mean of 21.23% (32.55%). This figures confirming their exposure to asset expropriation vis-à-vis blockholders.

However, less than absolutely powerful dominant shareholders may decide to collude with the second or the third largest shareholder in the firm, depending of their identities and discrepancy between

Table 3. Frequency distribution and percentage of voting rights and cash-flow rights by shareholder type.

	Family	Institutional	Corporate	Government	Sample	Float
Voting rights						
Frequency	368	540	1,023	225	—	1,116
Minimum	0.01	0.04	0.3	0.06	5.68	0.01
Maximum	99.99	100	96.28	99.86	100	94.32
Average	25.82	33.39	58.44	30.64	63.91	21.23
Cash-flow rights						
Frequency	370	552	1,026	236	—	1,142
Minimum	0.01	0.04	0.3	0.06	2.25	0.15
Maximum	99.85	99.51	91	94.42	100	94.32
Average	17.06	27.98	43.15	23.74	48.6	32.55

Note: Number of observations, minimum, maximum, and average voting rights and cash-flow rights, by shareholder category for non-floating shares and floating shares. The column "Sample" refers to all identifiable shareholders (non-floating shares) independently of their identities.

voting rights and cash-flow rights, to obtain, maintain or strengthen the control of the firm, and/or expropriate minority shareholders. Table 4, Panel A, shows that there are independent shareholders, as well as business group members in all four categories for the three largest shareholders. In addition, there are only 944 observations with a second largest shareholder — in terms of voting rights — that may monitor, challenge, or collude with dominant shareholders, out of the 1,179 observations. Similarly, there are only 764 third largest shareholders.

Table 4, Panel B, shows the percentage of voting rights and cash-flow rights by shareholder type, for the three largest shareholders.[14] The dominant shareholder in these firms has between 4.99% (1.1%) and 100% (99.85%) of voting rights (cash-flow rights), and on average has 55.78% (39.48%). On average, the three largest shareholders have more voting rights than cash-flow rights independent of its identity (except by the government as the second largest shareholder). Thus dominant shareholders have not only incentives to divert assets from the firm, but they may also count with the

[14]Claessens *et al.* (2002) calculate the wedge just for the larger shareholder.

Table 4. Frequency and percentage of voting rights and cash-flow rights by shareholder type, for the three largest shareholders.

Panel A. Distribution of observations for the three larger (aggregated) shareholders, by category. Only non-null holdings are reported in this table.

	Family	Institutional	Corporation	Government	Total
Largest Shareholders	133	191	772	83	1,179
Group members	114	174	342	54	684
Independents	19	17	430	29	495
2nd Largest Shareholders	55	184	629	76	944
Group members	40	131	170	33	374
Independents	15	53	459	43	570
3rd Largest Shareholders	62	201	457	44	764
Group members	18	143	69	22	252
Independents	44	58	388	22	512

Panel B. Voting rights and cash-flow rights for the three larger (aggregated) shareholders, by category. Only non-null holdings are reported in this table.

Largest Shareholders	Family	Institutional	Corporation	Government	Sample
Minimum VR	12.28	8.16	4.99	8.93	4.99
Maximum VR	99.99	99.51	100	99.86	100
Mean voting rights	58.42	60.72	53.68	59.67	55.78
Mean cash-flow rights	37.33	52.29	36.36	42.52	39.48
Maximum CFR	99.85	99.49	99.71	94.42	99.85
Minimum CFR	6.21	1.54	1.1	8.93	1.1
2nd Largest Shareholders	Family	Institutional	Corporation	Government	Sample
Minimum VR	0.08	0.07	0.04	0.06	0.04
Maximum VR	37.34	40	50	42.27	50
Mean voting rights	10.69	12.77	14.84	15.63	14.26
Mean cash-flow rights	8.08	10.9	11.74	16.44	11.74
Maximum CFR	37.34	56.02	54.81	42.27	56.02
Minimum CFR	1.05	0.07	0.04	0.06	0.04
3rd Largest Shareholders	Family	Institutional	Corporation	Government	Sample
Minimum VR	0.01	0.05	0.01	0.65	0.01
Maximum VR	18.49	20.52	28	16.22	28
Mean voting rights	8.97	7.51	8.48	7.82	8.22
Mean cash-flow rights	6.73	6.08	7.27	6.735	6.88
Maximum CFR	16.17	18.17	27.47	16.22	27.47
Minimum CFR	0.01	0.003	0.04	0.65	0.003

complicity of other blockholders. For example, when the dominant shareholder is a corporation (772 observations), on average it has 53.68% of voting rights and only 36.63% of cash flow rights. However, from Table 4, Panel A, there are only 629 cases, where the second larger shareholder is a corporation. Chances are that some of the 772 dominant corporate shareholders do not have a second largest shareholder to deal with, or that when it exists, it is not also a corporation, then communication and collusion for expropriation may be more difficult.

5. Results

The structure of the ownership database allows for a panel data analysis. This is one of the first corporate governance studies to apply panel data techniques to a set of firms in different emerging countries.[15] *A priori*, the OLS variance matrix based on iid errors may be inadequate since the errors for a given firm are likely to be correlated over time (Petersen, 2009). First, assuming homoskedastic disturbances, I perform Breusch-Pagan (1980) LM tests for firm-specific effects (not reported), and the pooled OLS specification is rejected due to the presence of unobserved heterogeneity. Unobserved heterogeneity refers to unobserved individual firm effects, which are omitted random variables potentially correlated with the regressors. The choice to compute the regression coefficients rests between a random effects and a fixed effects specification. The former assumes that the unobserved firms-specific effects are uncorrelated with all the regressors (a strong assumption) while the later allows for unspecified forms of covariance. However, with the fixed effects specification, the coefficients of time-invariant regressors are not identified. Second, having confirmed the presence of unobservable heterogeneity, I use a Hausman (1978) type test to distinguish between random and fixed effects. Under the null hypothesis of the test, both the random-effect estimator and the fixed-effect estimator are consistent but the random-effect estimator is efficient; thus any

[15]See also Gottesman *et al.* (2007).

difference in the estimated variance is due to sampling error. The test statistic is χ^2 distributed with degrees of freedom equal to the number of time-varying regressors. Under the alternative hypothesis, the random-effect estimator is inconsistent. A large test statistic rejects the null hypothesis for given confidence levels. The test (unreported) rejects the random effects specification.

The fixed effect specification, which is retained, allows for the inclusion of firm-specific effects not only in the computation of the regression coefficients, but also in the calculation of the standard errors. It allows for disturbances that are heteroskedastic and autocorrelated across time for each firm, but uncorrelated across firms. However, Driscoll and Kraay (1998) approach allows for standard errors, which are robust to general forms of cross-sectional and temporal dependence. This spatial correlation may compensate for the restriction to directly control for country or industry effects under the fixed effect specification. Moreover, the ownership concentration and interconnectedness of firms in the Latin-American sample revealed in Fig. 1 suggest contemporaneous cross-sectional correlations for the disturbances.

The Driscoll and Kraay's covariance estimator is implemented in Stata for pooled and fixed-effects (within) regression. Driscoll and Kraay (1998) approach uses a GMM estimator in which the orthogonality conditions have been averaged across firms in each year (cross-sectionally). Then a consistent estimator of the variance is estimated using Newey-West (1987) spectral density matrix estimation techniques. The structure of standard errors for coefficient estimates is assumed to be heteroskedastic, autocorrelated up to lag ($T-1=6$), and possibly correlated between firms. I report the pooled regressions estimates along with the within regression estimates, to directly include the country effects with dummy variables.

The focus of the regression analysis is to show evidence of the market anticipation for potential conflict of interests between large shareholders in a highly concentrated market. Investors would judge the managerial ability of dominant shareholders and his collaborators along with its appetite for extracting large benefits of control. In addition, other large stakeholders may influence the management of such firms.

I regress a proxy for firm value (Tobin's Q) on several ownership variables, which characterize the holdings and identity of dominant shareholders:

- RAT1, the ratio of the percentage of cash-flow rights to the percentage of voting rights held by the dominant shareholder. The larger the ratio, the lower the incentives for private consumption.
- GAP1, the difference of the percentage of voting rights and the percentage of cash-flow rights held by the dominant shareholder. The larger the gap, the higher the incentives for private consumption.
- Cfcon1, a dummy variable that takes the value of 1 if the dominant shareholder is a corporation or member of a family group, and zero otherwise.

Then, I examine the role of large stakeholders and their potential for monitoring or colluding with dominant shareholders:

- TOP2_3, the percentage of voting rights held by the second largest shareholder provided that it is not an institutional investor or government (if the second largest shareholder is an institutional investor or government, I take the percentage voting rights held by the third largest shareholder provided that it is not an institutional investor or government).
- BHS, the sum of the percentage of voting rights held by all large blockholders (Family + Corp + Other) excluding dominant shareholders.
- BHD, an indicator variable equal to 1 if an aggregated blockholder exists, as defined in BHS, 0 otherwise.
- INSOWN, the percentage of voting rights held by institutional investors excluding dominant shareholders.
- GOVOWN, the percentage of voting rights held by governments excluding dominant shareholders.
- CIGOWN = INSOWN + GOVOWN, the percentage of voting rights held by combined institutional investors and governments excluding dominant shareholders.

The regressions' specification includes year dummies, and for the pooled regressions country dummies. The country and year of comparison are Brazil and year 2000, respectively. I control for differences in firm size (log of total assets), leverage, and firms' idiosyncratic risk.

Table 5 provides the simple correlation matrix of the variables in the regression analysis. The negative relationship between firm value and the dominant shareholder's voting rights is already found on the bivariate correlations. Similarly, a positive relationship between firm value and voting rights for blockholders is advanced by the correlation coefficients suggesting a potential monitoring role for the later. Similarly, notice the negative correlation between dominant shareholders' voting rights and other blockholders' voting rights as an indication of the ownership concentration in these markets as was shown in Figs. 1 and 2. Finally, the negative correlation involving dominant shareholders' discrepancy between voting rights and cash-flow rights and other blockholders' voting rights may reflect the resistance from blockholders to invest in firms with already large potential private consumption by dominant shareholders.

The negative signs for the coefficient of GAP1 in Table 7 indicate the pessimism from market participants about large ownership concentration. Consistently, the cash-flow rights/voting rights ratio (RAT1) is positively related to firm value in Table 6. Since asset diversion is inefficient, market participants seem to appreciate that dominant shareholders accumulate cash-flow rights reducing their own incentives for consumption.

The positive coefficient of cfcon1 suggests that despite the stake of the dominant shareholder, market participants prefer the dominant stakeholder to be a corporation or a family member as opposed to a government or an institutional investor. Firms dominated by a government agency may pursue a political agenda that is not necessarily consistent with shareholders' wealth maximization. The limited confidence toward institutional investors as effective managers may reflect the small weight on the total portfolio that its stake on the firm represents. Therefore, despite the difficulty for institutional shareholders to divert funds away from the firm, the management may

Table 5. Correlation matrix of the variables in the regression analysis. 1,179 observations, 242 firms, 5 countries, 2000–2006.

	Tobin's Q	Top1VR	gap1	RAT1	TOP2_3	BHS	BHD	CIGOWN	INSOWN	GOVOWN	Cfcon1	Lsize	Leverage
Tobin's Q	1												
Top1VR		1											
gap1		0.4638*	1										
RAT1		−0.1872*	−0.8782*	1									
TOP2_3		−0.3943*	−0.2174*	0.1011*	1								
BHS	0.0608*	−0.6090*	−0.3158*	0.1519*	0.8026*	1							
BHD		−0.4742*	−0.2492*	0.0807*	0.5575*	0.5974*	1						
CIGOWN		−0.3454*	−0.2313*	0.1324*	−0.0962*		0.0856*	1					
INSOWN		−0.3140*	−0.2174*	0.1273*	−0.0971*		0.1141*	0.8605*	1				
GOVOWN		−0.1250*	−0.0711*					0.4471*	−0.0709*	1			
Cfcon1	0.1228*	−0.0999*	0.1332*	−0.1504*	0.0999*	0.1846*	0.1504*	−0.0989*	−0.0972*		1		
Lsize		0.0809*	0.1200*	−0.1425*	−0.0566	−0.0896*	−0.1115*		−0.0651*	0.0980*	−0.2662*	1	
Leverage	0.0678*	0.1799*	0.1552*	−0.1411*				−0.1083*	−0.1365*		−0.0812*	0.2243*	1
Volatility	−0.0511	0.1128*	0.1527*	−0.1363*		−0.0593*	−0.1359*	−0.1343*	−0.1899*	0.0704*	0.0789*	−0.1949*	0.1634*

Note: Tobin's Q = (Total liabilities + market value of equity)/(total assets). TOP1VR, the percentage of voting rights held by the dominant shareholder. GAP1, the difference of the percentage of voting rights and the percentage of cash-flow rights held by the dominant shareholder. RAT1, the ratio of the percentage of cash-flow rights to the percentage of voting rights held by the dominant shareholder. TOP2_3, the percentage of voting rights held by the second largest shareholder provided that it is not an institutional investor or government (if the second largest shareholder is an institutional investor or government, I take the percentage voting rights held by the third largest shareholder provided that it is not an institutional investor or government). BHS, the sum of the percentage of voting rights held by all large blockholders (Family + Corp + Other) excluding dominant shareholders. BHD, an indicator variable equal to 1 if an aggregated blockholder exists, as defined in BHS, 0 otherwise. INSOWN, the percentage of voting rights held by institutional investors excluding dominant shareholders. GOVOWN, the percentage of voting rights held by governments excluding dominant shareholders. CIGOWN = INSOWN + GOVOWN, the percentage of voting rights held by combined institutional investors and governments excluding dominant shareholders. Cfcon1, a dummy variable that takes the value of 1 if the dominant shareholder is a corporation or member of a family group, and 0 otherwise. Lsize = log (total assets). Leverage = total liabilities/total assets. Volatility = standard deviation of monthly stock price returns for the past 24 months. The stars denote a significance level of 5%. Values omitted are not significant at the 10% level.

Table 6. Effects of block holding on firm value. 1,179 observations, 242 firms, 5 countries, 2000–2006.

	OLS	OLS	OLS	OLS	OLS	OLS	OLS	FE	FE	FE	FE	FE	FE	FE
RAT1	0.237	0.23	0.221	0.239	0.238	0.24	0.239	0.536	0.542	0.543	0.54	0.52	0.525	0.535
	0.040**	0.050**	0.067*	0.037**	0.040**	0.040**	0.038**	0.003***	0.001***	0.001***	0.002***	0.003***	0.003***	0.003***
TOP2_3		0.002							0.004					
		0.000***							0.007***					
BHS			0.002							0.003				
			0.006***							0.010**				
BHD				0.033							0.048			
				0.381							0.053*			
CIGOWN					0							−0.004		
					0.538							0.113		
INSOWN						0.001							−0.003	
						0.063*							0.12	
GOVOWN							−0.002							−0.001
							0.018**							0.446
Cfcon1	0.207	0.203	0.188	0.201	0.208	0.209	0.207	0.121	0.135	0.138	0.118	0.146	0.132	0.124
	0.000***	0.000***	0.000***	0.000***	0.000***	0.000***	0.000***	0.001***	0.000***	0.000***	0.001***	0.000***	0.000***	0.000***
Lsize	−0.026	−0.026	−0.025	−0.025	−0.026	−0.025	−0.025	−0.074	−0.075	−0.076	−0.077	−0.071	−0.072	−0.074
	0.012**	0.013**	0.017**	0.026**	0.011**	0.011**	0.017**	0.019**	0.016**	0.015**	0.017**	0.029**	0.025**	0.019**

(Continued)

Table 6. (*Continued*)

	OLS	OLS	OLS	OLS	OLS	OLS	OLS	FE	FE	FE	FE	FE	FE	FE
Volatility	−0.087	−0.085	−0.081	−0.082	−0.088	−0.086	−0.081	0.258	0.262	0.259	0.262	0.254	0.256	0.258
	0.148	0.151	0.163	0.146	0.136	0.163	0.163	0.000***	0.000***	0.000***	0.000***	0.000***	0.000***	0.000***
Leverage	0.211	0.208	0.2	0.207	0.212	0.214	0.21	0.585	0.585	0.584	0.582	0.594	0.588	0.587
	0.000***	0.000***	0.000***	0.000***	0.000***	0.000***	0.000***	0.000***	0.000***	0.000***	0.000***	0.000***	0.000***	0.000***
R-sq	0.169	0.17	0.172	0.17	0.169	0.17	0.17							

Note: This table reports regression results of pooled OLS and fix-effects (FE) regression using Driscoll and Kraay (1998) estimation. The dependent variable is Tobin's Q = (total liabilities + market value of equity)/(total assets). The explanatory variables are: RAT1, the ratio of the percentage of cash-flow rights to the percentage of voting rights held by the dominant shareholder. TOP2_3, the percentage of voting rights held by the second largest shareholder provided that it is not an institutional investor or government (if the second largest shareholder is an institutional investor or government, I take the percentage voting rights held by the third largest shareholder provided that it is not an institutional investor or government). BHS, the sum of the percentage of voting rights held by all large blockholders (Family + Corp + Other) excluding dominant shareholders. BHD, an indicator variable equal to 1 if an aggregated blockholder exists, as defined in BHS, 0 otherwise. INSOWN, the percentage of voting rights held by institutional investors excluding dominant shareholders. GOVOWN, the percentage of voting rights held by governments excluding dominant shareholders. CIGOWN = INSOWN + GOVOWN, the percentage of voting rights held by combined institutional investors and governments excluding dominant shareholders. Cfcon1, a dummy variable that takes the value of 1 if the dominant shareholder is a corporation or member of a family group, and 0 otherwise. Lsize = log (total assets). Leverage = total liabilities/total assets. Volatility = standard deviation of monthly stock price returns for the past 24 months. Country dummy variables and year dummy variables coefficients and the constant are not reported. *p*-values are reported in parenthesis; ***, ** and * indicate that the coefficient is statistically different from 0 at the 1%, 5%, and 10% levels, respectively.

Table 7. Effects of block holding on firm value. 1,179 observations, 242 firms, 5 countries, 2000–2006.

	OLS	OLS	OLS	OLS	OLS	OLS	OLS	FE	FE	FE	FE	FE	FE	FE
GAP1	−0.003	−0.003	−0.002	−0.003	−0.003	−0.003	−0.003	−0.004	−0.004	−0.004	−0.004	−0.004	−0.004	−0.004
	0.015**	0.025**	0.074*	0.035**	0.014**	0.016**	0.013**	0.000***	0.000***	0.000***	0.000***	0.000***	0.000***	0.000***
TOP2_3		0.001							0.003					
		0.072*							0.014**					
BHS			0.002							0.002				
			0.102							0.034**				
BHD				0.006							0.034			
				0.904							0.164			
CIGOWN					0							−0.005		
					0.737							0.013**		
INSOWN						0.001							−0.003	
						0.278							0.010***	
GOVOWN							−0.002							−0.001
							0.004***							0.475
Cfcon1	0.201	0.198	0.185	0.2	0.2	0.201	0.201	0.097	0.109	0.11	0.095	0.128	0.112	0.1
	0.000***	0.000***	0.000***	0.000***	0.000***	0.000***	0.000***	0.000***	0.000***	0.000***	0.000***	0.000***	0.000***	0.000***
Lsize	−0.027	−0.027	−0.027	−0.027	−0.027	−0.027	−0.027	−0.066	−0.067	−0.068	−0.069	−0.063	−0.064	−0.066
	0.013**	0.014**	0.016**	0.023**	0.013**	0.013**	0.018**	0.044**	0.040**	0.038**	0.043**	0.063*	0.056*	0.044**

(*Continued*)

Table 7. (*Continued*)

	OLS	OLS	OLS	OLS	OLS	OLS	OLS	FE	FE	FE	FE	FE	FE	FE
Volatility	−0.089	−0.087	−0.083	−0.088	−0.088	−0.088	−0.082	0.25	0.253	0.25	0.253	0.245	0.248	0.25
	0.133	0.132	0.139	0.104	0.13	0.139	0.153	0.000***	0.000***	0.000***	0.000***	0.000***	0.000***	0.000***
Leverage	0.215	0.213	0.205	0.214	0.214	0.216	0.214	0.597	0.596	0.596	0.594	0.606	0.6	0.598
	0.000***	0.000***	0.000***	0.000***	0.000***	0.000***	0.000***	0.000***	0.000***	0.000***	0.000***	0.000***	0.000***	0.000***
R-sq	0.168	0.168	0.169	0.168	0.168	0.168	0.168							

Note: This table reports regression results of pooled OLS and fix-effects (FE) regression using Driscoll and Kraay (1998) estimation. The dependent variable is Tobin's Q = (total liabilities + market value of equity)/(total assets). The explanatory variables are: GAP1, the difference of the percentage of voting rights and the percentage of cash-flow rights held by the dominant shareholder. TOP2_3, the percentage of voting rights held by the second largest shareholder provided that it is not an institutional investor or government, (if the second largest shareholder is an institutional investor or government, I take the percentage voting rights held by the third largest shareholder provided that it is not an institutional investor or government). BHS, the sum of the percentage of voting rights held by all large blockholders (Family + Corp + Other) excluding dominant shareholders. BHD, an indicator variable equal to 1 if an aggregated blockholder exists, as defined in BHS, 0 otherwise. INSOWN, the percentage of voting rights held by institutional investors excluding dominant shareholders. GOVOWN, the percentage of voting rights held by governments excluding dominant shareholders. CIGOWN = INSOWN + GOVOWN, the percentage of voting rights held by combined institutional investors and governments excluding dominant shareholders. Cfcon1, a dummy variable that takes the value of 1 if the dominant shareholder is a corporation or member of a family group, and zero otherwise. Lsize = log (total assets). Leverage = total liabilities/total assets. Volatility = standard deviation of monthly stock price returns for the past 24 months. Country dummy variables and year dummy variables coefficients and the constant are not reported. *p*-values are reported in parenthesis; ***, ** and * indicate that the coefficient is statistically different from zero at the 1%, 5% and 10% levels, respectively.

find more freedom for decision making and returning to traditional forms of conflicts of interest.

The positive coefficient of TOP2_3 and BHS in Tables 6 and 7 indicates that blockholders may exercise effective monitoring and collaborate with dominant shareholders providing managerial expertise and access to markets. This conclusion is consistent with the finding in Lins (2003). However, their influence is conditioned by their identity relative to other corporations or family members. Moreover, the effect is characterized by the size of their stake. The mere presence of a potential monitor is not sufficient to booster market confidence, as the insignificance of the coefficient for BHD indicates.

The role of institutional investors and governments as efficient monitoring agents is again questioned by the negative signs and often insignificant coefficients for CIGOWN, INSOWN, and GOVOWN. In fact, they are perceived not only as poor monitors, but also as potential obstacles to pursue investment projects with positive net present value, for they would be extra-conservative (extremely risk averse) or would lengthen vital decision-making processes.

6. Concluding Remarks

I find that in a context of weak protection for minority shareholders and high ownership concentration, a discount is imposed on the value of firms in which the voting rights of dominant shareholders exceed their cash-flow rights. However, the valuation discount is mitigated when dominant shareholders are family groups or corporations rather than institutional investors or governments. Such preference may reflect managerial expertise, efficiency and/or enhanced access to product markets. The evidence suggests that the stock market discount is also lower when other family groups and corporations assume monitoring roles. On the other hand, institutional investors and governments are not perceived as efficient corporate monitors. Collusion between blockholders and dominant shareholders for the purpose of extracting private benefits, to the detriment of minority shareholders, is not evident.

References

Agrawal, A and CR Knoeber (1996). Firm performance and mechanisms to control agency problems between managers and shareholders. *Journal of Financial and Quantitative Analysis*, v31 (3, Sep.), 377–397.

Bennedsen, M and D Wolfenzon (2000). The balance of power in closely held corporations. *Journal of Financial Economics*, v58 (1, 2, Jan.), 113–139.

Breusch, T and A Pagan (1980). The Lagrange-multiplier test and its applications to model specification in econometrics. *Review of Economic Studies*, 47, 239–253.

Claessens, S, S Djankov, JPH Fan and LHP Lang (2002). Disentangling the incentives and entrenchment effects of large shareholdings. *Journal of Finance*, v57 (6, Dec.), 2741–2771.

Dahya, J, O Dimitrov and JJ McConnell (2008). Dominant shareholders, corporate boards and corporate value: A cross-country analysis. *Journal of Financial Economics*, 87, 73–100.

Demsetz, H and B Villalonga (2001). Ownership structure and corporate performance. *Journal of Corporate Finance*, v7 (3, Sep.), 209–233.

Driscoll, JC and AC Kraay (1998). Consistent covariance matrix estimation with spatially dependent panel data. *Review of Economics and Statistics*, v80 (4, Nov.), 549–560.

Faccio, M and LHP Lang (2002). The ultimate ownership of western European corporations. *Journal of Financial Economics*, 65 (3), 365–395.

Gottesman, A, M Morey, E Baker and B Godridge (2007). Corporate governance ratings in emerging markets. Working Paper.

Hausman, JA (1978). Specification tests in econometrics. *Econometrica*, 46 (6), 1251–1271.

La Porta, R, F Lopez-de-Silanes and A Shleifer (1998). Law and finance. *Journal of Political Economy*, 106 (6), 1113–1156.

La Porta, R, F Lopez-de-Silanes and A Shleifer (1999). Corporate ownership around the world. *Journal of Finance*, 54, 471–517.

Lefort, F and E Walker (1999). Ownership and capital structure of Chilean conglomerates: Facts and hypotheses for governance. *Revista ABANTE*, 3 (1), 3–27.

Lins, KV (2003). Equity ownership and firm value in emerging markets. *Journal of Financial and Quantitative Analysis*, 38 (1), 159–184.

McConnell, JJ and H Servaes (1990). Additional evidence on equity ownership and corporate value. *Journal of Financial Economics*, v27 (2), 595–612.

Miller, D, I Le Breton-Miller, R Lester and A Cannella (2007). Are family firms really superior performers? *Journal of Corporate Finance*, 13 (5), 829–858.

Morck, R, A Shleifer and R Vishny (1988). Management ownership and market valuation: An empirical analysis. *Journal of Financial Economics*, 20, 293–315.

Nenova, T (2003). The value of corporate voting rights and control: A cross-country analysis. *Journal of Financial Economics*, 68 (3), 325–351.

Newey, WK and KD West (1987). A simple, positive semi-definite, heteroskedasticity and autocorrelation consistent covariance matrix. *Econometrica*, 55 (3), 703–708.

Petersen, MA (2009). Estimating standard errors in finance panel data sets: Comparing approaches. *Review of Financial Studies*, 22 (1), 435–480.

Switzer, LN and C Kelly (2006). Corporate governance mechanisms and the performance of small-cap firms in Canada. *International Journal of Business Governance and Ethics*, 2(3/4), 329–340.

Valadares, SM and RPC Leal (2000). Ownership and control structure of Brazilian companies. Available at SSRN: http://ssrn.com/abstract=213409 or DOI: 10.2139/ssrn.213409.

14

Asymmetric Impact of News on Stock Return Volatility

Joon-Young Song

1. Introduction

Most researchers agree that the volatility of stock returns and the expected returns are predictable in short-time horizon periods and that the process governing volatility over time is similar across markets; however, they disagree on how this process should be modeled. Conrad and Kaul (1988, 1989) argue that time variation in expected returns accounts for substantial proportions (in excess of 25% for small firms) of the variance of both weekly and monthly portfolio returns.

On the other hand, Lo and MacKinlay (1990a) point out that the return on a portfolio of small stocks correlates with the lagged return on a portfolio of large stocks. Lo and MacKinlay also uncover a size asymmetry, noting that the return on a portfolio of large stocks is not correlated with the lagged return on small stocks. In addition, Conrad *et al.* (1991) and Kroner and Ng (1998) also confirm an asymmetric feature in the dynamics of the stock volatility spillover between small firms and large firms.

It is surprising that although many studies focus on the predictability of small stock returns by large stock returns, called "cross-autocorrelation", previous research has not shown whether the asymmetric cross-autocorrelation can be found across portfolio returns of stocks sorted by several categories including stock market affiliation or industry classifications, other than firm size or market capitalization. This approach of examining, a wider range of portfolio groups could create different views of the essence of the cross-autocorrelation.

Additionally, I examine the asymmetric cross-autocorrelation called volatility spillover across firm size-sorted portfolios. The goal of this chapter is to answer the question of how stock return volatility is deployed and what return volatility implies in the context of time-varying asset pricing. Furthermore, I attempt to ascertain whether the volatility spillover phenomenon is attributable to the difference in firm size. In doing this, I extend the analysis to the difference in market affiliation and industry.

As Barberies and Huang (2001) and Malkiel and Xu (2002) argue, the volatility spillover should be captured in the asset pricing model because it is considered a risk factor that has not been reflected in the traditional pricing models. As such, it is a good reason to establish possible patterns of volatility spillovers across stock markets and industries. In fact, many studies have documented the volatility spillovers of international stock returns,[1] whereas few papers have studied the volatility spillovers across domestic equity markets.

Another objective of this chapter explores the possibility of the asymmetry of the volatility spillover (i.e., leverage effect), since uncovered by Black (1976). This phenomenon posits that a negative return shock (unexpected price drop) will lead to a higher subsequent volatility than a positive return shock (unexpected price rise) of the same magnitude. It is generally observed that large negative stock returns are more common than large positive ones, so stock returns are negatively skewed. This phenomenon can be explained by the leverage hypothesis raised by Black (1976).

A number of researchers have attempted to attribute the "negative skewness" to volatility feedback (French *et al.*, 1987). However, some studies document that the leverage effect is too small to fully account for such a phenomenon (Poterba and Summers, 1986). Interestingly, few studies in the time-varying volatility spillover area incorporate explicitly the possibility of the leverage effect in volatility spillovers. The rationale underlying leverage effect, however, could be extended in the context of the volatility spillovers. It is hypothesized that bad (or good) news shock to a given portfolio increases (or decreases) the leverage ratio of not only the firms in the portfolio but also the firms in *other* portfolios, thus raising (or lowering) the future volatility and riskiness of not only the portfolio but also *other* portfolios. This hypothesis could help explain the negative skewness of stock returns.

Lastly, some variants of the GARCH-in-Mean (hereafter, GARCH-M) model are adopted to conduct the empirical works. One of the models to examine the volatility spillovers is similar to the one employed by Conrad *et al.* (1991). However, unlike Conrad *et al.* (1991), the model employs a market equilibrium model such as the Sharpe-Lintner model to distinguish between the residuals resulting from bad news event and those caused by good news event. A variant of the asymmetric GARCH-M model combined with the Glosten, Jagannathan and Runkle model (Glosten *et al.*, 1993) is also employed to capture the spillover of the leverage effects. Their model will be referred to as GJR model.

Anticipating the results, I find strong evidence on a stable, but asymmetric dynamic relationship of volatility spillovers between large and small firms. I claim that there also exists a specific pattern of return volatility spillovers across portfolios sorted by the stock market affiliation such as the NYSE, AMEX and NASDAQ and industries such as manufacturing, financial, service, utility and miscellaneous industries. This finding of the spillovers across market affiliation, industry and firm size implies that the volatility spillovers cannot be attributed solely to the difference in firm size.

Furthermore, I find that the conditional volatility of smaller firms (or NASDAQ or AMEX listed stocks) tends to be higher after bad news event (or NYSE listed stocks) than after good news event of larger firms. Thus, the asymmetric news impact on the volatility spillover as well as the spillover itself should be considered in the time-varying asset pricing process of a given stock, particularly small stocks, so that its aggregate volatility may not be underestimated. This finding of the asymmetric impact of good or bad news on volatility spillovers helps explain the negative skewness of stock returns, particularly small stocks.

The remainder of the chapter proceeds as follows. Section 2 presents the data and empirical design with some descriptive statistics of the sample data. In Sec. 3, formulations of models employed in this chapter and results of the diagnostic tests for fitness of the specified models are introduced. In Sec. 4, empirical tests for the spillover effects across firm size-, market- and industry-based portfolios are given. Section 5 concludes the chapter.

2. Data

I focus on portfolio returns of stocks sorted on market capitalization (size), stock market affiliation and industry classification. In particular, industry classification is chosen because industries have varying exposures to economic factors. For the empirical analysis, I use the Center for Research in Securities Prices (CRSP) daily return file, which contains data for the New York Stock Exchange (NYSE), American Stock Exchanges (AMEX) and NASDAQ to calculate daily portfolio returns over the sample period of 1997 through 2001. Portfolio returns, rather than individual stock returns, are used here because it is difficult to extract the (expected return) signal from noisy returns of an individual stock: I avoid the potential problem of serial correlation in daily returns series by constructing the portfolio.

Unlike previous studies, this study uses daily returns rather than weekly or monthly returns in generating portfolio returns in that daily returns may assimilate the possible volatility spillover better than weekly or monthly returns. However, the adoption of daily frequency may worsen a problem of non-synchronous trading. Since non-synchronous trading can cause a bias in the estimation of correlation in portfolio returns, it has been argued that non-synchronous trading of stocks on the stock market could cause asymmetric volatility spillover effects (Scholes and Williams, 1977). Prior works, however, document that non-synchronous trading has not been shown to generate spurious lagged cross-correlation in portfolio returns. Lo and MacKinlay (1990a,b) rule out non-synchronous trading as the only explanation of cross-autocorrelation because unreasonably high levels of non-trading are needed to explain the lagged cross-correlation if non-trading is homogeneous.

Furthermore, Conrad *et al.* (1991) report that non-trading is an unlikely source of the asymmetric volatility spillover effects; Mech (1993) finds that the cross-autocorrelation exists in NASDAQ stock returns even after he controls for non-synchronous trading. Nonetheless, several attempts are made to control for this market microstructure bias: (1) using portfolio returns, rather than daily returns, to avoid putting too much weight on small illiquid stocks, (2) rebalancing portfolios at the end of each year during the sample period to minimize micro-structure bid-ask bounce effect and (3) eliminating stocks whose average daily trading volumes over the sample period are less than 0.5 million from the sample. Additionally, since the stocks with too small trading volumes have lots of missing data and might cause a biased effect on the results, the stocks which have less than 200 daily returns are not included in the sample data. After screening, a total of 865 firms are included in the sample data. These sample stocks are divided into several groups to form size, market and industry portfolios.

A set of portfolios sorted on the value-weighted firm size is created. All 865 sample firms are classified into quintiles on the basis of a value-weighted average of daily market values calculated as of the end of the year. The results fall into one of five size-sorted portfolios; largest (referred to as "p_sz_xl"), large ("p_sz_l"), medium ("p_sz_m"), small ("p_sz_s") and smallest ("p_sz_xs") portfolios. Thus, each portfolio contains exactly 173 stocks, but the individual stocks contained in each portfolio may vary every year depending on their market value at the end of each year. For the second set of portfolios, the sample stocks are classified as NYSE ("p_mkt_nyse"), AMEX ("p_mkt_amex") or NASDAQ ("p_mkt_nasdaq") portfolios depending on their market affiliation.

The third set of portfolios is based on the Standard Industrial Classification (SIC) codes. Following French's five portfolio index based on five industry classifications, the sample stocks are grouped into the following five representative industries: manufacturing (SIC = 2000–3999, "p_sic_manuf"), utilities (4900–4999, "p_sic_util"), services, shop wholesale and retail (5000–5999, 7000–7999, "p_sic_svc"), money and finance (6000–6999, "p_sic_fin") and miscellaneous ("p_sic_oth"). Stocks that do not fall into a specific industry classification are assigned to the miscellaneous industry. Last, the CRSP's value-weighted market index is adopted as the market portfolio return in forming the market model to capture the variation caused by unexpected news shocks. Brief summary statistics of the portfolios described above are given in Table 1.

3. Models

3.1. *Models for Return Volatility Spillovers*

To formally address the issue of volatility spillovers across stocks, a variant of GARCH (1,1) model with the Sharpe-Lintner's market model as a mean equation is considered. I begin by specifying the market model with a binary variable to capture any potential holiday effect.

$$R_{i,t}^{V} = a_i + c_i D_t + b_i R_t^{VM} + \varepsilon_{i,t}, \quad \varepsilon_{i,t}|\Omega_{t-1} \sim N(0, \sigma_i^2), \tag{1}$$

where $R_{i,t}^{V}$ is the market-value-weighted daily returns on portfolio i and R_t^{VM} is the CRSP value-weighted daily market returns. D_t represents a binary variable that takes a value of 1 on days following weekends and holidays and a value of 0 otherwise. Equation (1) is a traditional asset-pricing model with constant variance. Here, assuming that the variance changes with time, the model should be changed to the ARCH type model as addressed in the previous section. Furthermore, the standard (G) ARCH model is modified to capture the spillover effects among the portfolios.

In order to analyze the volatility spillovers across size-, exchange market- and industry-sorted portfolios, the following two versions of an estimation model are considered. One is for the "pairwise spillover effects" and the other is for the "simultaneous spillover effects". Equations (2) and (3) estimate the relationship between the conditional variance of a portfolio i and the lagged squared shocks to *each* of the other portfolios (pairwise spillovers). This model is referred to as "Spillover GARCH-M model" throughout this chapter.

Table 1. Summary statistics of the sample portfolios.

	1997–2001							
	Stocks	Avg. beta	Avg. volume ($1,000)	Avg. price ($)	Avg. cap ($1,000)	Market_I[4]	Standard deviation	Market_II[5]
MKT Index						0.00039		0.00093
Panel A: Size[1]								
p_sz_xl	173	1.08	5,292,989	59.09	53,397,681	0.0011	0.0137	0.0006
p_sz_l	173	1.02	1,607,538	44.04	7,605,218	0.0014	0.0133	0.0006
p_sz_m	173	1.10	1,108,605	37.12	3,153,395	0.0020	0.0160	0.0008
p_sz_s	173	1.19	741,761	34.03	1,174,891	0.0028	0.0195	0.0014
p_sz_xs	173	1.38	399,458	19.95	241,746	0.0047	0.0234	0.0030
Sum	865							
Panel B: Market[2]								
p_mkt_nyse	475	1.04	1,458,542	42.13	14,050,345	0.0011	0.0116	0.0008
p_mkt_amex	6	1.07	748,894	14.57	1,606,849	0.0014	0.0230	0.0008
p_mkt_nasdaq	384	1.31	2,127,762	33.87	5,585,086	0.0021	0.0255	0.0019
Sum	865							
Panel C: Industry[3]								
p_sic_manuf	340	1.12	2,033,573	42.21	13,190,315	0.0012	0.0141	0.0014
p_sic_util	35	1.04	813,883	33.68	6,178,555	0.0007	0.0114	0.0006
p_sic_svc	242	1.23	1,877,095	33.75	8,437,922	0.0017	0.0175	0.0014
p_sic_fin	96	1.00	1,226,987	47.20	13,399,088	0.0011	0.0161	0.0008
p_sic_oth	152	1.20	1,283,060	33.01	7,063,234	0.0010	0.0136	0.0010
Sum	865							

Note: This table contains the descriptive statistics of market capitalization-, stock market affiliation and industry-sorted portfolios. Data are sampled daily returns from January 1997 to December 2001. The number of sample stocks is 865. The returns of each portfolio are calculated using 1,257 daily returns (five years) obtained from the CRSP files. All average figures of each portfolio are computed based on a firm. Portfolio returns are formed based on both market value-weighted and equally weighted methods. Standard deviations are computed based on the market value-weighted portfolio returns. Also, CRSP market index is adopted as a proxy for the market portfolio return.

[1]p_sz_xl = portfolio of the 173 largest market value stocks (quintile 5), p_sz_l = portfolio of the next 173 large market value stocks (quintile 4), p_sz_m = portfolio of the 173 intermediate market value stocks (quintile 3), p_sz_s = portfolio of the 173 small market value stocks (quintile 2), p_sz_xs = portfolio of the 173 smallest market value stocks (quintile 1).

[2]p_mkt_nyse = portfolio of the NYSE stocks, p_mkt_amex = portfolio of the AMEX stocks, p_mkt_nasdaq = portfolio of the NASDAQ stocks.

[3]p_sic_manuf = portfolio of the stocks in manufacturing industry (SIC = 2000–3999), p_sic_util = portfolio of the stocks in utility industry (4900–4999), p_sic_svc = portfolio of the stock in service industry (5000–5999, 7000–7999), p_sic_fin = portfolio of the stocks in financial industry (6000–6999), p_sic_oth = portfolio of the stocks in any industries other than the above industries.

[4]Market_I = average of market value-weighted portfolio returns (daily).

[5]Market_II = average of equally-weighted portfolio returns (daily).

3.1.1. *Model I-A: Spillover GARCH(1,1)-M for Pairwise Effects*

1st stage: GARCH (1,1) process

$$R^V_{j,t} = a'_j + c'_j D_t + b_j R^{VM}_t + \nu_{j,t} \quad \text{where } \nu_{j,t}|\Omega_{t-1} \sim N(0, \mu_{i,t}) \qquad (2)$$

$$\mu_{j,t} = \alpha'_j + \delta'_j \mu_{j,t-1} + \omega'_j \nu^2_{j,t-1}$$

2nd stage: GARCH (1,1) — M process

$$R^V_{i,t} = a_i + c_i D_t + d_i h_{i,t} + b_i R^{VM}_t + \varepsilon_{i,t} \quad \text{where } \varepsilon_{i,t}|\Omega_{t-1} \sim N(0, h_{i,t})$$

$$h_{i,t} = \alpha_i + \delta_i h_{i,t-1} + \omega_i \varepsilon^2_{i,t-1} + \theta_{ij} \nu^2_{j,t-1} \quad j \neq i, \qquad (3)$$

where i stands for size-, market- and industry-sorted portfolios. θ_{ij} is the coefficient of the spillover from past volatility shocks to portfolio j to the conditional variance of portfolio i. ω_i, δ_i and d_i represent ARCH, GARCH and GARCH-M effect. The estimated lagged squared term for each portfolio will proxy for the news shocks that may spillover to the volatility of the other portfolios. The terms are plugged into the second-pass model as lagged squared errors.[2] In the second stage, GARCH (1,1)-M model with spillover effects is estimated. The model allows the conditional variances to affect the conditional mean equation. This two-stage procedure is similar to the models used by Hamao *et al.* (1990) and the univariate model employed by Conrad *et al.* (1991).[3]

It is worthwhile to note several distinct modifications of the models used in previous studies. Unlike these studies, I impose an equilibrium model of a market model to identify news shocks. This aims to distinguish the return volatility caused by a news surprise from the volatility raised by mere adjustment for the deviation from equilibrium. Since the variance of price changes is related directly to the rate of flow of information, mere adjustment of the deviation of the price from an equilibrium price that may dilute the spillover effects should be ruled out when the volatility spillovers across various portfolios are examined. Also, the GARCH model rather than GARCH-M is employed to measure pure impact of the news shock by preventing conditional variance from affecting the mean equation.

The key parameter in the model is the coefficient of spillover effect, which represents the degree of the influence of the past volatility surprises to the portfolio j on the conditional variances of the portfolio i. Thus, the relative magnitude of θ_{ij} and θ_{ji} can help determine whether aggregate shocks have differential effects across portfolios. Following the approach conducted by Conrad *et al.* (1991), I also estimate the *simultaneous* effects of volatility surprises to the other portfolios on the conditional volatility of portfolio i by estimating the following equations.

3.1.2. *Model I-B: Spillover GARCH(1,1)-M for Simultaneous Effects*

1st stage: GARCH (1,1)—M process
the same as Eq. (2)

2nd stage: GARCH (1,1)—M process

$$R_{i,t}^{V} = a_i + c_i D_t + d_i h_{i,t} + b_i R_t^{VM} + \varepsilon_{i,t} \quad \text{where } \varepsilon_{i,t}|\Omega_{t-1} \sim N(0, h_{i,t})$$

$$h_{i,t} = \alpha_i + \delta_i h_{i,t-1} + \omega_i \varepsilon_{i,t-1}^2 + \sum_{\substack{j=1 \\ j\neq i}}^{n} \theta_{ij} \nu_{j,t-1}^2, \tag{4}$$

where n = number of size-, stock market- or industry-sorted portfolios and θ_{ij} is joint impact coefficient of past volatility shocks to portfolio j on the conditional variance of portfolio i (simultaneous spillover effects).

3.2. *Models for the Asymmetric News Impact on Volatility Spillovers*

The traditional ARCH, GARCH or (G) ARCH-M models cannot capture some important features of the data generating process. The most interesting feature not addressed by these models is the leverage or asymmetric effect discovered by Black (1976) and confirmed by the findings of French *et al.* (1987), Nelson (1991) and Schwert (1990).[4] This effect occurs when an unexpected drop in prices (due to bad news event) increases predictable volatility more than an unexpected increase in price (due to good news event) by the same magnitude.

This effect suggests that a symmetry constraint on the conditional variance function in past error terms is inappropriate.

Earlier studies have mainly accommodated asymmetric volatility to their models in the context of the return series of individual stocks or portfolios and specific market indices (e.g., Nelson, 1991; Glosten *et al.*, 1993; Bekaert and Wu, 2000; Ang and Chen, 2002; Dean and Faff, 2004). With a few exceptions, it is surprising that many applications of GARCH models to the spillover effects have not embraced asymmetric volatility models (Hamao *et al.*, 1990; Conrad *et al.*, 1991). Even a few studies with asymmetric GARCH models mainly focus on the spillovers across international stock markets (Bae and Karolyi, 1994).

The goal of this chapter begins with the question: can the leverage effect uncovered in the volatility in stock returns also be found in the spillovers of the return volatility across pre-sorted portfolios? It is conjectured that the pattern of the spillovers across pre-classified portfolios could be different depending on whether the volatility of a portfolio results from a negative or positive news shock. The estimation models in Eqs. (5) and (6) are established to answer this question. For the purpose of the above issues, a variant of GJR model, named "Spillover GJR-GARCH (1,1)-M model".

3.2.1. *Model II: Spillover GJR-GARCH (1,1)-M for Pairwise Effects*

1st stage: GARCH (1,1) process
the same as Eq. (2)

2nd stage: GJR–GARCH (1,1)—M process

$$R_{i,t}^{V} = a_i + c_i D_t + d_i h_{i,t} + b_i R_t^{VM} + \varepsilon_{i,t}$$
$$\varepsilon_{i,t} | \Omega_{t-1} \sim N(0, h_{i,t}) \tag{5}$$
$$h_{i,t} = \alpha_i + \delta_i h_{i,t-1} + \omega_i \varepsilon_{i,t-1}^2 + \gamma_{ij} S_{j,t-1}^{-} \nu_{j,t-1}^2 + \theta_{ij} \nu_{j,t-1}^2, \quad (\textit{Negative Innovations}) \tag{6}$$
$$S_{j,t-1}^{-} = 1 \quad \text{if} \quad \nu_{j,t-1} < 0, \quad \text{and} \quad 0 \text{ otherwise},$$

where γ_{ij} is the coefficient of leverage effect of the shock to portfolio j. θ_{ij} is the coefficient of spillover impact of past volatility shock to portfolio j on the conditional variance of portfolio i. The conditional variance equation in the Spillover GARCH (1,1)-M model is expanded to account for the leverage effect in the volatility spillover caused by "good news" or "bad news" on the volatility of other portfolios. The model in the second stage includes a binary variable to distinguish the negative innovations from the positive innovations. This term has a value of 1 if the lagged residual $v_{j,t-1}$ is negative (i.e., negative innovations) and 0 otherwise. The binary variable aims to compare the impact of the positive shocks of portfolio j on the future volatility of the other portfolio i with that of the negative shocks on the future volatility of the other portfolio i.

In the similar manner, the Spillover GJR-GARCH (1,1)-M model can be modified with respect to "positive innovations" by simply replacing $S^-_{j,t-1}$ with $S^+_{j,t-1}$. Intuitively, it can be conjectured that the coefficients of $S^-_{j,t-1}$ for negative innovations and $S^+_{j,t-1}$ for positive innovations are likely to show a positive sign (increase the volatility) and a negative sign (decrease the volatility), respectively if there exists the leverage effect in volatility spillover. Although the GJR-GARCH (1,1)-M model is applied for both "pairwise" and "simultaneous effects", the model for pairwise effects only is presented. The Spillover GJR-GARCH (1,1)-M model for "simultaneous effects" can be obtained by replacing the terms of $\gamma_{ij}S^-_{j,t-1}\nu^2_{j,t-1}$ and $\theta_{ij}\nu^2_{j,t-1}$ in Eq. (6) are replaced with $\sum_{\substack{j=1\\ j\neq i}}^{n} \gamma_{ij}S^-_{j,t-1}\nu^2_{j,t-1}$ and $\sum_{\substack{j=1\\ j\neq i}}^{n} \theta_{ij}\nu^2_{j,t-1}$, respectively.

4. Empirical Results

4.1. *Size-Sorted Portfolios*

4.1.1. *Volatility Spillover Effects*

The results of estimating the Spillover GARCH (1,1)-M for both pairwise and simultaneous effects are presented in Table 2. According to the residual diagnostics for the model that capture the volatility spillovers, Durbin Watson statistics, Ljung-Box Q values and Engle's LM test results indicate no significance in the autocorrelation and heteroskedasticity in the estimation model. All Q-statistics of the

Table 2. Estimated parameters: Model I-A&B, spillover GARCH(1,1)-M model for five size-sorted portfolios.

Model		d	a	c	b	α	ω (ARCH)	δ (GARCH)	θ_{ij}				LL[1]	DW[2]	Q(6)_I[3]	Q(6)_II	LM[4]
	P_SZ_XL								θ (XL,L)	θ (XL,M)	θ (XL,S)	θ(XL,XS)					
GARCH(1,1)-M	Coefficient	32.981	0.000	0.001	1.110	0.000	0.151	0.798					5449.46	1.775	16.313	5.897	0.078
	z Statistic	(2.270)	(−0.838)	(4.159)	(220.879)	(5.514)	(8.1919)	(33.756)									
Spillover GARCH(1,1)-M																	
Simultaneous	Coefficient	30.691	0.000	0.001	1.108	0.000	0.070	0.661	0.021*	0.017**	−0.001	0.007	5486.58	1.753	15.119	6.502	0.1560
	z Statistic	(2.253)	(−0.044)	(3.801)	(192.19)	(4.387)	(3.505)	(14.362)	(2.081)	(2.408)	(−0.386)	(4.333)					
Pairwise	Coefficient								0.038***	0.034***	0.013***	0.007					
	z Statistic								(3.883)5	(5.570)	(6.434)	(5.886)					
	P_SZ_L								θ (L,XL)	θ (L,M)	θ (L,S)	θ (L,XS)					
GARCH(1,1)-M	Coefficient	29.406	0.000	0.000	0.974	0.000	0.071	0.928					5123.49	2.006	8.754	5.085	0.023
	z Statistic	(3.660)	(1.902)	(−1.453)	(149.443)	(1.988)	(7.158)	(95.909)									
Spillover GARCH(1,1)-M																	
Simultaneous	Coefficient	17.403	0.001	0.000	0.973	0.000	0.055	0.856	0.021	0.025**	−0.001	0.004	5148.52	2.006	5.441	1.432	0.0162
	z Statistic	(1.917)	(3.317)	(−1.580)	(117.62)	(−0.842)	(3.574)	(36.787)	(1.416)	(3.812)	(−0.739)	(3.308)					
Pairwise	Coefficient								0.043***	0.038***	0.006***	0.006					
	z Statistic								(3.640)	(5.869)	(3.687)	(6.130)					
	P_SZ_M								θ (M,XL)	θ (M,L)	θ (M, S)	θ (M,XS)					
GARCH(1,1)-M	Coefficient	27.911	0.000	−0.001	1.078	0.000	0.060	0.936					4607.52	1.929	3.030	3.171	0.032
	z Statistic	(4.137)	1.170	(−3.338)	(77.400)	(1.745)	(6.836)	(92.161)									
Spillover GARCH(1,1)-M																	
Simultaneous	Coefficient	21.120	0.001	−0.001	1.070	0.000	−0.002	0.779	0.050	0.093***	0.053***	0.009	4645.83	1.914	3.781	2.592	0.9420
	z Statistic	(3.156)	(2.686)	(−3.388)	(73.366)	(1.619)	(−0.163)	(26.150)	(0.930)	(2.856)	(4.293)	(2.084)					
Pairwise	Coefficient								0.049**	0.043***	0.048***	0.013					
	z Statistic								(2.194)	(3.086)	(5.764)	(4.991)					

Table 2. (*Continued*)

Model		d	a	c	b	α	ω (ARCH)	δ (GARCH)	θ_{ij}				LL[1]	DW[2]	Q(6)_I[3]	Q(6)_II	LM[4]
	P_SZ_S								θ(S, XL)	θ(S,L)	θ(S,M)	θ(S,XS)					
GARCH(1,1)-M	Coefficient	15.589	0.001	−0.002	1.169	0.000	0.122	0.863					4116.035	1.827	8.0468	20.788***	0.272
	z Statistic	(3.516)	(2.049)	(−3.251)	(56.834)	(2.773)	(7.560)	(46.927)									
Spillover GARCH(1,1)-M																	
Simultaneous	Coefficient	12.034	0.001	−0.002	1.175	0.000	0.065	0.780	0.063	−0.062	0.196***	0.038	4150.41	1.8219	5.310	24.766	2.0835
	z Statistic	(2.895)	(3.188)	(−3.063)	(53.567)	(0.750)	(3.875)	(22.651)	(0.645)	(−1.215)	(4.067)	(3.612)					
Pairwise	Coefficient								0.377***	0.125**	0.220***	0.048					
	z Statistic								(3.736)	(2.564)	(4.874)	(4.981)					
	P_SZ_XS								θ(XS, XL)	θ(XS,L)	θ(XS,M)	θ(XS,S)					
GARCH(1,1)-M	Coefficient	6.963	0.003	−0.001	1.224	0.000	0.115	0.861					3732.444	1.636	26.22***	2.945	0.639
	z Statistic	(2.690)	(5.767)	(−1.792)	(50.002)	(3.502)	(7.689)	(49.382)									
Spillover GARCH(1,1)-M																	
Simultaneous	Coefficient	5.381	0.003	−0.001	1.234	0.000	0.031	0.616	0.498	0.531***	0.288***	0.343	3784.539	1.6495	22.793***	8.333	2.3207
	z Statistic	(1.999)	(7.391)	(−1.722)	(45.380)	(0.941)	(1.343)	(10.794)	(1.500)	(3.260)	(2.715)	(4.978)*					
Pairwise	Coefficient								1.106***	0.459***	0.458***	0.371**					
	z Statistic								(4.560)	(4.106)	(5.579)	(6.695)*					

Note: Table presents the results of estimating the spillover GARCH (1,1)-M model for both pairwise and simultaneous effects of the volatility spillovers. Also, some diagnostic tests are conducted to see the appropriateness of the model. The results of the test are given as well. The size-sorted portfolios are rebalanced using rankings of yearly average market value of the sample stocks of 856 at the end of each year during the sample period of 1997 through 2001. The estimated parameters of the standard GARCH (1,1)-M model are also presented for the purpose of comparison with those of the GARCH (1,1)-M containing spillover terms, that is, the Spillover GARCH (1,1)-M model.

1) LL = Log likelihood 2) DW = Durbin-Watson statistics 3) Q (6)_I and Q (6)_II are the Ljung-Box Q statistics with the degrees of six, for the standardized residuals and standardized squared residuals, critical values = 10.64(10%), 12.59(5%), 16.81(1%) 4) LM = Engle's LM test statistics. The numbers in parentheses below the estimated coefficients are z statistics. *, **, and *** denote significance of the statistics at the 10%, 5% and 1% levels, respectively.

GARCH (1,1)-M Without Spillover Term

$$R^V_{i,t} = a_i + c_i D_t + d_i h_{i,t} + b_i R^{VM}_t + \varepsilon_{i,t}$$

where $\varepsilon_{i,t}|\Omega_{t-1} \sim N(0, h_{i,t})$

$$h_{i,t} = \alpha_i + \delta_i h_{i,t-1} + \omega_i \varepsilon^2_{i,t-1}$$

Spillover GARCH (1,1)-M for Pairwise Effects

$$R^V_{i,t} = a_i + c_i D_t + d_i h_{i,t} + b_i R^{VM}_t + \varepsilon_{i,t}$$

where $\varepsilon_{i,t}|\Omega_{t-1} \sim N(0, h_{i,t})$

$$h_{i,t} = \alpha_i + \delta_i h_{i,t-1} + \omega_i \varepsilon^2_{i,t-1} + \theta_{it} v^2_{t,t-1} \quad t \neq i, \quad i, t = 1-5$$

Spillover GARCH (1,1)-M for Simultaneous Effects

$$R^V_{i,t} = a_i + c_i D_t + d_i h_{i,t} + b_i R^{VM}_t + \varepsilon_{i,t}$$

where $\varepsilon_{i,t}|\Omega_{t-1} \sim N(0, h_{i,t})$

$$h_{i,t} = \alpha_i + \delta_i h_{i,t-1} + \omega_i \varepsilon^2_{i,t-1} + \sum^5_{\substack{t=1 \\ t \neq i}} \theta_{it} v^2_{t,t-1} \quad i, t = 1-5$$

i = size-, stock market- and industry-sorted portfolio; $R^V_{i,t}$ = market value weighted daily returns on portfolio i; R^{VM}_t = CRSP value-weighted daily market returns;

$D_t = 1$, if it is a day following weekends or holidays, 0 otherwise; $v_{j,t-1}$ = the residuals generated from the standard GARCH (1,1); θ_{ij} = the coefficient of the spillover from the volatility of portfolio j at time $t-1$ to the conditional variance of portfolio i at time t.

portfolios, except for the smallest portfolio (p_sz_xs), show statistical insignificance ($p = 0.01$). Furthermore, the Engle's LM statistics for ARCH effects indicates no significant heteroskedasticity in the residuals from the model across all portfolios ($p = 0.05$). Even in contrast with the basic GARCH-M model without spillover term, the spillover model seems to be better specified. Furthermore, the spillover model has higher values of log likelihood than the basic GARCH-M model for all size-sorted portfolios.

Estimates of the spillover GARCH (1,1)-M model provide strong evidence that conditional variances vary with size-sorted portfolios. All ARCH and GARCH effects represented by ω and δ are statistically significant. The sum of the estimated coefficients of ω and δ is less than unity, which means that the conditional variance follows a stationary process. It is noted that the coefficients of GARCH-M term d_i are significantly positive. This finding is consistent with the positive relationship between the expected market risk premium and the predictable volatility of stock returns. Thus, the expected return on a particular portfolio is a function of its own conditional variance which is also a function of the lagged unexpected changes in volatility of the *other* portfolios as well as its own past-realized variances. The GARCH-M effect is also significantly positive in the conditional mean equation of the spillover model for pairwise effects, though not reported here.

Now, the estimated coefficients of spillover effects are discussed. For the convenience of comparison, the coefficients of the spillover term θ_{ij} are summarized in Table 3. The estimated coefficients of the simultaneous spillover term in Panel A of Table 3 show spillover effects across all five size-sorted portfolios. The results indicate the existence of the asymmetric pattern of the spillover effects across the five size-based portfolios; the values of most of the spillover coefficients below the diagonal of the matrix of Panel A are larger than those above the diagonal. In other words, the lagged shocks to the larger firms have greater impact on the current conditional variance of smaller firms than the lagged shocks to the smaller firms on the larger firms. In addition, the volatility spillover effect from larger to smaller firms is consistently greater than that from smaller to larger firms. This result may be attributable to the fact that extremely small firms are not sampled to avoid nontrading problems.

Table 3. Estimates of volatility spillover effects: Size-sorted portfolios.

$i \backslash j$	$\nu^2_{xl,t-1}$	$\nu^2_{l,t-1}$	$\nu^2_{m,t-1}$	$\nu^2_{s,t-1}$	$\nu^2_{xs,t-1}$
Panel A: Simultaneous spillover effects					
$h_{xl,t}$	—	0.02119**	0.016785**	−0.000561	0.0066***
		(2.081)	(2.408)	(−0.386)	(4.333)
$h_{l,t}$	0.021275	—	0.025289***	−0.001216	0.003962***
	(1.416)		(3.812)	(−0.739)	(3.308)
$h_{m,t}$	0.049839	0.093264***	—	0.052621***	0.008592**
	(0.930)	(2.856)		(4.293)	(2.084)
$h_{s,t}$	0.062761	−0.062342	0.195636***	—	0.037848***
	(0.645)	(−1.215)	(4.067)		(3.612)
$h_{xs,t}$	0.497577	0.531137***	0.288432***	0.343392***	—
	(1.500)	(3.260)	(2.715)	(4.978)	
Panel B: Pairwise Spillover Effects					
$h_{xl,t}$	—	0.037836***	0.033823***	0.012582***	0.006937***
		(3.884)	(5.570)	(6.434)	(5.886)
$h_{l,t}$	0.042864***	—	0.037697***	0.005606***	0.005633***
	(3.640)		(5.869)	(3.687)	(6.130)
$h_{m,t}$	0.048532**	0.042904***	—	0.047656***	0.012924***
	(2.194)	(3.086)		(5.764)	(4.991)
$h_{s,t}$	0.376674***	0.124817**	0.220031***	—	0.048347***
	(3.736)	(2.564)	(4.874)		(4.981)
$h_{xs,t}$	1.10584***	0.459147***	0.458126***	0.370516***	—
	(4.600)	(4.106)	(5.579)	(6.695)	

Note: Table summarized the estimated coefficients of spillover effects. The coefficients of the simultaneous spillover term in Panel A show spillover effects across all five size-sorted portfolios while the coefficients in Panel B measure the volatility spillover effects between a pair of portfolios. The estimated coefficients presented in this table means the spillover effect of past volatility of portfolio j (i.e., $\nu^2_{i,t-1}$) on the future volatility of portfolio i (i.e., $h_{i,t}$). The numbers in the parenthesis are z statistics. *, ** and *** denote significance of the statistics at the 10%, 5% and 1% levels, respectively.

Another interesting finding is that the spillover effect from largest firms to the other firms is not statistically significant. It may be explained by a kind of "volatility spillover interaction". In the spillover model for simultaneous effects, the shocks to the largest portfolio would affect the contemporaneous conditional variance of other portfolios. In other words, the shock to the largest portfolio that should have been transmitted to the lagged conditional variance of a particular portfolio i may be absorbed in the lagged residuals of other portfolios.

Since the spillover model with simultaneous effects allows the spillovers to circulate in all other portfolios, the significance of the spillover term of a particular portfolio depends on the interaction of the spillovers across portfolios. The spillover effects from larger portfolios to smaller portfolios are strong enough for the shock to larger portfolios to be conspicuously carved in the lagged residuals of other smaller portfolios. Therefore, the spillover term of the larger portfolio may lose explanatory power. Conversely, since the spillover from smaller to larger portfolios tends to be weak, the spillover term of the smaller portfolio may not lose much explanatory power. The results of estimating the spillover model for pairwise effects reported in Panel A of Table 3 support the explanation given above.

The estimated coefficients of the pairwise spillover term are more distinct and consistent than those of the simultaneous spillover term and the result of Conrad *et al.* (1991). As shown on Panel B of Table 3, all estimated coefficients below the diagonal of the matrix are much larger than those above the diagonal. The spillover effects from larger to smaller firms significantly dominate those from smaller to larger firms without any exception. For example, the estimated effect of $v_{xl,t-1}^2$ on $h_{xs,t}$ (1.10584) is almost 160 times as large as the effect of $v_{xs,t-1}^2$ on $h_{xl,t}$ (0.006937). Moreover, this asymmetric pattern of the spillover effects is displayed consistently across all five size-sorted portfolios. Unlike the result from the spillover model for simultaneous effects, all pairwise spillover effects from larger portfolios to smaller portfolios are statistically significant. This significant time-varying co-movement between large- and small-firm return volatility is exactly consistent with Ang and Chen (2002), Kroner and Ng (1998) and Conrad *et al.* (1991).

4.1.2. *Asymmetric Impacts of News on Volatility Spillovers*

The spillover GJR-GARCH (1,1)-M model described earlier is applied to investigate whether or not the leverage effects of volatility spillover across the size-based quintile portfolios. The estimated coefficients are given in Table 4. For the model specifications, several diagnostic test results such as Ljung-Box Q value and Engle's LM statistics show no serious problems in the model specification. Compared with

Table 4. Estimated parameters: Model II, spillover GJR-GARCH(1,1)-M model for five size-sorted portfolios.

Model		d	a	c	b	α	ω (ARCH)	δ (GARCH)	γ_{ij} (Leverage effects)				LL[1)]	DW[2)]	Q(6)_I[3)]	LM[4)]
GJR-GARCH (1,1)-M																
	P_SZ_XL								γ(XL,L)	γ(XL,M)	γ(XL,S)	γ(XL,XS)				
Simultaneous	Coefficient	87.788	−0.001	0.001	1.103	0.000	0.035	0.658	0.097	0.026	0.008	0.009	5530.044	1.882	9.892	0.007
	z Statistic	(6.127)	(−4.917)	(3.854)	(172.567)	(2.761)	(2.335)	(14.354)	(4.761)	(2.424)	(2.247)	(3.102)				
Pairwise	Coefficient								0.131	0.050	0.036	0.001				
	z Statistic								(3.067)	(2.953)	(3.520)	(0.211)				
	P_SZ_L								γ(L,XL)	γ(L,M)	γ(L,S)	γ(L,XS)				
Simultaneous	Coefficient	16.858	0.001	−0.0003	0.971	0.000	0.042	0.870	−0.012	0.010	−0.005	−0.004	5151.385	1.999	5.243	0.082
	z Statistic	(1.796)	(3.451)	(−1.485)	(116.251)	(−0.612)	(2.639)	(38.018)	(−0.369)	(0.807)	(−1.118)	(−1.449)				
Pairwise	Coefficient								0.518	0.044	0.027	0.021				
	z Statistic								(6.078)	(3.338)	(3.626)	(2.923)				
	P_SZ_M								γ(M,XL)	γ(M,L)	γ(M,S)	γ(M,XS)				
Simultaneous	Coefficient	26.983	0.000	−0.001	1.068	0.000	−0.004	0.780	0.000	−0.076	−0.055	0.004	4651.293	1.938	3.809	0.891
	z Statistic	(3.885)	(1.512)	(−3.429)	(72.810)	(2.328)	(−0.362)	(27.968)	(0.001)	(−1.100)	(−3.327)	(0.487)				
Pairwise	Coefficient								0.332	0.104	0.020	−0.004				
	z Statistic								(4.986)	(3.235)	(4.498)	(−1.045)				
	P_SZ_S								γ(S,XL)	γ(S,L)	γ(S,M)	γ(S,XS)				
Simultaneous	Coefficient	16.948	0.001	−0.001	1.173	0.000	0.059	0.754	0.072	0.004	−0.272	−0.015	4156.649	1.846	4.617	1.695
	z Statistic	(4.008)	(1.682)	(−2.889)	(54.036)	(1.497)	(3.033)	(19.799)	(0.270)	(0.032)	(−2.431)	(−0.719)				
Pairwise	Coefficient								0.487	0.131	0.088	0.017				
	z Statistic								(4.933)	(2.695)	(4.033)	(2.581)				

(Continued)

Table 4. (*Continued*)

Model		d	a	c	b	α	ω (ARCH)	δ (GARCH)	γ_{ij} (Leverage effects)				LL[1]	DW[2]	Q(6)_I[3]	LM[4]
	P_SZ_XS								γ(XS,XL)	γ(XS,L)	γ(XS,M)	γ(XS,S)				
Simultaneous	Coefficient	4.888	0.003	−0.001	1.239	0.000	0.033	0.625	0.572	0.561	0.258	0.027	3786.693	1.647	23.414	2.458
	z Statistic	(1.742)	(7.712)	(−1.836)	(46.146)	(0.268)	(1.366)	(10.788)	(0.843)	(1.633)	(1.197)	(0.249)				
Pairwise	Coefficient								0.629	0.362	0.163	0.122				
	z Statistic								(10.222)	(4.767)	(5.105)	(4.512)				

Note: Table 4 presents the results of estimating the spillover GJR-GARCH(1,1)-M model in order to detect the asymmetric impact of good or bad news events on the volatility spillovers. For brevity, the estimated coefficients of the spillover terms θ_{ij} are omitted from the table. The estimation model used here is as follows:

$$R_{i,t}^{V} = a_i + c_i D_t + d_i h_{i,t} + b_i R_t^{VM} + \varepsilon_{i,t}, \quad \textit{where}, \varepsilon_{i,t}|\Omega_{t-1} - N(0, h_{i,t})$$

$$h_{it} = \alpha_i + \delta_i h_{i,t-1} + \omega_i \varepsilon_{i,t-1}^2 + \gamma_{ij} s_{j,t-1}^- v_{j,t-1}^2 + \theta_{j,t-1} v_{j,t-1}^2, \quad \text{for pairwise effects}$$

$$h_{i,t} = \alpha_i + \delta_i h_{i,t-1} + \omega_i \varepsilon_{i,t-1}^2 + \sum_{\substack{j=1 \\ j\neq i}}^{n} \gamma_{ij} s_{j,t-1}^- v_{j,t-1}^2 + \sum_{\substack{j=1 \\ j\neq i}}^{n} \theta_{ij} v_{j,t-1}^2, \quad \text{for simultaneous effects}$$

i = size-, stock market- and industry-sorted portfolio; $R_{i,t}^V$ = market value weighted daily returns on portfolio i; R_t^{VM} = CRSP value − weighted daily market returns; $D_t = 1$, if it is a day following weekends or holidays, 0 otherwise; $v_{j,t-1}$ = the residuals generated from the standard GARCH (1,1); θ_{ij} = the coefficient of the spillover from the volatility of portfolio j at time $t-1$ to the conditional variance of portfolio i at time t; $s_{j,t-1}^-$ (binary variable) = 1 *if* $V_{j,t-1} < 0$, and 0 otherwise; i, j = 1(p_sz_xl), 2(p_sz_l), 3(p_sz_m), 4(p_sz_s), 5(p_sz_xs); $R_{i,t}^V$ = market value weighted daily returns on portfolio i; R_t^{VM} = CRSP value − weighted daily market returns; θ_{ij} = spillover effect from portfolio j to portfolio i; γ_{ij} = leverage effect from portfolio j to portfolio i.

1) LL = Log Likelihood 2) DW = Durbin-Watson statistics 3) Q (6)_I and Q (6)_II are the Ljung-Box Q statistics with the degrees of six, for the standardized residuals and standardized squared residuals, critical values = 10.64(10%), 12.59(5%), 16.81(1%) 4) LM = Engle's LM test statistics. The numbers in parentheses = z statistics. *, **, and *** denote significance of the statistics at the 10%, 5% and 1% levels, respectively.

Table 2, this model appears to fit better than the GARCH (1,1)-M spillover model.

The Spillover GJR-GARCH (1,1)-M model considers a binary variable $s_{j,t-1}^{-}$, to capture an asymmetric reaction of the conditional volatility to the arrival of a news event in the context of spillovers. As addressed in Sec. 1, this study is motivated to further examine how differently the return volatility of portfolio spillovers across other portfolios depending on the quality of a news event to the portfolio. This possibility can be explained by the leverage effect. A change in the financial leverage of a firm trigger a change in the covariance between the return on the stock of the firm and the returns on other stocks which in turn leads other firms to adjust their financial leverage. Similarly, it is hypothesized that a news event to a firm may cause a change in the risk of the firm as well as the other firms and a bad news event tends to lead to a higher subsequent volatility of the firms than a good news event.

The binary variable $S_{j,t-1}^{-}$ (or $S_{j,t-1}^{+}$) in the conditional variance equation takes a value of 1 for negative (or positive) portfolio return innovation (i.e., the lagged residual term $V_{j,t-1}$) and a value of 0 otherwise. If the hypothesis is true, the signs of the estimated coefficients γ_{ij} of the model are expected to be positive for negative innovations and negative for positive innovations. The coefficient γ_{ij} is referred to as "leverage term" throughout this paper in contrast to the coefficient Q_{ij} of "spillover term". In other words, unexpected negative and positive excess return on a portfolio changes *asymmetrically* the conditional volatility of the excess return on other portfolios for the next period.

Although the estimates for both pairwise and simultaneous effect are reported in Table 4, our discussion is concentrated on the estimates of the model for pairwise effects. Also, Table 4 includes the estimates of the model for the leverage effect of bad news.[5] Table 5 summarizes the estimated coefficients of the leverage term for both negative and positive innovations. It is found that there exists a leverage effect in the volatility spillover. Both positive and negative throughout this chapter in contrast to the coefficient Q_{ij} of "spillover term". In other words, unexpected negative and positive excess return on a portfolio changes *asymmetrically* the conditional volatility of the excess return on other portfolios for the next period.

Although the estimates for both pairwise and simultaneous effect are reported in Table 4, our discussion is concentrated on the estimates of the model for pairwise effects. Also, Table 4 includes the estimates of the model for the leverage effect of bad news.[5] Table 5 summarizes the estimated coefficients of the leverage term

Table 5. Estimates of leverage effects on volatility spillover: Size-sorted portfolios.

$i\backslash j$	γ (,XL)	γ (,L)	γ (,M)	γ (,S)	γ (,XS)
Panel A: $S^{-}_{j,t-1}\nu^2_{j,t-1}$					
$h_{xl,t}$	—	0.131***	0.050***	0.036***	0.001
		(3.067)	(2.953)	(3.520)	(0.211)
$h_{l,t}$	0.518***	—	0.044***	0.027***	0.021***
	(6.078)		(3.338)	(3.626)	(2.923)
$h_{m,t}$	0.332***	0.104***	—	0.020***	−0.004
	(4.986)	(3.235)		(4.498)	(−1.045)
$h_{s,j}$	0.487***	0.131***	0.088***	—	0.017**
	(4.933)	(2.695)	(4.033)		(2.581)
$h_{xs,t}$	0.629***	0.362***	0.163***	0.122***	—
	(10.222)	(4.767)	(5.105)	(4.512)	
Panel B: $S^{+}_{j,t-1}\nu^2_{j,t-1}$					
$h_{xl,t}$	—	−0.084***	−0.074***	−0.030***	−0.012***
		(−4.825)	(−7.541)	(−5.831)	(−4.755)
$h_{l,t}$	−0.020	—	−0.008	0.002	0.004**
	(−0.799)		(−0.739)	(0.613)	(2.088)
$h_{m,t}$	−0.170***	0.042	—	0.036***	0.013***
	(−3.001)	(1.062)		(2.960)	(2.898)
$h_{s,t}$	−0.464**	0.038	0.150*	—	0.031*
	(−2.076)	(0.345)	(1.934)		(1.847)
$h_{xs,t}$	−0.048	−0.421*	−0.317**	−0.099	—
	(−0.117)	(−1.752)	(−2.566)	(−1.147)	

Note: Table summarizes the estimated coefficients associated with the impact of bad or good news on the volatility spillovers among the firm size-sorted portfolios. The coefficients γ_{ij} in the spillover GJR-GARCH (1,1)-M model for pairwise effects measure the leverage effect from portfolio j to portfolio i for both negative and positive innovations. In other words, the positive (or negative) sign of the coefficients means unexpected bad (or good) news to a particular portfolio j tends to increase (or decrease) the volatility of the returns on other portfolio i. The estimate coefficients for bad news (i.e., negative innovations) and good news (i.e., positive innovations) are presented in Panels A and B, respectively.

The numbers in parentheses below the estimated coefficients are z statistics. *, ** and *** denote significance of the statistics at the 10%, 5% and 1% levels, respectively.

for both negative and positive innovations. It is found that there exists a leverage effect in the volatility spillover. Both positive and negative portfolio returns innovations are asymmetrically transmitted among portfolios. The signs of the coefficients of the leverage term for the negative shock are consistently positive and statistically significant. In the case of positive shock, some coefficients show negative signs. Although some coefficients have positive signs, most of them do not seem to be statistically significant. It is noteworthy that leverage effect is much more outstanding for negative innovations than for positive innovations.

In addition, such leverage effects show an asymmetric pattern. The coefficients below the diagonal in Panel A of Table 5 are consistently larger than those above the diagonal. Hence, past negative shock to larger portfolios causes more volatility of other portfolios than the negative shock to smaller portfolios does. In fact, increase in the conditional volatility of smallest portfolio (p_sz_xs) induced by a negative shock to largest portfolio (p_sz_xl), which is 0.629 of $\gamma_{xs,xl}$, is almost twice as large as that induced by a negative shock to large portfolio (p_sz_l), which is 0.362 of $\gamma_{xs,l}$. A similar story can be posed for the case of positive innovation, though the results are not quite consistent and statistically significant. It is noted that past positive shock to largest portfolio tends to reduce the conditional volatility of smaller portfolios.

The signs of the estimated coefficients reported in Panel A and B of Table 5 indicate that unexpected bad news to a particular portfolio tends to increase the volatility of the returns on other portfolios, whereas unexpected good news to a particular portfolio (in particular largest portfolio) reduces the volatility of the returns on other portfolios.

Unexpected negative and positive returns have vastly different effects on the volatility spillovers across firm size-sorted portfolios. The results support that the conditional volatility of smaller firms tends to be higher after bad news events than after good news events of larger firms. The asymmetry of the leverage effect in volatility spillover appears to render smaller stocks more volatile than larger stocks.

4.2. *Market- and Industry-Sorted Portfolios*

4.2.1. *Volatility Spillover Effects*[6]

I examine possible volatility spillovers, both among three stock markets, including the NYSE, AMEX and NASDAQ and among five representative industries including manufacturing, financial, utility (including regulated industry), service and miscellaneous industry. The estimates of the spillover GARCH (1,1)-M model are presented in Table 6.

The format of the table is identical to that of Table 2. The diagnostics of autocorrelation and autoregressive heteroskedasticity show that the Spillover GARCH (1,1)-M model fits better than the basic GARCH (1,1)-M model that does not include the spillover term. Table 6 reports the presence of serial correlation in the market-sorted portfolios and utility industry portfolio. With respect to the spillover model for simultaneous effect, most of the GARCH-M effects consistently indicate positive signs. The estimated coefficient of GARCH-M term in the NASDAQ portfolio shows a negative sign, but it is not significant. For simplicity, the estimated coefficients of spillover terms for the market- and industry-sorted portfolios are summarized in Tables 7 and 8, respectively.

Table 7 indicates that volatility spillovers are found both among and between the three stock market affiliations. Unexpected volatility surprises originating in the NYSE portfolio significantly effect the future volatilities of the AMEX and NASDAQ portfolios for both simultaneous and pairwise effects ($p = 0.05$). With respect to pairwise effect, in particular, the return volatility spillover from the NYSE to the NASDAQ (0.41851) is about 2.5 times larger than that from the NYSE to the AMEX (0.179283). This means that the NYSE is more closely synchronized with the NASDAQ market than with the AMEX. This is consistent with the finding that the spillover effect coefficients from the AMEX to the NYSE (0.000577) is less than those from the NASDAQ to the NYSE (0.004741). For the spillover effects between the AMEX and the NASDAQ, the effect from the NASDAQ to the AMEX (0.010705), though insignificant, is about 30 times greater than the effect from the AMEX to the NASDAQ (0.003393). To summarize, the return volatility spillover effect from the NYSE

Table 6. Estimated parameters: Model I, spillover GARCH (1,1)-M model for market- and industry-sorted portfolios.

Model		d	a	c	b	α	ω (ARCH)	δ (GARCH)	θ_{ij}		LL[1]	DW[2]	Q(6)_I[3]	Q(6)_II	LM[4]
Panel A: Markets															
	P_MKT_NYSE								θ(nyse, amex)	θ(nyse, nasdaq)					
GARCH(1,1)-M	Coefficient	10.488	0.000	0.000	0.990	0.000	0.125	0.869			5432.2	1.927	4.159	33.844***	0.432
	z Statistic	(1.262)	(2.024)	(2.979)	(220.910)	(3.022)	(7.650)	(50.055)							
Spillover GARCH(1,1)-M															
Simultaneous	Coefficient	18.159	0.000	0.000	0.975	0.000	0.138	0.790	0.001	0.006	5450.15	1.937	2.704	19.368***	1.577
	z Statistic	(2.074)	(1.478)	(2.558)	(173.910)	(−2.593)	(6.599)	(32.325)	(5.251)	(5.050)					
Pairwise	Coefficient								0.001	0.005					
	z Statistic								(4.623)	(4.482)					
	P_MKT_AMEX								θ(amex, nyse)	θ(amex, nasdaq)					
GARCH(1,1)-M	Coefficient	−0.981	0.002	−0.003	0.665	0.000	0.032	0.953			3065.1	1.972	17.159***	4.3662	0.894
	z Statistic	(−0.196)	(1.030)	(−2.577)	(16.030)	(2.397)	(3.885)	(81.293)							
Spillover GARCH(1,1)-M															
Simultaneous	Coefficient	4.227	0.000	−0.003	0.674	0.000	0.027	0.947	0.174	−0.008	3065.184	1.977	18.352***	5.2557	1.264
	z Statistic	(0.865)	(0.006)	(−2.545)	(15.847)	(2.544)	(3.239)	(69.040)	(2.003)	(−0.702)					
Pairwise	Coefficient								0.179	0.011					
									(2.125)	(0.956)					
	P_MKT_NASDAQ								θ(nasdaq, nyse)	θ(nasdaq, amex)					
GARCH(1,1)-M	Coefficient	1.359	0.001	0.000	1.682	0.000	0.061	0.914			3791.3	1.967	3.756	3.2687	1.348
	z Statistic	(0.224)	(1.615)	(−0.608)	(74.471)	(2.374)	(4.683)	(43.409)							
Spillover GARCH(1,1)-M															
Simultaneous	Coefficient	−0.481	0.002	0.000	1.658	0.000	0.057	0.685	1.168	−0.002	3813.51	1.975	5.028	15.657**	6.942***
	z Statistic	(−0.094)	(2.215)	(−0.581)	(65.747)	(3.838)	(2.282)	(9.541)	(4.066)	(−0.604)					
Pairwise	Coefficient								0.419	0.003					
	z Statistic								(3.403)	(1.921)					

(Continued)

Table 6. (*Continued*)

Model		d	a	c	b	α	ω (ARCH)	δ (GARCH)	θ_{ij}				LL[1]	DW[2]	Q(6)_I[3]	Q(6)_II	LM[4]
Panel B: Industries																	
	P_SIC_MANUF								θ(manuf, util)	θ(manuf, svc)	θ(manuf, fin)	θ(manuf, oth)					
GARCH(1,1)-M	Coefficient	−49.767	0.001	0.001	1.077	0.000	0.082	0.862					5136.7	1.813	19.153***	0.958	0.150
	z Statistic	−3.389	(4.493)	(3.687)	(149.144)	(4.077)	(6.089)	(35.315)									
Spillover GARCH(1,1)-M																	
Simultaneous	Coefficient	33.169	−0.0001	0.001	1.088	0.000	0.031	0.679	0.006	0.014	0.024	0.011	5189.6	1.931	5.850	0.782	0.034
	z Statistic	(2.546)	−0.347	(3.052)	(128.167)	(3.125)	(1.361)	(12.254)	(2.611)	(2.533)	(3.791)	(2.357)					
Pairwise	Coefficient								0.007	0.017	0.020	0.012					
	z Statistic								(3.438)	(4.518)	(4.079)	(4.950)					
	P_SIC_UTIL								θ(util, manuf)	θ(util, svc)	θ(util,fin)	θ(util, oth)					
GARCH(1,1)-M	Coefficient	3.740	0.000	0.000	0.370	0.000	0.138	0.862					4069.6	1.696	30.749***	13.976**	6.003**
	z Statistic	(0.990)	(0.076)	(0.857)	(19.331)	(2.653)	(8.369)	(56.474)									
Spillover GARCH(1,1)-M																	
Simultaneous	Coefficient	4.261	0.000	0.001	0.366	0.000	0.106	0.820	0.225	0.070	0.023	0.012	4091.1	1.698	24.795***	12.726**	4.692
	z Statistic	(1.093)	(0.068)	(1.076)	(17.039)	(−1.530)	(5.654)	(32.038)	(3.111)	(2.673)	(1.959)	(0.539)					
Pairwise	Coefficient								0.286	0.113	0.048	0.065					
	z Statistic								(4.432)	(4.089)	(3.398)	(3.292)					
	P_SIC_SVC								θ(svc. manuf)	θ(svc, util)	θ(svc, fin)	θ(svc, oth)					
GARCH(1,1)-M	Coefficient	8.898	0.001	−0.001	1.263	0.000	0.076	0.891					4580.7	1.862	9.541	3.198	0.038
	z Statistic	(0.740)	(1.891)	(−1.915)	(105.324)	(3.509)	(7.799)	(54.013)									
Spillover GARCH(1,1)-M																	
Simultaneous	Coefficient	18.977	0.0005	−0.001	1.271	0.000	0.055	0.652	0.115	0.015	0.018	0.064	4619	1.866	8.555	2.395	0.265
	z Statistic	(1.873)	(1.169)	(−1.588)	(87.839)	(3.754)	(2.572)	(10.584)	(2.452)	(2.890)	(2.128)	(3.828)					
Pairwise	Coefficient								0.156	0.033	0.017	0.081					
	z Statistic								(4.842)	(4.747)	(2.851)	(6.273)					

(*Continued*)

Table 6. (*Continued*)

Model		d	a	c	b	α	ω (ARCH)	δ (GARCH)	θ_{ij}				LL^1	DW^2	Q(6)_I³	Q(6)_II	LM⁴
	P_SIC_FIN								θ(fin, manuf)	θ(fin, util)	θ(fin, svc)	θ(fin, oth)					
GARCH(1,1)-M	Coefficient	1.616	0.0003	0.001	1.090	0.000	0.067	0.927					4216.47	1.916	3.174	1.471	0.001
	z Statistic	(0.367)	(0.876)	(1.382)	(67.688)	(3.166)	(6.109)	(85.607)									
Spillover GARCH(1,1)-M																	
Simultaneous	Coefficient	1.600	0.0003	0.0005	1.111	0.000	0.059	0.876	0.155	0.001	0.068	0.032	4233.64	1.916	2.854	3.119	0.905
	z Statistic	(0.375)	(1.039)	(1.081)	(55.778)	(−3.451)	(4.142)	(47.263)	(3.289)	(0.160)	(4.384)	(2.395)					
Pairwise	Coefficient								0.129	0.009	0.068	0.055					
	z Statistic								(3.522)	(2.244)	(5.358)	(4.622)					
	P_SZ_OTH								θ(oth, manuf)	θ(oth, util)	θ(oth, svc)	θ(oth, fin)					
GARCH(1,1)-M	Coefficient	0.311	0.001	0.0002	0.925	0.000	0.041	0.952					4431.07	1.935	9.797	8.109	7.812***
	z Statistic	(0.032)	(1.001)	(0.470)	(69.142)	(1.982)	(5.126)	(104.427)									
Spillover GARCH(1,1)-M																	
Simultaneous	Coefficient	6.089	0.000	0.000	0.931	0.000	0.039	0.797	0.077	0.002	0.082	0.020	4454.53	1.937	10.377	4.498	3.061
	z Statistic	(0.710)	(0.429)	(0.809)	(58.974)	(2.416)	(3.104)	(19.382)	(1.848)	(0.434)	(3.649)	(2.073)					
Pairwise	Coefficient								0.118	0.017	0.089	0.038					
	z Statistic								(3.139)	(3.264)	(5.036)	(3.123)					

Note: Daily estimates of the spillover GARCH(1,1)-M model for three market-sorted portfolios of the NYSE (p_mkt_nyse), AMEX (p_mkt_amex), and NASDAQ (p_mkt_nasdaq) portfolios (Panel A) and five industry-sorted portfolios of the manufacturing (p_sic_manuf), utilities (p_sic_util), services (p_sic_svc) , financial (p_sic_fin), and miscellaneous (p_sic_oth) portfolios (Panel B). The estimation models and all pertinent notations follow those described in Table 2.

1) LL = Log Likelihood 2) DW = Durbin-Watson statistics 3) Q(6)_I and Q(6)_II are the Ljung-Box Q statistics with the degrees of six, for the standardized residuals and standardized squared residuals, critical values = 10.64(10%), 12.59(5%), 16.81(1%) 4) LM = Engle's LM test statistics. The numbers in parentheses below the estimated coefficients are z statistics. *, **, and *** denote significance of the statistics at the 10%, 5% and 1% levels, respectively.

Table 7. Estimates of volatility spillover effects: Market-sorted portfolios.

j/i	$\nu^2_{nyse,t-1}$	$\nu^2_{amex,t-1}$	$\nu^2_{nasdaq,t-1}$	$\nu^2_{nyse,t-1}$	$\nu^2_{amex,t-1}$	$\nu^2_{nasdaq,t-1}$
	Panel A: Simultaneous effects			Panel B: Pairwise effects		
$h_{nyse,t}$	—	0.0001***	0.001***	—	0.001***	0.005***
		(5.251)	(5.050)		(4.623)	(4.482)
$h_{amex,t}$	0.174**	—	−0.008	0.179**	—	0.011
	(2.003)		(−0.702)	(2.125)		(0.956)
$h_{nasdaq,t}$	1.168***	−0.002	—	0.419***	0.003*	—
	(4.066)	(−0.604)		(3.403)	(1.921)	

Note: Table summarized the estimated coefficients of spillover effects. The coefficients of the simultaneous spillover term in Panel A show spillover effects across all three market-sorted portfolios of the NYSE (p_mkt_nyse), AMEX (p_mkt_amex) and NASDAQ (p_mkt_nasdaq) stocks. The coefficients in Panel B measure the volatility spillover effects between a pair of the market-sorted portfolios. The estimated coefficients presented in this table means the spillover effect of past volatility of portfolio j (i.e., $\nu^2_{i,t-1}$) on the future volatility of portfolio i (i.e., $h_{i,t}$). The numbers in the parenthesis are z statistics. *, ** and *** denote significance of the statistics at the 10%, 5% and 1% levels, respectively.

market (p_mkt_nyse) to the NASDAQ (p_mkt_nasdaq) and AMEX (p_mkt_amex) markets and that from the NASDAQ to the AMEX are observed to be relatively strong, while the spillover from the AMEX or the NASDAQ to the NYSE appears to be weak.

Table 8 presents the estimates of the Spillover GARCH (1,1)-M model applied to the industry-sorted portfolios. The estimated coefficients of the spillover term show a distinct asymmetric volatility spillover effect of a particular portfolio at time $t-1$ on the conditional variance of other portfolios at time t. Specifically, spillover effects from the manufacturing industry (p_sic_manuf) to the others are unambiguously greatest. In particular, spillover effects from the utility industry portfolio (p_sic_util) to the other portfolios are very small relative to those from the other portfolios to the utility industry portfolio. Note that the estimated coefficients of the spillover term of the model for simultaneous and pairwise effects below the diagonals are larger than those above the diagonals with a few exceptions. Setting aside the miscellaneous industry (p_sic_oth), the impact of a past shock to a particular portfolio on the conditional variance is strong in the order of manufacturing, financial, service and utility industry. For example, with respect to the pairwise effect, the spillover effect from the manufacturing industry to the utility industry is almost 40 times

Table 8. Estimates of volatility spillover effects: Industry-sorted portfolios.

$i\backslash j$	$\nu^2_{manuf,t-1}$	$\nu^2_{oth,t-1}$	$\nu^2_{fin,t-1}$	$\nu^2_{svc,t-1}$	$\nu^2_{util,t-1}$
Panel A: Simultaneous spillover effects					
$h_{manuf,t}$	—	0.011**	0.024***	0.014**	0.006***
		(2.357)	(3.791)	(2.533)	(2.611)
$h_{oth,t}$	0.077	—	0.02**	0.082***	0.002
	(1.848)		(2.073)	(3.649)	(0.434)
$h_{fin,t}$	0.155***	0.032	—	0.068***	0.001
	(3.289)	(2.395)		(4.384)	(0.16)
$h_{svc,t}$	0.115**	0.064***	0.018**	—	0.015***
	(2.452)	(3.828)	(2.128)		(2.89)
$h_{util,t}$	0.225***	0.012	0.023	0.07	—
	(3.111)	(0.539)	(1.959)	(2.673)	
Panel B: Pairwise spillover effects					
$h_{manuf,t}$		0.012***	0.02***	0.017***	0.007***
		(4.95)	(4.079)	−4.518	(3.438)
$h_{oth,t}$	0.118***		0.038***	0.089***	0.017***
	(3.139)		(3.123)	(5.036)	(3.264)
$h_{fin,t}$	0.129***	0.055***		0.068***	0.009**
	(3.522)	(4.622)		(5.358)	(2.244)
$h_{svc,t}$	0.156***	0.081***	0.017***		0.033***
	(4.842)	(6.273)	(2.851)		(4.747)
$h_{util,t}$	0.286***	0.065***	0.048***	0.113***	
	(4.432)	(3.292)	(3.398)	(4.089)	

Note: Estimates of the spillover GARCH (1,1)-M model for five industry-sorted portfolios of the manufacturing (p_sic_manuf), utility (p_sic_util), services (p_sic_svc), financial (p_sic_fin) and miscellaneous (p_sic_oth) industry portfolios. The estimated coefficients presented here mean the spillover effect of past volatility of portfolio j on the future volatility of portfolio i (from j to i). The numbers in the parenthesis are z statistics. *, ** and *** denote significance of the statistics at the 10%, 5% and 1% levels, respectively.

larger than that from the utility industry to the manufacturing industry (0.286 vs. 0.007). The spillover effects from the financial industry (p_sic_fin) and the service industry (p_sic_svc) to the utility industry are 5.3 and 3.4 times larger than those from the utility industry to the financial industry and the service industry, respectively. Therefore, it is found that there exist asymmetric volatility effects among the five industry-sorted portfolios. In short, a shock to the firms in the manufacturing industry have the greatest impact on the future return volatility of the firms in other industries, while a shock to the firms in the utility industry appears to have minimal impact on the future conditional volatility of the firms in other industries.

Although the results of the spillover model for the market- and industry-sorted portfolios show distinct volatility spillovers and their asymmetry pattern, it is not easy to offer a substantive economic explanation underlying these findings. Several studies document the volatility spillover effect as an important feature of international stock return volatility processes (e.g., Hamao *et al.*, 1990; Bae and Karolyi, 1994). These studies present that the spillover phenomenon across international stock markets seems to be related to the subsequent reflection of information with time lag because of the different market operation times among the markets. Indeed, their argument could be an explanation for the volatility spillovers, but not for the asymmetry of the spillovers. A key clue to a plausible explanation of the asymmetric volatility spillovers emerges in Table 1. The order of average market capitalizations of the stocks in the portfolios given in Table 1 is exactly consistent with the direction of the asymmetric volatility spillovers among size-, market- and industry-sorted portfolios. This finding sheds an important light on the phenomenon of the asymmetric volatility spillovers; asymmetric spillovers observed across market- and industry-sorted portfolios may be mainly attributable to the difference in firm size of the stocks of the portfolios, rather than the difference in stock market affiliation or industry.[7] Hence, it is likely to appear that the asymmetry in volatility spillovers are mainly influenced by the difference in firm size. Thus, the size of a firm seems to play the role of "information reference". This "size effect" in the asymmetric spillovers may cast a serious doubt on prior literature about the volatility spillovers across international stock markets. The volatility spillovers across international markets documented by previous studies might be a spurious result due to no control for the size difference of the stock markets. It is noteworthy that asymmetry in volatility spillovers is more pronounced in the size-sorted portfolios than the market- or industry-sorted portfolios.

4.2.2. *Asymmetric Impacts of News on Volatility Spillovers*

Table 9 reports the estimates of the Spillover GJR-GARCH (1,1)-M model along with diagnostic test results for the goodness-of-fit of the model. The Spillover GJR-GARCH (1,1)-M model seems to fit better

Table 9. Estimated parameters: Model II, spillover GJR-GARCH (1,1)-M model for market- and industry-sorted portfolios.

Model		d	a	c	b	α	ω (ARCH)	δ (GARCH)	γ_{ij} (leverage effects)				LL[1)]	DW[2)]	Q(6)_I[3)]	Q(6)_II	LM[4)]
Panel A: Market-Sorted Portfolios																	
GJR-GARCH(1,1)-M																	
	P_MKT_NYSE								γ(nyse, amex)	γ(nyse, nasdaq)							
Simultaneous	Coefficient	19.198	0.0001	0.0005	0.978	0.0000	0.141	0.796	0.001	0.0002			5452.4	1.938	2.187	11.511*	1.547
	z Statistic	(2.213)	(1.261)	(2.629)	(160.917)	(−2.543)	(6.690)	(33.370)	(2.782)	(0.097)							
Pairwise	Coefficient								0.000	−0.001							
	z Statistic								(1.926)	(−0.770)							
	P_MKT_AMEX								γ(amex, nyse)	γ(amex, nasdaq)							
Simultaneous	Coefficient	1.441	0.001	−0.003	0.668	0.0000	0.022	0.961	0.085	−0.080			3067.4	1.974	18.018***	6.429	1.730
	z Statistic	(0.310)	(0.599)	(−2.462)	(15.306)	(2.569)	(2.813)	(72.599)	(0.330)	(−2.198)							
Pairwise	Coefficient								0.537	−0.053							
	z Statistic								(1.615)	(−1.470)							
	P_MKT_NASDAQ								γ(nasdaq, nyse)	γ(nasdaq, amex)							
Simultaneous	Coefficient	−31.499	0.006	−0.001	1.689	0.00002	0.046	0.780	−0.098	−0.011			3798.6	1.908	4.968	6.802	1.709
	z Statistic	(−4.485)	(5.758)	(−0.828)	(70.308)	(2.821)	(2.337)	(11.526)	(−0.387)	(−1.564)							
Pairwise	Coefficient								0.453	−0.003							
	z Statistic								(0.780)	(−0.525)							
Panel B: Industry-Sorted Portfolios																	
GJR-GARCH(1,1)-M																	
	P_SIC_MANUF								γ(manuf, util)	γ(manuf, svc)	γ(manuf, fin)	γ(manuf, oth)					
Simultaneous	Coefficient	49.132	−0.0003	0.001	1.083	0.0000	0.033	0.662	0.005	−0.021	0.010	0.030	5195.85	1.947	5.114	1.750	0.019
	z Statistic	(3.745)	(−1.537)	(2.768)	(120.798)	(3.391)	(1.523)	(11.955)	(1.202)	(−1.556)	(1.081)	(2.796)					
Pairwise	Coefficient								−0.003	−0.003	0.005	0.007					
	z Statistic								(−1.064)	(−0.447)	(0.709)	(1.156)					

(Continued)

Table 9. (*Continued*)

Model		d	a	c	b	α	ω (ARCH)	δ (GARCH)	γ_{ij} (leverage effects)				LL[1)]	DW[2)]	Q(6)_I[3)]	Q(6)_II	LM[4)]
	P_SIC_UTIL								γ(util, manuf)	γ(util, svc)	γ(util, fin)	γ(util, oth)					
Simultaneous	Coefficient	3.236	0.0001	0.0005	0.369	0.0000	0.095	0.836	−0.119	−0.091	−0.064	−0.043	4095.03	1.698	22.446***	11.867*	4.116**
	z Statistic	(0.842)	(0.336)	(0.913)	(16.499)	(−0.712)	(5.246)	(34.021)	(−0.723)	(−1.993)	(−2.233)	(−1.255)					
Pairwise	Coefficient								−0.100	−0.095	−0.026	0.004					
	z Statistic								(−0.685)	(−2.214)	(−1.006)	(0.121)					
	P_SIC_SVC								γ(svc. manuf)	γ(svc, util)	γ(svc, fin)	γ(svc, oth)					
Simultaneous	Coefficient	34.722	−0.0002	−0.001	1.269	0.0000	0.056	0.578	0.180	0.015	0.058	0.037	4623.78	1.902	7.089	2.823	0.033
	z Statistic	(3.236)	(−0.515)	(−1.694)	(86.839)	(4.083)	(2.351)	(8.812)	(2.103)	(1.375)	(2.828)	(1.032)					
Pairwise	Coefficient								0.015	0.025	−0.002	−0.017					
	z Statistic								(0.215)	(2.480)	(−0.186)	(−0.748)					
	P_SIC_FIN								γ(fin, manuf)	γ(fin, util)	γ(fin, svc)	γ(fin, oth)					
Simultaneous	Coefficient	3.810	0.0002	0.0005	1.107	0.0000	0.057	0.881	−0.010	−0.023	0.083	0.018	4238.89	1.919	2.892	3.259	1.335
	z Statistic	(0.890)	(0.521)	(1.020)	(57.392)	(−3.559)	(3.886)	(44.012)	(−0.128)	(−1.891)	(2.808)	(0.647)					
Pairwise	Coefficient								0.005	−0.027	0.062	−0.020					
	z Statistic								(0.074)	(−2.758)	(2.444)	(−0.955)					
	P_SIC_OTH								γ(oth, manuf)	γ(oth, util)	γ(oth, svc)	γ(oth, fin)					
Simultaneous	Coefficient	5.996	0.0002	0.0003	0.929	0.0000	0.042	0.771	−0.138	0.017	0.033	0.002	4456.31	1.938	10.165	3.317	2.213
	z Statistic	(0.690)	(0.475)	(0.639)	(57.594)	(2.733)	(3.080)	(16.351)	(−1.349)	(1.319)	(0.839)	(0.091)					
Pairwise	Coefficient								−0.081	0.010	0.005	0.011					
	z Statistic								(−1.031)	(0.955)	(0.202)	(0.678)					

Note: Table shows the results of estimating the spillover GJR-GARCH(1,1)-M model for market- and industry-sorted portfolios in order to detect the asymmetric impact of good or bad news events on the volatility spillovers. For brevity, the estimated coefficients of the spillover terms θ_{ij} are omitted from the table. The model specifications and all pertinent notations follow those described in Table 4. 1) LL = Log Likelihood 2) DW = Durbin-Watson statistics 3) Q (6)_I and Q (6)_II are the Ljung-Box Q statistics with the degrees of six, for the standardized residuals and standardized squared residuals, critical values = 10.64(10%), 12.59(5%), 16.81(1%) 4) LM = Engle's LM test statistics. The numbers in parentheses = *z* statistics. *, **, and *** denote significance of the statistics at the 10%, 5% and 1% levels, respectively.

compared with the Spillover GARCH (1,1)-M model. No serious misspecifications are found in market- and industry-sorted portfolios.[8]

The estimated coefficients of leverage terms γ_{ij} in the model for pairwise effects are summarized in Tables 10 and 11. Table 10 indicates the presence of the leverage effect in volatility spillovers among the market-sorted portfolios as observed in the model for the size-sorted portfolios. The leverage effects in volatility spillovers are observed between the NYSE portfolio and other market-sorted portfolios. For instance, bad news shock to the NYSE firms causes subsequently higher conditional volatility of the NADAQ and AMEX firms (i.e., positive sign of $\gamma_{NASDAQ,NYSE}$ and $\gamma_{AMEX,NYSE}$ as appeared in Panel A of Table 10). In particular, the leverage effect is more pronounced between the NYSE and NASDAQ market than between the NYSE and AMEX market. In contrast, the leverage effects between the NASDAQ and AMEX portfolios are reversed from my expectation.[9] However, those estimates are not statistically significant.

The estimated coefficients of GJR-GARCH (1,1)-M model for five industry-based portfolios are presented in Table 11. The results appear to be far from consistent with the leverage effects. Moreover, most coefficients are not statistically significant. It is, however,

Table 10. Estimates of leverage effects on volatility spillover: Market-sorted portfolios.

$i\backslash j$	γ(,nyse)	γ(,amex)	γ (,nasdaq)	γ (,nyse)	γ (,amex)	γ (,nasdaq)
	Panel A: $S^{-}_{j,t-1}v^{2}_{j,t-1}$ (negative innovations)			Panel B: $S^{+}_{j,t-1}v^{2}_{j,t-1}$ (positive innovations)		
$h_{nyse,t}$	—	0.0005*	−0.001	—	−0.0005**	0.001
		(1.926)	(−0.770)		(−2.01)	(0.712)
$h_{amex,t}$	0.537	—	0.053	−0.701*	—	0.042
	(1.615)		(−1.470)	(−1.670)		(1.237)
$h_{nasdaq,t}$	0.453	−0.003	—	−1.322**	0.003	—
	(0.780)	(−0.525)	—	(−2.113)	(0.656)	

Note: Table summarizes the estimated coefficients associated with the impact of bad or good news on the volatility spillovers among the market sorted-portfolios. The coefficients γ_{ij} in the spillover GJR-GARCH (1,1)-M model for pairwise effects measure the leverage effect from portfolio j to portfolio i for both negative and positive innovations. In other words, the positive (or negative) sign of the coefficients means unexpected bad (or good) news to a particular portfolio j tends to increase (or decrease) the volatility of the returns on other portfolio i. The estimate coefficients for bad news (i.e., negative innovations) and good news (i.e., positive innovations) are presented in Panels A and B, respectively.
The numbers in parentheses below the estimated coefficients are z statistics. *, **, and *** denote significance of the statistics at the 10%, 5% and 1% levels, respectively.

Table 11. Estimates of leverage effects on volatility spillover: Industry-sorted portfolios.

$i \backslash j$	$\gamma(\,,\text{manuf})$	$\gamma(\,,\text{oth})$	$\gamma(\,,\text{fin})$	$\gamma(\,,\text{svc})$	$\gamma(\,,\text{util})$
Panel A: $S^{-}_{j,t-1}\nu^{2}_{j,t-1}$					
$h_{manuf,t}$		0.007	0.005	−0.003	−0.003
		(1.156)	(0.709)	(−0.447)	(−1.064)
$h_{oth,t}$	−0.081		0.011	0.005	0.01
	(−1.031)		(0.678)	(0.202)	(0.955)
$h_{fin,t}$	0.005	−0.02		0.062**	−0.027***
	(0.074)	(−0.955)		(2.444)	(−2.758)
$h_{svc,t}$	0.015	−0.017	−0.002		0.025**
	(0.215)	(−0.748)	(−0.186)		(2.48)
$h_{util,t}$	−0.1	0.004	−0.026	−0.095**	
	(−0.685)	(0.121)	(−1.006)	(−2.214)	
Panel B: $S^{+}_{j,t-1}\nu^{2}_{j,t-1}$					
$h_{manuf,t}$		−0.006	−0.005	0.003	0.003
		(−0.948)	(−0.674)	(0.462)	(0.947)
$h_{oth,t}$	0.073		−0.009	−0.004	−0.01
	(0.939)		(−0.595)	(−0.136)	(−0.960)
$h_{fin,t}$	−0.0004	0.022		−0.062**	0.027***
	(−0.006)	(1.136)		(−2.445)	(2.757)
$h_{svc,t}$	−0.016	0.018	0.003		−0.025**
	(−0.231)	(0.768)	(0.244)		(−2.477)
$h_{util,t}$	0.103	−0.003	0.026	0.095**	
	(0.708)	(−0.098)	(1.011)	(2.222)	

Note: The estimated coefficients relating to the impact of bad or good news on the volatility spillovers among the industry sorted-portfolios. The coefficients γ_{ij} in the spillover GJR-GARCH (1,1)-M model for pairwise effects measure the leverage effect from portfolio j to portfolio i for both negative and positive innovations.
The numbers in parentheses below the estimated coefficients are z statistics. *, ** and *** denote significance of the statistics at the 10%, 5% and 1% levels, respectively.

interesting that the signs of the estimated coefficients in Panel A (for negative innovations) are opposite to those in Panel B (for positive innovations). So, it seems to depend on the relationship between two industries whether or not a bad (or good) news shock to an industry increases (or decreases) the future volatility of the stock return of the firms in other industry.

5. Conclusions

I investigated the dynamic behavior of the stock return volatility of firms sorted on several firm characteristics such as firm size of capitalization, stock market affiliation and industry. The results confirm that there exists a stable and asymmetric pattern of the volatility spillovers between large and small firms. That is, large-firm returns tend to affect the subsequent volatility of small-firm returns, but small-firm returns do not have much effect on the volatility of large-firm returns. A variant of the GARCH model employed in this study provides a more consistent pattern of the volatility spillovers across firm-size sorted portfolios than prior studies do.

Applying the same empirical models, it is also uncovered that there exists a specific pattern of return volatility spillovers across portfolios sorted on the market affiliation and industry. I found that the shocks to the firms in the NYSE market significantly affect the subsequent conditional return volatility of the firms in the AMEX and NASDAQ markets, while the surprises to the firms in the AMEX and NASDAQ market do not have much impact on the conditional volatility of the firms in the NYSE. With respect to industry-sorted portfolios, it is found that the volatility spillover from manufacturing industry to other industries is most pronounced among the spillovers observed among any other industries.

I also document that the spillover effect becomes weak when the impact of volatility shocks to a portfolio on the rest of portfolios are considered in the conditional equation of the model (i.e., the model for simultaneous effects) compared to the spillover effect when the volatility spillover between a pair of portfolios is taken into account (the model for pairwise effects). It is believed that a shock to a particular portfolio may affect the subsequent volatility of *all* other portfolios, which in turn may trigger multiple repercussive spillovers among the portfolios.

It is also worthy to note that the volatility spillovers across the portfolios sorted by firm size are more pronounced than those across the portfolios sorted by stock market affiliation and industry. Interestingly, the asymmetric direction of the spillovers observed in market- and industry-based portfolios is found to be almost consistent with the order of the average firm size of the portfolios. This finding implies that the asymmetric volatility spillovers observed in the market and industry portfolios would more likely depend on the difference in firm size, rather than market affiliation or industry.

I modified the Spillover GARCH (1,1)-M model to allow an important asymmetry in the conditional variance equation, often called the "leverage effect", thus examining whether the leverage effects spillover across portfolios. The results show that the leverage effect in volatility spillovers is found across size and market sorted portfolios. In particular, the leverage effect appears to be most conspicuous between the largest and smallest-size portfolios. The existence of the leverage effect in volatility spillovers implies that the conditional co-movement between large-firm returns and small-firm returns tends to be higher after bad news event than after good news event of the large firms.

Following the logic of the leverage hypothesis claimed in Black (1976), this finding is interesting because a bad (or good) news shock to a given firm increases (or decreases) raises (or lowers) the future volatility and riskiness of not only the firm but also *other* firms. This finding of the asymmetric impact of bad or good news on volatility spillovers helps us explain the negative skewness of stock returns and why the leverage effect is stronger for small firms compared to large firms.

The findings documented in this chapter have some implications for asset pricing. The empirical results of this study demonstrate that the conditional volatility of a stock is a function of not only its own past realized variances but also the past realized variances of the other stocks. Also, the impact of variances of other stocks have asymmetric pattern depending on whether the variances are caused by good news or bad news. Therefore, the volatility spillover effect as well as the asymmetric news impact on the volatility spillover should be considered in the time-varying asset-pricing process of a given stock so that its aggregate volatility may not be underestimated.

Endnotes

1. King *et al.* (1990) report the link between international stock markets. This linkage is investigated further by Hamao *et al.* (1990), who examine the issue of volatility spillovers among international stock markets using ARCH-M model on daily open and close prices. A similar approach is taken in Engle and Susmel (1990) and Ng *et al.* (1991) report the volatility spillovers between the U.K. and U.S. stock

markets and among the Pacific Rim countries, respectively. Chan *et al.* (1990) analyze the relationship between the S&P 500 stocks index and the stock index futures markets.

2. Put differently, the surprises of the other portfolios are treated as exogenous variables and the volatility spillover effects for each portfolio are estimated separately. Joint estimation by the multivariate model is omitted because the results documented by the univariate model are not far different from those by the multivariate model (Conrad *et al.*, 1991).
3. The model used in this study is constructed on the basis of the GARCH (1,1)-M, while Hamao *et al.* (1990) and Conrad *et al.* (1991) employ the MA(1)-GARCH(1,1)-M and the ARIMA(1,1)-GARCH(1,1)-M model, respectively.
4. According to Rabemananjara and Zakoian (1993) and Fonari and Mele (1997), the asymmetric effect of the volatility (called leverage effect) could be reversed. High negative shocks increase future volatility more than high positive ones while small positive shocks too often produce a stronger impact on future volatility than negative shocks of the same size.
5. The estimates for the leverage effect of good news are not reported here.
6. The same model is also applied for equally weighted returns series (portfolio and the CRSP market returns). The results are not documented here because diagnostic statistics show significant misspecification of the model.
7. It suggests that the research regarding volatility spillovers may need to control for size in order to gauge precise spillover phenomenon associated with a specific characteristics of firms.
8. The estimates for the leverage effect of good news are not reported here.
9. The reversed signs of estimates could be explained using a concept of "*reversed* (*or switching*) leverage effect" between the AMEX and NASDAQ markets. If the negative or positive innovations are sufficiently small, the reversals of the asymmetric leverage reaction of the conditional volatility to the sign of past news events may occur (Rabemananjara and Zakoian, 1993; Fornari and Mele, 1996, 1997).

References

Ang, A and J Chen (2002). Asymmetric correlation of equity portfolios. *Journal of Financial Economics*, 63, 443–494.

Bae, KH and GA Karolyi (1994). Good news, bad news and international spillovers of stock return volatility between Japan and the U.S. *Pacific-Basin Finance Journal*, 2, 405–438.

Barberies, N and M Huang (2001). Mental accounting, loss aversion, and individual stock returns. *Journal of Finance*, 60, 905–929.

Bekaert, G and G Wu (2000). Asymmetric volatility and risk in equity markets. *Review of Financial Studies*, 13, 1–42.

Black, F (1976). Studies in stock price volatility changes. Proceedings of the 1976 Business Meeting of the Business and Economic Statistics Section. *American Statistical Association*, 177–181.

Chan, K, KC Chan and GA Karolyi (1990). Intraday volatility in the stock index and stock index futures markets. Unpublished manuscript, Ohio State University, Columbus, Ohio.

Conrad, J and G Kaul (1988). Time-variation in expected returns. *Journal of Business*, 61, 409–425.

Conrad, J and G Kaul (1989). Mean reversion in short-horizon expected returns. *Review of Financial Studies*, 2, 225–240.

Conrad, J, MN Gultekin and G Kaul (1991). Asymmetric predictability of conditional variances. *Review of Financial Studies*, 4, 597–622.

Dean, WG and RW Faff (2004). Asymmetric covariance, volatility, and the effect of news. *Journal of Financial Research*, 27, 393–414.

Engle, RF and R Susmel (1990). Intraday mean and volatility relations between US and UK stock market returns. Unpublished manuscript, University of California, San Diego, California.

Fornari, F and A Mele (1996). Modeling the changing asymmetry of conditional variances. *Economic Letters*, 50, 197–203.

Fornari, F and A Mele (1997). Sign and volatility-switching arch models: Theory and applications to international stock markets. *Journal of Applied Econometrics*, 12, 49–65.

French, K, GW Schwert and R Stambaugh (1987). Expected stock returns and volatility. *Journal of Financial Economics*, 19, 3–29.

Glosten L, R Jaganathan and DE Runkle (1993). On the relation between the expected value and the volatility of the nominal excess returns on stocks. *Journal of Finance*, 48, 1779–1801.

Hamao, Y, RW Masulis and V Ng (1990). Correlations in price changes and volatility across international stock markets. *Review of Financial Studies*, 3, 281–307.

King, MA, E Sentana and SB Wadhwani (1990). A heteroscedastic factor model for asset returns and risk premia with time-varying volatility: An application to sixteen world stock markets. Unpublished manuscripts, London School of Economics, London, U.K.

Kroner, KF and V Ng (1998). Modeling asymmetric comovements of asset returns. *Review of Financial Studies*, 11, 817–844.

Lo, AW and AC MacKinlay (1990a). When are contrarian profits due to stock market overreaction? *Review of Financial Studies*, 3, 175–205.

Lo, AW and AC MacKinlay (1990b). An econometric analysis of nonsynchronous trading. *Journal of Econometrics*, 45, 181–211.

Malkiel, BG and Y Xu (2002). Idiosyncratic risk and security returns. Unpublished manuscript, University of Texas at Dallas, Dallas, Texas.

Mech, T (1993). Portfolio return autocorrelation. *Journal of Financial Economics*, 34, 307–344.

Nelson, D (1991). Conditional heteroskedasticity in asset returns: A new approach. *Econometrica*, 59, 347–370.

Ng, V, RP Chang and R Chou (1991). An examination of the behavior of international stock market volatility. *Pacific-Basin Capital Markets Research*, II, 245–260.

Poterba, JM and LH Summers (1986). The persistence of volatility and stock market fluctuations. *The American Economic Review*, 76, 1142–1151.

Rabemananjara, R and JM Zakoian (1993). Threshold ARCH models and asymmetries in volatility. *Journal of Applied Econometrics*, 8, 31–49.

Scholes, M and J Williams (1977). Estimating betas from nonsynchronous data. *Journal of Financial Economics*, 5, 309–327.

Schwert, GW (1990). Stock volatility and the crash of 87. *Review of Financial Studies*, 3, 77–102.

Index